BELIN sup
Langues

English for Today's World

Society

J.-M. DUBÉ
W. MARSHALL
avec la participation de
S. ASLANIDES

Belin

Photo de couverture : Getty Images/Thinkstock/iStockphoto.

 ISSN 1158-3762 ISBN 978-2-7011-5699-6

Sommaire

Avant-propos

Ce manuel est destiné aux élèves de classes préparatoires économiques (ECS/ECE) préparant les concours d'entrée aux écoles de commerce, aux élèves et étudiants préparant les concours d'entrée des différents Instituts d'études politiques (IEP), ainsi qu'aux étudiants en cursus Licence des facultés de Langues étrangères appliquées (LEA) et de Droit, et plus généralement à tous les étudiants de filières générales souhaitant améliorer leur maîtrise linguistique sur les grands sujets de l'actualité socio-culturelle du monde anglophone.
L'ouvrage est articulé sur une double visée : l'amélioration des compétences linguistiques (acquisition de vocabulaire spécifique de base, révision-consolidation des structures de la langue) et l'acquisition de méthodes et techniques – les exercices proposés correspondant aussi bien aux épreuves des concours d'entrée aux grandes écoles qu'à des savoir-faire professionnels.

Les unités traitent 55 sujets d'actualité, illustrés par des textes anglais et français très récents. Ils suivent tous le même modèle :
• la présentation d'un fait de langue (*Language focus*) ;
• 50 termes du vocabulaire spécifique (*Wordbank*) ;
• 5 phrases de thème grammatical (*Translation*) ;
• un texte anglais authentique de 450 à 700 mots avec un appareil pédagogique en deux parties (A. Recherche de synonynes/antonymes dans le texte ; B. Trois questions de compréhension détaillée [réponses courtes]) ou une question amenant à reformuler une partie précise du texte [réponse longue]) et/ou l'explication d'une citation longue issue du texte ;
• un court texte français à traduire (dans les chapitres ou le texte anglais est court) ;
• un point thématique pour apporter davantage d'informations sur le sujet ou pour problématiser la thématique dans la perspective de l'épreuve d'expression écrite (*Overview*) ;
• un point phonologique avec des exercices de répétition (*Pronunciation*) enregistrés sur le CD qui accompagne le manuel. La progression du module phonologie est organisée en 74 unités (55 + 19 en annexe) allant du plus simple (différenciation de phonèmes) au plus complexe (accent de mot et accent de phrase).
Les annexes sont entièrement consacrées aux méthodes d'expression écrite et au contenu lexical nécessaire à l'étude et l'exploitation de textes issus de la presse anglo-saxonne.

Le manuel peut être utilisé soit en accompagnement du cours, soit en auto-formation, et peut donner lieu à deux types de parcours : une approche thématique (unité par unité), ou une approche méthodologique (entraînement systématique à un type d'exercices sur de multiples sujets).

Les corrigés de tous les exercices sont téléchargeables à partir du site Belin (www.editions-belin.com).

Les Auteurs

Chapter 1

The monarchy

Language focus

Auxiliaires vs *verbes lexicaux*

• Les verbes peuvent se classer en deux catégories.

1. Les auxiliaires (*be, have, do* et les modaux). Ils sont suivis d'un participe ou d'une base verbale :

be	*I **am reading** a book. It **was published** in England.* (participes)
have	*We **have made** a mistake.* (participe passé)
do	*They **don't write** very often.* (base verbale)
can	*She **can find** the answer.* (base verbale)
will	*You won't like it.* (base verbale)

2. Les verbes lexicaux (autonomes) :

like	*I **like** physics. I **don't like** playing chess.*
listen	*She's **listening**. Does she often **listen** to the radio? …*

• Certains peuvent être tantôt l'un, tantôt l'autre :

Have you seen the report? (auxiliaire *have*, verbe *see*)
Do you have classes here? (auxiliaire *do*, verbe *have*)
What do you do on Saturdays? (auxiliaire *do*, verbe *do*)

Wordbank

to abdicate	*abdiquer*
the accession	*l'avènement*
an adviser	*un conseiller*
affairs of state	*des affaires d'État*
to appoint	*nommer (le Premier minister, par exemple)*
to ascend the throne	*monter sur le trône*
a baroness	*une baronne*
a birthright	*un droit d'aînesse*
blue blood	*le sang bleu*
by royal appointment to H.M. The Queen	*fournisseur commercial attitré*
a claimant to the throne	*un prétendant*
the coronation	*le couronnement*
the coronation oath	*le serment du couronnement*
crown lands	*les terres royales*
Defender of the Faith	*Défenseur de la foi*
a duke	*un duc*
an earl	*un comte*

ER	*Elizabeth Regina*
expenditure	*les dépenses*
a figurehead	*une figure de proue*
the gentry	*la petite noblesse*
HRH (His/Her Royal Highness)	*Son Altesse royale*
the king's/royal coffers	*les fonds royaux*
a kingdom	*un royaume*
knight (*n.*, *v.*)	*un chevalier ; adouber*
a marquess, a marchioness	*un marquis, une marquise*
to name	*nommer*
next in line of succession	*prochain dans l'ordre de succession*
the nobility	*la noblesse*
the Order of the Bath	*l'Ordre du Bain (Ordre de Chevalerie)*
the Order of the Garter	*l'Ordre de la Jarretière (Ordre de Chevalerie)*
a peer of the realm	*un pair du royaume*
a private secretary	*un secrétaire particulier*
the Privy Council	*le conseil privé*
public engagements	*les obligations officielles*
the Queen's (birthday) honours list	*la liste de distinctions honorifiques*
the Queen's speech	*le discours du début et de la clôture du parlement*
reign (*n.*, *v.*)	*le règne ; régner*
royal assent	*la signature royale validant tout document officiel*
the royal crest	*les armoiries royales*
the royal estate	*le domaine royale*
the royal household	*les biens et membres de la famille royale*
royal pageantry	*l'apparat, la pompe*
the sovereign	*le souverain*
to succeed to the throne	*accéder au trône*
to summon parliament	*convoquer le parlement*
the upkeep	*l'entretien*
Westminster Abbey	*l'Abbaye de Westminster (lieu de couronnement)*

Translation

Translate the sentences into English.

1. Quel est le rôle du monarque ? La reine incarne l'unité nationale et représente la nation à l'étranger mais ne dirige pas le pays.

2. Un prétendant peut monter sur le trône à condition d'être l'héritier suivant dans l'ordre de succession.

3. Elizabeth II règne sur la Grande-Bretagne depuis 1952, le soixantième anniversaire de son couronnement aura donc lieu en 2012.

4. Lorsque le résultat des élections législatives est connu, la reine doit nommer le Premier ministre en le choisissant dans le parti majoritaire.

5. Les fonds royaux sont utilisés pour financer l'entretien des biens et le train de vie des membres de la famille royale.

Read and answer

Read the article and then do activities A and B that follow.

David Cameron risks Queen's impartiality over hung parliament

David Cameron risks jeopardising the Queen's traditional political impartiality if he challenges a convention that would allow Gordon Brown to remain prime minister in the event of a hung parliament, according to constitutional experts.

Amid signs that the Conservative leader might declare himself the winner of the election, even if Brown decides to remain in office to try to form a coalition with the Liberal Democrats, advisers to Whitehall say the Tories will need to tread with care. The Conservatives fear a repeat of February 1974, when Ted Heath remained in office for four days after losing the election as he tried to negotiate a deal with the Liberals.

Some Tories say that Cameron is prepared to declare himself the winner if he comes first but fails to secure an overall parliamentary majority. They have been studying the experience of Alex Salmond, the SNP first minister in Scotland, who runs a minority administration. Salmond flew into Edinburgh by helicopter after the 2007 election to declare himself the winner, after the SNP won one more seat than Labour.

Lord Armstrong of Ilminster, who was Heath's principal private secretary during the 1974 negotiations, defended the convention. "The prime minister is the prime minister until he resigns," he said. "It is his duty not to put the Queen into a position where she might be appearing to take political decisions. If and when he does come to resign, it is his responsibility to recommend to the Queen whom she should send for as her new prime minister. I don't see how you protect the Queen from becoming over-involved in political decisions unless you can do it like that."

Senior Tory shadow ministers have indicated that they are unhappy with a new rule which will delay the return of parliament by a week. They say this could check any momentum Cameron might have from an election win as Brown is given extra time to negotiate a coalition with the Liberal Democrats.

Opinion polls indicate that the Tories are on course to come first in the election but fall short of an overall majority. There is even the possibility that Labour could perform poorly in the national vote but come first in the share of seats or win enough seats to allow Brown to form a coalition with the Lib Dems.

Armstrong's comments were echoed by Peter Hennessy, the Attlee professor of contemporary British history at Queen Mary University of London. He said: "Do they want to put the monarchy in danger of being politicised? It is not a good idea to appear to tangle with the palace, is it, and put the Queen in any danger of appearing to be politicised? Clegg and Cameron have had a whinge. It may not seem perfect to them, but I'm afraid that is what the British constitution is." [...]

Professor Robert Hazell, director of the constitution unit at University College London, said the convention was not just designed to protect the Queen. "Yes, it is in order not to leave the Queen in the lurch. But, just as important, it is in order not to leave us in the lurch. What the Queen is there to ensure is stability and continuity. In the old high Tory phrase: the Queen's business must be carried on. We must always have a

...

...

government. It isn't just Brown's privilege or right to remain in office as the incumbent prime minister. It is actually his duty, because we must always have a government."

The Guardian, (guardian.co.uk), 4/5/2010

A. Language

1. Find synonyms in the first five paragraphs of the article for the following: *endangering, he questions, pundits, an alliance, to progress cautiously, to summon, to restrain, impetus.*

2. Find antonyms in paragraphs 3, 4 and 5 of the article for the following: *he manages to, lose/put it at risk, attacked, satisfied, will hasten.*

B. Questions

Use information in the article to answer but do not copy sentences directly: use your own words.

1. Why is Gordon Brown's position compared to Mr Heath's in 1974 ? (50 words)

2. Why do Lord Armstrong and Professor Hennessy advise David Cameron not to challenge the convention? (50 words)

3. What is the role of the Queen as defined by the writer? (50 words)

Translation

Translate the article into English.

La reine d'Angleterre a reçu 500.000 euros de subventions agricoles en 2008

La reine Elizabeth d'Angleterre, une des femmes les plus riches du Royaume-Uni, a perçu plus de 500.000 euros de subventions agricoles européennes en 2008, selon les chiffres communiqués jeudi par le ministère de l'Agriculture.

La reine Elizabeth a reçu en 2008 un total de 473.583,31 livres (environ 530.000 euros) pour son domaine privé autour du château royal de Sandringham, dans l'est de l'Angleterre.

Le prince Charles, son fils aîné, a reçu 95.222,56 livres pour son duché de Cornouailles, et 86.262,98 livres pour la ferme du Duché, soit un total de 181.485,54 livres.

La reine, 214ème fortune de son royaume, avec 270 millions de livres selon un classement du *Sunday Times*, perçoit les aides européennes de la politique agricole commune (PAC) comme n'importe quel propriétaire terrien ou agriculteur. Elle est loin de bénéficier de la plus forte somme.

Ainsi, les groupes agroalimentaires Nestlé et Tate & Lyle perçoivent respectivement 1.018.459,69 livres et 965.796,78 livres.

Le duc de Westminster, troisième personne la plus riche du Royaume-Uni (derrière les magnats indien et russe Laskhmi Mittal et Roman Abramovich) avec 6,5 milliards de livres, a bénéficié pour sa part en 2008 de 486.534,15 livres via ses fermes.

Un total de 2,674 milliards de livres de ces subventions agricoles européennes a été distribué au Royaume-Uni l'an dernier.

AFP (dans *Le Point* [lepoint.fr]), 30/04/2009

Overview

Read a general overview of the subject.

God Save the Monarchy?

It may be hard to believe when you see Queen Elizabeth II sitting in an open horse-drawn carriage waving to crowds as she is driven through the streets of London, that it was less than 400 years ago that her ancestor, Charles I, became so unpopular that he ended up on the scaffold. His younger son, James, was also deposed but in this case (the Glorious Revolution of 1688) the monarch was unharmed and it was his own heirs, William and Mary, who succeeded him (albeit prematurely) and brought constitutional monarchy to Britain.

Since then, monarchs have, generally speaking, been loved and respected by their subjects.This does not mean that *everyone* loved them: Queen Victoria, for example, survived eight assassination attempts and Edward VIII was vilified in the press for his abdication and marriage to an American divorcee. It does mean, however, that, these days, about 60 to 70% of the British population believe that the monarchy should be preserved.

But does it serve a vital purpose? The sovereign may be Head of the Church, Head of State and Commander-in-Chief of the Armed Forces, but what if he or she ordered the airforce to bomb Parliament? One step outside the ceremonial role and that would be the end of the monarchy.

The present queen fully appreciates this and it is largely due to her that the Royal Family still enjoys such popularity. Ever since coming to the throne in 1952, she has never been so foolish as to express a controversial opinion in public. She has never antagonised a foreign leader or shown anything but the utmost courtesy to all those she has come into contact with. Her personal reputation is spotless. And although she holds no effective political power, it is certainly due to her diplomatic skills that relationships with certain countries have remained firm and that the Commonwealth has held in place for so long.

More recently – by agreeing to pay income tax (1993) and by expressing grief over the death of Princess Diana (1997) – she has learnt how to walk the tightrope between keeping one's royal distance and making it clear that one understands how ordinary English people feel.

...

Pronunciation

Listen and repeat.

back [bæk], **pack** [pæk]

- cubs/cups, bears/pairs, beach/peach, cab/cap.
- A pair of bears bumped into the wolfcubs on the beach.

2 Chapter

Parliament

Language focus

A. Questions fermées, questions ouvertes

• Les questions fermées (*Yes/No questions*).

Can you speak Chinese? (auxiliaire déjà disponible: *I can speak Chinese.*)

Did you see that car ? (auxiliaire *do* au prétérit à insérer : *I saw that car.*)

• Les questions ouvertes. Inversion auxiliaire sujet, sauf si la question porte sur le sujet :

*What have you eaten? When did you arrive? Who saw you? (*sujet)

B. Tags et réponses courtes

• Si un auxiliaire est disponible, on le reprend :

"It's a great movie, isn't it?" "Yes, it is./No, it isn't."

"Have you seen it?" "Yes, I have./No, I haven't."

• S'il n'y en a pas, on utilise *do/did* et on lui ajoute les marques de temps nécessaires :

You liked it, didn't you? He liked it and I did too.

• Le *question tag* prend le contrepied de la question principale (phrase affirmative/*tag* négatif, phrase négative/*tag* affirmatif). Attention aux « négations cachées » :

They never go abroad, do they? (*never* est négatif)

He hardly ever sees his sister, does he? (hardly ever est négatif.

Wordbank

an Act of Parliament	*une loi adoptée par le parlement*
the agenda	*l'ordre du jour*
an amendment	*une modification de projet de loi*
a backbencher	*un député de base*
to bar someone from doing sthg	*interdire à quelqu'un de faire qch.*
the back/front benches	*les bancs des députés sans responsabilités ministerielles/des ministres*
a Bill	*un projet de loi*
a cabinet reshuffle	*un remaniement ministériel*
to chair	*présider*
the Chief Whip	*le chef de file et responsable de la discipline d'un parti*
a constituency	*une circonscription électorale*
to dissolve	*dissoudre*
the electoral register	*la liste électorale*
eligible	*éligible*
an emergency debate	*une session extraordinaire*
an expenses allowance	*une allocation pour dépenses professionnelles*

first-past-the-post	*attribué à la personne pour qui on a le plus voté*
the floor of the House	*le lieu du débat au parlement*
the government/opposition benches	*(dans la chambre des Communes) les bancs du parti qui gouverne/d'opposition)*
hard-line, hard-liner	*dur, un dur du parti*
the House of Commons	*la Chambre des Communes*
the House of Lords	*la Chambre des Lords*
a hung parliament	*un parlement dans lequel aucun parti n'a une majorité de sièges*
a joint committee	*une commission mixte*
to keep/to lose a seat	*garder/perdre un siège au parlement*
to lodge a deposit	*payer une caution*
the maiden speech	*le premier discours d'un député*
Prime Minister's Question Time	*le temps dédié aux questions pour le Premier ministre*
a parliamentary session	*une session parlementaire*
to pass/to throw out a Bill	*voter et accepter/rejeter un projet de loi*
a postal vote, a proxy vote	*un vote postal, un vote par procuration*
to prorogue	*proroger*
public borrowing	*les emprunts publics*
rank and file members	*la base du parti*
to scrutinise government plans	*examiner de très près les projets du gouvernement*
a select committee	*une commission parlementaire*
the Shadow Cabinet	*le gouvernement fantôme*
the Speaker	*le président/la présidente de l'assemblée*
a spokesman	*un porte-parole*
to take one's seat	*prendre son siège au parlement*
a three-line whip	*les consignes de vote*
in the wake of	*dans le sillage de, à la suite de*
Westminster	*terme (géographique) utilisé pour évoquer le parlement britannique*
a wimp *(fam.)*	*un indécis*

Translation

Translate the sentences into English.

1. Les députés de la majorité qui n'ont pas de responsabilité ministérielle peuvent difficilement voter contre les projets de loi du gouvernement.

2. Le gouvernement fantôme ne peut jamais empêcher le gouvernement de déposer un projet de loi, n'est-ce pas ?

3. Les chefs de file de chaque parti ne sont-ils pas censés faire appliquer les consignes de vote ? Oui, en effet.

4. Le système électoral britannique est-il juste ? Non, car le nombre de sièges ne correspond pas au nombre de votes.

5. Comment le public peut-il contrôler les allocations versées aux parlementaires et vérifier qu'ils ne s'en mettent pas plein les poches ?

Read and answer

Read the article and then do activities A and B that follow.

An unlikely partnership that could mark the start of a treacherous era

In the end, the progressive coalition failed the stress test. The parliamentary arithmetic for a Labour-Liberal Democrat coalition simply did not add up to "strong and stable" government. The prospect of such an administration being forced to rely, vote after vote, on the capricious support of Scottish Nationalists and Ulster Unionists was too off-putting even for those from both parties who yearned for this historic partnership of the two progressive forces of British politics. Just a dozen more seats for the Liberal Democrats might have made the alliance feasible. But that was not the hand the parties were dealt by the election result.

This is a cause for real regret. A Conservative-Liberal Democrat coalition will not serve the cause of progressive politics in the way that a Labour-Liberal Democrat alliance would have. Liberal Democrat and Labour policies are closer and sounder on a host of crucial areas, from the approach to the economy to our relations with Europe. And of the two larger parties, Labour offered by far the more serious package on electoral reform. A Labour-Liberal Democrat coalition would have left Britain thrillingly close to the long-sought goal of a fair voting system. The Conservatives' pledge to hold a referendum on moving to the Alternative Vote - though better than nothing - leaves us with a mountain to climb as far as serious political reform is concerned.

Yet there are reasons why progressives should not be entirely crushed by this outcome. What many Liberal Democrat and indeed Labour voters feared in the run-up to this election was a rampant and doctrinaire Conservative government of the sort experienced by Britain in the 1980s. This is not what they will now get. David Cameron does not swagger into Downing Street, but rather limps across the threshold. This politician, who once thought power was heading inexorably in his direction, this week briefly stared into the political abyss. That should be a chastening experience for the new Prime Minister.

And Mr Cameron remains very much on probation. The wilder excesses of what is still, in many ways, an ideologically hard-line Tory party should be curbed by the presence of the Liberal Democrats. The fact that there will be Liberal Democrat ministers in the new Cabinet ought to act as a restraining influence. It is hard to see any stunts to repatriate powers from Brussels with pro-Europeans such as Nick Clegg and Chris Huhne in positions of authority. And George Osborne will find it much harder to unleash his right-wing ideological furies on a still fragile British economy with Vince Cable at his elbow. A shackled Conservative government is not a prize to bear comparison with a historic progressive coalition, but it is a prize nonetheless. And the presence of the Liberal Democrats might, ironically, make it easier for David Cameron to face down his own vociferous right wing. This coalition might end up helping to civilise the Conservative Party.

Yet we should not imagine for a moment that this will be an easy arrangement. The social democratic wing of the Liberal Democrats and the unreconstructed Thatcherites of the Conservatives will make for awkward benchfellows in the Commons. And the Labour Party, some of whose MPs are already savouring the prospect of being the "progressive opposition", will not make life easy for the new coalition government.

...

...

There is also likely to be considerable external pressure on the Liberal Democrats in the coming months. This ideologically uneasy coalition will severely test the unity of Mr Clegg's party. It will also test the Liberal Democrat support in the wider country. Few people voted Liberal Democrat last week in the hope that it would help deliver a Tory government. Yet that is what their vote has ended up doing. This is a perilous moment for Mr Clegg's party. Smaller coalition partners have a habit of getting squeezed. The Liberal Democrats will have to be careful that they do not get outmanoeuvred by the Conservatives and end up taking the blame for unpopular decisions.

There will be those from across the political spectrum and in all parties who hope this alliance will be strangled at birth. But they should be careful what they wish for. We have heard a great deal of talk about the "national interest" from our political leaders in recent days. It is easy to be cynical about this phrase. But a national interest – shared goals above partisan politics – does exist. And it exists especially on the economy at the moment.

Britain's public borrowing is at record levels and there is a mighty economic storm on the Continent that could easily turn our way. This new government needs to make it clear to the financial markets and the wider public that it will do what it takes to get the deficit under control. This does not necessarily mean cuts this year, despite what the Tories have argued. It means a coherent plan to reassure investors in British debt that our politicians are capable of working together and making the inevitably unpopular decisions.

The Independent (independent.co.uk), 12/5/2010

A. Language

Find synonyms in paragraphs 1 and 3 of the article for the following: *union, outlook, inconstant/fickle, help, to crave, demoralised, result, unrestrained, dogmatic, bottomless pit, humbling.*

B. Questions

Use information in the article to answer but do not copy sentences directly: use your own words.

1. According to the writer, what will make it difficult for the coalition to be effective? (250 words)

2. What does the following sentence mean: "In the end [...] strong and stable government (ll. 1-3)? (100 words)

Overview

Read a general overview of the subject.

Parliament and the British Constitution

The British Parliament is one of the oldest legislative bodies in the world, dating back to 1801 in its present form. However, its roots go back much further than that – to the 1265 Parliament convened by Simon de Montfort, a noble who led a revolt against the King and then brought together nobility, clergy and commoners in order to reform the way the monarch ruled.

Parliament is made up of two chambers – the House of Lords and House of Commons – of which only the lower chamber is elected (by universal suffrage and a first-past-the-post system). Each piece of new legislation – a Bill – is presented in the House of Commons. If passed, it has to be approved by the Lords and signed by the monarch before it becomes an Act.

The British Constitution dates back to *Magna Carta*, signed in 1215 by King John. This document, which limited the authority of the monarch, is the first of the many documents that make up the Constitution – a hotch-potch of laws, legal decisions and opinions that does not exist in a single printed form. Curiously, although it has served as the model for a great many parliamentary democracies, the Constitution is no longer a subject taught in school, there is no organisation in the UK that examines Acts of Parliament to make sure they in no way contravene the Constitution, and you rarely hear it mentioned in a British court of law – in contrast to the USA with regard to the celebrated 5th Amendment.

One of the cornerstones of the Constitution is the *Habeas Corpus* Act of 1679, which officialised a right that had been legally admitted as far back as 1305: the right not to be detained without justification.

The other Acts usually quoted as the backbone of the Constitution are the Bill of Rights of 1689 and the two Parliament Acts of 1911 and 1949. The Bill of Rights was a massive extension of *Magna Carta* in that it stated that the Crown had to obtain the consent of the people in order to reign, and that this consent was manifest in Parliament. After this severe restriction on the powers of the monarch, Parliament had to wait over 200 years before being able to limit the powers of the House of Lords: since the 1911 Parliament Act, the Lords have in effect no power to veto legislation emanating from the House of Commons.

Pronunciation

Listen and repeat.

rice [raɪs], **rise** [raɪz]

- place/plays, loose/lose, price/prize, he sat/he's at.
- He's at my place, where he often plays poker and loses.

Chapter 3

Political parties

Language focus

Les verbes à un complément

• Le complément peut être direct (pas de préposition) ou indirect (introduit par une préposition). La construction est propre à chaque verbe, il faut donc l'apprendre ; elle ne peut pas se déduire de la construction du verbe français de sens analogue :

listen ***to****/look* ***at****/wait* ***for*** *(so./sthg)*
écouter, regarder, attendre (qqn/qqch.)

mais :

obey/ask/answer so.
obéir à/demander à/répondre à qqn

• Ce complément peut souvent être absent (emploi intransitif) :

I'm listening.
I've been waiting since yesterday.

Wordbank

an activist	*un militant*
the agenda	*le programme politique*
backstabbing	*les coups de poignard, le trahison*
the ballot box	*l'urne*
to be accountable to	*être responsable envers*
a bold move	*une action/décision audacieuse*
the by-elections	*les élections partielles*
a buzzword	*une petite phrase à la mode*
to call someone's bluff	*prouver que quelqu'un bluffe*
to canvass voters	*démarcher les électeurs*
the Chancellor of the Exchequer	*le Ministre des Finances*
Conservative *(n., adj.)*	*(du parti) conservateur*
to enfranchise	*accorder le droit de vote*
to expose sleaze	*faire éclater un scandale au grand jour*
the Government Chief Whip	*le deputé chargé de faire respecter la discipline et la ligne du gouvernement lors de votes au parlement*
the grassroots	*la base (d'un mouvement, d'un parti)*
a handout	*une aide, une subvention*
ideological strands	*les courants idéologiques*
internecine strife	*les luttes intestines*
a keynote speech	*un discours-programme*

Labour *(n., adj.)*	*(du parti) travailliste*
a landslide	*un raz de marée (électoral)*
Lib-Dem *(Liberal Democrat)*	*(du parti) libéral-démocrate*
a marginal/safe seat	*une circonscription à faible/forte majorité*
an MP (Member of Parliament)	*un député*
a new dawn	*une ère nouvelle*
an ombudsman	*un médiateur*
to oust from the party	*évincer du parti*
the party congress	*la conférence du parti*
the party faithful	*les fidèles du parti*
party headquarters	*le siège social du parti*
the political agenda	*le programme*
a political soundbite	*une petite phrase*
the political spectrum	*l'échiquier politique*
a polling station	*un bureau de vote*
a rainbow coalition	*une coalition « arc en ciel », rassemblant plus d'un parti politique*
a rosette	*une cocarde*
a secret ballot	*un vote à bulletin secret*
a showdown	*une épreuve de force*
a spokesman, a spokeswoman, a spokesperson	*un porte-parole*
a staunch supporter	*un fidèle partisan*
to step out of line	*refuser de se conformer*
the swing vote	*le vote décisif*
to toe the line	*se plier à la ligne politique du parti*
Tory *(n., adj.)*	*Tory, conservateur*
the turn-out	*le taux de participation*
a ward	*une section électorale*

Translation

Translate the sentences into English.

1. Les militants participent aux campagnes électorales en démarchant les électeurs.

2. Les cadres du parti fixent le programme politique pour les élections dans un discours-programme.

3. Les médias écoutent les dirigeants politiques pour rapporter leurs petites phrases alors que les divers porte-paroles utilisent les médias pour repérer les mots à la mode.

4. Ses plus fidèles partisans n'ont pu empêcher l'ancien chef du parti d'être évincé du pouvoir à jamais.

5. Le Premier ministre a été capable d'en finir avec les luttes intestines au sein de son gouvernement.

Read and answer

Read the articles and then do activities A and B that follow.

Tory-Lib Dem coalition: the verdict

Compared to Tony Blair's triumphant entrance to Downing Street back in 1997, tonight's coronation of the new prime minister seemed a downbeat affair. That's hardly surprising, since the full details of the government David Cameron hopes to lead remain opaque. It's less a sense of marching to a brave new dawn; instead, we seem to be limping to a tired, confused twilight. The big question hanging on the announcement of the details of the arrangement is: who won and who lost? Undoubtedly, there are some in the Conservative party who believe David Cameron has conceded too much. Until the full policy commitments are known, it's hard to say which side fought for and won the hardest bargain.

Yet, the early signs are that the Lib Dems, famous for their ferocious tactics at local level, may have proved the tougher negotiators. For all that Nick Clegg was beginning to look like a ditherer as he swung between the Conservatives, to Labour and back to the Conservatives again, it is quite possible that the shenanigans of the last few days were simply part of a clever Lib Dem plot.

Certainly, Labour's negotiating team came away with the impression that the Lib Dems were not very serious about striking a deal with Labour. What seems to have happened is that Labour's team did reach out first to the Lib Dems last weekend, when they picked up reports of discontent among Lib Dem activists at the prospect of a blue-yellow deal.

But the Lib Dems, so Labour believe, seized on this offer of secret talks more in the hope of winkling more concessions out of the Conservatives than from any real belief that the so-called "rainbow coalition" of progressive parties might succeed.

If that was the case, the bluff-calling undoubtedly worked: early suggestions are that the Lib Dems have up to six cabinet seats and have forced concessions from the Conservatives on inheritance tax, favouring married couples in the tax system and, crucially, a referendum on electoral reform.

An extraordinary coup by Tory modernisers

This is a revolutionary moment: the day Tory modernisation became real. What has just happened is so startling that even now, it is hard to take in. A Liberal-Conservative alliance with an agreed long-term programme for government, Lib Dem ministers, and shared liberal values light years away from the centralising social democracy that has dominated Britain for more than a decade. Of course, it may falter – indeed, tonight it has not even been formally confirmed by the Liberal Democrat parliamentary party and executive. Of course, there will be unpleasant policy compromises. But no one can question the ambition.

Only David Cameron could have taken his party boldly into an alliance with the Liberal Democrats – and perhaps, only Nick Clegg could have agreed to one. Other Tory leaders, faced with this situation, would have shunned a Lib Dem coalition and tried to rule alone in a reactionary minority – perhaps turning to the Ulster unionists for support. [...]

All Tories were dismayed by last week's failure to win a majority, but some – mostly those close to Cameron – saw the benefit of coming close to power, but not quite close ...

...

enough. They pushed that advantage in coalition negotiations that few people, before this election, thought could ever succeed. A Tory government with a small majority would have been trapped by its own parliamentary extremists. A coalition with the Lib Dems will – at least, at the start – be stronger in parliament and more ideologically centred, too. Anyone who had been dismayed by the prospect of untrammelled Tory rule should wish this alliance well, even if, in the end, they cannot bring themselves to support it.

Any government supported by 306 Conservative MPs must draw on Tory traditions and values: and this will be the Conservative government that more voters last week supported than any other alternative. But not wholly a Conservative government, and not wholly formed from the Conservative party of old.

Jackie Ashley, Julian Glover, *The Guardian* (guardian.co.uk), 11/5/2010

A. Language

Find synonyms in the first three paragraphs of the first article for the following: *victorious, gloomy, barely, sunrise, just after sunset, yielded, pledges, fierce, an indecisive person, trickery, coming to an agreement.*

B. Questions

Use information in the articles to answer: use your own words.

1. According to the first article, why did the Lib Dems agree to talk with the defeated Labour party after the general election? (50 words)

2. According to the second article, why should the coalition benefit the Tories? (100 words)

Translation

Translate the article into English.

Conservateurs et travaillistes doivent réinventer le modèle britannique

Il y a bien longtemps que la vieille démocratie britannique n'a plus peur de rien. C'est heureux, car, au terme d'un combat électoral sans merci, le nouveau gouvernement devra présider aux destinées d'un pays qui traverse bien plus qu'une crise économique. Dans un système où plus de 20 % du PIB national proviennent des flux financiers engendrés par la City, où 20 % des emplois relèvent de la finance et de l'immobilier (contre 4 % en France), l'impact du marasme international se fait sentir cruellement. L'emploi manufacturier n'occupe que 10 % de la population active (pour 20 % en Allemagne) et le déclin industriel s'est poursuivi sous les gouvernements travaillistes Blair et Brown.

Le modèle du *hedge fund* conquérant et de la fiscalité matée fait des envieux en engendrant une prospérité visible, fondée sur une multiplication des services et un gonflement de la bulle immobilière. Le résultat s'est traduit par une croissance soutenue et l'explosion des hauts revenus, mouvement que le Labour a largement accompagné et encouragé, mais aussi par la grande dépendance des classes moyennes par rapport à la bulle financière, autant de catégories sociales que Gordon Brown ne pouvait que décevoir en cas de chute de la croissance.

Christian Makarian, *L'Express* (lexpress.fr), 5/5/2010

Overview

Read a general overview of the subject.

Current British politics

There are 367 registered political parties in Great Britain. Fortunately, not all of them manage to win seats in general elections, or else the country would be ungovernable. Britain is essentially a two-party system but the coalition formed in 2010 was a reminder that, since the 1920s, there have been *three* major parties: the Conservatives (also known as the Tories), the Labour Party, and the Liberal Party – now called the Liberal Democrats.

The Labour Party began in the 1920s as a party financed by trades unions and other organisations interested in social reform. Originally greatly attached to socialist principles, it had some success in the 1920s and 30s but first came to real power after World War II when it introduced the National Health Service. Successful again in 1964 and 1974, it was ironically trade union strike action in 1978-9 (the "Winter of Discontent") that led to its downfall and its "Wilderness Years" of 1979-1997. Then came Tony Blair and the "third way". By calling the party New Labour and veering towards the centre, he managed to attract more middle-class votes and won a landslide victory in 1997. The honeymoon lasted until the Iraq war – when Blair was seen to be acting as President Bush's puppet – but New Labour struggled on until 2010, finally brought down by the MPs' expenses scandal and what was perceived as PM Gordon Brown's incompetence in handling the world financial crisis.

Whilst Labour had its roots in the trade union movement, Tory support originally came from landowners and the moneyed classes in general. This has changed quite a bit since right-wing 1980s Thatcherism has turned into so-called "compassionate conservatism". In fact it is now difficult to see any difference whatsoever between the two main parties, although Tories tend to be tougher on crime and policing and harder on Europe, and Labour shies away from any policies that might disadvantage the "working man".

As for the Lib Dems, up until the 2010 elections, the only policy they had which distinguished them from the two other main parties was the introduction of proportional representation, which was hardly surprising since the Lib Dems held so few seats. But now, with 57 seats and places on the front benches (i.e. ministerial posts) in a coalition government, could this be the turning point? Or is it just a flash in the pan? Were the Tories and the Lib Dems voted in or was Labour voted out?

Pronunciation

Listen and repeat.

down [daʊn], **town** [taʊn]

- die/tie, dry/try, send/sent, wide/white.
- He sent me downtown and I tried not to die.

4 Chapter

Religion

Language focus

Les verbes à deux compléments

- La construction est propre à chaque verbe ; il faut l'apprendre.
- Certain verbes n'ont qu'une seule construction :

to steal sthg from so.	voler qqch. à qqn
to blame so. for sthg	reprocher qqch. à qqn
to remind so. of so./sthg	rappeler qqch./qqn à qqn
to explain sthg to so.	expliquer qqch. à qqn

- Certains verbes ont deux constructions :

  She gave the book to the student./She gave him the book.
  She sent the email to her friend./She sent him the email.

Wordbank

an archbishop	*un archevêque*
to baptise, to christen	*baptiser*
bigotry	*le fanatisme, l'étroitesse d'esprit*
a bishop	*un évêque*
blasphemy	*le blasphème*
a blessing	*une bénédiction*
a breakaway movement	*un mouvement séparatiste*
canon law	*le droit canon*
a cassock	*une soutane*
celibacy	*le célibat*
the Church of England	*l'Église d'Angleterre*
a churchgoer	*un pratiquant*
a congregation	*une assemblée de fidèles*
to convert	*convertir*
a creed	*une croyance, un credo*
a cult	*une secte*
a deacon	*un diacre*
Defender of the Faith	*Défenseur de la foi*
a denomination	*une confession*
a diocese	*un diocèse*
to disestablish	*séparer l'Église de l'État*
to do a balancing act	*faire de l'équilibrisme*

enlightenment	*l'édification*
to entrench	*ancrer*
the established church	*l'église établie*
evil	*le mal*
faith	*la foi*
far-reaching	*d'une portée considérable*
the Holy See	*le Saint-Siège*
in holy orders	*dans les ordres*
a lapsed believer	*un croyant qui ne pratique plus*
a layman	*un laïc*
the oath of allegiance	*le serment d'allégeance*
the papal will	*la volonté du pape*
a parish	*une paroisse*
a pew	*un banc d'église*
the priesthood	*la prêtrise*
holy scripture	*les Saintes Écritures*
secular, secularity	*laïc, la laïcité*
a set of beliefs	*un ensemble de croyances*
a splinter group	*un groupe dissident*
a teaching	*un enseignement*
a tenet	*une doctrine*
traditional values	*les valeurs traditionnelles*
to unfrock	*défroquer*
a vicar	*un pasteur*
a vicarage	*un presbytère de l'Église d'Angleterre*
women priests	*les femmes-prêtres*
to worship	*vénérer*
a worshipper	*un fidèle*

Translation

Translate the sentences into English.

1. Certains groupes dissidents reprochent à l'Église d'Angleterre d'abandonner ses valeurs traditionnelles.

2. Contrairement à la France où il y a eu séparation de l'Église et de l'État au début du XXe siècle, le souverain est le chef de l'Église d'Angleterre.

3. Les églises établies ont du mal à garder leurs fidèles à l'heure où les sectes se multiplient.

4. Le pasteur expliqua à ses fidèles qu'il pensait que l'Église d'Angleterre devait donner le droit aux femmes de devenir évêque.

5. L'archevêque de Cantorbéry rappela aux laïcs les croyances et les valeurs qui fondent la société britannique depuis des siècles.

Read and answer

Read the article and then do activities A and B that follow.

The Roman Catholic and Anglican churches: Unleashing the Counter-Reformation

Since the Church of England voted 17 years ago to admit women to the priesthood, disenchanted individual members of the 80m-strong worldwide Anglican Communion have been quietly converting to Roman Catholicism. Since 2003, when the Episcopalian church, the American branch of the Communion, first ordained an openly gay bishop, the number of alienated conservatives has been swollen by those dismayed by their Church's growing tolerance of homosexuality.

Many traditionalist Anglicans, nevertheless, have held back, reluctant to sacrifice their liturgy and heritage. On October 20th Pope Benedict offered them a way out of their unease and into the Catholic church. In so doing, he created a new headache for the beleaguered Anglican leadership – and resuscitated an old conundrum for the Vatican.

For years, the pope's officials have been mulling over what to do about Anglican splinter groups which sought to join the Catholic church as a body. Foremost among these is the Traditional Anglican Communion (TAC), led by an Australian archbishop, John Hepworth. It had been thought the pope might offer the TAC a status within the Roman Catholic Church like that given to the conservative fellowship, Opus Dei – one that gives its members their own pastors rather than putting them under the local diocesan bishop.

But the papal decree goes much further. It enables not just the TAC, but any Anglican group – community, parish, even an entire diocese – to enter into communion with Rome without sacrificing its traditions. The so-called Apostolic Constitution (the highest form of pontifical ordinance) creates a new entity that transcends diocesan boundaries: the "personal ordinariate", similar to the "military ordinariates" for Roman Catholics in the armed forces. In charge of each will be a former Anglican prelate. The Vatican has already taken, following reordination, several dozen rebel Anglican priests, some of them married. It makes a similar exception to its rule of priestly celibacy for the Eastern Catholic churches (which recognise the pope but use their own rites). The Vatican does not, however, permit married bishops. So the pastors of these new "personal ordinariates" must either be unmarried bishops or married priests.

Archbishop Hepworth declared himself "profoundly moved by the generosity" of Pope Benedict. But Rowan Williams, the leader of the Anglicans' mother Church, seemed stunned. Writing to his bishops, he complained he had been informed only at "a very late stage".

No wonder he was shocked. The pope's scheme will make it even harder for the Anglican leader to sustain an already difficult balancing act. To keep his worldwide Communion together, he is hewing to a relatively conservative line on homosexuality that would involve gay-friendly Americans settling for a sort of associate status. But in his own Church, he has gone along with a liberal policy on women. Preparations are in train for the ordination of female bishops. And there is likely to be an end to the procedural devices allowing traditionalist clergy to avoid serving alongside (or, in future, under) women. That may have persuaded the Vatican to act: it had to decide how to respond to conservatives who felt the Church of England was about to make their position untenable.

Hitherto, an uneasy alliance of low-church evangelicals and Anglo-Catholics has struggled to resist liberal Anglicanism. "This will change the balance in the Church of England

...

in favour of the liberals," says Jonathan Bartley of Ekklesia, a think-tank. "The evangelicals won't go to Rome and they may now be abandoned by their Anglo-Catholic allies." Some think (or fear) that as many as one in seven Church of England priests could convert.

The Economist (economist.com), 22/10/2009

A. Language

1. Find synonyms in the first three paragraphs of the article for the following: *disappointed, top officials, problem, thinking over, one united group, to propose, granted, brotherhood.*

2. Find antonyms in the first three paragraphs of the article for the following: *to reject, relieved, bigotry, dissatisfaction, modern/progressive, keen to, to leave.*

B. Questions

Use information in the article to answer but do not copy sentences directly: use your own words.

1. Describe the relationship between Anglicans and the Catholic Church over the last 2 decades. (200 words)

2. What does the following sentence mean : "The pope's scheme will make it even harder for the Anglican leader to sustain an already difficult balancing act." (100 words)

Translation

Translate the article into English.

Quand l'Église anglicane décide de parler sexe

Londres. Face à l'augmentation des divorces et au manque de communication dans les couples, l'Église anglicane estime que le temps est venu de parler sexe.

Elle publie un manuel du mariage, intitulé « Grandir ensemble », qui invite notamment les couples mariés à aborder de manière franche et directe les questions sexuelles.

« Le sexe, loin d'être quelque chose de mal, est tout à fait merveilleux et doit être célébré », précise ce guide d'un nouveau genre fort éloigné de la pudibonderie victorienne mais qui n'a quand même rien à voir avec le Kama Sutra.

« Comme toutes les autres facultés, il faut l'enseigner et chacun doit l'enseigner à l'autre. »

L'auteur de ce bréviaire inhabituel, Andrew Body, un pasteur du sud de l'Angleterre, est marié depuis 39 ans, comme l'autorise la religion anglicane pour les ministres du culte.

« Je ne voudrais pas que les gens pensent que l'Église cherche ainsi à faire irruption dans les chambres sans y être invitée », a-t-il dit à Reuters.

« Ce n'est pas du tout ça – nous voulons simplement que les gens se parlent. Ce n'est pas à l'Église anglicane de publier un manuel de technique sexuelle. »

Le guide cite le cas d'un couple qui s'étonnait de ne pas avoir d'enfant. Et pour cause, ajoute-t-il : « il s'est avéré que l'homme et la femme n'avaient jamais eu de rapports sexuels aboutis ».

Reuters (dans *Le Point* [lepoint.fr]), 10/3/2008

Overview

Read a general overview of the subject.

Multi-faith Britain or no-faith Britain?

In the 16th century, religion was inextricably bound up with politics. When the Pope excommunicated Henry VIII in 1533, Henry put the Church of England under his own control: henceforth all British sovereigns were also Head of the Church. His subjects were told to follow suit and deny the Pope's authority or else… After a few ups and downs, the Church of England established itself under Elizabeth I as the official – Protestant – religion. Elizabeth was shrewd enough to tolerate Catholics rather than persecute them and the tradition of tolerance continued over the centuries, but only up to a point: it is still forbidden for a Catholic to succeed to the throne. Not that many people would seem to care much about that any more… after all, 43% of Britons never go to a religious service and only 12% belong to a church. But beware of laying a finger on traditions, however obsolete they may seem! Much of British culture and civilisation is built on longstanding ties between the established Church and daily life: national events still go hand in hand with hymns and prayers that are part of the collective consciousness. Remove such markers and symbols and you attack the very foundations of a civilisation.

Until recently, these religious foundations have not been under threat from anything more serious than satire or the occasional sex scandal, but now things are happening that are beginning to concern even those who have never been to Church in their lives, except perhaps to attend a wedding or a funeral. It is all because certain elements of the Establishment think that Britain should be overtly multicultural, and this is what is upsetting the applecart.

For example, when the annual Christmas Nativity Play at a primary school is abandoned in favour of an entertainment celebrating multiculturalism, or when a nurse is prosecuted for wearing a crucifix on duty, what do the vast majority of Britons think? Are these examples of the desire not to exclude or offend any member of British society, or are they examples of the gradual removal of Judeo-Christian traditions from British everyday life in the interests of accommodating the sensibilities of an alien, immigrant minority? For the first time in centuries, the man on the Clapham omnibus* is actually thinking about religion and wondering if things he has always taken for granted are under fire.

* *A term sometimes used in law and in politics to mean an ordinary intelligent reasonable person.*

Pronunciation

Listen and repeat.

few [fju:], **view** [vju:]

- fan/van, knife/knives, ferry/very, first/versed.
- There were few vans on the first ferry. It was very quiet despite the football fans.

Chapter 5

Education

Language focus

Dénombrables vs indénombrables

- Les noms anglais ont une caractéristique : ils sont soit dénombrables *(countable)* soit indénombrables (*uncountable*). Selon qu'ils sont l'un ou l'autre, certains déterminants sont possibles, d'autres non :

Dénombrable	Indénombrable
a/the cat ø/the bread/	*money/love*
many/three cats	*much bread/money/love*

- Les noms indénombrables ne se mettent jamais au pluriel.

Wordbank

A-levels	*la série d'examens subie au même âge que le baccalauréat mais comportant 3 ou 4 matières*
an academy	*un établissement à fonds publics et avec une gestion pédagogique autonôme*
a budding scientist	*un scientifique en herbe*
a careers master	*un conseiller d'orientation*
to chop a budget	*supprimer des fonds*
a co-ed(ucational) school	*une école mixte*
a comprehensive school	*une école ouverte à tous (école d'état)*
continuous assessment	*le contrôle continu*
the core	*la partie obligatoire du programme scolaire*
a crammer	*une boîte à bac*
the curriculum	*le programme scolaire*
the Department for Education	*le ministère de l'Éducation*
a disadvantaged background	*un milieu défavorisé*
to ditch	*abandonner*
a drop-out	*un laissé pour compte*
to enrol	*s'inscrire*
an entrance examination	*un concours d'entrée*
exam pass-rates	*les taux de réussite aux examens*
to fall behind	*décrocher*
a form teacher	*un professeur principal*
GCSE (General Certificate of Secondary Education)	*une série d'examens (minimum 5) que les élèves passent à 16 ans*
the governors, the governing body	*le conseil d'administration*

a grammar school	*un lycée classique*
a Headmaster/Headmistress, a Head Teacher	*un principal, un proviseur*
illiteracy	*l'illettrisme*
an independent school	*une école indépendante et « privée »*
key stage exams	*les examens qui jalonnent la scolarité depuis KS 1, le cycle des 3 ans a 7 ans, à KS 4, le cycle des 14 à 16 ans*
the LEA (Local Education Authority)	*l'autorité locale chargée de l'enseignement*
obligatory/compulsory schooling	*la période de scolarisation obligatoire*
Ofsted (Office for Standards in Education, Children's Services and Skills)	*l'agence de surveillance éducative (l'inspectorat)*
parental choice	*le choix parental*
a prep(aratory) school	*une école primaire privée*
a primary school	*une école primaire (généralement publique)*
Year One	*première année : à partir de 5-6 ans*
a public school	*un collège/lycée privé*
a pupil premium	*un fonds pour des écoles inscrivant des élèves de milieux défavorisés*
a scholarship	*une bourse*
the school staff	*les effectifs professionnels d'une école*
to set up a school	*fonder une école*
a sink school	*une école en grave échec*
the sixth form	*le cursus de deux ans à la suite du GCSE*
skills	*les connaissances, les compétences*
to slash budgets	*tailler dans les budgets*
a star	*un point de mérite*
a state (secondary) school	*un lycée public*
state-funded	*financé par l'État*
a subsidy	*une subvention*
a "Superhead"	*un « super-proviseur » recruté pour améliorer l'image et les performances d'une école en échec*
tuition fees	*les frais de scolarité*
vocational training	*la formation professionnelle*

Translation

Translate the sentences into English.

1. Le système éducatif offre de nombreux moyens aux élèves pour leur permettre de devenir des scientifiques en herbe.

2. Le gouvernement a supprimé des fonds pour les universités, et de nombreux élèves ne peuvent pas trouver de place en fac.

3. Le savoir et les compétences pédagogiques sont tous les deux nécessaires pour enseigner avec efficacité.

4. Il y a tant de pression sur les « super-proviseurs » recrutés pour améliorer les résultats des écoles publiques.

5. Les forts taux de réussite au bac semblent donner raison aux critiques qui dénoncent le nivellement par le bas.

Read and answer

Read the article and then do activities A and B that follow.

Cutting the knot

Plans to give excellent schools the freedoms already enjoyed by dire ones

A silver thread of accountability runs through the fabric of education in England. Schools are held to account through a regime of inspections introduced almost two decades ago. The previous Labour government used the system to take over schools that fell short, reorganising and reopening them as "academies" that have greater control over what they spend their money on and how doggedly they pursue the national curriculum. On May 27th the new education secretary, Michael Gove, was due to introduce legislation to let schools deemed outstanding by inspectors join the ranks of these favoured few.

Academies were a pet scheme of Tony Blair's, introduced in 2000 to redeem failing state secondary schools in poor inner-city areas by handing over their management to sponsors who could appoint excellent head teachers and give them the freedom to do much as they pleased. Once a school had repeatedly failed to impress inspectors, a sponsor – usually a charity or philanthropist – was allowed to take it over. The sponsor controls the governing body of an academy, which holds some power over admissions, decides how to deal with bad behaviour and what, outside the core curriculum, is taught.

The powerful teaching unions dislike academies because they need not hire staff registered with the General Teaching Council, as other state schools do, and they can opt out of national pay agreements. There are now more than 200 of them, and exam pass-rates are far better than at the schools they replaced.

The thread of accountability that informs parental choice has now been picked up by Mr Gove. In the expectation that his bill will be passed, he has written to the governing bodies of the 2,200 state primary and secondary schools that have won inspectors' top rating, asking them whether they would like to become academies. Hundreds are expected to accept the offer at once. Separate legislation in the autumn will allow parents, teachers, charities, other schools and religious groups to set up new state-funded schools, the most radical reforming policy espoused by the Conservatives before the election. But the move to let schools turn themselves into semi-autonomous academies is likely to prove far more popular.

The creation of academies has already tempted new providers into establishing schools. Kunskapsskolan, a Swedish for-profit company, is due to open two academies in London in September. University College London is in the process of setting up an academy intended to boost the numbers of teenagers who study science and modern languages in the capital.

Other universities might be advised to follow suit, for the government is ring-fencing spending in this financial year on schools. Universities are not so lucky. English institutions had already had their budgets chopped by £1.3 billion over three years by the previous government; they learned on May 24th that they are losing a further £200m this year. Plans for an extra 20,000 places for students anxious to avoid the dole queues have been slashed to 10,000, and these will be limited to budding scientists and mathematicians.

The creation of more academies will increase parents' choice of where their children are educated. Mr Gove intends to provide more information on how schools com-

...

pare with one another. Any school that starts to slide down the league tables will be inspected promptly. So will those where a suspicious proportion of the teachers quit.

Whether having more academies will close the growing gap in academic performance between rich and poor children is moot; the new academies are more likely than existing ones to end up teaching well-off ones. Patricia Sowter, head of Cuckoo Hall primary school in north London, reckons that if her school becomes an academy, as she intends, she could ditch prescriptions on providing one-to-one tuition to certain children in favour of supplying more of it to the neediest, for example. It would be a start.

The Economist (economist.com), 27/5/2010

A. Language

1. Find synonyms in the first three paragraphs of the article for the following: *responsibility, structure, to take control of, obstinately, estimated, a favourite program/a priority, to rescue/improve, empowering, has authority over, resent, employ.*

2. Find antonyms in paragraphs 2 and 3 of the article for the following: *successful, occasionally, managed to, miser, was forbidden to, optional subjects, weak, they have to.*

B. Questions

Use information in the article to answer but do not copy sentences directly: use your own words.

1. What is an "academy"? (50 words)

2. Describe the British education system's "thread of accountability". (50 words)

3. According to *The Economist,* why should the principles of academies be applied to the whole system? (200 words)

Translation

Translate the article into English.

Recettes anglaises

Londres. Ragoût d'agneau, paella, risotto de champignons ou spaghettis bolognaise... Il s'agit là de quelques recettes que les collégiens britanniques auront bientôt pour devoir d'apprendre dans le cadre de leurs études. Le but ? Enseigner à la génération fast-food les règles du bien-manger... Le ministre de l'Education, Ed Balls, a ainsi annoncé le 11 septembre que les cours de cuisine allaient devenir obligatoires à partir de 2011 pour tous les écoliers âgés de 11 à 14 ans. Le gouvernement britannique consacre 150 millions de livres à la construction de cuisines d'apprentissage dans les écoles et au recrutement de 800 professeurs de cuisine, dans le cadre de sa politique de lutte contre l'obésité, qui avoisine 20 % chez les jeunes. Un livre de cuisine financé par le gouvernement et destiné aux adolescents, qui regroupe 32 recettes sélectionnées par le public, est d'ores et déjà disponible sur Internet, et sera distribué dès cette année à tous les élèves de sixième.

Frédérique Andréani, *Le Point* (lepoint.fr), 24/09/2008

Overview

Read a general overview of the subject.

Falling standards in a confused system

Up until the early 1960s, the education system was simple: there was a state sector and a private sector. In the state sector, where education was free, children went to primary school and then on to grammar school (if they passed an exam at age 11) from which they might go on to university, or to secondary modern school where they would most likely leave and get a job before they were 18. In the private sector, children started at preparatory ("prep") school and went on to public school (the name for a private, or independent, secondary school) at the age of 13.

Powerless to get rid of private education, Labour governments tried at least to get rid of selection in secondary education to provide children from disadvantaged backgrounds with better educational opportunities. But, although many secondary schools became "comprehensive" schools (i.e. schools without selection), it soon became apparent that standards were falling. Successive governments tried to restore confidence in the system by imposing a national curriculum and widening the range of subjects that could be taken at the GCSE (General Certificate of Secondary Education). Unfortunately, this only led to more controversy and no halt to the falling standards in state secondary schools. Furthermore, the universities, who were concerned about these standards, began to impose higher entry requirements on candidates. This, together with the disappearance of university grants (replaced by loans which had to be repaid…) meant that people from poorer backgrounds were becoming even less willing to apply for university. The irony is that student loans were introduced by a Labour government: the perfect example of an "own goal".

These days, only 13% of working-class children go to university as opposed to 44% of middle-class children. This is practically no improvement at all on figures from 30 years ago.

Other "own goal" policies of the recent past include a renewed concentration on exams, curricula with a feel-good content and not much else, new types of educational establishments, league tables… In all, the state system seems to have lost any sense of direction.

It is hardly surprising, therefore, that the private sector is booming. If someone like Diane Abbott, candidate for the leadership of the Labour Party in 2010 and noted for her criticism of private education, sends her own son to a private school at a cost of £10,000 a year – a fact which caused her a great deal of political embarrassment – then there is something profoundly wrong somewhere.

Pronunciation

Listen and repeat.

gate [geɪt], **Kate** [keɪt]

- bag/back, dog/dock, goat/coat, glass/class.
- Katy stood at the gate with her bag and coat.

6 Chapter

Oxbridge

Language focus

Singuliers et pluriels particuliers

- Certains noms singuliers ont un pluriel inhabituel :
  woman/women, foot/feet, mouse/mice, child/children, life/lives, wife/wives.
- Certains noms ressemblent à des pluriels mais sont en fait singulier :
  physics (et autres noms en *–ics*)
  news
- Certains noms ont la même forme au singulier et au pluriel :
  sheep, series, means…
- Certains noms pluriels n'ont pas de singulier correspondant :
  belongings, leftovers, riches, surroundings, jeans…

Wordbank

the academic year	*l'année universitaire*
to attend classes	*suivre les cours*
to apply for	*se porter candidat*
attainment, achievement	*la réussite*
to award a degree	*donner la licence*
B.Sc. (Bachelor of Science)	*licence ès science*
B.A. (Bachelor of Arts)	*licence ès lettres*
cap *(n., v.)*	*un plafond, imposer un plafond*
a Chancellor	*un recteur*
a course	*un cursus*
cushioned	*protégé*
a degree	*une licence*
to devise	*inventer*
a don	*un professeur d'université (notamment à Oxford et Cambridge)*
a double first	*une mention très bien dans un double cursus*
to drop out	*abandonner ses études*
enrolment	*l'inscription*
expectations	*les attentes*
a fee-paying student	*un étudiant devant régler des droits*
a fellow	*un chargé de cours*
a first-class honours degree	*une licence avec mention très bien*

graduate *(n., v.)*	*un diplômé ; obtenir son diplôme*
a grant	*une bourse*
a Hall of Residence	*une résidence universitaire*
the intake	*les admissions*
the league table ranking	*le rang dans les classements*
a (senior/junior) lecturer	*un maître de conférence*
a lecture	*un cours magistral*
the student loan system	*le système de prêts*
to major in	*se spécialiser en*
the old school tie network	*le réseau des anciens (qui se reconnaissent grâce à leur cravate distinctive)*
the Open University	*l'université d'enseignement à distance*
Oxbridge	*Oxford et Cambridge*
to pass an exam	*être reçu à un examen*
a polytechnic	*une université d'enseignement technologique (IUT/IUP)*
a postgraduate	*un étudiant de master/doctorat*
practicals	*les travaux pratiques*
a professor	*un professeur d'université*
a reader	*un chargé d'enseignement*
a seminar	*un séminaire, un colloque*
to read for a degree	*préparer une licence*
top-up fees	*les frais complémentaires*
a tutorial	*un cours (de travaux dirigés) par groupes de 2 ou 3*
a tutor	*un tuteur, un directeur d'études*
an undergraduate	*un étudiant qui prépare une licence*

Translation

Translate the sentences into English.

1. Il y a beaucoup d'entreprises de nouvelles technologies dans les environs d'Oxford – c'est l'extremité ouest de la banane bleue européenne.

2. Les étudiants préparant une licence doivent passer une série d'examens chaque année pendant trois ans pour décrocher leur diplôme.

3. Le meilleur moyen de réussir ses études universitaires est de suivre les cours avec assiduité et de travailler dur sous la tutelle de son directeur d'études.

4. L'information la plus importante en Grande-Bretagne au mois d'août est le nombre (grandissant) de candidats brillants qui n'arrivent pas à entrer à Oxbridge.

5. Du fait de la hausse des frais de scolarité et des frais complémentaires, le gouvernement a dû inventer un système de prêt étudiant.

Read and answer

Read the article and then do activities A and B that follow.

A degree of honesty is needed

It may be a case of stating the obvious to say that a first-class degree from Oxford and Cambridge is always going to count for more than one from a "bog-standard" university - to plagiarise Alastair Campbell's famous phrase. Yet earlier this year, a Commons select committee, spurred on by tales of universities putting pressure on their academics to mark students more leniently to secure high league table rankings, made the case for consistent national standards across the sector.

Yesterday's report from the Higher Education Policy Institute, one of the most revered higher education think tanks, argues that not only is this "not feasible" but it is also not "desirable". The institute is certainly right to say it is not feasible. Put your hand on your heart and admit that you can never envisage a situation where an employer faced with rival applications from Oxbridge and a university at the foot of the league tables - both with first-class degree passes - would not give more weight to the Oxbridge candidate. [...]

There has been a lot of heated debate over the past few months over whether Britain will be able to retain its world-class universities in the wake of the £1.1 billion spending cuts imposed on them in this year's Budget. One way to ensure this in the 21st century is raising funds from alternative sources to the taxpayer - and one of these areas has to be through the recruitment of international students. If they perceive our top-performing universities - Oxford, Cambridge, Imperial College London and University College London - are not retaining their rankings in world league tables, they will be less likely to come here and the universities will be in danger of losing world-class status. Remember, we are facing increased competition from a massive growth in the higher education sector in countries like India and China.

That having been said, there are some points raised by the Commons inquiry into standards that the report does have to address. With the introduction of top-up fees, students have a higher expectation of their degree courses than they had previously and this does not mean making it easier for them to obtain a first-class degree. They deserve to have an assurance that their degree course conforms to robust standards and that is where the HEPI report's recommendation that there should be minimum standards for all courses at universities across the country comes in.

This will be easier to say than achieve. Universities are proud of their autonomy and will oppose attempts to impose a minimum curriculum on them. That said, it should not be beyond the wit and wisdom of academics to devise an external system of assessment which can rate courses in different subject areas according to whether they meet a minimum criteria. The proof of the pudding will be in the eating.

The reform of the degree classification system is not a good pointer to success in this field. Everyone agrees that the current classification system – devised when only a tiny proportion of the number who attend higher education now graduated from our universities – is not fit for purpose.

Richard Garner, *The Independent* (independent.co.uk), 3/6/2010

A. Language

Find synonyms in the first two paragrphs of the article for the following: *to be more valuable than, to borrow, stimulated by, less severely, to obtain, unvarying, respected, groups of experts, possible, beneficial, contemplate, at the bottom of, applicant.*

B. Questions

Use information in the article to answer but do not copy sentences directly: use your own words.

1. Why does the Higher Education Policy Institute oppose the idea of "consistent national standards"? (50 words)

2. Why are universities also likely to oppose the idea? (50 words)

3. What are the difficulties British universities have to face? (50 words)

Translation

Translate the article into English.

« Oxbridge », l'ÉNA des Britanniques

À chacun son « énarchie ». La Grande-Bretagne a beau être dirigée depuis dix-sept ans par des Premiers ministres issus de milieux modestes et apôtres de la méritocratie (successivement Margaret Thatcher et John Major), la prééminence d'une certaine élite sur les affaires du pays n'a jamais été aussi forte. C'est la conclusion d'une enquête mettant en évidence le rôle croissant des universités d'Oxford et de Cambridge, qui sont, de fait, à la Grande-Bretagne ce que l'École nationale d'administration est à la France. Selon cette étude, seuls 20 % des décideurs du monde politique, économique ou culturel étaient issus d'« Oxbridge » en 1830, contre le double aujourd'hui. Entre ces deux dates, la proportion n'a cessé de croître régulièrement, et rien ne permet de penser que la tendance doive s'inverser à brève échéance. À titre indicatif, 38 % des nouveaux noms apparus dans la dernière édition du *Who's Who* étaient issus d'Oxford ou de Cambridge.

En revanche, ces universités ne sont plus des bastions de l'aristocratie britannique. Le spectre social y est aujourd'hui beaucoup plus large qu'à l'époque victorienne et la proportion de femmes admises représente près de la moitié du nombre total d'étudiants. On assiste également à une certaine réorientation des champs d'activités : alors qu'à la génération précédente les anciens d'Oxbridge étaient particulièrement nombreux dans l'enseignement, chez les hauts fonctionnaires et les militaires, ils s'affirment désormais plus volontiers dans les affaires, la justice et les médias.

Au niveau inférieur, le rayonnement des *public schools* est tout aussi impressionnant, notamment pour la plus prestigieuse d'entre elles, Eton. Toujours selon le *Who's Who*, référence en la matière, ce collège privé, qui compte environ 1 200 élèves, fournirait bon an mal an 5 % de l'élite de la nation.

Le Point (lepoint.fr), 25/1/2007

Overview

Read a general overview of the subject.

Shared values and a shared reputation

Oxford came first. People were already teaching there in the 11th century; then, in 1231, it gained university status. Meanwhile, scholars who had fled from Oxford (because of a murder investigation…) had founded the university of Cambridge in 1209. Both universities developed a collegiate system which continues today within the university structure. The university lays down the guidelines for syllabuses, organises lectures and takes charge of examinations; on the other hand, it is each individual college that deals with tuition: tutors (or supervisors) are paid by the college, not by the university. It is also still the case that one officially applies to an individual college for entrance, not simply to the university. The choice of college may be fairly abritrary or may depend on family tradition, links with one's school or the college's reputation in a certain areas.

Although praised for their academic excellence, the two universities are also criticised by some for being elitist. It has to be said that, up until the 1970s, and despite rigorous entrance exams that had been introduced to sort out the wheat from the chaff, certain scions of wealthy families still managed to end up at Oxbridge by means of parental influence. Ironically, the entrance exams themselves were dropped in the 1990s because they were considered elitist: after all, in order to sit the exams, you needed to have studied Latin (not generally taught in comprehensive schools…), and you had to have studied one subject to a level which demanded specialised teaching – something that was not within the capabilities of the run-of-the-mill public sector teacher. Conclusion: these exams went against the principle of equal opportunity. However – another twist of fate – Oxbridge entrance exams are now likely to be reintroduced in the face of falling standards in national GCE "A-level" exams.

Whilst resisting the overall dumbing-down of educational standards, Oxbridge has however followed other major social trends: most colleges are now "mixed" (i.e. for both sexes) and the erstwhile aristocratic lifestyle has become more middle-class (i.e. fewer servants and more hot water). But defenders of what Oxbridge stands for live in fear of the advocates of mediocrity getting the upper hand and obliging the two universities to become more like the redbrick and new universities where uninspired students are put through their paces and given a degree whose only real purpose is to get them a job.

Pronunciation

Listen and repeat.

hear [hɪəː], **we're** [wɪə], **year** [jɪə]

- here/ear, heart/art, hear/year, hair/air.
- Did you hear that we're here for a year?

Chapter 7

The Welfare State

Language focus

L'article indéfini

• L'article indéfini devant un nom dénombrable permet d'introduire un objet ou un fait nouveau :

*I met **an** interesting lecturer yesterday.*

• Il peut également servir à faire une référence générale :

***An** elephant never forgets.*

• Attention à certains emplois différents du français :

*I am **a** painter.*	Je suis peintre.
*As **a** painter, he is very talented.*	Comme peintre, il est très talentueux.
*Without **an** umbrella, I'm lost.*	Sans parapluie, je suis perdu.

• L'équivalent de l'article indéfini pour les noms indénombrables est l'article ø (« article zéro »).

Wordbank

A & E (Accident and Emergency) Unit	*les urgences*
to be on a drip	*être sous perfusion*
a blood donor	*un donneur de sang*
care	*les soins*
a CAT scan	*un scanner*
the charges	*les frais, les honoraires*
a charity, a charitable organisation	*une oeuvre caritative*
child benefit	*les allocations familiales*
cover	*la couverture (= assurance)*
a crackdown on spending	*une réduction draconienne des dépenses*
day care	*l'hôpital de jour*
dental treatment	*les soins dentaires*
a disability	*une incapacité*
a district nurse	*une infirmière visiteuse*
a doctor's surgery	*un cabinet médical*
to dole out	*donner parcimonieusement*
an emergency	*une urgence*
exemption	*l'exonération*
from the cradle to the grave	*du berceau au tombeau*
a GP (general practitioner)	*un généraliste*

housing benefit	*l'allocation logement*
an injection	*une piqûre*
an in-patient	*un patient hospitalisé*
a marked increase	*une augmentation sensible*
market forces	*les forces/mécanismes du marché*
medical fees	*les frais médicaux*
the nanny state	*l'état-nounou*
the NHS (National Health Service)	*Le Service de santé national*
a nursing practitioner	*infirmière pouvant assumer quelques tâches du médecin*
an OAP (Old Age Pensioner)	*un retraité*
old age insurance	*l'assurance veillesse*
an out-patient	*un malade externe*
to overspend	*trop dépenser*
the patients' charter	*la charte des patients*
a prescription	*une ordonnance*
a private patient	*un patient privé*
public health care	*le système de santé public*
self-governing	*(administration) autonome*
a senior citizen	*une personne agée, un senior*
sickness benefit	*l'allocation maladie*
council housing	*le logement social*
a social worker	*un assistant social*
spiralling costs	*les côuts qui montent en flèche*
a state pension	*une pension de la sécurité sociale*
a stitch	*un point de suture*
a surgeon	*un chirurgien*
treatment	*les soins*
a trust	*un hôpital public à gestion autonome*
unemployment insurance	*l'assurance chômage*
a waiting list	*une liste d'attente*
the Welfare State	*l'état providence*
wide-ranging social cover	*une couverture sociale large*

Translation

Translate the sentences into English.

1. Il est médecin généraliste à Dartmouth alors qu'il voulait être dentiste à Harley Street pour le gratin londonien.

2. Le système de santé doit faire face à des coûts qui montent en flèche à un moment où de moins en moins de travailleurs cotisent au financement des soins.

3. En tant qu'infirmière visiteuse, Sandra n'a pas le droit de donner des médicaments ou de prescrire une ordonnance à ses patients.

4. Si un hopital public à gestion autonome dépense trop, soins et traitements seront donnés avec parcimonie.

5. En tant que chirurgien en chef, il doit être prêt pour toutes les urgences, de simples points sutures aux opérations à cœur ouvert.

Read and answer

Read the article and then do activities A and B that follow.

Less nanny state, more caring mate

Welfare was designed to improve our lives, but hasn't. What we need is a compromise between Fabian-style state socialism and naked Thatcherism. Enter the new era of volunteering.

Over most of the past century, the liberal democracies of the west were distinguished from totalitarian regimes in eastern and central Europe – communist, but also at one time fascist and National Socialist – by representative government and a rule of law. But the democracies themselves were increasingly divided by the Atlantic. The countries that now form the core of the European Union developed elaborate systems of public health care, education and welfare funded by taxation and directed by the state (as indeed did those dictatorships). The United States did not.

During the astonishing three decades after 1945 – with the German Wirtschaftswunder and what the French called les Trente Glorieuses – Europeans believed that they could indefinitely combine rapid growth with public welfare. This was what the historian Tony Judt has called the "social-democratic moment", although it was in many ways also the work of Christian Democratic leaders and governments, as most European politicians on all sides accepted a Keynesian-interventionist consensus. In 1956, Anthony Crosland published *The Future of Socialism*, making the egalitarian case while deriding the puritanical-bureaucratic traditions of "total abstinence and a good filing system", but also assuming that rapid growth and widening prosperity would continue in any foreseeable future.

Then, in the 1970s, the "Glorious 30" ended with both a bang and a whimper: economic crisis followed by social unrest. The social-democratic moment was over, and governments of a reinvigorated populist right came to power - notably Margaret Thatcher's in 1979 - and assaulted that Keynesian consensus. The future now belonged to markets rather than planning, privatised rather than nationalised industry, the individual rather than the collective ("There is no such thing as society") and, it turned out, the rich rather than the poor.

Thus it is, Judt asserts in his remarkable new book, *Ill Fares the Land*, that "something is profoundly wrong with the way we live today". Even ardent free-marketeers scarcely foresaw the astonishing increase in disparity of income, particularly in the US. In 1968, the chief executive of General Motors was paid 66 times as much as an average worker on his payroll; in 2005, the head of Wal-Mart made 900 times as much. No politician is very keen to defend this now; the deadly sin of avarice appears more sinful than ever in the lurid light of bankers' bonuses, not to mention BBC salaries and MPs' expenses.

For Judt, the answer to this ill is a renewed commitment to social democracy, which European countries continue to practise but "have forgotten how to preach". Even after the greatest financial crisis in generations, the left is curiously reticent and bedraggled, though in this country the deeply demoralising effect of New Labour might have something to do with that. It is significant that this clarion call comes not from a Westminster politician but from a historian, a Londoner who has spent more than 20 years in exile as a professor at New York University.

...

. . .

In truth, the death of the welfare state has been much exaggerated, at least here and elsewhere in Europe, if not in America. Thatcher's enemies concede that she couldn't dismantle the welfare state, but did she really try? Often we mistake rhetoric for reality, and despite Thatcher's supposed "cuts" and her trumpeting of the virtues of self-help and individual responsibility, spending on the National Health Service increased by 60 per cent in real terms while she was prime minister. Overall public spending as a proportion of GDP was almost the same when she left Downing Street as when she entered it.

The United States was a different story. From the Marxist left, Perry Anderson has observed that, in terms of domestic policy, the Nixon administration was decidedly more progressive than the Clinton administration (one of those truths that conventional American liberals are incapable of digesting). And Judt mocks the Orwellian name of Clinton's Personal Responsibility and Work Opportunity Act 1996, which, a century and a half after the New Poor Law of 1834, followed the Whig legislation in using the lashes of hunger and humiliation to drive the undeserving poor to work.

But perhaps part of our real problem is something different from an imaginary assault on public welfare. Could it be that the welfare state itself has gone wrong, with consequences unintended as well as malign? Judt's book is dedicated to his schoolboy sons, with his awareness of "how inadequately we have furnished them with the means to improve" the world they will inherit. Some of the reasons for that problematic legacy are discussed in another new book, *The Pinch*, by the Conservative frontbencher David Willetts. He shows how the baby-boom generation, born in the 20 years after the end of the Second World War (which includes Judt, Willetts and myself), has been selfish and thriftless in ways that have greatly attenuated prospects for the next generation, while welfare may have discouraged social mobility, or even the well-being of the masses.

New Statesman (newstatesman.com), 29/3/2010

A. Language

1. Find synonyms in the subtitle and first paragraph of the article for the following: *was planned to, to better, a settlement, tolerant, are the pillars, complex, financed, run by.*

2. Find antonyms in the second paragraph of the article for the following: *slow decline, elitist, respecting, excess/intemperance, narrowing, poverty.*

B. Question

Use information in the article to answer but do not copy sentences directly: use your own words.

What does the historian Tony Judt advocate to improve the Welfare State ? (250 words)

Overview

Read a general overview of the subject.

The NHS: the flagship that lost its way

For Britons in 1948 – still enduring rationing and other post-war restrictions – the newly-founded National Health Service was nothing short of astonishing. Before, many people could simply not afford medical treatment. Now, suddenly, it was all free at point of use: nothing to pay the doctor and nothing to pay the chemist for a prescription. As a result, "baby boomers" were the healthiest generation ever to grow up in Britain: they even got free orange juice as babies and free milk at school... When some charges had to be introduced in the 1960s (notably prescription charges and visits to the dentist), there was an outcry from the idealists, but the average Briton still believed the NHS was the best in the world and that British doctors and nurses were practically infallible and never to be questioned.

Then things changed. It became obvious in the 1970s that the NHS was costing far too much, that the service was deteriorating and that public perception of the service was changing. By the 1980s, everyone had heard about someone who had been kept waiting for hours in Accident & Emergency before getting treatment, or had waited 6 months for a hip replacement... There were even reports of dirty bed linen and wards not being properly cleaned. A new breed of hospital managers, brought in to cut the costs, succeeded mostly in outsourcing as many support services as possible (often to rather dubious enterprises) and in demotivating staff.

No longer the recipients of automatic respect, medical staff complained of being undervalued. This was remedied (on the surface anyway) by some inspired terminology: ambulance men became paramedics, matrons became nurse managers, and anyone from a cleaner to a consultant became a health care worker or, better still, a "health professional". They also got a bit more money, but not enough to attract enough new recruits into health care jobs. Things went from bad to worse. Dissatisfied patients, faced with falling care standards, interminable waits for attention or surgery, and doctors and nurses they couldn't communicate with because they'd come from abroad to relieve the staff shortages, were beginning to resort to suing for incompetence and malpractice – already a national pastime in the USA. Many used the private sector if they could afford it, or even resorted to going abroad for treatment.Once the flagship of Labour party policy, the NHS is now adrift in a very rough sea...

Pronunciation

Listen and repeat.

sheep [ʃiːp], **jeep** [dʒiːp], **cheap** [tʃiːp]

- watch/wash, cheese/Jeez, ridge/rich
- The sheep blocked my jeep. Jeez! I had to watch out not to fall over the ridge!

8 Chapter

Social ills

Language focus

The, this *ou* that *devant un nom singulier ?*

• On emploie *the* devant un nom singulier s'il s'agit d'un objet déterminé par le contexte :

I saw an elephant yesterday. The elephant was pink.

ou par la situation :

Look! The bus is right there!

ou encore pour faire référence à l'objet générique :

The lion is the king of animals.

• Certains noms sont presque toujours employés avec *the* parce qu'ils renvoient à des objets uniques :

the president, the earth, the west…

• *This* et *that* partagent avec *the* le renvoi à un objet déterminé, avec une précision supplémentaire : *this* lie l'objet à la sphère de celui qui parle (espace, temps, affect), *that,* à l'extérieur de sa sphère (ou à celle de son interlocuteur) :

Look at this! (en brandissant l'objet)
Look at that! (en montrant quelque chose à mon interlocuteur)
this week (la semaine en cours)
That week, John was abroad.
Cette semaine-là, John était à l'étranger (dans un récit au passé).
This is my daughter.
Je vous présente ma fille.

Wordbank

anguish	*l'angoisse*
an ASBO (Antisocial Behaviour Order)	*une ordonnance contre les comportements antisociaux*
better policing	*des méthodes policières mieux adaptées*
binge-drinking	*l'excès d'alcool, la beuverie*
on the breadline	*sans un sou*
a breakdown in the community	*une ligne de fracture*
to bridge a divide	*établir un rapprochement*
a broken society	*une société désunie*
child abuse	*la maltraitance d'enfant, les abus sexuels contre les enfants*
to commit a crime	*commettre un délit/crime*

in dire need	*dans le besoin extrême*
to fragment	*fragmenter*
gun crime	*la violence par arme à feu*
heightened fears	*les peurs intensifiées*
to hold down a job	*garder un travail*
the Home Office	*le ministère de l'Intérieur*
the homeless	*les SDF*
a housing estate	*un lotissement*
knife crime	*le crime à l'arme blanche*
a lager lout	*un ivrogne agressif*
to live on handouts	*vivre de la mendicité*
a low achiever, an under-achiever	*celui qui est peu doué pour les études*
to move out	*partir, déménager*
the needy	*ceux qui sont dans le besoin*
neglectful parents	*les parents négligeants*
to reach a peak	*atteindre un sommet*
to regenerate a neigbourhood	*réhabiliter un quartier*
a single-parent family	*une famille mono-parentale*
to shine the spotlight on	*mettre la lumière sur*
shoddy housing	*le logement de mauvaise qualité*
a sick society	*une société malade*
to spark (off) trouble	*mettre le feu au poudre*
to stab	*poignarder*
to strangle	*étrangler*
sub-standard housing	*le logement qui n'est pas aux normes*
to take someone into care	*prendre quelqu'un en charge*
the teenage pregnancy rate	*le taux de grossesse chez les adolescentes*
truancy	*l'absentéïsme scolaire*
the underclass	*la classe défavorisée*
to unravel the social fabric	*détricoter le tissu social*
a volunteer	*un bénévole*
a yawning gap	*un écart béant*
a yob	*un voyou*

Translation

Translate the sentences into English.

1. Ce projet bénévole peut favoriser un rapprochement entre les différentes communautés.

2. Il faut des méthodes policières mieux adaptées pour lutter contre la délinquance qui prolifère dans la classe défavorisée.

3. Le taux de grossesse chez les adolescentes a atteint un sommet en Grande-Bretagne.

4. Le Premier ministre et son gouvernement conservateur veulent durcir la lutte contre les voyous et les actes d'incivilité.

5. Cette société d'abondance est malade de ses inégalités croissantes et de sa culture de l'excès.

Read and answer

Read the article and then do activities A and B that follow.

Britain's "broken society": Through a glass darkly

It is hard to believe that such appalling crimes could have been committed by anyone so young. Two boys in the north of England were subjected to a sadistic attack that caused parents across the country to shudder. The anguish of the children was awful enough. But in a grotesque twist, their tormentor was also a child, not yet even a teenager. The attacks had been carried out "solely for the pleasure and excitement" of it, the judge in the case said. What has society come to when such evil is found in those so young?

That was in 1968. Mary Bell, the daughter of a Tyneside prostitute and supposedly the victim of repeated abuse herself, became Britain's most famous child-killer when, just 11 years old, she was convicted of strangling two young boys. Now, a similar case is causing people to wonder again whether society has gone to the dogs. Two brothers from the South Yorkshire village of Edlington, aged ten and 11, were convicted on January 22nd of torturing and sexually abusing two younger boys in an ordeal that left one of them close to death.

The case was highlighted by David Cameron, the leader of the opposition, who on the day the boys were sentenced launched a chapter of his Conservative Party's election manifesto dedicated to dealing with what he calls Britain's "broken society". The Edlington case was not "just some isolated incident of evil", Mr Cameron said. Connecting it to four other infamous examples of callous brutality, he declared that it raised "deep questions about what is going wrong in our society". Britain is experiencing a social recession to match the economic one, he reckons.

Was Mary Bell's Britain better than today's version? An increasing number of people seem to think so. Opinion pollsters around the world find that people are usually gloomy about the future, perhaps because it is inherently more uncertain than the past. But Britons are getting even more downbeat. When Labour came to power in 1997, 40% of the population thought the country was becoming a worse place to live in. By 2007 that had risen to 60%. A year on, and a year into Gordon Brown's spell as prime minister, the malcontents numbered 71% – and that was before the financial crash. There has been a "surge of nostalgia" for the good old days, says Ben Page, head of Ipsos-Mori, a polling firm.

Chief among people's worries is their security. Under Labour, fear of crime climbed until by 2007 it had become the issue that pollsters identified as the main complaint among voters. (Since then worries about the economy have eclipsed all else.) The heightened fears are a puzzle to criminologists, who point out that over the past 15 years Britain has experienced a steady, deep fall in crime. The statistics are notoriously hard to interpret, but according to the British Crime Survey, the Home Office's most reliable measure though still far from perfect, crime overall has dropped by 45% since its peak in 1995. A big chunk of that fall is owing to reductions in vehicle theft and domestic burglary, for which alarm manufacturers and increased householder vigilance probably deserve as much credit as the police. But violent crime has fallen too. It is now almost half what it was in 1995, and no higher than in 1981.

...

. . .

Looking more carefully, the big fall in brutality has been in domestic violence, which has dropped by a staggering 70%. (No one is sure why; the best guess is that an improving economy has kept men out of the house and given women enough money to escape if they need to.) Violence at the hands of strangers – the prospect that probably drives fear of crime more than anything else – has fallen by far less, and in fact rose in the most recent reporting period. Robbery has not gone down as much as burglary, perhaps because personal security has not improved in line with domestic security. But it too has been falling.

This sort of upbeat, wonkish analysis enrages those who insist that, for ordinary people, Britain is a more frightening place than it once was, whatever official statistics might say. In parts of the country, and some of the time, that is bound to be true. Until recently the Home Office crime survey did not interview under-16s. Nor does it weight serious crimes more heavily than mild ones, which means that a drop in bicycle theft could cancel out an increase in assaults. The Conservatives say that this has masked a rise in rare but serious crimes – particularly gun and knife crime.

The evidence is mixed. Gun crime has in fact been pretty flat nationwide. Data on knife crime are poor, but some doctors say that they are dealing with more stabbings, and the number of murders involving "sharp instruments" (bottles as well as knives) has risen slightly. Murders using guns increased alarmingly during the first few years of Labour's time in office, but have since dropped back down. Indeed, the day before Mr Cameron made his "broken society" pitch it was announced that the total number of homicides recorded by the police was at its lowest in 19 years.

The Economist (economist.com), 4/2/2010

A. Language

1. Find synonyms in the first two paragraphs of the article for the following: *horrifying, made shiver, distress, dreadful, bizarre and abnormal, adolescent, assaults, allegedly, found guilty of.*

2. Find antonyms in paragraphs 3 and 4 of the article for the following: *was downplayed, follower, common/widespread, glorious, gentle, decreasing, seldom, optimistic, satisfied people, boom.*

B. Question

Use information in the article to answer but do not copy sentences directly: use your own words.

To what extent is David Cameron justified in saying Britain is "a broken society"? (250 words)

Overview

Read a general overview of the subject.

Never had it so good?

In 1959, despite signs that wartime solidarity was disintegrating a little, the advent of the Welfare State, a boom in the world economy and increased social, geographical and occupational mobility led Prime Minister Harold McMillan to declare that Britons had "never had it so good".

This optimism lasted until the late 60s, but things began to change when inflation, unemployment and strikes – all largely associated with the oil crisis of the 70s – began to tear at the fibre of society. It became common to find families "living on benefit", to hear of dissatisfied people losing respect for traditional values, to observe community spirit disappearing fast… Joblessness and bad housing (notably in tower blocks of council flats) gave rise to phenomena that are now common features of inner-city life: drug-dealing and related violent crime, binge-drinking, truancy, gang warfare, inadequate parenting, no-go areas for police… Young people are the vast majority of offenders and, in an attempt to deal with behaviour that has plagued inner cities and council house estates for decades, the ASBO (Anti-Social Behaviour Order) was introduced in 1998.

During the Thatcher years (1979-1990) the rift between the "haves" and the "have nots" widened (it is now the widest in the EU). Union powers were truncated by the Employment Acts of 1980 and 1982, making it easy to sack people and difficult for unions to operate a closed shop. And, while more people were having to fight to keep body and soul together, at the other end of the scale, "golden boys" were making fortunes on the stock market and consumerism was running wild, replacing traditional upper-class values of moderation, discretion and thrift.

In circumstances like these, it is not surprising that anger and frustration should come to the fore. But not since the 19th century has Britain seen such urban violence: gangs of youths roaming city streets at night, random knife attacks, violent behaviour in hospitals, at sports grounds and on public transport…

According to a recent survey, Britain is on the edge of some form of social upheaval. Various social groups have reached breaking point: union members who have seen their power and influence dwindle, unemployed youths who see no future for themselves, couples who were given a mortgage by a greedy bank and whose home has been repossessed because they couldn't keep up the payments… And, at the bottom of the heap, an underclass of people who find themselves excluded from the society they grew up in.

Pronunciation

Listen and repeat.

flies [flaɪz], **fries** [fraɪz]

- correct/collect, flight/fright, jaw/draw, surprise/supplies
- Supplies of French fries came as a nice surprise on our flight!

Chapter 9

Social classes

Language focus

ø ou the devant un nom pluriel ?

- Comparez ces quatre phrases :

  1. *There were* **ø** *bus drivers among the strikers.*
  Il y avait des chauffeurs de bus parmi les grévistes.
  2. **ø** *Bus drivers don't earn much money.*
  Les chauffeurs de bus ne gagnent pas beaucoup d'argent.
  3. ***The*** *bus drivers who refused to work were sacked.*
  Les chauffeurs de bus qui ont refusé de travailler, furent licenciés.
  4. ***The*** *Greeks drink ouzo,* ***the*** *French drink wine.*
  Les Grecs boivent de l'ouzo, les Français boivent du vin.

- Dans la phrase n° 1, *bus drivers* est le pluriel de ***a*** *bus driver*, tout comme « des chauffeurs » est le pluriel de « un chauffeur ». Puisqu'il n'existe pas de forme pluriel de l'article indéfini *a/an*, on utilise « l'article zéro » – c'est-à-dire, pas d'article – que l'on indique par le symbole ø.
- Dans la phrase n° 2, on parle des chauffeurs de bus en général. Quand on parle de généralités, on ne met pas d'article défini (*the*) devant le nom pluriel.
- Dans la phrase n° 3, on utilise *the* parce qu'on parle d'un groupe de chauffeurs bien identifié. Il ne s'agit pas des chauffeurs en général.
- Dans la phrase n° 4, on utilise *the* + un adjectif au pluriel pour caractériser un générique pluriel, qui va servir à contraster deux classes, par exemple.

Wordbank

anti-poverty measures	*des mesures pour combattre la pauvreté*
to bequeath	*léguer*
a burden	*un fardeau*
a class-bound/-ridden society	*une société bloquée/minée par l'idée de classe*
the class struggle	*la lutte des classes*
a classless society	*une société sans classes sociales*
the cornerstone of society	*la pierre angulaire*
to decay	*décliner*
the fabric of society	*la structure de la société*
to foster resentment	*alimenter le ressentiment/les frustrations*
a framework	*un cadre, une structure*
hardship	*la pauvreté*
high society	*la haute société*

the inner city	*le centre-ville (= le quartier défavorisé)*
the ladder of success	*l'échelle sociale*
a landowner	*un propriétaire foncier*
the lower/working class	*la classe ouvrière*
to make ends meet	*joindre les deux bouts*
to make it to the top	*arriver en haut de l'échelle*
a manual job	*un poste manuel*
a means test, means-tested	*une enquête de ressources, basé sur les ressources*
the middle class	*la classe moyenne*
the minimum wage	*le salaire minimum*
the offspring	*la progéniture*
a policy-maker	*un décideur politique*
posh	*chic, snob, distingué*
the roots of poverty	*les racines de la pauvreté*
a row of terraced houses	*une rangée de maisons mitoyennes*
the ruling class	*la classe gouvernante*
to shrink the state	*réduire l'intervention de l'État*
the social fabric	*le tissu social*
a social indicator	*un indicateur social*
to squander	*gaspiller*
a standard of living	*un niveau de vie*
tax relief	*des dégrèvements d'impôts*
the suburbs	*la banlieue*
to map out	*tracer les grandes lignes*
a top civil servant	*un mandarin de la fonction publique*
the top drawer	*le gratin, la haute*
to underpin	*étayer, sous-tendre*
unfairness	*l'injustice*
the upper class	*la grande/haute bourgeoisie et l'aristocratie*
upwardly mobile	*en pleine ascension sociale*
well-heeled	*nanti*
well-off	*aisé*
a widening gap	*un écart grandissant*

Translation

Translate the sentences into English.

1. L'écart entre les riches et les pauvres grandit dans les pays occidentaux depuis le début des années 80.

2. Les valeurs communes qui étayent les structures sociales ont changé depuis la création de l'État-providence dans les années 40.

3. Les étudiants issus de la classe ouvrière ont beaucoup moins de chances que la progéniture des nantis de grimper l'échelle sociale.

4. Malgré les mesures mises en œuvre pour combattre la pauvreté, de nombreux foyers n'arrivent pas à joindre les deux bouts.

5. Le Rêve américain était fondé sur la réussite sociale par le travail alors que la société britannique était restée minée par la conscience de classe.

Read and answer

Read the article and then do activities A and B that follow.

Budget 2010: The very fabric of society will be put at risk by this unfair Budget

Britain would be on the road to ruin but for the diversion signs to be laid down in the most vicious Budget in memory. That warning will, George Osborne hopes, be enough to convince the public that there is no other track to recovery. Forget the less barren pathways selected by Labour or the scenic routes once mapped by the Lib Dems. The only chance, the Chancellor will tell us, is to ride the fairness freeway to salvation. He is wrong.

The promised land to which Mr Osborne points would be neither fair, nor free. On the contrary, this Budget risks tearing society apart. Economic interests and human instincts alike decree that we must create a secure destiny for our children and their children. And yet, bizarrely, the chief targets of the Coalition's economic policy are the young. Already, 500,000 needy children have been denied free school lunches and child trust funds have gone. The Future Jobs Fund, created to get 150,000 young people into work, has been ditched and free swimming sunk.

The Budget is likely to cut deeper, with Mr Osborne eroding child tax credits and, later if not now, child benefit for all. Forget the argument that middle-class handouts represent a couple of bottles of chardonnay. As the Child Poverty Action Group points out, families on £30,000 a year find it hard to make ends meet, and reintroducing a means-tested system would impose stigma, expensive bureaucracy and the severing of a universal principle that binds citizens together.

Keeping children in poverty, which already costs £25 billion a year, benefits no one. Nor are Mr Osborne's likely measures aimed only at the poor. Despite youth unemployment at a 17-year high and rising, 10,000 university places have been cut. The loan-burdened students on whose education the future prosperity of Britain will rest have been called a burden on the taxpayer by David Willetts, the universities minister. [...]

Yet this Budget risks entrenching an unfairness, the effects of which will last long after economic upturn. The signs are that it will penalise the young both directly and indirectly, through raising VAT, throwing people out of work and punishing families on modest incomes. Poverty, however you define it, is mainly miserable for the poor. Unfairness tarnishes the affluent and the destitute alike. [...)

You might imagine, from government preamble, that the financial crisis was incubated not in bank boardrooms but in benefit offices, or that the instruments of economic destruction were dreamed up in Sure Start centres and youth clubs rather than over Krug on financiers' yachts. [...]

Mr Osborne could take another path. As the Institute for Public Policy Research suggests, a staged 3p increase in the basic and higher rates of income tax would raise £15 billion and rebalance the planned 80:20 split between cuts and tax rises that makes it virtually impossible to shield the less well-off. He could also impose a tougher levy on bankers and financial institutions. All would produce howls of pain, but anything would be better than a fate that threatens all citizens, irrespective of age or wealth.

In the name of averting ruin, Mr Osborne risks rounding up the generation on whom the future of this nation depends and forcing it down the long road to perdition.

Mary Riddell, *The Daily Telegraph* (telegraph.co.uk) 21/6/2010

A. Language

Find synonyms in the title and the first two paragraphs of the article for the following: *structure, jeopardised, infertile/devoid of interest, planned/charted, unravelling the social fabric, in the same way, safe, oddly, have been refused, has been given up.*

B. Questions

Use information in the article to answer but do not copy sentences directly: use your own words.

1. What are the measures the Chancellor of the Exchequer is likely to take to save the country's economy? (50 words)

2. Why is the writer critical of such a policy ? (150 words)

3. What does the following sentence mean: "The very fabric of society will be put at risk by this unfair budget"? (100 words)

Translation

Translate the article into English.

Grande-Bretagne : les différences sociales pourraient peser sur l'issue du scrutin

Londres. Le milieu nanti auquel appartient David Cameron, ses manières distinguées et son parler chic pourraient bien le desservir aux législatives de jeudi en Grande-Bretagne, les plus serrées depuis des décennies. Dans une société hiérarchisée, le chef de file des conservateurs semble prisonnier des clichés de classe et de l'image qu'il renvoie.

Bien que les Tories aient été adoubés par *The Economist* pour leur projet de réduction du déficit et de relance de l'économie, leur leader âgé de 43 ans n'a pas réussi à gagner les cœurs des électeurs des classes ouvrière et moyenne dans les circonscriptions cruciales où l'issue du vote est indécise, alors même que ces électeurs se sentent abandonnés par le Labour et s'inquiètent pour leur emploi.

Voilà plusieurs mois, les sondages prédisaient que ces élections seraient celles de David Cameron, après le plongeon du Labour au bout de 13 ans de pouvoir. Mais un nouveau sondage ICM/Guardian diffusé lundi suggère que les conservateurs, crédités de 33 % des suffrages, n'atteindront pas la majorité, tandis que le Parti travailliste du Premier ministre Gordon Brown et les Libéraux démocrates de Nick Clegg sont à égalité, à 28 %. L'enquête a été réalisée du 20 avril au 2 mai par téléphone auprès de 1.026 personnes âgées de 18 ans et plus.

Les contrastes de classe abondent au Royaume-Uni, de la monarchie aux différences d'accents – de l'anglais chic de David Cameron à l'accent cockney de Londres, en passant par les dialectes du nord à Liverpool et Manchester. Des études à Oxford et Cambridge sont toujours considérées comme la crème de la crème, et préférer le polo au football, ou la chasse au renard aux courses de chiens peut en dire beaucoup sur le milieu social d'une personne.

AP (dans *Le Nouvel Observateur* [nouvelobs.com]), 4/5/2010

Overview

Read a general overview of the subject.

Money, class and power

The most important thing to understand about being upper class is that it has little or nothing to do with money or power. It's not what you've got but where you come from, where you went to school, how you speak and what you like or dislike. If you were born a working class man and think that you've become upper class because you've made a fortune making fur-covered toilet seats and now have an Aston Martin, a flat in Kensington and a villa in Tuscany, you've got another think coming. In your position, you may well socialise with upper class people who will probably treat you as their equal, but you can be sure that, behind their well-bred smiles, they are looking at your gold taps and silk suits and thinking: "not one of us".

Of course, you can't actually mention class in Britain these days: the very word is taboo. We are supposed to be living in a classless society with equal opportunity for all and limitless social mobility; at least, that is what the lower classes are encouraged to believe… The truth of the matter is that there are still three basic classes in Britain: the upper, middle and lower (or working) class.

The true upper class consists only of the aristocracy. It does not include all those who were given titles for doing lengthy service to government, industry or the arts. Former Prime Minister Margaret Thatcher, for instance, is not upper class despite her title of Baroness (conferred on her in 1992). As the daughter of a north-country grocer, she started life as lower-middle class and rose – by means of careful diction and doggedness – to just about upper-middle class. Even though she used upper-class models when choosing her politics, her accent and her hats, she is definitely "not one of us".

Progressing from working class to middle class is a different matter because middle class describes the great majority of Britons, from the humble clerk to the highest civil servant, and entry requirements are minimal: it simply means reading the *Guardian* instead of the *Daily Mirror* and shopping in Sainsbury's rather than Tesco's. Notice, however, that the *Guardian* costs more than the *Daily Mirror* and Sainsbury's is more expensive than Tesco's… Although wealth is not synonymous with class, the traditional pursuits and preoccupations of the upper-middle class (education, travel, the arts, philanthropy, entertaining…) do not come cheap.

Pronunciation

Listen and repeat.

Arthur [ˈɑːθə], **mother** [ˈmʌðə]

- thick, both, three, breathe, then, than.
- Arthur followed his father Uther through thick and thin back then.

10 Chapter

Devolution

Language focus

Le présent simple

• Le présent simple anglais a 2 valeurs.

1. On l'emploie pour parler d'une propriété du sujet, une vérité générale ou un fait de fréquence variable (de nulle à infinie) :

Mrs S. teaches English.
Elephants never forget.
Mrs S. never lies. She seldom cheats. She never cries.

2. On l'emploie pour raconter une histoire (on l'appelle alors le *present dramatic)* ou commenter un événement :

(documentaire TV) *In 1066 William now has enough ships and so he decides to invade England.*
(commentaire d'un match de football) *He's running towards the goal… he gets past one defender, two defenders, and he shoots!*

Wordbank

to adopt a stance	*prendre position*
an advocate of decentralisation	*un décentralisateur*
the aspirations	*les espoirs*
an assembly	*une assemblée*
to back an idea	*soutenir une idée*
a bitter pill to swallow	*une pilule amère, difficile à avaler*
a block grant	*une enveloppe financière globale*
the break-up of the UK	*la fragmentation du Royaume-Uni*
to conduct business	*conduire les affaires*
a cross-party committee	*une commission constituée de personnes de plusieurs courants politiques*
to decentralise	*décentraliser, déconcentrer (une administration)*
decentralisation	*la déconcentration administrative*
a devolved matter	*une activité déconcentrée*
a difficult relationship	*des rapports difficiles*
to draft legislation	*rédiger une législation*
emphatically opposed	*totalement opposé*
empowerment	*la délégation de pouvoir*
to empower	*déléguer du pouvoir, donner le pouvoir*
financial autonomy	*l'autonomie financière*

a first minister	*un premier ministre, le premier des ministres*
to grant powers	*accorder des pouvoirs*
to hail a success	*saluer une réussite*
the Holyrood administration	*le gouvernement de l'assemblée écossaise qui siege à Holyrood*
home rule	*l'autonomie*
horse-trading	*le marchandage*
legislative powers	*les pouvoirs législatifs*
legal powers	*les pouvoirs juridiques*
a mandatory commission	*une commission obligatoire*
MLA (Member of the [Northern Ireland] Legislative Assembly)	*député : assemblée de l'Irlande du nord*
MSP (Member of the Scottish Parliament)	*député : assemblée de l'Écosse*
MWA (Member of the Welsh Assembly)	*député : assemblée du pays de Galles*
outstandingly successful	*exceptionnellement réussi*
the political agenda	*l'ordre du jour politique*
to poll votes	*recueillir des voix*
to press	*mettre la pression sur*
to put forward legislation	*proposer une législation*
the standing orders	*le règlement intérieur*
reserved matters	*les questions réservées*
Royal Assent	*l'approbation royale*
to scotch	*étouffer, réprimer*
self-determination	*l'auto-détermination*
to shelve a project	*mettre un projet en suspens*
a steering group	*une commission de pilotage*
to stick to plans	*s'en tenir aux plans*
to strike a deal	*conclure un accord*
to tender one's resignation	*donner sa demission*
transferred matters	*les questions déléguées (à l'assemblée d'Irlande du nord)*
to vindicate	*justifier, faire valoir*
to vote in favour of	*voter pour*

Translation

Translate the sentences into English.

1. La décentralisation a donné aux assemblées d'Écosse et du Pays de Galles le pouvoir de gérer de façon autonome leurs propres affaires.

2. Le processus de décentralisation lancé par le gouvernement travailliste de Tony Blair à la fin des années 90 a requis l'accord de la reine pour être voté au parlement.

3. Les Écossais élisent leurs députés, et le gouvernement de l'assemblée écossaise propose des lois sur les questions sociales de l'Écosse.

4. Pour certains parlementaires anglais, l'autonomie politique et financière accordée à l'Écosse fut une pilule qui eut du mal à passer.

5. Les commissions de pilotage sont parfois obligées de mettre un projet en attente parce qu'il requiert l'accord du parlement à Londres.

Read and answer

Read the article and then do activities A and B that follow.

Ten Years of Devolution

This is a day for anniversaries: my 35th and the Scottish Parliament's 10th. The latter is, I concede, the more significant milestone. Once upon a time George Robertson, then Shadow Scottish Secretary, declared that devolution would kill the demand for independence "stone dead". His Labour colleague, Tam Dalyell, disagreed predicting that devolution would put us on the "motorway" towards independence. Well, a decade later, neither man has been vindicated and, indeed, the case remains Not Proven.

Scotland does not stand where once she did, but nor has her future path been determined. It is still too soon to say whether devolution has been a success, but some myths concerning it deserve to be, forgive me, scotched. The first of these - one that one has frequently been aired in the pages of the Daily Telegraph and the Daily Mail - is that devolution was part of a Blairite plot to destroy Britain. Not so. Indeed, if Tony Blair could have avoided devolution he would have done so. But it was part of his inheritance and could not be avoided. There was, whether England realised it or not, a genuine demand for Home Rule.

Not that this was a new idea. Indeed, Labour had technically been in favour of devolution since the party's foundation. Nonetheless, Labour's conversion to the idea of Home Rule was built upon an essentially negative analysis of British politics and political trends. On the one hand devolution was supposed to shoot the nationalist fox; on the other it was a means of protecting Scotland against the supposed ravages of Conservative rule at Westminster.

So it was not a great surprise that Labour, though committed by 1997 to the idea of a parliament in Edinburgh, had little idea as to what it might do with that parliament once it came into being. This was partly, though not only, because the best and the brightest members of the Scottish Labour party were more concerned with what Labour might do once given the chance to rule the whole of the United Kingdom.

Nonetheless, most of Scottish Labour's talent remained in London, ensuring that, with the exception of Donald Dewar, it was largely the B Team that entered government, in coalition with the Liberal Democrats, in Edinburgh. In truth, the new parliament had a pretty modest agenda and the new First Minister had few more powers than he would have done had he merely been administering Scotland as Secretary of State. [...]

Devolution also recognised an important political and psychological point often, I think, overlooked or ignored in England: the United Kingdom is a Union, not England with a few Scots and Welsh and Irish added on. It's easy to understand why the English, being so numerically superior, might forget this but it's not something so easily ignored on this side of the Tweed. Pierre Trudeau's famous quip about being "In bed with an elephant" resonates in Scotland. And reasonably so.

This is something that is sometimes forgotten in England. It is not always easy or comfortable to be part of a political entity in which you are outnumberd 10:1. That discomfort is exacerbated when the majority partner seems, as is often the case, to conflate English with British. The Union may be something of an abstract notion in England,

...

but it's concrete up here. Britain is a multi-national state with all the layered, complex and sometimes contradictory loyalties that implies.

I use the word partner deliberately. The idea of a voluntary union existed in Scotland well before the actual Union came into being. (Successive English monarchs, of course, had a different view.) Indeed the idea of Union predates even the Union of the Crowns in 1603. But my sense is that many English people do not see the Union as a partnership and, instead, assume that Great Britain is really Greater England. Not so! [...]

Britain and Britishness are ideas and powerful ones at that. But they are not necessarily undermined by devolution. Nor, it should be said is Scottishness undermined by Britain. Not for nothing does Alex Salmond often sweeten the independence pill by stressing that the "social Union" between Scotland and England would continue. He's right to say this, not least because our histories and cultures are so intertwined. Indeed, though they might dispute it, the Irish are still in important and significant respects British. The same would be true of any putative independent Scotland. [...]

Devolution has been, despite the long list of terrible bills passed at Holyrood (terrible in my estimation of course), a success and a welcome affirmation of the fact that Britain is, as I say, a multi-nation state. There are, for sure, flaws in the current arrangements but these can be worked out in the years to come. Devolution then may have, paradoxical as it may seem, weakened Britain in order to save it. Time will tell. What it has done, however, is make what was always true, clear: Britain is not England and England is not Britain.

Alex Massie, *The Spectator* (spectator.co.uk), 1/7/2009

A. Language

Find synonyms in the first two paragraphs of the article for the following: *birthdays, meaningful, watershed, foreseeing, decentralisation of power, proved right, decided, stopped, has been expressed, conspiracy, legacy, real/honest.*

B. Questions

Use information in the article to answer but do not copy sentences directly: use your own words.

1. How does the writer justify his support of the devolution process? (250 words)

2. What were the arguments used by those who opposed the idea of devolution? (50 words)

Overview

Read a general overview of the subject.

The West Lothian Question

During the election campaign of 1997, Tony Blair promised that, if the Labour Party won, devolution would be granted to Scotland, Wales and Northern Ireland.

Although Northern Ireland politics were very sensitive, Scotland and Wales were not exactly hotbeds of revolt. But there had been bomb attacks by Welsh terrorists in the 1960s provoked by the flooding of a Welsh valley to provide water for an English city and, since the 1970s, there had been concerns in Scotland that its rights to the income from North Sea oil were being usurped by the English. This was also a time when "control over one's one destiny" had become the battle-cry of the dissatisfied, so it was hardly surprising that the 1997 referendums showed majorities in favour of national assemblies.

The subsequent creation of the Scottish Parliament, the National Assembly for Wales and the Northern Ireland Assembly did not attract much attention from the average English person. After all, these assemblies could only legislate on what were essentially local matters; Westminster could veto any legislation it thought went against the interests of the Union. But then people realised that there was the "West Lothian question", a problem raised back in 1977 when the first debates about devolution had taken place.

The problem is that the Westminster Parliament is made up of MPs from England, Scotland, Wales and Northern Ireland. They vote on matters concerning all of those countries in all areas of policy. Therefore a Scottish MP at Westminster can vote on something that affects, say, the opening hours of shops in an English town. However, because of devolved powers, Westminster no longer votes on the opening hours of shops in *Scotland*. So, Scottish MPs at Westminster have a say in what happens in England, but English MPs at Westminster do *not* have a say in what happens in Scotland. This is obviously unfair, and has triggered politicians into suggesting a variety of solutions ranging from the creation of an English Assembly – dealing exclusively with English problems – to the abandonment of devolution. Many think that the bureaucracy involved in the former solution would make it totally impractical; others think that the latter solution might lead to demands for Welsh, Scottish and Northern Irish independence... One thing is sure, a solution has to be found: the English think the present situation is not fair play – and they don't like it.

Pronunciation

Listen and repeat.

ship [ʃɪp], **sheep** [ʃiːp]

- bin/bean, mill/meal, hit/eat, chick/cheek, hill/heal.
- Good evening, this week we'll be speaking to Jean and Peter Smith.

Chapter 10

Britishness

Language focus

Be + V-ing

• *Be* + V-*ing* (ou la forme progressive, *the present continuous*) s'emploie pour mettre l'accent sur l'activité en cours de déroulement (passé, présent ou futur) :

Janet's in the garden. She's watering the flowers.
Janet est dans le jardin. Elle est en train d'arroser les fleurs.
I was watering the garden when the doorbell rang.
J'étais en train d'arroser le jardin quand on a sonné à la porte.
We'll be arriving in ten minutes.
On va arriver dans dix minutes.

ou pour ajouter une nuance de jugement critique, en particulier associée à l'adverbe *always* :

She's always cheating!
l faut toujours qu'elle triche !

• Certains verbes sont dits récalcitrants à la forme *be* + V-*ing* de par leur sens : verbes d'état (*seem*), d'état mental (*know*), de perception involontaire (*hear*), de sentiment (*love*).

Wordbank

a bank holiday	*un jour férié*
the BBC (British Broadcasting Corporation)	*l'Office de la radiodiffusion et télévision britannique*
to bestow on	*octroyer, conférer*
binding values	*les valeurs communes*
a (true) Brit	*un Britannique (patriotique)*
britpop	*la musique pop britannique des années 1990*
caning	*le chatiment corporel (la punition à coups de baguette à l'école)*
(a) Cockney	*un habitant d'un quartier populaire de Londres et son accent*
common law	*le droit coutumier*
to crack something up to be	*vanter les mérites de quelque chose*
fair play	*le respect des règles*
a farmers' market	*un marché de produits du terroir*
fish and chips	*poisson frit et frites*
chicken tikka masala	*curry de poulet tikka masala*

to fly the flag	*arborer le drapeau*
the fragmentation	*la destructuration*
freedom of expression	*la liberté d'expression*
God-given	*donné par Dieu*
to hark back to Empire	*avoir la nostalgie de l'Empire*
hooliganism	*le vandalisme*
an identity crisis	*une crise d'identité*
to keep a stiff upper lip	*rester impassible*
a limey *(US fam., vieilli)*	*un Anglais*
multicultural	*multiculturel*
the National Trust	*l'association pour la préservation de sites et monuments*
nationhood	*le sentiment d'identité nationale*
an open economy	*une économie ouverte*
a pom *(Aust., fam.)*	*un Anglais*
Poppy Day	*le jour où on porte un coquelicot à la boutonnière en souvenir des morts au combat (le 11 novembre)*
(the pound) sterling	*la livre britannique*
a press magnate/baron	*un magnat de la presse*
a professional army	*une armée de métier*
Remembrance Sunday	*le dimanche du souvenir des morts au combat (le 11 novembre)*
Royal Ascot	*des courses hippiques en juin à Ascot*
the rule of law	*l'autorité de la loi*
school uniform	*l'uniforme scolaire*
a shareholder	*un actionnaire*
a pub	*un pub, un bar*
the right accent	*le bon accent*
a thorny issue	*une question épineuse*
trooping the colour	*la présentation des couleurs de régiment*
unarmed police	*la police non-arméee*
the Union Jack/Union Flag	*le drapeau britannique*
the WI (Women's Institute)	*l'association volontaire de femmes*

Translation

Translate the sentences into English.

1. Une question épineuse est en train d'être débattue au parlement : faut-il remettre le bœuf bouilli aux carottes au menu des écoles britanniques ?

2. Mary LeBow n'est pas vraiment cockney, elle traverse juste une crise d'identité culturelle.

3. Il faut toujours qu'il clame sa nostalgie des jours glorieux de l'empire britannique et monte les couleurs devant la maison.

4. Les dizaines d'ivrognes agressifs en train d'envahir les pubs du centre-ville sont un triste exemple de la culture de la beuverie qui mine le pays depuis une décennie.

5. Je ne pense pas que les britanniques vantent les mérites de leur système de sélection universitaire en ce moment.

Read and answer

Read the article and then do activities A and B that follow.

Who are we?

Immigration yielded the worst gaffe of the campaign on April 28th, when a microphone caught Gordon Brown describing as "bigoted" a widow who had just complained to him about it. For the most part, however, one of the biggest issues facing Britain (so people tell opinion pollsters) has been ignored in the run-up to the election on May 6th. Immigration merits about a page in each of the Labour, Conservative and Liberal Democrat manifestos.

Such reticence makes political sense. Labour largely ducked talking about the issue as it presided over the biggest influx Britain has ever seen: 5.6m people have come to the country for at least a year since 1997. Much of this was down to a decision by the government not to impose temporary restrictions on migrants from the central and eastern European countries that joined the European Union in 2004.

The Tories, meanwhile, avoid the subject for fear of reviving their old image as the "nasty party" – an image assiduously softened under the leadership of David Cameron. The Lib Dems' caginess is similarly political: their relatively relaxed line on immigration, which includes an earned amnesty for some illegal migrants, does not go down well with most voters.

Compared with a decade ago, the *laissez-faire* approach to immigration has fewer takers, even on the left. Influential writers such as Polly Toynbee of the *Guardian* and David Goodhart of *Prospect* worry that the welfare-state consensus may not hold if those paying for it feel less connection to those benefiting from it. Britain's liberal culture may be compromised as migrants with illiberal values arrive. And MPs such as Frank Field and Jon Cruddas, at the cerebral end of the Labour Party, talk of the stress that immigration puts on public services.

This change in elite opinion has something to do with the lack of conclusive academic evidence that the past decade's influx has been the economic boon it was cracked up to be. To be sure, migrants have not "stolen" jobs from Britons. Employers need the newcomers, especially in sectors such as agriculture where many of the low-paid jobs migrants take would not make sense at the higher wages needed to attract natives from unemployment and other benefits. And talented, educated foreigners have made up for a lack of highly skilled local workers too. But although immigration has contributed to economic growth overall, there is no evidence that income per person has gone up greatly as a result. And if the argument for immigration is utilitarian – that is, that some people lose out from it but the economy benefits overall – this matters.

Britain's new points system, which sets educational and other restrictions on non-EU immigrants, may have started to make a dent in the numbers, as would the absolute cap on arrivals suggested by the Tories. More importantly, the slower economy and weaker pound of recent years have cut inflows and encouraged some migrants in Britain to move on. The lion's share of immigration is from the EU and cannot be restricted; even if it could, EU rules also let Britons move the other way. Some 5.5m of them now live abroad, many in Europe, according to the Institute for Public Policy Research, a ...

...

think-tank. The absence of a proper system for recording the flow of migrants, and for preventing illegal entry, is troubling.

But if there is little the government can do to cut the number of immigrants, it may be able to do more to integrate them once they arrive. The shift in opinion away from open borders has been matched by a move away from Britain's traditionally hands-off approach to identity. Unequivocal defenders of multiculturalism are now hard to find; even its advocates concede the need for newcomers to learn to speak English, and, to a degree, for values and institutions to bind together a diverse population.

Much of this is happening: language tests, exams on life in Britain, citizenship ceremonies and a nascent idea of civic service for young people may, slowly, build a richer idea of citizenship. "Britain is engaged in a mild form of nation-building," says Mr Goodhart. "We didn't even use the term 'citizen' very much in 1997."

Most countries that try to assimilate immigrants, such as France and America, can point to a defining event when their national identity "began"; Britain did not have the same kind of revolution. But it has much else to inspire newcomers: a sweeping history that is also broadly progressive, a language everyone wants to speak, longer experience of racial diversity than most European nations. And "Britain" itself is a civic invention rather than an ethnic community, created in 1707 to supersede more blood-based notions of Englishness and Scottishness. [...]

Civic nationalism is no longer easily dismissed as a French or American notion, not least because attitudes were changed by the events of July 7th 2005, when Britain became the first and so far only Western country to suffer suicide bombings by people born and raised at home. Mr Brown's own attempts to put "Britishness" on the table also played their part. Sadly, his contribution to matters of immigration and identity is likely to be reduced to a petulant quip during a losing campaign.

The Economist (economist.com), 29/4/2010

A. Language

Find synonyms in the first three paragraphs of the article for the following: *blunder, intolerant, moaned, problems, polling agencies, reluctance, is logical from a political point of view, avoided, was due to, limits, became members of, shun, industriously, cautious behaviour, tolerant stance, is not appreciated by.*

B. Questions

Use information in the article to answer but do not copy sentences directly: use your own words.

1. Describe the impact that immigration has had on Britishness, according to the writer. (250 words)

2. What do the following sentences mean: "One of the biggest issues facing Britain has been ignored in the run-up to the elction. Immigration merits about one page in each of the Labour, Conservative and Liberal Democrat manifestos"? (100 words)

Overview

Read a general overview of the subject.

What it means to be British

"British" is an adjective often used when national pride or status is involved: a British passport, the British Olympics team, British beef, the British Empire, the British Embassy... But ask "British" people what nationality they are and you will get a variety of answers.

More than two-thirds of white people born and bred in England will answer "English." Black, Asian, mixed-race or foreign-born citizens living in England will most probably answer "British," as will some Scots and Welsh people, although many of these prefer to be identified with their individual country first and the UK second. As for the Northern Irish... well, you have to tread very carefully there.

The fact that most white English people call themselves "English" rather than "British" is undeniably linked to the historical supremacy of England in the British Isles and and to the fact that being "British" has no real specificity in terms of national character except for tenacity and courage in adversity. To put it bluntly: when you're faced by a common enemy, you're British; when you're defining your individual identity, you're English. Foreigners unaware of this subtlety frequently confuse "British" and "English" and will say of someone who, for example, is understating his own merit: "That's so British", whereas being self-deprecating is an English stereotype, not a British one.

In 1968, the government tried to make the English, Welsh, Scots and Northern Irish think of themselves as British and buy British goods in order to improve the Balance of Trade. The "I'm Backing Britain" campaign was taken seriously by some, but the main campaign symbol – the British flag – was adopted (tongue-in-cheek) by youth culture and millions of Union Jack T-shirts, Union Jack mugs, in fact Union Jack anythings... appeared in trendy shops. Since most of these were made abroad and not in Britain, this rather defeated the original object. The campaign soon lost ground and "Britishness" went underground for a bit. It was time to try and blend in with Europe...

At the present time, after several decades of frustration, anger and fear caused by the flow of directives from Brussels, lax immigration laws, the excesses of multiculturalism and the reality of terrorism, there has arisen a new definition of Britishness which involves not so much character as behaviour. Despite the sinister overtones of such views, they seem to be permeating British society in a climate of uncertainty about the future.

Pronunciation

Listen and repeat.

sit [sɪt], **set** [set]

- miss/mess, nick/neck, fill/fell, mint/meant, hill/hell.
- Will Ted sing to Kim in his bed?

12 Chapter

Immigration

Language focus

La transposition

• La transposition est la technique qui consiste à traduire un terme d'une langue source par un terme d'une catégorie grammaticale différente dans la langue cible :

– nom => verbe

I threatened him with divorce.

Je l'ai menacé de divorcer.

– adjectif => nom

I met him in the late 90s.

Je l'ai rencontré à la fin des années 90.

– adverbe => verbe

I finally managed to write it.

J'ai fini par arriver à l'écrire.

– préposition => verbe

She appeared in a beautiful dress.

Elle entra, portant une robe magnifique.

Wordbank

to apply for settlement	*demander le droit de s'installer*
to acquire citizenship	*obtenir la citoyenneté*
an asylum seeker	*un demandeur d'asile*
to beg	*quémander, mendier*
to blend in	*s'intégrer*
border control	*la surveillance des frontières*
a border check	*un contrôle à la frontière*
to cap	*plafonner*
citizenship by descent	*la citoyenneté par filiation*
a common travel area	*une zone de libre circulation*
to comply with the rules	*observer les règles*
to deport	*expulser, renvoyer hors des frontières*
deportation	*l'expulsion*
to deprive someone of their basic rights	*priver quelqu'un de ses droits fondamentaux*
to detain	*détenir*
dual citizenship	*la double nationalité*
entry clearance	*la procédure d'admission*
fast-track deportation	*l'expulsion rapide*

to flee oppression	*fuir l'oppression*
HSMP (Highly-Skilled Migrant Programme)	*procédure pour encourager l'immigration de migrants qualifiés*
illegal employment	*l'emploi illégal*
an immigration removal centre	*un centre de rétention administrative*
insalubrious/insanitary accommodation	*le logement insalubre*
a last-ditch appeal	*un appel de dernière minute*
leave to enter/remain/work	*la permission d'entrer/de s'installer/de travailler*
the life in the UK test	*le test passé par des migrants souhaitant s'établir au Royaume-Uni*
a low-paid job	*un emploi mal payé*
a menial job	*un petit boulot*
migratory flows	*les flux migratoires*
moonlighting	*le travail au noir*
the oath of allegiance	*le serment de loyauté*
a points-based screening	*une sélection basée sur un classement par points*
a removal centre	*un centre de transit*
a resident worker	*un travailleur résident*
to scrounge	*vivre aux crochets de quelqu'un*
self-sufficient	*auto-suffisant*
to send back	*renvoyer*
to settle (down)	*s'installer*
a skilled migrant	*un immigrant ayant des savoir faire*
a smuggling ring	*un réseau de passeurs*
to sneak past	*passer discrètement*
stateless	*apatride*
to throw out	*mettre à la porte*
the tier system	*le classement d'immigrants selon leurs savoir faire*
to screen	*passer en revue, sélectionner*
to toughen the rules	*durcir les règles*
to unroll/roll up the welcome mat	*dérouler/remballer le tapis rouge*
a visa holder	*un détenteur d'un visa*
to welcome	*accueillir*
a work permit	*un permis de travail*

Translation

Translate the sentences into English.

1. Le gouvernement britannique a menacé les immigrés clandestins de les expulser vers leur pays d'origine.

2. Au début des années 2000, la Grande-Bretagne a accepté d'accueillir des milliers de travailleurs immigrés d'Europe de l'est.

3. Sous la pression des médias hostiles à une nouvelle vague d'immigrants, le gouvernement a fini par remballer le tapis rouge.

4. En laissant entrer davantage de main d'œuvre qualifiée, la Grande-Bretagne a amélioré la productivité de son économie.

5. Le gouvernement a voulu préserver des emplois pour ses chômeurs en refoulant presque tous les demandeurs d'asile.

Read and answer

Read the articles and then do activities A and B that follow.

This sceptical isle

"The old, honest English stock" is being diluted by asylum seekers of a "different and base species". So complained Francis Atterbury, the Bishop of Rochester, in a 1714 moan about the Palatine refugees from the Rhineland. Immigrants have always and everywhere had a rough time. But a poll published on December 3rd suggested that today's Britons are particularly hostile. Of six European countries plus America and Canada, Britain emerged as by far the least happy about immigration.

Britons felt most strongly that there were too many immigrants in their country, and disapproved most categorically of their government's management of inflows. Worries focused on jobs and resources: Britons were the most likely to say that immigrants were taking jobs and the least likely to say they should have access to the same state benefits as natives. Social issues were less sensitive: immigrants were not blamed for crime as they were in Germany, say, and Britons were not especially likely to complain about cultural clashes. And, interestingly for the MPs currently lobbying for the adoption of a "guest-worker" scheme, a (slim) majority said they preferred permanent migration to the temporary sort.

The overall message, though, was an overwhelming thumbs-down. Why? Britain does not have an unusually high proportion of migrants among its population (higher than France and Italy, but lower than the other five countries in the sample). But it has recently fielded a big, visible rush from eastern Europe, which by some measures is its biggest influx since the Huguenots in the 17th century.

The unpopular 12-year-old government may be another reason for the bolshie sentiment, as may be a recent slight increase in the willingness of the Tories to talk about this sensitive subject. Britons expressed enthusiasm for stronger border-policing to reduce illegal migration, a longstanding Tory theme (and a nonsense, as most illegals are overstayers rather than sneakers-in).

Newspapers also play a part. British ones are shriller and more widely read than in most countries. And national papers are more popular than regional ones, meaning that even people in areas with low immigration read about it every day. Roughly 10% of people in Britain are immigrants; the average Briton believed the figure to be 27%.

The Economist (economist.com), 3/12/2009

Theresa May: immigration cap will not harm UK economy

The Home Secretary, Theresa May, insisted today that the coalition government's immigration cap would not be economically damaging to the UK. May will confirm this morning that immediate restrictions will limit the number of workers entering the UK from outside the Europe Union to 24,100 before April 2011, a fall of 5% on last year.

"Introducing this temporary limit is necessary to ensure that we don't get a rush of people trying to come through into the UK before that permanent limit is put in place next year," the Home Secretary told BBC Radio 4's Today programme. "What we have

...

as an aim is indeed to bring immigration down from the hundreds of thousands that it became under Labour to the tens of thousands that it used to be. There are various ways in which we do that."

The immigration cap was one of the Conservatives' flagship policies during the election campaign but there has been speculation that it could be watered down in the face of opposition from the City and some Tory ministers.

May rejected the idea that a cap would be harmful to business, arguing that it had not affected the competitiveness of other economies.

"I don't think that anybody would ever suggest that Australia or the United States or New Zealand, in operating an annual limit, weren't able to get into the country the skilled people that they need and that their economies were somehow suffering from that annual limit," she said.

The Home Secretary rebuffed suggestions that the policy would be ineffective because it could not restrict the number of immigrants from the EU.

May said that, according to the most recent immigration figures, just over half – 52% – came from outside the EU.

Net migration to the UK was 142,000 in the year to September 2009, down from 160,000 in the previous 12 months.

Labour claimed the fall was due to its tough immigration policies, but the Tories said it was a result of the economic downturn.

The Lib Dems were opposed to a cap during the election campaign but it was included in the agreement with the Tories that formed the basis for the coalition government.

The Guardian (guardian.co.uk), 28/6/2010

A. Language

1. Find synonyms in the first paragraph of the first article for the following: *race/ancestry, contemptible, a complaint, a testing time, unfriendly, the most critical of.*

2. Find antonyms in the first six paragraphs of the second article for the following: *beneficial, leaving, permanent, to boost, endorsed/supported the idea, harmless, unskilled, welcomed, effective.*

B. Questions

Use information in the articles to answer but do not copy sentences directly: use your own words.

1. First article. Why are the Btitish hostile to immigration ? (150 words)

2. Second article.What is the recently-elected government aiming to do? (50 words)

3. Second article. For what reasons is the immigration cap criticised? (50 words)

Translation

Translate the article into English.

La Grande-Bretagne veut réduire l'immigration

En raison du ralentissement de l'économie et de la montée du chômage, la Grande-Bretagne prévoit de limiter le nombre d'étrangers sur son territoire, déclare le ministre de l'Immigration, Phil Woolas, dans une interview publiée samedi par *The Times*.

« Quand les gens sont sans emploi, la question de l'immigration devient extrêmement épineuse. Il a été trop facile dans le passé d'entrer dans ce pays et cela va devenir plus difficile », prévient-il.

« Ce gouvernement ne va pas laisser la population s'accroître jusqu'à 70 millions. Il doit y avoir un équilibre entre les gens qui arrivent et les gens qui partent », souligne Woolas.

En période de difficultés économiques, poursuit-il, les employeurs doivent privilégier les Britanniques faute de quoi ils risquent d'alimenter le racisme.

Woolas se prononce enfin contre toute régularisation des immigrants illégaux pour éviter d'encourager l'immigration clandestine.

La population britannique est estimée à 61 millions d'habitants. Selon le *Times*, l'immigration nette est de plus 200.000 personnes par an.

Reuters (dans *Le Point* [lepoint.fr]), 18/10/2008

Overview

Read a general overview of the subject.

The cost of immigration

Immigration in Britain has been hitting the headlines on and off for about 50 years. It started in 1948 when the British Nationality Act made it possible for citizens of the British Empire – around 800 million people – to live and work in the UK without a visa. Altruistic? Not really. The aim of the Act was to attract enough colonial manpower to rebuild Britain's war-damaged economy.

But immigration numbers soared. Economic migrants from the Caribbean combined with refugees from the conflict in India and Pakistan following separation (there are now 2 million UK residents of Indian or Pakistani origin). Concerns about these rising numbers led to the Commonwealth Immigrants Act of 1962 which required would-be immigrants to have jobs waiting for them in the UK or special skills that were needed on the labour market. Finally, as from 1972 (the Immigration Act), all distinctions between Commonwealth and non-Commonwealth citizens were dropped, making it obligatory for immigrants to have a work permit and/or parents or grandparents in the UK.

During the Cold War period, there was relatively little immigration from non-Commonwealth countries, except for political refugees – for example, after the Hungarian uprising in 1956. But then came the Common Market and the European Union. In

...

compliance with the "Four Freedoms" of the EU, the UK has admitted large numbers of immigrants from Eastern Europe over recent years. A "points system" based on job prospects does however restrict the numbers.

The result is that, out of a total of over 60 million, about 7 million UK residents are non-white and 3 million are white but not British. More than 8% of UK residents were born abroad. The question is: is this a problem? Racists will of course answer yes, and so will those who believe – quite wrongly according to recent statistics – that immigrants are a burden on the Welfare State. Others, who believe that Britain has been enriched by immigration, will not agree.

Illegal immigration is a different matter. Whether or not one sympathises with Britain's 500,000 or so illegal aliens, it has been calculated that to deport them would cost over £10 billion. By legalising them, the government would get over £1 billion a year in additional tax revenue but might lose a few billion every year in health care… But should financial considerations dominate what is, after all, a moral problem?

Pronunciation

Listen and repeat.

bed [bed], **bad** [bæd]

- pen/pan, shell/shall, said/sad, beg/bag, ten/tan.
- Ten pence for an apple? That's expensive!

13 Chapter

Personal freedom

Language focus

Adjectifs et pronoms possessifs

• Les possessifs ont le genre du possesseur (contrairement au français) :

le père de Jane/son père

Jane's father/her father (parce Jane est une fille)

le père de John/son père

John's father/his father (parce que John est un garçon)

• Quand il y a plusieurs possesseurs, même si chacun ne possède qu'un exemplaire, le nom est au pluriel en anglais :

*Three men came in. They kept their **hats** on.*

Trois hommes sont entrés. Ils ont gardé leur chapeau.

• Les pronoms possessifs remplacent le groupe « adjectif possessif + nom » :

This car is mine (= my car)

Those socks are yours (= your socks)

Etc.

Wordbank

the accused, the defendant	*l'accusé, le prévenu*
arbitrary search and arrest	*la perquisition et l'arrestation arbitraires*
a Big Brother state	*un état où on est constamment surveillé (cf.* 1984 *de George Orwell)*
to bug a phone	*mettre une ligne téléphonique sur écoute*
to catch someone out	*prendre quelqu'un en défaut*
a CCTV camera	*une caméra en circuit fermé*
checks and balances	*contrôle mutuel (cf. le système judiciaire des États-Unis)*
a civil liberties campaign	*une campagne pour des libertés civiles*
to come under fire	*être sous le feu des critiques*
a controversial idea	*une idée controversée*
core values	*les valeurs de base/fondamentales*
a Crown Prosecutor	*un procureur*
to curb	*freiner*
electronic eavesdropping	*l'écoute électronique*
to enfranchise	*accorder, affranchir*
to enshrine	*conserver religieusement*
to enter a plea	*plaider*

a flaw	*un vice de forme, un défaut, une faille*
to gag/muzzle the press	*museler/baillonner la presse*
a hidden camera	*une caméra masquée/cachée*
to hide from	*se cacher de*
to hold in custody	*garder à vue*
a hotbed of trouble	*un nid de problèmes*
to intrude	*s'ingérer, s'immiscer*
invasive	*envahissant*
a law court	*un tribunal*
a lawyer	*un avocat*
legal aid	*l'assistance judiciaire*
a loophole	*une faille*
narrow-minded	*borné*
to obtain a warrant	*obtenir un mandat*
phone bugging	*la mise sous écoute d'une ligne téléphonique*
a police state	*un état policier*
to prohibit	*interdire*
to rein in	*restreindre*
to relax the rules	*assouplir les règles*
to relinquish control	*renoncer au contrôle*
a safeguard	*une sauvegarde*
to scrap a scheme	*arrêter un projet*
to snoop on	*espionner*
the "snooper society"	*la société de surveillance*
a solicitor	*un notaire pouvant plaider*
to sue for damages	*poursuivre pour dommages et intérêts*
to take into custody	*mettre en état d'arrestation*
to take legal action against	*intenter un procès contre*
to tighten up the rules	*durcir les règles*
to trace, to track	*suivre à la trace de*
to trample on	*piétiner, fouler aux pieds*
under threat	*menacé*
unlawful arrest	*l'arrestation illégale*

Translation

Translate the sentences into English.

1. Les citoyens britanniques seraient-ils sous surveillance ? La plupart de leurs déplacements en zone urbaine sont filmés par des réseaux de caméras.

2. Ce projet controversé est le tien : tu dois assumer la responsabilité de tes idées.

3. L'avocat a expliqué à son client que les écoutes téléphoniques sont illégales – même au sein de sa famille.

4. Ce gouvernement va durcir ses mesures contre l'excès d'alcool pour obliger les consommateurs à changer leurs habitudes de consommation.

5. Nos valeurs fondamentales ne sont pas compatibles avec les vôtres – si vous persistez à prôner l'instauration d'un état policier omniprésent.

Read and answer

Read the article and then do activities A and B that follow.

Clegg to roll back 'Big Brother state'

Nick Clegg is on collision course with the police and security services after he said that the authorities would "not hold people's internet and e-mail records when there is just no reason to do so". Mr Clegg made his comments in his first big speech as deputy prime minister, in which he promised civil liberties measures to roll back Labour's "Big Brother state".

The Liberal Democrat leader is in charge of what he calls "the biggest shake-up of our democracy" for more than 150 years, setting out an agenda spanning House of Lords and electoral reform and plans to curb "the surveillance state". His promise not to store internet and e-mail records suggested the new government has plans to scrap the £2bn Home Office "intercept modernisation programme", which aims to bring wire-tapping into the internet age.

However, Home Office officials were at pains yesterday to point out the debate on the project's survival was still "very much on". The country's most senior police officers and the security services have said it will be impossible to do their jobs without having the ability to track internet traffic.

Talks between the government and senior MI5 and Scotland Yard officials are expected to go on for a week, with a resolution expected before next week's Queen's Speech.

Intelligence officials have asked for the records of all internet, e-mail and telephone traffic to be stored for a year by telecoms companies such as BT, Virgin Media and BSkyB, as well as social networking sites such as Facebook and Twitter. However, the companies have argued the plans go "far beyond" the current regime for tracking telephone calls and would be cripplingly expensive.

Mr Clegg, speaking at a north London college, said the Conservative-Lib Dem coalition would undertake a "power revolution", proposing fixed-term parliaments, an elected House of Lords and a referendum on changing the voting system.

The deputy prime minister also said the government was "not insecure about relinquishing control", although it remains to be seen whether his Tory coalition partners share his urgency on the need for reform. David Cameron's aides have said the government's "ultimate aim" is to introduce an elected House of Lords, although the prime minister insisted before the election that reform of the upper house was "a third-term issue".

Mr Clegg said a review of different options for Lords reform would be complete by the end of the year.

He wants legislation to be ready by the third year of the coalition government's planned five-year term, allowing time for it to be forced through a resistant House of Lords.

Other proposed measures include scrapping the ID card scheme and the accompanying national identity register, all future biometric passports and the children's ContactPoint database, and curbs on closed-circuit television cameras.

Mr Clegg, who once worked for a Brussels lobbying company, also called for his former industry to be made "completely transparent", though he said it would be wrong to think the sector was "all sleazy".

James Boxell & George Parker, *Financial Times* (ft.com), 20/5/2010

A. Language

Find synonyms in paragraphs 2 and 3 of the article for the following: *reorganisation, schedule, to keep in check, pledge, to accumulate to get rid of, whose goal is to, went out of their way to.*

B. Question

Use information in the article to answer but do not copy sentences directly: use your own words.

What are the options Mr Clegg is likely to take up in order to bridle the "Big Brother" policies of the former Labour government? (150 words)

Translation

Translate the article into English.

Vidéo-surveillance : « Mains en l'air, vous allez commettre un crime »

Un nouveau système de vidéo-surveillance installé en Grande-Bretagne permet d'analyser les mouvements des individus et d'alerter la police en cas de comportement suspect. Toute personne repérée par le réseau de caméras peut ensuite être forcée de justifier son comportement devant les forces de l'ordre.

Selon le *Daily Mail*, les principaux critères d'alerte retenus par le système de surveillance « Perceptrak » sont les démarches lentes et les attitudes des « rôdeurs », qui s'attardent dans des lieux sans raison apparente. Dans un premier temps, seule la ville de Portsmouth teste des caméras offertes par l'entreprise Smart CCTV, qui espère promouvoir son nouveau produit en Europe.

Le concept de prévention des crimes et délits fait inévitablement penser au film de science-fiction *Minority Report*, de Steven Spielberg (2002). Dans un futur pas si lointain, la police s'est dotée d'une unité de prévision des crimes : elle arrête et condamne les citoyens pour des actes qu'ils n'ont pas encore commis, mais qu'ils commettront à coup sûr… selon l'ordinateur.

Même si le système britannique n'en est pas encore à condamner les citoyens sur la foi d'une prévision informatique, l'installation d'un tel mécanisme d'analyse est un premier pas. Selon Smart CCTV, il sera bientôt possible de supprimer le maillon humain dans la chaîne de la vidéo-surveillance, en laissant carte blanche à l'ordinateur.

Toutefois, l'entreprise reconnaît qu'elle ne peut pas tout deviner. « Ce que je ne peux pas faire, c'est dire si un homme attend sa petite amie ou est sur le point de commettre un crime », concède Nick Hewitson, de Smart CCTV, à Sky News.

Des versions moins développées du système d'anticipation Perceptrak avaient été installées avec succès à New York, Washington et Chicago. La Grande-Bretagne est régulièrement pointée du doigt, comme étant la plus avancée des sociétés de surveillance du monde, avec plus de 4,2 millions de caméras pour surveiller ses soixante millions d'habitants.

Guerric Poncet, *Le Point* (lepoint.fr), 3/12/2008

Overview

Read a general overview of the subject.

More or less free than before?

Britain has been witnessing two contrasting trends in official attitudes to individual freedom. The long-term trend has been one of liberalisation. You can now publish obscene prose if it has literary merit (Obscene Publications Act 1959), there is no theatre censorship (Theatres Act 1969), you can distribute any video if it is classified correctly (Video Recording Act 1984) and you only have to adhere to "generally accepted standards" on radio and television (Communications Act 2003). And, of course, you have been able to say what you like in Parliament since 1689 (Bill of Rights) – so long as you don't call MPs liars, rats, swine or traitors...

However, this general trend has not stopped governments from issuing DA notices (official requests not to print something) or from attempting to smother scandals by enforcing the Official Secrets Act, the law that covers the divulging of sensitive material or national secrets by civil servants. The latest version of the Act (1989) removed the "public interest" clause, which means that whistle-blowers can no longer justify their action by saying it is in the public interest.

Then, in the aftermath of the July bombings in London in 2005, came the inevitable backlash: the Terrorism Act of 2006. It introduced new terrorist offences, an extended detention period (up from 14 to 28 days) and new police powers. Although the provisions of the Act worry certain people, most law-abiding citizens are more likely to be concerned by the disappearance of another personal freedom: the right to privacy, currently being invaded by CCTV. With more than 4 million CCTV units in operation, Britain has more surveillance cameras than any other country. It is said that they act as a deterrent to would-be criminals and help identify offenders, but crime figures don't seem to bear this out. What is clear is that a great many citizens feel they are living in a Big Brother era where their every move is being watched.

Finally, the tyranny of political correctness has also hit British freedom. The Racial and Religious Hatred Act of 2008, whose intention was supposedly to free minority groups from being verbally attacked, has put a nail in the coffin of free expression. Under previous libel and slander acts and common law judgments related to public insults, an offence was only committed if the words harmed the person in some way. The new Act changed "harm" to "offend"... Humorists, satirists and other defenders of free expression are up in arms.

Pronunciation

Listen and repeat.

hat [hæt], **heart** [hɑːt]

- match/march, bad/bard, back/bark, scat/scar, pat/par.
- The dark cat scarred Mark's bat.

Chapter 14

Northern Ireland

Language focus

Verbes suivis de to, *verbes suivis de V*-ing

• Certains verbes sont suivis d'un infinitif en *to* :

*He **promised to be** there before midnight.*
*They **planned to leave** the following day.*

• D'autres sont toujours suivis de la forme *V-ing* :

*I **quit/stopped* smoking** yesterday.*
*We **enjoy eating** out in restaurants.*

• D'autres verbes encore permettent les deux constructions, sans grande différence de sens :

I love dancing/I love to dance.
It started raining/It started to rain.

• La dernière catégorie comprend les verbes qui permettent les deux constructions, mais avec changement de sens :

*I **remembered to lock** the door.* (= ne pas oublier de…)
*I **remembered locking** the door.* (se rappeler de…)
*We **stopped looking** at it.* (arrêter de faire quelque chose)
*We **stopped to look** at it.* (s'arrêter pour faire quelque chose)

* Attention ! Ne pas confondre avec *I stopped to smoke* où le *to* marque l'expression du but = « Je me suis arrêté pour fumer ».

Wordbank

a hearing	*une audition, une audience*
to achieve (a) lasting peace	*parvenir à une paix durable*
bloodshed	*l'effusion de sang*
a car bomb	*une voiture piégée*
to blunder along	*avancer à l'aveuglette*
a border community	*une communauté vivant sur la frontière*
a casualty	*une victime, un mort, un blessé*
a ceasefire	*un cessez-le-feu*
civil strife	*la dissension sociale*
a cross-border commission	*une commission trans-frontalière*
a curfew	*un couvre-feu*
to decommission weapons	*mettre des armes hors d'usage*
direct rule	*l'administration directe*
a disturbance	*une perturbation*

to draw up legislation	*rédiger des lois*
to enhance cooperation	*améliorer la coopération*
gerrymandering	*le truquage de circonscription*
the Good Friday Agreement	*l'Accord du vendredi saint (le 10 avril 1998)*
internment without trial	*l'emprisonnement sans procès*
the linen industry	*l'industrie du lin*
the mainland	*(ici) la Grande-Bretagne*
media censorship	*la censure médiatique*
a mural	*une fresque murale*
the Parades Commission	*la commission qui règle les défilés*
the peace process	*le processus de paix*
a petrol bomb	*un cocktail molotov*
power-sharing	*le partage du pouvoir*
proximity talks	*des pourparlers qui ne sont pas en face à face*
to retaliate	*riposter*
retaliation	*des représailles*
a rift	*une division*
a riot	*une émeute*
a roadmap	*un plan d'action*
to scrap a system	*mettre fin à un système*
a sectarian school	*une école confessionnelle*
a setback	*un revers*
a settlement	*un règlement*
the shipbuilding industry	*les chantiers navals*
the Six Counties	*les six comtés d'Irlande du Nord*
a stalemate	*un point mort*
strife	*le conflit*
to strive for peace	*lutter pour la paix*
the "Troubles"	*la période de conflit en Irlande du nord*
to undergo a trial	*subir un procès*
urban warfare	*la guérilla urbaine*
war-torn	*déchiré par la guerre*
to yield benefits	*donner des points positifs*

Translation

Translate the sentences into English.

1. Les deux camps ont promis d'assurer une paix durable bien que le conflit ait fait rage pendant des années.

2. Le gouvernement d'Irlande du nord projette d'améliorer la coopération avec la République d'Irlande.

3. Les deux camps ont arrêté de riposter et ont commencé à respecter le couvre-feu.

4. Le processus de paix a pour objectif de mettre fin au cercle vicieux de la violence et des représailles.

5. Les six comtés d'Irlande du nord ont commencé à vivre en paix après l'accord de 1998.

Read and answer

Read the article and then do activities A and B that follow.

"Today our political process comes of age"

Devolution deal to yield benefits on both sides of border

The Government believes the agreement reached in Northern Ireland yesterday will result in greater co-operation on economic development and fighting crime. Policing and justice powers will be transferred from London to Belfast in just two months' time, following a deal agreed by the DUP and Sinn Fein, after 130 hours of talks.

In what was viewed by the Government as a significant and symbolic gesture in response to the agreement, US President Barack Obama last night invited Taoiseach Brian Cowen to the White House for St Patrick's Day. Mr Obama also extended the invitation to the North's First Minister Peter Robinson and Deputy First Minister Martin McGuinness.

Mr McGuinness, meanwhile, said that compared to the Good Friday Agreement and St Andrews Agreement, "this could turn out to be maybe the most important agreement of all". He added: "This might just be the day, this might just be the day, when the political process in the North came of age." The earlier than expected devolution date of April 12 was accompanied by an agreement to look at new ways to referee the routes of contentious Orange Order parades. Setting a date for devolution was vital to Sinn Fein, while the DUP wanted the existing Parades Commission system scrapped.

After 10 days of negotiations, Taoiseach Brian Cowen and British Prime Minister Gordon Brown joined Mr Robinson and Mr McGuinness at Hillsborough Castle to sign-off on the agreement.

But the agreement was not greeted with universal approval as the UUP, the unionist party which negotiated the Good Friday Agreement in 1998, did not turn up for the announcement of the Hillsborough Agreement yesterday. The Government expects the deal will enhance cross-border cooperation as it ensures the stability of the North's power-sharing government.

According to a government source, a justice minister operating in Belfast, solely dealing with Northern Ireland, rather than in Westminster dealing with the whole of Britain, will lead to greater co-operation, particularly in relation to cross-border crime and sex offenders.

On a practical level, justice legislation will be drawn up and passed in the North and security and policing policy will be decided there, rather than in London, making consultation and co-operation easier.

But there will also be an economic benefit, as another source said the agreement ensures that North-South co-operation across a range of departments will continue.

"That will benefit border communities, for example, and, in particular, the opening up of the north-west corridor," the source said.

Justice Minister Dermot Ahern's spokesman said co-operation with Northern Ireland is already at a high level, but the Government sees devolution as presenting opportunities for improving this work.

...

"We believe it ultimately will lead to harmonisation of legislation where appropriate. Significant efforts are already under way in this regard in relation to the management of sex offenders," the spokesman said.

"The Government looks forward to increased co-operation to build on significant progress in cross-border justice issues."

Mr Cowen said the fair and balanced compromises were required in the agreement so that gaps could be bridged and different perspectives accommodated.

"The completion of the devolution of policing and justice in a matter of weeks is an essential step for peace, stability and security in Northern Ireland," the Taoiseach said.

"It consolidates the operation of devolved government and closes the circle in the transformation of policing structures in Northern Ireland."

Mr Cowen paid tribute to Northern Secretary Shaun Woodward and Foreign Affairs Minister Micheal Martin. "I want to thank Micheal particularly and thank him for the political skills he's displayed in recent days," he said.

Mr Brown said what had been seen was a determination to resolve issues that had been "outstanding for too long".

"We have had decades of violence, we had years of talks, and we had weeks of stalemate, but the determination that's been shown in the last day or two in particular to try and get over these unresolved issues is one that I both applaud and commend to the people of Northern Ireland," he said.

Fionnan Sheahan, *The Irish Independent* (independent.ie), 6/2/2010

A. Language

Find synonyms in the first five paragraphs of the article for the following: *assumes, lead to, an agreement, negotiations, was seen as, meaningful, this could prove, itineraries, controversial, crucial, was not received, did not come, will improve.*

B. Questions

Use information in the article to answer but do not copy sentences directly: use your own words.

According to the writer, what are the benefits of the devolution process in Northern Ireland? (150 words)

Translation

Translate the article into English.

David Cameron s'excuse pour les événements du Bloody Sunday

Le Premier ministre britannique David Cameron a lourdement condamné, mardi 15 juin, l'action des soldats britanniques lors du « Bloody Sunday », qui désigne la mort de quatorze catholiques le 30 janvier 1972 lors de la répression d'une manifestation à Londonderry, en Irlande du Nord.

…

« Ce qui s'est passé le jour du Bloody Sunday était non justifié et non justifiable. C'était mal », a déclaré David Cameron devant la chambre des Communes, chambre basse du Parlement, en annonçant les conclusions de l'enquête publique sur le « Dimanche sanglant ».

La responsabilité du drame incombe aux soldats qui « ont perdu le contrôle d'eux-mêmes », a expliqué le nouveau premier ministre britannique. Au nom du pays, « je suis profondément, profondément désolé », a déclaré le chef du gouvernement.

Son discours, retransmis en direct à Londonderry, a soulevé des hourras d'enthousiasme dans le millier de personnes regroupées devant l'écran géant diffusant l'adresse du chef du gouvernement.

« Ce qui s'est passé n'aurait jamais dû se passer », a ajouté David Cameron dans un discours au ton étonnamment dur. « Je n'ai jamais eu pour intention de remettre en question le comportement de nos soldats », mais les conclusions du rapport Saville, du nom du président de la commission d'enquête Mark Saville, sont « absolument claires », a reconnu le Premier ministre conservateur. « Il n'y a aucun doute, aucune équivoque, aucune ambiguïté », a-t-il asséné.

Le rapport, diffusé après le discours de David Cameron, a conclu qu'aucun des treize catholiques tués le jour-même, et un quatorzième mort plusieurs mois plus tard, « ne représentait une menace de mort ou risquait de provoquer des blessures graves ».

Le Nouvel Observateur (nouvelobs.com), 16/6/2010

Overview

Read a general overview of the subject.

Troubles of all sorts

Administratively made up of 6 counties, Northern Ireland, with its population of almost 1.8m people, lies in the north-eastern corner of the island of Ireland.

Education policy does not follow the exact pattern of that for the rest of the UK, although Northern Ireland students do sit A-levels just like their UK counterparts. Primary and secondary schools are for the most part denominational, children being able to commence schooling at 4 and go on to the province's own two universities and colleges of further education.

Partition of Ireland occurred in 1921 leaving one part of the island British crown territory. The Stormont parliament came into being following the Government of Ireland Act (1920) and legislated in matters of import to the province, defence and foreign affairs being the domain of the Westminster parliament.

At that time, the Royal Irish Constabulary was disbanded, leaving in its place, and responsible for policing operations in the six counties, the Royal Ulster Constabulary. That force had for long shown itself to be a bone of contention with many Nationalist-leaning residents before being renamed, following a decade of debate and reform, as the PSNI (Police Service of Northern Ireland) in 2001.

…

...

In a country ruled by the same party for its entire existence, the first civil rights march took place in August 1969. Parliament, whose buildings stand outside Belfast, N.I.'s capital, was suspended by the Westminster government in 1972 and abolished one year later with today's present assembly, bringing together 108 elected MLAs, coming into existence following the Good Friday agreement of April 1998. That agreement and the Peace Process were major landmarks in the history of the "Troubles" , from the 1960s onwards, which have seen almost 3,500 violent deaths, thousands of injuries and millions of pounds of destruction.

The period saw deployment of the British army in August 1969 followed by internment without trial in August 1971, "Bloody Sunday" with its 14 civilian deaths taking place in 1973. The "Peace People" movement was to take off from 1975. Prison hunger strikes in 1980/81 left 10 prisoners dead. Many paramilitary groups were active throughout the period, bombs exploding in Northern Ireland, the Irish Republic and Great Britain. A ceasefire was announced by the IRA in July 1997 and weapons decommissioned from 2001. The economy of the province, with the help of incentives from the UK, EU and US had been on its way to recovery before being hit again by the worldwide economic crisis and credit crunch of 2008/2009.

Pronunciation

Listen and repeat.

mad [mæd], **mud** [mʌd]

- lack/luck, cat/cut, match/much, bat/but, track/truck.
- The white rabbit ran out of the hut and jumped back in the hat.

Chapter 15

Britain and the European Union

Language focus

Le present perfect : have + *V*-en

• Le *present perfect* sert à marquer l'impact au présent d'un événement passé non daté :

I ***have seen*** *that movie. I don't want to go again.*

J'ai vu ce film ; je ne veux pas le revoir.

The manager ***has left****. (= he's not here.)*

Le directeur est parti. (= il n'est plus là.)

• Le *present perfect* peut aussi vouloir dire qu'une action ou un état a commencé dans le passé et se prolonge dans le présent, si un complément de temps en *since* ou *for* décrit l'intervalle de temps concerné :

He ***has been*** *on sick leave* ***for*** *three weeks/since the end of May.*

Il est en congé de maladie depuis 3 semaines/depuis fin mai.

Wordbank

the administrative apparatus	*la machine administrative*
to apply for membership	*poser sa candidature*
to avoid huge surpluses	*éviter d'énormes surplus de production*
to boost European businesses	*redynamiser les entreprises européennes*
the CAP (Common Agricultural Policy)	*la PAC*
chauvinistic, jingoistic	*chauvin, nationaliste*
a common foreign/trade policy	*une politique extérieure/commerciale commune*
a customs union	*une union douanière*
to cut export subsidies	*réduire les subventions à l'exportation*
to draw up a directive	*rédiger une directive*
the ECB (European Central Bank)	*la banque central européenne*
to enforce common rules/regulations	*faire appliquer la réglementation commune*
to enhance economic ties	*renforcer les liens economiques*
the enlargement process	*le processus d'élargissement*
an EU commissioner	*un commissaire européen*
a eurocrat	*un eurocrate/bureaucrate de l'Union européenne*
a European army corps	*un corps d'armée européen*
the euro zone, Euroland	*la zone euro*
excise duties	*les droits de régie*
to fit into a European personality	*se couler dans le moule européen*
to hamstring a policy	*faire obstacle à une politique*
to honour one's commitments/pledges	*tenir ses engagements*

to introduce new aid mechanisms	*mettre en place un nouveau dispositif d'aide*
to join the EU	*adhérer à l'UE*
to meet the challenges ahead	*faire face aux défis qui s'annoncent*
to meet the conditions	*remplir les critères*
to meet the membership requirements	*répondre aux critères d'adhésion*
a member state	*un État membre*
to muster a majority	*rassembler une majorité*
to opt in	*choisir de participer*
to opt out	*choisir de ne pas participer*
the quota regulation	*la réglementation par les quotas*
to ratify a treaty	*ratifier un traité*
to reach a compromise	*aboutir à un compromis*
to safeguard one's national sovereignty	*préserver sa souveraineté nationale*
to sell out sovereignty	*sacrifier sa souveraineté*
on the sidelines	*sur la touche*
the single currency	*la monnaie unique*
the single market	*le marché unique*
the social chapter	*la charte sociale*
to stand aside	*se tenir à l'écart*
a subsidy	*une subvention*
to transfer powers	*transférer des pouvoirs*
a two-speed/two-tier(ed) Europe	*une Europe à deux vitesses*
a variable speed/geometry Europe	*une Europe à vitesse/géométrie variable*
to vet a bill	*vérifier/évaluer une proposition de loi*
to veto a bill	*opposer son véto à une proposition de loi*
to withdraw	*se retirer*

Translation

Translate the sentences into English.

1. La Grande-Bretagne et la France ont trouvé un accord satisfaisant sur la politique agricole commune.

2. La Grande-Bretagne est membre de l'Union européenne depuis 1973.

3. Le parti conservateur a toujours été méfiant vis à vis des institutions européennes.

4. Cela fait plus de trente ans que les eurosceptiques accusent les technocrates européens de Bruxelles de vouloir contrôler la politique intérieure britannique.

5. Le parlement européen est basé à Strasbourg depuis plus de vingt ans.

Read and answer

Read the article and then do activities A and B that follow.

David Cameron's splendid isolation

Sometimes politics can be like watching a car crash in slow motion. Take for instance Britain and the European Union. The imminent British election campaign will barely mention Europe, but it could well produce a Conservative government with the rare distinction of being both the most Eurosceptic in the EU's history and the least loved in mainland Europe. The new prime minister, David Cameron, will then go to Brussels with a series of demands that his European peers – for good and bad reasons – will take great pleasure in rejecting. Britain's already awkward relationship with Europe will hit a new low. That so much of this is avoidable makes it even worse. Both the Tories and the current leaders of the EU need to start paying a little more attention to what each other is up to.

Begin with British Euroscepticism. At its best, it can set a good example. Think, for instance, of the impetuous way in which Greece, Portugal and Spain rushed unprepared into Europe's single currency, the euro. Britain has a better record than most of applying the EU's rules, whereas many others sign up for commitments that they then gaily flout. There are also understandable geographical and historical explanations for British ambivalence towards Europe. But there is something else, too: a suspicion of the entire European project that has sunk especially deeply into today's Conservative Party.

This newspaper has no regrets about opposing both the draft EU constitution and the Lisbon treaty. It remains appalled about the way the reform was pushed through without a referendum in Britain. But given the choice between putting up with a mildly awful treaty (and the moderately ineffective politicians it has installed in Brussels) or getting out of the EU, we would far sooner stay in. By contrast 40% of Tory candidates favour either "fundamental" renegotiation of Britain's membership or withdrawal. Add in an often xenophobic Tory press and Mr Cameron's decision to desert the main centre-right European People's Party (EPP) for a more extreme new group and it is not hard to see why many continental Europeans and some Britons worry that a Tory government would be a platoon of little Englanders. [...]

Mr Cameron's public pronouncements on Europe rightly raise eyebrows. But there is no point in exaggerating the problem. When contemplating Tories, too many "sophisticated" European politicians abandon their usually acute pragmatism. To begin with, Europe has cost several Conservative leaders their jobs; that is not an incentive for Mr Cameron to make it a central part of Tory policy. And he has sensibly ditched any notion of holding a referendum on Lisbon, now it has been ratified. What he is seeking is opt-outs from swathes of social and employment policy and from chunks of justice and home-affairs legislation – something he may stand precious little chance of getting, but it would hardly be the end of the EU if he did.

In truth, both sides to this looming quarrel should do more to accommodate each other. On the European side, it would be a mistake to sit back and wait for a sea-change in Tory attitudes once the party is in power. Britain is not about to join the euro or the Schengen passport-free zone; nor is Mr Cameron about to take his party back into the EPP. Every club member has his eccentricities. Rather than working out ...

how to skewer Mr Cameron, European leaders would do better thinking what they can offer him that might get him off the hook with his more rabid backbenchers. One example might be accepting that it would be wrong in principle to impose new financial regulations by a majority vote against the wishes of the country with the biggest financial-services industry in Europe.

Mr Cameron, however, is the one who has to do the most thinking. When it comes to negotiation, it would be hard to retreat from asking for those opt-outs, but he should not make too much of a failure to win. (There is precious little new social legislation in the pipeline, and Britain already has the right to opt out of most new judicial measures.) A reprieve for the City from the proposed financial rules would be a coup. He could also make much more of the areas where even the Tories consider that Europe can add value. These include a more coherent EU approach to foreign policy and greater co-operation in defence. The only two EU countries that count militarily are France and Britain: it makes obvious sense for them to work together, especially in procurement, as even the Eurosceptic shadow defence secretary, Liam Fox, understands.

Sooner or later, though, Mr Cameron has some home truths to tell his own backbenchers. These surely include the fact that on many issues Euroscepticism has won. After the damp squib of Lisbon, further big treaties look unlikely. Thanks to a changed intellectual climate, to enlargement that took in ten largely free-market countries from central and eastern Europe, and not least to Britain's own influence, the EU has become both more liberal and keener on competition – not a million miles away from the club the Tories always wanted. If they would only look and learn, the Conservatives could find some strong allies in Brussels, not just implacable enemies.

The Economist (economist.com), 31/3/2010

A. Language

1. Find synonyms in the first two paragraphs of the article for the following: *fast approaching, hardly, opposite numbers, difficult, rash, putting into effect, pledges, disregard.*

2. Find antonyms in the fourth paragraph of the article for the following: *minimising, naïve, idealism, a peripheral element, taken on, have a very high possibility of.*

B. Questions

Use information in the article to answer but do not copy sentences directly: use your own words.

1. According to *The Economist,* what are the EU's basic flaws ?

2. Why should both EU officials and Tory MPs seek to mend fences?

3. What are the different opt-outs the British Conservatives are likely to contemplate?

4. In 200-250 words, give the reasons for David Cameron's "splendid isolation" on EU matters?

Overview

Read a general overview of the subject.

Why is Great Britain so different from other EU members?

It was Robert Schuman who suggested the creation of a European organisation for the production and consumption of coal and steel. It would be open to all European countries in an effort to prevent another major conflict from breaking out in Europe. In 1951, 6 countries (France, West Germany, Italy, the Netherlands, Luxembourg and Belgium) signed a treaty setting up the ECSC, thus agreeing to delegate part of their national sovereignty. Britain could not accept this, so it limited itself to a customs union.

In August 1961, Britain applied for entry to the EEC. However, the special treatment it requested led to doubts as to Britain's desire and ability to join the community. It was not until 1973 that Britain officially became a member.

Over the 30-odd years of internal EU diplomatic activity, several bones of contention have set Great Britain and other members poles apart. The Single European Act in 1987 raised fears that its real aim was to pave the way for further political integration. The then Conservative Prime Minister Margaret Thatcher made it plain that Britain would resist all attempts to reduce its national sovereignty and declared the idea of a federal Europe unacceptable.

Then came the so-called "beef crisis" which erupted in 1996. The EU banned all exports of British beef until British cattle were culled after an outbreak of "mad cow disease". Prime Minister John Major's government's obstruction policy was seen as further evidence of Britain's refusal to play by the rules. The Major government also fiercely opposed the Social Chapter which was meant to enforce a common European policy concerning workers' wages, pensions and safety.

The launch of the new European currency in 1999 transformed the EU into a euroland which Britain refused to join. The British government objected on the grounds that Britain would lose its freedom to determine its economic policy and that the financial supremacy of the City of London would be eroded.

Prime Minister Tony Blair's unflinching support for George W. Bush and the subsequent attack on Iraq in 2003 provoked deep divisions within the EU. Britain's commitment to the EU appeared clearly to come far behind its submission to the USA and their long-standing "special relationship".

Tory leader David Cameron's recent coming to power at 10 Downing Street in May 2010 may spell further trouble since some of his backbenchers are poles apart from the European Union's guiding principles.

Pronunciation

Listen and repeat.

dark [dɑːk], **duck** [dʌk]

- barn/bun, bark/buck, cart/cut, park/puck.
- Ducky Duck parked the cart by the barn.

16 Chapter

The special relationship

Language focus

Le present perfect continuous : have+ *V*-en + be + *V*-ing

Les valeurs des deux formes se combinent. *Be* + V-*ing* va ajouter au *present perfect* un aspect : l'action n'est pas terminée, ou elle a laissé des traces visibles. Comparez :

*You **have drunk** the whole bottle.*
Tu as bu toute la bouteille. (= Il n'en reste plus.)
*You **have been drinking**!*
Tu as bu ! (= Tu ne marches pas droit, tu as une diction pâteuse, etc.
*I **have painted** the garage door.* (= Elle est repeinte.)
*I **have been painting** the garage door.* (= Elle n'est peut-être pas complètement repeinte, mais j'ai de la peinture sur les doigts, les cheveux, je suis fatigué, etc.)

Wordbank

to beef up troops	*renforcer les troupes/la présence militaire*
the Berlin airlift	*le pont aérien de Berlin*
to bond together	*former des liens*
the Chief of Staff	*le Chef d'état-major*
CND (Campaign for Nuclear Disarmament)	*une association contre les armes nucléaires*
a cosy relationship	*des rapports chaleureux*
a cruise missile	*un missile de croisière*
a demo(nstration)	*une manif(estation)*
to deter	*dissuader*
an even-handed view	*un point de vue impartial*
to follow blindfolded	*suivre les yeux fermés*
to forge a relationship	*forger des rapports*
give and take	*des concessions (mutuelles)*
a hallmark	*une marque distinctive*
a hard-headed approach	*une approche réaliste*
high stakes	*des enjeux de taille*
to house nuclear bases	*accueillir des bases nucléaires*
joint	*commun, combiné*
the Intelligence Services	*les services secrets/de renseignement*
the Iron Curtain	*le rideau de fer*
a landmark decision	*une décision qui fait date*
the lynchpin	*le point central, le pilier, la base*

military procurement	*l'approvisionnement militaire*
the most reliable ally	*l'allié le plus fiable*
no grounds for	*sans fondements*
the nuclear deterrent	*la dissuasion nucléaire*
a nuclear warhead	*une ogive nucléaire*
one-sided	*déséquilibré, unilatéral(e)*
two-sided	*à double sens, équitable*
a peace camp	*un camp pour la paix*
peacekeeping	*le maintien de la paix*
to pool intelligence	*partager des renseignements*
to sanction	*approuver*
scaremongering	*l'alarmisme*
self-seeking	*intéressé*
to stand shoulder to shoulder	*rester solidaire*
a strained relationship	*des rapports difficiles*
to supply military hardware	*fournir du materiel militaire*
a task force	*une force d'intervention*
tight military cooperation	*une proche coopération militaire*
trading links	*des liens commerciaux*
to trigger a war	*déclencher une guerre*
a whirlwind/whistlestop tour	*une tournée/visite éclair*
willing to wage war	*prêt à entrer en guerre*
to withdraw troops	*retirer des troupes*
to work hand in hand	*travailler de pair/de concert*
a working relationship	*des rapports de travail*

Translation

Translate the sentences into English.

1. Les États-Unis et la Grande-Bretagne ont renforcé leur présence militaire en Afghanistan depuis l'élection d'Obama.

2. Depuis la marée noire de Deepwater en juin 2010, les rapports entre les deux alliés sont de moins en moins chaleureux.

3. La Grande-Bretagne est l'alliée la plus fidèle des États-Unis depuis la Seconde Guerre mondiale : elle « regardera toujours vers l'Ouest » pour citer Winston Churchill.

4. Comme les armes nucléaires sont des armes de dissuasion à l'échelle planétaire, elles sont souvent au cœur des relations internationales.

5. Chaque nouveau film de James Bond vient nourrir le mythe d'une collaboration équitable basée sur des concessions réciproques.

Read and answer

Read the article and then do activities A and B that follow.

It's over: MPs say the special relationship with US is dead

Britain's special relationship with the US – forged by Winston Churchill and Franklin Roosevelt in the Second World War – no longer exists, says a committee of influential MPs. Instead, America's relationship with Britain is no more special than with its other main allies, according to a report by the Commons Foreign Affairs Committee published today.

The report also warns that the perception of the UK after the Iraq war as America's "subservient poodle" has been highly damaging to Britain's reputation and interests around the world. The MPs conclude that British prime ministers have to learn to be less deferential to US presidents and be "willing to say no" to America.

The report, entitled Global Security: UK-US Relations, says Britain's relationship with America is "extremely close and valuable" in a number of areas, particularly intelligence co-operation. However, it adds that the use of the phrase special relationship, in its historical sense, "is potentially misleading and we recommend that its use should be avoided". It does not reflect the "ever-evolving" relationship between the two countries and raises unrealistic expectations, the MPs say. "Over the longer term, the UK is unlikely to be able to influence the US to the extent it has in the past," the committee adds.

In an apparent rebuke to Tony Blair and his relationship with President George W. Bush, the report says there are "many lessons" to be learnt from Britain's political approach towards the US over Iraq.

"The perception that the British government was a subservient poodle to the US administration is widespread both among the British public and overseas," the MPs say. "This perception, whatever its relation to reality, is deeply damaging to the reputation and interests of the UK."

While the relationship between the American president and the British prime minister was an important part of dealings between the two countries, the cabinet and parliament also had a role to play. "The UK needs to be less deferential and more willing to say no to the US on those issues where the two countries' interests and values diverge," the MPs say.

They are also critical of the US use of extraordinary rendition and torture. The report calls for a comprehensive review of the use by the CIA of British bases, such as that on the Indian Ocean island of Diego Garcia, to carry out extraordinary rendition.

"The issues relating to rendition through Diego Garcia to which we have previously drawn attention raise disturbing questions about the uses to which US bases on British territory are put", the MPs say.

They express regret at "considerable restraints" on the ability of both the government and parliament to scrutinise US activities carried out on British territory.

"We recommend that the government should establish a comprehensive review of the current arrangements governing US military use of facilities within the UK and in British overseas territories." The review should "identify shortcomings in the current system of scrutiny and oversight… and report to parliament on proposals to remedy these".

The report also demands a statement from the government on the implications of the Court of Appeal judgment regarding the alleged collusion of MI5 in the torture of Binyam Mohamed, a British resident.

…

Last month the court ordered the government to release evidence from American intelligence reports which showed that MI5 was aware of the torture.

Senior US officials subsequently suggested that releasing such evidence might prevent the US from sharing some intelligence with Britain.

Michael Smith, *The Sunday Times* (thesundaytimes.co.uk), 28/3/2010

A. Language

Find synonyms in the first four paragraphs of the article for the following: *created, friends, released, reminds/informs (us), docile/obedient, image, precious, (confidential) information, deceptive, we advise, translate, hopes, to sway, criticism of.*

B. Question

Use information in the article to answer but do not copy sentences directly: use your own words.

What explanation can be given for the British political establishment's U-turn with regard to its relationship with the USA (150w)

Translation

Translate the article into English.

Fuite de pétrole : Barack Obama s'entretient avec David Cameron

Barack Obama a affirmé à David Cameron que sa frustration à l'égard de la fuite de pétrole n'était pas une attaque contre la Grande-Bretagne, selon le bureau du Premier ministre britannique.

Au cours de cet entretien « chaleureux et constructif » de plus d'une demi-heure, David Cameron a fait part de sa tristesse devant la catastrophe. Quant au président américain, il a reconnu que British Petroleum était une compagnie multinationale, et précisé que la frustration ressentie par les États-Unis « n'avait rien à voir avec l'identité nationale » mais avec le fait de s'assurer qu'une entreprise « grande et riche se montre à la hauteur de ses obligations », a précisé un haut responsable de l'administration. [...]

Les critiques américaines ont été parfois mal perçues en Grande-Bretagne, où BP reste considérée comme l'un des piliers de l'industrie nationale. Des millions de retraités britanniques dépendent des dividendes de BP nombre de fonds de pension ayant investi largement dans la compagnie, le troisième groupe pétrolier du monde.

David Cameron s'est efforcé de trouver un juste milieu. Il a dit partager la « frustration » des Américains devant les efforts infructueux pour arrêter la fuite et leur inquiétude devant les dommages écologiques causés par les milliers de barils de pétrole qui s'écoule du puits.

Mais le Premier ministre britannique a également souligné qu'il considère BP comme une « compagnie importante économiquement », non seulement au Royaume-Uni mais aussi aux États-Unis et dans d'autres pays, selon Downing Street. « Il est dans l'intérêt de tout le monde que BP continue d'être une compagnie financièrement forte et stable », a souligné M. Cameron.

AP (dans *Le Nouvel Observateur* [nouvelobs.com]), 12/6/2010

Overview

Read a general overview of the subject.

Till Death Us Do Part?

The term "special relationship" was first used by Sir Winston Churchill in 1945. The phrase was not controversial or even original at the time, and yet it has endured, much as his other famous phrase "the iron curtain". Churchill's mother was American so it was natural that his feeling for the USA would be a special one, and the British people had just come out of a European war which could not have been won without US aid, so the idea of a special relationship seemed appropriate.

Since then, Britain and the US have not always seen eye to eye. They were at their closest during the Thatcher-Reagan years when the ideologies of both leaders was similar: free trade, low taxes and "small" government (i.e. removing government interference from as many areas as possible). The relationship was probably at its lowest point when President Clinton clashed with John Major (and Mitterrand) over policy in Bosnia in 1993, but other problems had arisen during the intervening years, notably Britain's involvement with the EU, the US's invasion of Grenada in 1983 and various US actions in the Middle East.

However, the relationship has always survived such crises and rose to a new high under the unlikely – and some say unholy – alliance of George W. Bush and Tony Blair in the Iraq war. UK support for the war was highly contested in Britain and many accused Blair of making Britain into the USA's poodle.

Despite the highs and lows of the relationship, often due to the personalities of the two countries' leaders, the main basis of the official military relationship – the mutual defence agreement of 1958 which covers nuclear arms development – remains solid, as do commercial ties. Close financial links have their downside, as in the recent financial crisis when the first country to be affected by the US mortgage loan crash was, of course, Britain.

Finally and perhaps most importantly, there are the linguistic and cultural links, whose importance cannot be overemphasised. Although George Bernard Shaw said that we were "two countries separated by a common language," it is certainly the reverse that is true, and the fact that the values and structure of American society are much closer to those of Britain than to any other country, with the exception perhaps of Canada, make it difficult to envisage a time when the US and the UK would ever be anything other than allies.

Pronunciation

Listen and repeat.

sharp [ʃɑːp], **shop** [ʃɒp]

- clerk/clock, dark/dock, guard/god, lark/lock, parks/pox.
- Tom the clerk rocked around the clock in the parking lot.

Chapter 17

The Constitution

Language focus

Les pronoms réfléchis et réciproques

• On emploie les pronoms réfléchis lorsque le sujet et un complément (ou un autre élément de la phrase) renvoient à la même personne ou chose :

She sent a message to herself.
Elle s'est envoyé un message à elle-même.
I'll keep the cake for myself.
Je garderai le gateau pour moi.
They called themselves The Beach Boys.
Ils se faisaient appeler les Beach Boys.

• Attention : ce n'est pas parce que le français marque explicitement le réfléchi avec le pronom « se » que l'anglais fait de même :

He dressed quickly.
Il s'est habillé rapidement.

• Les constructions réciproques (*each other* ou *one another*) s'utilisent quand au moins deux individus sont en jeu :

They dream a lot about each other.
Chacun des deux rêve de l'autre.

Wordbank

to adjourn	*suspendre, interrompre, lever*
to adjudicate	*déclarer, se prononcer*
an amendment	*un amendement, un changement*
to appoint a judge	*nommer un juge*
bi-cameral	*à deux chambres législatives*
the Bill of Rights	*les 10 premiers amendements*
a binding clause	*une clause obligatoire*
common law	*le droit coutumier*
case law	*la jurisprudence*
checks and balances	*l'équilibre des pouvoirs*
to collect taxes	*percevoir des impôts*
the commander-in-chief	*le commandant en chef (= le président)*
Congress	*le Congrès*
a constitutional amendment	*un amendement à la constitution*
an electoral college	*un collège électoral*
eligible	*éligible*

to establish rules	*établir des règles*
the executive branch	*le pouvoir exécutif*
the framers of the constitution	*les rédacteurs de la constitution*
a framework	*une structure, un cadre*
gerrymandering	*le redécoupage des circonscriptions*
the gubernatorial election	*l'élection du gouverneur*
the House	*le Congrès*
the House of Representatives	*la Chambre des députés*
human rights abuse	*la violation des droits de l'homme*
to impair	*affaiblir*
an impeachment	*une procédure d'accusation d'un président*
the incumbent president	*le président sortant/en exercice*
the judicial branch	*le pouvoir judiciaire*
the legislative branch	*le pouvoir législatif*
to levy taxes	*lever des impôts*
the lower House	*la Chambre basse, la Chambre des députés*
to nominate a judge	*nommer un juge*
to remove a president	*écarter un président du pouvoir*
a repeal	*une abrogation*
to require consent	*exiger le consentement*
to requisition troops	*réquisitionner des troupes*
to rule on	*statuer sur*
to run for Congress	*être candidat au Congrès*
the Senate	*le Sénat*
the separation of powers	*la séparation des pouvoirs*
the State of the Union Address	*le discours presidentiel sur l'état de l'Union*
a state official	*un élu d'un État*
a statute	*une loi, une ordonnance*
The Supreme Court	*la Cour suprême*
to topple a tyrant	*renverser un tyran*
the upper house	*la chambre haute, le Sénat*
to veto a bill	*mettre son véto*
the winner-take(s)-all system	*le système du tout au vainqueur*
the yoke of tyranny	*le joug de la tyrannie*

Translation

Translate the sentences into English.

1. C'est le Président en personne qui a ouvert le bal à West Point.

2. Le Président lui-même peut être écarté du pouvoir s'il est mis en examen.

3. Les membres du Sénat ne peuvent s'en prendre qu'à eux-mêmes d'avoir rejeté ce projet de loi sur les énergies renouvelables.

4. Les rédacteurs de la Constitution s'inspirèrent des philosophes des Lumières anglais et français pour établir les fondations de la démocratie américaine.

5. Le Président s'habilla rapidement avant de rédiger sa déclaration pour les médias.

Read and answer

Read the article and then do activities A and B that follow.

Free speech in the state : Liberty, privacy and some bottles of beer

Want to talk politics with your neighbour? Better ask permission

Pat Murakami runs a small computer repair shop and does a little political agitating on the side. She worries about her neighbourhood, a vibrant area full of Vietnamese shops and veiled women waiting at bus stops. The city of Seattle tried to declare parts of it "blighted", which would have enabled it to seize people's homes and hand the land to private developers.

Mrs Murakami started a group called "Many Cultures, One Message", to rally her neighbours in protest. She prevailed. Or at least, the plan to knock down chunks of her neighbourhood was shelved in 2007. But she worries that the politicians and their developer chums may try again, so she wants to reform Washington state's rules on "eminent domain", which give local government extraordinary powers to condemn private property.

She ran into a second little-known state law. If she prints some flyers, calls some meetings and urges her neighbours to write to their state representative demanding change, she has to register as a "grassroots lobbyist". This rule applies to any group that spends more than $500 in any given month trying to influence the legislature. That sum includes not only cash but also anything else of value.

To comply with the law, Mrs Murakami must provide details such as the name, address and occupation of everyone who helps organise her campaign or who contributes more than $25 in cash or kind to it. All this information is then made public on the internet. She must also provide monthly reports on all the group's activities and expenditures. Failure to follow the rules can result in ruinous fines; $10,000 per violation, which could mean every time she sends out a mailshot. Mrs Murakami is suing to have this law overturned.

If the first amendment means anything, she reckons, it surely protects the right of Americans to talk politics with their neighbours. Many of Mrs Murakami's supporters are recent refugees from autocratic regimes. If getting involved means having their personal details published, they would rather not.

The same worry afflicts supporters of unpopular causes. Alfred Petermann, who runs a discussion group called "Conservative Enthusiasts", says it is "unbelievable" that he has to publish the name, address and occupation of anyone who brings $25-worth of beer to a meeting. "Conservative" is a dirty word in Seattle, he says. Some in his group fear repercussions at work if they are outed.

All states regulate professional lobbyists: ie, paid agents who communicate directly with politicians in the hope of swaying them. Fair enough. But a new report from the Institute for Justice, a libertarian group, reveals that 36 states also impose restrictions on "grassroots lobbying", meaning people like Mrs Murakami. The rules are often complex and unclear. The first sentence of the Massachusetts guidelines for grassroots lobbyists is but a whisker shorter than the Gettysburg address and comprehensible only to a lawyer. Small groups cannot afford lawyers. Yet a few states even threaten criminal penalties for breaking the rules. In Alabama, the maximum sentence is 20 years in jail.

...

. . .

The most severe punishments are seldom, if ever, applied. But they still have a chilling effect on the exercise of free speech. The constitution says people have a right "peaceably to assemble, and to petition the government for a redress of grievances". Politicians hate that.

The Economist (economist.com), 20/5/2010

A. Language

1. Find synonyms in paragraphs 1, 2 and 4 of the article for the following: *lively district, excessively damaged, offer to, gather, demolish, she fears, to abide by the law, supply information, can lead to, is going to court/is filing a lawsuit.*

2. Find antonyms in paragraphs 2, 3 and 5 of the the article for the following: *was defeated, deters her neighbours from, threatens the right, democratic.*

B. Questions

Answer each of the following questions in 50 words. Use information in the article to answer but do not copy sentences directly: use your own words.

1. What must grassroots lobbysists do to abide by the law?
2. What are grassroots lobbysits worried about?
3. To what extent are the rules on grassroots lobbying flawed?

Overview

Read a general overview of the subject.

What the US Constitution says

The United States Constitution is the oldest written constitution in use today. It was drafted in Philadelphia in 1787, ratified by nine states in 1788 and implemented in 1789. It reflects the reasons which led up to the War of Independence, notably the desire for freedom from what was seen as unjustifiable and arbitrary taxation by Britain and its monarch, King George III, who was personally hated. Inspired largely by French and English Enlightenment thinkers, it was also the result of compromise between the states after the first attempt at establishing the articles of confederation had failed in the 1780s.

Its seven Articles lay down the principles of the separation of powers (legislative, executive and judicial) and the establishment of a "checks and balances" system making each branch a counterbalance to the others. A bicameral Congress with a Senate and House of Representatives is set up (= the legislative branch). The President (= the executive branch) is given the power to veto bills passed by Congress but can only nominate officials with the "advice and consent" of the Senate. The court system (= the judiciary branch) is set up and guarantees the right to trial by jury in all criminal cases. One article has the famous "supremacy clause", establishing the hierarchy of legal authority, with the Constitution at the top. It also states that qualification for public office cannot

. . .

be based on any religious criteria. The document also deals with relations between the federated states and procedure for amendment and ratification of the Constitution.

In 1791, ten Amendments were added which make up what is known as the Bill of Rights, largely based on the English Bill of Rights of 1689. Since then, other Amendments have been added, making a total of 27.

The Bill of Rights gives people the right to practise the religion they choose and to express the views they choose. All citizens are given the right to bear arms (i.e. to carry weapons). It also states that people's property may not be searched or seized without a warrant and that "due process" (i.e. the correct procedure) must always be observed in legal prosecution. Protection is given against double jeopardy (i.e. being tried twice for the same crime), against self-incrimination (i.e. you can refuse to give evidence that might incriminate you by "pleadling the Fifth Amendment") and against "cruel and unreasonable" punishments.

Pronunciation

Listen and repeat.

hot [hɒt], **hut** [hʌt]

- bog/bug, shot/shut, doll/dull, gone/gun, hog/hug, knots/nuts.
- My boss, a history buff, lost his guns in the bog.

18 Chapter

The Land of the Free

Language focus

Le passif

- Le passif se forme avec la forme approprié de l'auxiliaire *be*, suivi du participe passé du verbe :

  write : is written, has been written, was being written, etc.
- Le complément (direct ou indirect) du verbe se met en position sujet :

  They are decorating the room.

  The room is being decorated.

  La pièce est en cours de restauration.

  He broke into the house.

  The house was broken into.

  La maison a été cambriolée.
- Les verbes qui ont deux compléments directs peuvent être « passivés » de deux manières :

  John gave her a book. =

  1. *A book was given to her (by John).* 2. *She was given a book (by John).*

Wordbank

a beacon	*un guide*
a nation of plenty	*un pays de cocagne*
access to education	*l'accès à l'éducation*
affirmative action	*la discrimination positive*
to bind together	*rassembler*
blatant racism	*le racisme criant*
to bring a lawsuit	*intenter un procès*
censorship	*la censure*
to collate intelligence	*collationner des informations*
counter-terrorism measures	*des mesures anti-terroristes*
to cull intelligence	*sélectionner des informations*
to delve into secrets	*fouiller des secrets*
demeaning behaviour	*un comportement humiliant*
an economic opportunity	*une opportunité économique*
to enforce	*faire respecter*
equality under the law	*l'égalité aux yeux de la loi*
an ethnic enclave	*une enclave ethnique*
to fend off	*repousser*
to flee from	*fuir*

to foster a sense of identity	*stimuler un sentiment d'identité*
the Founding Fathers	*les Pères fondateurs*
a free press	*une presse libre*
free speech	*la liberté d'expression*
freedom of worship	*la liberté de culte*
a hallmark of democracy	*une marque de démocratie*
an illegal alien/immigrant	*un immigrant illégal*
an inalienable right	*un droit inaliénable*
to indict	*mettre en examen*
an obstacle course	*une série d'obstacles*
to outlaw	*mettre hors la loi*
a police check	*une vérification policière*
political dissent	*la dissension politique*
racial profiling	*établir des profils raciaux*
a radical conservative	*un conservateur farouche*
to restrain	*restreindre*
the right to bear arms	*le droit de porter des armes*
to rule out	*exclure*
a stringent law	*une loi stricte*
a strong civil society	*une société civile forte*
to temper	*tempérer*
the pursuit of happiness	*la poursuite du bonheur*
to thwart	*contrarier*
to undermine freedom	*saper la liberté*
the vanguard	*l'avant-garde*
to venerate	*vénérer*
a vibrant society	*une société dynamique*
to vilify	*calomnier*
a watchdog	*une agence de surveillance*
a witchhunt	*une chasse aux sorcières*
to tap/bug (a phone)	*mettre sur table d'écoute*
investigative journalism	*le journalisme d'investigation*

Translation

Translate the sentences into English.

1. Les mesures de discrimination positive auraient pu être contrariées par le racisme criant de certains décideurs locaux.

2. Le droit de porter des armes à feu a été limité dans certains états sous la pression des groupes militant contre le port d'armes à feu.

3. La poursuite du bonheur est vénérée comme l'emblème d'une société américaine prospère et dynamique.

4. Un procès a été intenté à cette usine de montage de l'Arizona car ses pratiques de management menaçaient les droits fondamentaux de certains travailleurs immigrés.

5. Les libertés individuelles seront préservées aux États-Unis tant que la presse et les comités de surveillance veilleront à les faire respecter.

Read and answer

Read the article and then do activities A and B that follow.

Afflictions of liberty

Obama may have grasped that the ideal of freedom Americans so fiercely cling to is fracturing their society

After a year of setback and struggle, Barack Obama last week sought to revive his programme, to reboot the American Dream. A generally solemn State of the Union address culminated in a rousing call to the nation "to start anew, to carry the dream forward, and to strengthen our union once more".

Commentary focused on the president's efforts to connect with the needs of middle-class America, those blue-collar workers whose lives are profoundly affected by the jobs market, taxation and interest rates.

But another feature of this address is just as remarkable – for its absence. The word "liberty" was entirely missing, and the term "freedom" was used only once.

Prior to Obama's election, these terms had been liberally sprinkled over every address for the last 25 years. They represent a mission statement for America that has become hardwired into its logic circuitry.

There is no way of knowing if Obama is seeking to wean his fellow citizens off the "f" word. But my analysis of the conflicted state of contemporary US society points to a country that is hooked on freedom – and suffering from the afflictions of liberty. This ideal has grown inflated and unstable, and is now fracturing the society it defines.

The US is not, of course, a Hobbesian dystopia. The Founding Fathers sought the perfect balance between liberation and regulation, and contemporary America can appear to fulfil this vision. A sense of consensus emerges in the give and take of the free market; shared narratives played out in the cinema; the ritualised battles of sport; and the year's cycle marked out by feast days and public holidays. But this doctrine of liberty has developed a bias towards hyper-individualism, engendering a sense of insecurity about personal and national identity.

The political scientist Louis Hartz described this condition as "psychic inflation" – a term that chimes with the Jungian concept of the neurotic who believes an idealised image to be the real self. This spirit of freedom is intoxicating, but it threatens to turn the American dream into a nightmare. For Jung, psychic inflation could be overcome through patience, humility and self-analysis, and there are countless US citizens practising these as they agonise about the unsettled states of America. No less a figure than President Obama stands in the vanguard for change.

But the steep decline of Obama's ratings in the polls and the apparent resistance to much of his programme – reflected in the loss of the Massachusetts senate seat to the Republicans – may suggest that millions of Americans regard their brand of liberty as a commodity that needs to be protected.

The idea of liberty beloved by the US seems quite different from the British conception. These two Anglo-Saxon cultures, characterised by the common law, representative government, strong civil society and traditions of individual freedom, adopt surprisingly different approaches. Hartz wrote of England containing "an indefinable germ

...

of liberty, a respect for the privacies of life" that the US cannot duplicate. American expatriates in the UK often praise the quality of tolerance in British society, and many cite this as a reason for migrating.

British society seems to have moved away from the libertarian tradition that was transported to America. There seems to have been a notable shift in British opinion in the 1880s. Gladstone shocked many in the Liberal party by supporting the agenda of collectivists in his cabinet. The individualist current abated, and while Lord Salisbury (leader of the Conservatives) proposed public grants for working class housing, the Fabian Society advanced principles of social democracy and laid the foundations of the Labour party.

Fifty years ago, the philosopher Isaiah Berlin provided a clue to these differences. He spoke of "negative" and "positive" attitudes to freedom – the difference between protecting and taking liberties. And he suggested liberty might need to be constrained so that all can be free – a liberal morality underpinned by notions of equality and social justice.

Western liberalism, as Berlin recognised, faces an irreconcilable dilemma: if we desire freedom to be the ultimate end for humanity, none should be deprived of it by others, nor should some enjoy it at the expense of others.

The radically positive approach contained in the idea of Land of the Free exacerbates this dilemma. An American pupil of Berlin, the philosopher John Rawls, seemed to agree. He argued that in order to achieve equality of liberty, the defining precept for a society like the US should not be freedom but justice: a shared conception of what is fair.

If America could adjust its frame of reference by tempering its brand of liberty, it might come closer to the vision of the Founding Fathers. Given the temper of the times and the mindset of so many American voters, however, this would be a brave change, indeed. But I suspect Barack Obama understands why it matters. And this might explain why the key omission from this year's address was any extensive reference to the great American fetish – freedom.

The Guardian (guardian.co.uk), 1/2/2010

A. Language

1. Find synonyms in the first five paragraphs of the article for the following: *hitch(es), efforts, reached a peak, stirring, to get in tune with, generously, to dissuade/discourage from using, addicted to, unravelling the social fabric, free market mechanisms, fostering/ creating, goes hand in hand with, among those in the front line.*

2. Find antonyms in paragraphs 2, 3 and 4 of the article for the following: *white-collar workers, superficially, utopia, flawed, imbalance, conflict, safety.*

B. Questions

1. According to the Guardian, to what extent is the American ideal of freedom basically flawed? (Answer in 200-250 words. Use information in the article but do not copy sentences directly: use your own words.)

2. Explain the following quotation (100 words): "If America could adjust its frame of reference by tempering its brand of liberty, it might come closer to the vision of the Founding Fathers."

Overview

Read a general overview of the subject.

The Land of the Free

The Land of the Free is an expression from *The Star-Spangled Banner* (the future US national anthem, written in 1814). At the end of every stanza, the writer imagines the US flag waving over the Land of the Free. But many Americans now wonder if the USA is really the seat of personal freedom that it has always set itself up to be.

The writers of the Declaration of Independence of 1776 stated that liberty was one of the unalienable rights of all men. Thirteen years later, the French Declaration of the Rights of Man and Citizen said pretty much the same thing. But these two declared national attachments to freedom have produced very different societies. Take the example of carrying a gun. Illegal in France for ordinary citizens, bearing arms is set down in the 2nd Amendment to the US Constitution as a right, still hotly defended by the four million members of the powerful National Rifle Association. And, whereas France has come to embrace "big government", state intervention is resented by a substantial percentage of Americans who believe, like the Founding Fathers – the Framers of the Constitution -- that government interference in private affairs is the first step to tyranny. "The land of the free has become the land of the government permit," said the libertarian Joseph Sobran.

The Supreme Court has ruled that, for "compelling" reasons, Americans' rights to certain freedoms can be withdrawn. Given the events of 9-11, such tampering with the Constitution may be understandable, but how, Americans ask, does the IRS's (Internal Revenue Service) right to examine their bank accounts have any relevance to the prevention of terrorism?

With increasing federal interference, there is a constant struggle going on to get the right balance between the maintenance of law and order and personal freedom. What's more, in a land made up of states which each have their own laws, freedom can vary from place to place. The fact that there is no national policy on issues as high-profile as same-sex marriage and abortion means that if you want certain freedoms in the USA, you had better choose your place of residence carefully.

And, although the right of states to make their own laws is empowering to the local population, it has also resulted in some very idiosyncratic laws, like the one in Kentucky which forbids you from selling ducks that have been artificially coloured – unless you are selling more than six at a time!

Pronunciation

Listen and repeat.

shot [ʃɒt], **short** [ʃɔːt]

- spot/sport, cot/caught, fox/forks, pot/port.
- She's got a soft spot for port-drinking sportsmen.

Chapter 19

Immigration

Language focus

Le prétérit vs le present perfect

• S'il y a dans la phrase des compléments qui datent l'événement dans le passé, on ne peut employer que le prétérit :

*Last year, I **saw** only three films.*
L'an dernier, je n'ai vu que trois films.
*Yesterday, I **went** to the park with the kids.*
Hier, je suis allé au jardin public avec les enfants.

• Le *present perfect*, qui est une forme du présent, n'est compatible qu'avec des expressions qui renvoient au présent :

*I **have** now **understood** the idea.*
J'ai compris l'idée maintenant. (= mon processus de réflexion est arrivé à son terme)

• Selon le point de vue que le locuteur privilégie, il choisira l'une ou l'autre forme verbale :
– récit au passé, suite d'actions détachée du présent = prétérit ;
– bilan dans le présent du passé = *present perfect*.

Wordbank

an alien	*un étranger*
a birthright	*un droit acquis à la naissance*
the border police	*la police des frontières*
caught in the snare	*pris au piège*
cheap labour	*la main d'œuvre à bas prix*
to curb the flow	*limiter l'afflux*
the customs	*la douane*
a dirty job	*un sale boulot*
a drop-house	*une maison de transit pour clandestins*
to enter illegally	*entrer en fraude*
everyone for himself	*chacun pour soi*
forged documents/papers	*de faux papiers*
to fence out	*exclure en érigeant une barrière*
to file for citizenship	*demander la citoyenneté*
to find one's marks	*trouver les repères*
a foreigner	*un étranger*
to gain a right	*obtenir un droit*

to get rid of	*se débarasser de*
to grant asylum	*accorder l'asile*
to grant authorisation to stay	*accorder le droit de résider*
a green card	*une carte verte (pour résidents permanents)*
to hail from	*être originaire de*
a hindrance	*une entrave*
the homeland	*la patrie*
ID (identification)	*des papiers d'identité*
an illegal alien	*un étranger sans papiers, un travailleur clandestin*
to issue a visa	*délivrer un visa*
to live side by side peacefully	*se côtoyer sans heurt*
to look back	*regarder en arrière*
a melting pot	*un creuset*
a neighbourhood	*un quartier*
a new departure	*un nouveau départ*
a nightmare	*un cauchemar*
a passer, a "coyote"	*un passeur, un trafiquant*
to process an asylum application	*examiner/traiter une demande d'asile*
to provide rights	*donner des droits*
to quarantine	*mettre en quarantaine*
red tape	*la bureaucratie*
to roam	*errer*
to send money home	*envoyer de l'argent à la maison*
to slacken rules	*assouplir les règlements*
to sneak across the border	*franchir la frontière clandestinement*
a social program	*un programme social*
to stay	*séjourner*
a stowaway	*un voyageur clandestin*
the struggle for life	*la lutte pour la vie*
a sweat shop	*un atelier clandestin*
unfettered access	*un accès sans obstacle*

Translation

Translate the sentences into English.

1. Pendant le XXe siècle, le creuset américain amena des immigrants venant des quatre coins du monde à se côtoyer sans heurt.

2. De tous temps, on a donné les sales boulots à des travailleurs immigrés.

3. Nous sommes entrés illégalement aux États-Unis en 1967, mais nous avons obtenu la carte verte dix ans plus tard.

4. On lui a fourni des faux papiers hier et il a disparu depuis ce matin.

5. Pour ne pas être pris au piège par la police des frontières, le passeur a abandonné les sans-papiers à leur sort dans le désert.

Read and answer

Read the article and then do activities A and B that follow.

Politicians hoped to avoid immigration issue in election year, but Arizona law changes that

TUCSON, Arizona. With the scrawl of a pen, GOP Gov. Jan Brewer of Arizona awakened the dormant but explosive issue of illegal immigration, sending shock waves across the political spectrum in an election year when both parties had hoped to sidestep the topic. Two months after Brewer signed a law instructing police to demand proof of a questionable person's legal status, voters have refocused on a topic that had faded into the background after Congress failed to overhaul the immigration system in 2007.

Protests have flared. Lawsuits have followed. Arizona boycotts are under way. More than 20 states are discussing similar efforts. Polls again put border security and immigration among voters' top concerns. "It's not just a problem in Arizona; it's a problem everywhere. People are just furious," Gary Widemann says of illegal immigration. "Something needs to be done."

He would know. Widemann, 59, splits his time between Arizona, a big gateway for illegal immigrants with an estimated 460,000 living there, and South Dakota, which has a small Hispanic population but relies on immigrants – legal or not – to fill jobs at its meatpacking plants. "What the Arizona law did tap into was the idea that we've got to control our borders," said Andrew Kohut, director of the nonpartisan Pew Research Center. "This law really galvanized public opinion on that one aspect of this issue."

Politicians from President Barack Obama down find themselves again wrestling with a topic that's politically perilous for Republicans and Democrats alike, particularly in an election year and as both parties seek to court Hispanics, the nation's fastest-growing minority group. They have little choice.

An Associated Press-GfK poll this month found that 85 percent of people now rank immigration as an important issue. Every spoke in the wheel of American life is touched by it. Porous borders and undocumented people have national security implications. Foreign workers become an important part of the economy, filling low-paying jobs and possibly depressing wage scales in higher-paying ones. Schools, businesses and most other entities are forced to adapt to immigrant-swelled populations. Family, race and social norms also are at play.

Senate Democratic leader Harry Reid, who faces a fierce re-election fight in Nevada, pushed for legislation in the spring to provide an eventual path to citizenship – what critics call amnesty – for many of the estimated 12 million illegal immigrants. Reid was accused of pandering and he shelved the plan when other Democrats declined to jump aboard. In Arizona, Attorney General Terry Goddard opposes the law in a state that overwhelmingly supports it. The Democratic nominee for governor, he's trying to figure out just how to challenge Brewer on the issue.

Republican candidates also find themselves in a tight spot. Social conservatives want a get-tough policy on illegal immigrants, agriculture operations fear it will be too tough and businesses want more visas for immigrants possessing high-tech skills.

...

. . .

Arizona Sen. John McCain, the GOP champion of a comprehensive immigration reform when Congress last debated the issue, now advocates securing the border first. "Complete the dang fence," McCain says in a TV ad in his GOP primary race against former Rep. J. D. Hayworth, a staunch border-security advocate.

"Would I have written the bill? Probably not," McCain said in a recent interview. "But the fact is people in Arizona are frustrated because the federal government didn't act. People feel very passionate about it, here and everywhere."

In California, Democratic Sen. Barbara Boxer's GOP challenger, Carly Fiorina, is finding that her defense of the Arizona law during the GOP primary could turn off Hispanics she needs to win in November. Meg Whitman, the state's GOP candidate for governor, shifted to the right on immigration during the primary but is now courting Hispanics with a TV ad that notes her opposition to the Arizona law.

Scorching now, the issue is certain to become even hotter as the nation's minority population steadily rises. Boosted by a surge in Hispanic births and people who call themselves multiracial, minorities now make up 35 percent of the U.S. population. Both parties are courting them.

Democrats have an edge. But Hispanic support isn't guaranteed. "This is a very tricky issue for the administration and for Democrats, in particular, because the Latino vote has been an important part of the Obama coalition," said Kohut.

Obama typifies the conflicted politicians. He called the Arizona law irresponsible. But he also dispatched 1,200 more National Guard troops to the southern border to show he's sympathetic to slowing the tide of illegal immigrants. Obama supports the same legislation that Reid advocates, but the president is not putting it at the top of his priorities.

Liz Sidoti, *Los Angeles Times/AP* (latimes.com), 25/6/2010

A. Language

Find synonyms in paragraphs 1, 3, 4, 5 and 6 of the article for the following: *woke up, inactive, highly sensitive, to avoid the issue, to require evidence, had vanished, main worries, divides, draw on/exploit, roused/excited, hazardous, indulging someone's desires, put on the back burner, illegal migrants, vastly, to understand.*

B. Questions

1. What is the impact of Arizona governor's move on immigration laws on the US national immigration policy? (Answer in 200-250 words. Use information in the article but do not copy sentences directly: use your own words.)

2. Explain the following quotation (100 words): "Scorching now, the issue is certain to become even hotter as the nation's minority population steadily rises."

Overview

Read a general overview of the subject.

People from all over the world

Practically all countries in the world have seen their citizens leave for American shores at one time or another throughout their history. Economic or political circumstances, or flight from religious persecution, have driven millions to cross oceans or land barriers, often at great peril to their lives, in their quest to enter America. Between the early 1500s and late 1600s the Dutch, English, French and Spanish had all established settlements in America vying with each for control of the vast territory, with England finally laying claim to large tracts of North America before being ousted, in its turn, at the American revolution. In the 1800s, poverty-stricken immigrants fled to America from Great Britain seeking a better life and, in the mid-1800s, countless numbers left rural Ireland stricken by potato famine. Some estimates put that flight at 25% of the adult population of Ireland over a 10-year period from 1845 – perhaps as many as 2 million adults. The 19th century saw millions leaving Germany, Italy and Russia, some after failed revolutions and with many Jews also looking at America as a safe haven from persecution. These different communities came at a time of internal economic expansion in the American Republic and worked long hours in unskilled jobs in cities and on railroads. Communities from different counties often found themselves sharing specific urban areas, and in conflict with each other over economic opportunities. In recent decades, European immigrants have been replaced by immigrants of Spanish-speaking origin and from Asia.

Immigrants to America have to cross many hurdles in their quest to settle in the USA. Living and working permanently in the USA requires the "Green Card" which may be obtained by family ties or company sponsorship. However, for every legal immigrant, there are as many illegal aliens ready to face extreme danger to get round police and border controls. And things have not changed much in 200 years: the immigrants of the past found themselves in the sweatshops of New York, today's Mexican immigrants can also be found working in insalubrious conditions for very low wages. Immigrants the world over are often rejected by would-be host countries, but very recently, the border state of Arizona took the rejection one step further by voting in a State Act that made illegal immigration a crime in the eyes of the law. Advocates of immigration point out its benefits in terms of culture, flexibility in the labour market and innovation.

Pronunciation

Listen and repeat.

fall [fɔːl], **full** [fʊl]

- Paul/pull, ball/bull, hawk/hook, talk/took, wall/wool.
- Captain Hook took a walk along the wall with Paul.

20 Chapter

The American Dream

Language focus

Le prétérit en be + V-ing (past continuous)

• C'est le temps de « l'arrière-plan » dans un récit au passé. Il se traduit presque toujours par l'imparfait en français :

It was a lovely day. The birds ***were singing*** *and the sun* ***was shining****.*

Il faisait très beau. Les oiseaux **chantaient** et le soleil **brillait**.

• Comparez ces phrases qui illustrent la différence entre le prétérit simple et le prétérit en *be* + V-*ing* :

1. *Mark* ***was singing*** *a song to the baby when it began to cry.*
2. *Mark* ***sang*** *a song to the baby when it began to cry.*

• Dans la phrase n° 1, Mark était déjà en train de chanter avant que le bébé ne pleure ; dans la phrase n° 2, Mark s'est mis à chanter lorsque le bébé a commencé à pleurer.

Wordbank

a quest for betterment	*une quête d'amélioration*
to achieve a goal	*atteindre un objectif*
an achiever	*un battant*
anchored in	*ancré dans*
an array of possibilities	*une gamme de possibilités*
to become a self-made man	*réussir par ses propres moyens*
bleak prospects	*des perspectives moroses*
a deep-rooted belief	*une croyance solidement ancrée*
drive	*l'énergie, la motivation*
an enduring appeal	*un attrait durable*
an entrenched belief	*une croyance enracinée*
the ethos of the people	*le génie du peuple*
fairness	*la justice*
fortitude	*la force, le courage moral*
from rags to riches	*de la misère à la richesse*
to fulfil a dream, to make a dream come true	*réaliser un rêve*
to grow weary	*se lasser*
hard work	*le dur labeur*
to hit the jackpot	*gagner/toucher le gros lot*
home ownership	*l'accession à la propriété, le fait d'être propriétaire de son logement*

a household	*un ménage*
an inalienable right	*un droit inaliénable*
an ingrained idea	*une idée tenace*
to lag (behind)	*être à la traîne*
the land of opportunity	*le pays de tous les possibles*
to make a quick buck	*gagner de l'argent facilement*
a misplaced idea	*une idée fausse*
to move ahead	*aller de l'avant*
to move up the ladder	*gravir les échelons*
a nightmare	*un cauchemar*
to overhaul the system	*réviser le système*
the pursuit of happiness	*la quête du bonheur*
to predict	*prédire*
a rate	*un taux*
a rising tide	*une marée montante*
a rung	*un barreau de l'échelle*
to shift	*faire bouger*
social mobility	*l'ascenseur social*
stamina	*l'endurance physique*
to strike it rich	*faire fortune*
to be stuck	*être bloqué*
to stuff one's pockets	*se remplir les poches*
thrift	*(le sens de) l'économie*
an unattainable goal	*un objectif irréalisable*
an uncrossable barrier	*un obstacle infranchissable*
to weave relationships	*tisser des liens*
white-collar	*col blanc*
a widening gap	*un écart grandissant*
within (one's) grasp	*à portée de main*

Translation

Translate the sentences into English.

1. En 1849 certains mineurs chanceux s'en mettaient plein les poches pendant que le père de Clementine creusait en vain en Californie.

2. Pendant la traversée entre Cork et Ellis Island les immigrants irlandais tissaient des liens qui leur seraient utiles plus tard en Amérique.

3. Les bouviers menaient le troupeau de bétail Longhorn sur la piste de l'Oregon quand ils furent pris dans une tempête de sable terrible.

4. La famille Earp était à la traîne loin derrière le convoi de chariots quand les Cheyennes se montrèrent.

5. À cette époque-là, Patrick économisait sou par sou pour réaliser son rêve : partir faire fortune en Amérique.

Read and answer

Read the article and then do activities A and B that follow.

Social mobility and inequality: Upper bound

CHICAGO. Americans are an optimistic lot. If there is one thing they believe in above all, it is the ability to move ahead. In poll after poll, a majority reject the notion that success is determined by forces beyond their control. In early 2009, hardly a sunny period, 71% still agreed that hard work and personal skill are the main ingredients for success. A high degree of social mobility has always defined American culture, from the work of Alexis de Tocqueville and Horatio Alger to the remarkable story of Barack Obama himself.

But the reality for most Americans is becoming more complicated. The recession came at the end of a period marked by record levels of inequality. Many Americans, lacking true upward mobility, bought its trappings, such as a bigger house or better car. Disaster duly followed. As a result, American optimism has been pierced by doubt. In a new poll for *The Economist* by YouGov, 36% of respondents said they had less opportunity than their parents did, compared with 39% who thought they had more. Half thought the next generation would have a lower standard of living, double the share that thought living standards would rise. As the country recovers, two problems cloud its future. Rates of social mobility are unlikely to grow. Inequality, however, may widen even further.

These trends have been building up for years. In 1963 John Kennedy declared that a rising tide lifts all boats. Indeed, in 1963 this was true. Between 1947 and 1973, the typical American family's income roughly doubled in real terms. Between 1973 and 2007, however, it grew by only 22% – and this thanks to the rise of two-worker households. In 2004 men in their 30s earned 12% less in real terms than their fathers did at a similar age, according to Pew's Economic Mobility Project. This has been blamed on everything from immigration to trade to declining rates of unionisation. But the driving factor, most economists agree, has been technological change and the consequent lowering of demand for middle-skilled workers.

The most highly skilled, meanwhile, have stuffed their pockets happily. Between 1970 and 2008 the Gini coefficient, a measure of income inequality, grew from 0.39 to 0.47. In mid-2008 the typical family's income was lower than it had been in 2000. The richest 10% earned nearly half of all income, surpassing even their share in 1928, the year before the Great Crash.

Compared with people in other rich countries, Americans tend to accept relatively high levels of income inequality because they believe they may move up over time. The evidence is that America does offer opportunity; but not nearly as much as its citizens believe.

Parental income is a better predictor of a child's future in America than in much of Europe, implying that social mobility is less powerful. Different groups of Americans have different levels of opportunity. Those born to the middle class have about an equal chance of moving up or down the income ladder, according to the Economic Mobility Project. But those born to black middle-class families are much more likely than their white counterparts to fall in rank. The children of the rich and poor, meanwhile, are less mobile than the middle class's. More than 40% of those Americans born in the bottom quintile remain stuck there as adults. [...]

...

…

How rising inequality affects social mobility is still unclear. Those born since inequality started to rise sharply are only just now becoming adults. However there are some troubling signs according to two papers to be presented at the Tobin Project, an alliance of scholars, this month. Christopher Jencks of Harvard University finds that income inequality has been accompanied by a widening gap in college attendance. […]

The recession, meanwhile, may have exacerbated trends in inequality. The capital markets, points out Timothy Smeeding of the University of Wisconsin, have recovered more quickly than the housing or labour markets. This is troubling for the poor and the middle class, since homes represent a greater share of their wealth. Unemployment has been concentrated in America's lower ranks. As the rich recover, poor and middle-class people may lag behind. Young workers may fare badly, too. Those who graduate in recessions have lower incomes in the long term, according to Lisa Kahn of Yale University.

The Economist (economist.com), 15/4/2010

A. Language

Find synonyms in paragraphs 1, 2, 4 and 8 of the article for the following: *to progress, dismiss the idea, decided, not exactly, status symbols, naturally, made plenty of money, the unequal distribution of income, oudoing, aggravated, may hit a rough patch/may meet difficulties.*

B. Question

According to the journalist, is the American Dream still valid? (Answer in 200-250 words. Use information in the article but do not copy sentences directly: use your own words.)

Translation

Translate the article into English.

Le « rêve américain » d'un entrepreneur français

Pour Stanislas Vilgrain, la *French Touch* fait bon ménage avec l'esprit d'innovation américain : cet entrepreneur français installé aux États-Unis est le leader du marché américain du cuisiné sous vide haut de gamme.

« Le rêve américain existe », dit cet héritier des minotiers nancéens des Grands Moulins de Paris qui a fondé il y a 21 ans à Alexandria (Virginie, est) « Cuisine Solutions », qui produit des bases cuisinées sous vide à basse température pour garder longtemps couleurs et saveurs. […]

La clé du succès : « Il faut trouver une niche pour le marché. Ce pays est un pays de niches », affirme M. Vilgrain.

« Aux États-Unis, on vous donne une chance. Ils vont essayer votre produit, surtout si c'est nouveau. En France l'approche est toujours plus dubitative, moins risquée », dit-il, dénonçant aussi, dans l'industrie de la transformation alimentaire française, les lourdeurs des inspections administratives et sanitaires. « En France, ce n'est pas le coût du travail qui est cher, c'est celui de l'administration », ajoute-t-il.

Virginie Montet, AFP (dans *Le Point* [lepoint.fr]), 28/3/2010

Overview

Read a general overview of the subject.

The reality of the American Dream?

The words American Dream were penned by J. T. Adams in 1931 in *The Epic of America*, but just how far back does one have to delve to find the origins of the idea of the American Dream? Was it with Puritan leader John Winthrop, who, in 1630, 10 years after the Mayflower landed, spoke of a "city upon a hill", or those who drafted the Declaration of Independence, adopted in 1776, which enshrines the rights to pursue life, liberty and happiness?

In the 18th and 19th centuries, immigrants came to carve out a successful life for themselves, free from hunger and unemployment. Newcomers from many lands found, after their passage through Ellis Island, a land which could offer hope. Life expectancy rose, as did health and education levels for settlers having to fend for themselves and their families on lands newly claimed from native Americans or bought at bargain-basement prices. On arriving in the USA, foreigners in their ragged clothes could always dream of finding their pot of gold and going from rags to riches like so many self-made men who through their industriousness were to become industrial magnates.

Threading itself through those centuries of mass immigration has been the idea that everything is possible for those who are ready to work long hard hours, and not squander their earnings but rather keep money aside for the future. But that protestant work ethic has in many circles disappeared, and has been watered down to fit into a society based on consumerism, keeping up with the Joneses and getting rich as quickly as possible.

The idealistic version of the dream excludes discrimination on grounds of colour, race, religion or origin, but unfortunately, if some have been able to live out their dream, others are living a nightmare. Access to health care and education remains a difficult issue for minorities, and, because competitiveness is at the very heart of US society, many remain locked in situations of intense poverty and deprivation. The American dream has long been based on hopes of economic freedom in a country of free enterprise but this also goes hand in hand with a system where welfare is not provided for all by "big government". And indeed, ideas of social Darwinism put forward by Spencer and Sumner preclude government intervention and lock the fragile and deprived into a system which some say favours only the well-heeled.

Pronunciation

Listen and repeat.

shut [ʃʌt], **short** [ʃɔːt]

- bud/bored, spun/sport, fudge/forge, dusk/dawn.
- Sporty Bud was bored until dawn.

Chapter 21

Mobility

Language focus

Le génitif N's N, *et la différence avec* N of N

• Le génitif marque une relation de possession et se forme en ajoutant *'s* au nom du possesseur :

John's car, my brother's car

• Si le nom possesseur est pluriel, on se contente d'ajouter une apostrophe après le *-s* du pluriel :

his parents' car

• Le génitif marque aussi un repérage dans le temps ou dans l'espace :

today's paper

New York's best restaurants

• Dans les autres cas, on préférera la structure *N of N* ou un nom composé :

the roof of the house

the table leg

Wordbank

an ability	*une compétence*
to borrow	*emprunter*
to bring public spending into line	*mettre les dépenses publiques en ordre*
a bubbling market	*un marché porteur*
climbing/rising unemployment	*le chômage à la hausse*
to climb the social ladder	*grimper l'échelle sociale*
a decline	*une chute*
a downward drift to failure	*une dérive vers l'échec*
a driving force	*une force agissante*
to drop out of school	*laisser tomber l'école*
a forecast	*une prévision*
a forecaster	*un prévisionniste*
a highly-skilled worker	*un ouvrier hautement qualifié*
the housing boom and bust	*la croissance et récession de l'immobilier*
an income gap	*un écart de revenus*
the lengthening dole queues	*les files grandissantes de chômeurs*
a low-skilled worker	*un ouvrier peu qualifié*
a magnet state	*un État attractif*
mainstream America	*l'Amérique profonde*
mired in poverty	*englué dans la pauvreté*

a mortgage	*une hypothèque*
to move house	*déménager*
a neighborhood	*un quartier*
a part-time job	*un travail à temps partiel*
a pattern	*une tendance*
pinned down	*bloqué dans une situation*
a population movement	*un mouvement de population*
to provide flexibility	*fournir une flexibilité*
a racial obstacle	*une barrière raciale*
from rags to riches	*de la misère à la richesse*
a recession-proof job	*un travail à l'épreuve de la récession*
reckless	*imprudent*
a spell of unemployment	*une période de chômage*
to spur on	*encourager*
to start from scratch	*partir de zéro*
a steady job	*un travail stable*
a structural hindrance	*une barrière structurelle*
to supplement an income	*compléter un revenu*
to switch careers	*changer de carrière*
a tax hike	*une augmentation d'impôts*
tough times	*les temps difficiles*
training	*la formation*
underemployed	*sous-employé*
to be on welfare	*vivre de l'aide sociale*
willingness	*la volonté*
to wrangle over	*se battre au sujet de/pour*

Translation

Translate the sentences into English.

1. Les compétences de cet employé qualifié lui ont permis de grimper l'échelle sociale.

2. L'Amérique profonde d'aujourd'hui n'a pas perdu foi dans ses rêves de réussite et de promotion sociale.

3. La maison des Bauer a été saisie par le directeur de la banque.

4. Le déclin de l'économie américaine menace même les emplois à l'épreuve de la récession.

5. La conclusion du rapport du FMI souligne que l'écart de revenus entre les riches et les pauvres s'est accru de façon dangereuse.

Read and answer

Read the article and then do activities A and B that follow.

House prices and mobility: Off the road

During this recession too many Americans are rooted to the spot

WASHINGTON DC. When the going gets tough, it's said, the tough get going. Sadly, this does not seem to apply to unemployed Americans any more. A high degree of population mobility has traditionally been one of America's great economic strengths, providing a flexibility that allows for more efficient labour markets and lower unemployment. However, during this recession Americans have been hunkering down, not moving on.

Declining mobility has in fact long been a feature of the post-war American economy, thanks to the ageing of its workforce and rising rates of home ownership. In the two decades after the second world war, the domestic migration rate hovered around 20%, but by 2000 it had fallen to under 15%. And amid the recent economic troubles mobility has declined even more.

There are exceptions. In the deep recession of 1981-82 domestic migration jumped from below 17% to almost 20%, driven by workers moving out of a deindustrialising Midwest. Between 2000 and 2001, in contrast, the migration rate fell from over 15% to under 14%. Today workers are all but stuck, thanks to the paralysing effect of the housing bust. Nearly one in four mortgage borrowers owe more on their loans than their homes are worth. These "underwater" borrowers face a stark choice: foreclosure or staying put. Millions of Americans now find themselves pinned down in places where unemployment rates are well above the national average. In 2008 the domestic migration rate was just under 12%, and the rate of migration between states fell to 1.6% – less than half the level that prevailed in the post-war decades.

One might expect the problem to be most severe in the bubbliest of markets, where homeowners routinely find themselves owing twice the value of their homes. In fact, the opposite is true. High rates of foreclosure in bubble states have freed workers to leave for more promising markets, including the once too-expensive cities from which such migrants previously fled. The reversal of fortune has been abrupt for former magnet states such as Florida and Nevada. In 2005, over a quarter of a million Americans moved to Florida. During the past two years the state has experienced a net population loss to other states of 50,000 people.

A few bright spots have managed to attract mobile Americans. Texas and Oklahoma weathered the downturn better than most, thanks to strong local energy industries and the absence of a housing boom and bust. The same is true for the Washington, DC, area, where an all-but-recession-proof economy based on the federal government has already managed a return to pre-downturn output levels.

Slowing migration has, ironically, helped California, among the most economically battered of states. California's housing boom coincided with a large increase in out-migration, as expensive housing drove residents to neighbouring states. Those neighbours no longer seem so attractive next to increasingly affordable, entertaining and

...

surf-fringed California. Between 2008 and 2009 fewer than 100,000 Californians left the state, the best performance since 2003.

In some parts of the country the decline in out-migration may be a welcome sign. In the north-east population loss began slowing in the middle of the decade, thanks to a broad-based economic revival. But elsewhere, falling migration means little more than pain. In Michigan the rate of population loss declined between 2008 and 2009, even as the unemployment rate soared above 15%. Workers whose jobs have disappeared for ever are, for a variety of reasons, unable to move on.

The Economist (economist.com), 30/12/009

A. Language

1. Find synonyms in the first three paragraphs of the article for the following: *when testing times come, jobless, standing/holding firm, a characteristic, remained steady, increased sharply, stuck.*

2. Find antonyms in paragraphs 3, 4 and 5 of the article for the following: *boom, lenders, moving (in any direction), rarely, gradual, have succeeded in putting off, upturn, input.*

B. Questions

Answer each of the following questions in 50 words. Use information in the article to answer but do not copy sentences directly: use your own words.

1. Why are Americans less mobile today?

2. Which states haves been hurt by the housing bust and why?

3. Which states have benefited from the bust and why?

Overview

Read a general overview of the subject.

Mobility: A myth to debunk?

Mobility – be it social, geographic or economic- is one of the key myths in American mythology : the United States is the quintesssential young nation always on the move – as opposed notably to Europe, "the old continent". From the conquest of the West, late 19th century "Manifest Destiny" to the 1969 moon landing, Americans – whether pioneers, cowboys, astronauts or visionary political and corporate leaders – have been charting their own course through the unknown, thus embodying the entrepreneurial spirit as they rightfully keep pursuing opportunities.

Such mobility is generally thought to be inherited from the 19th century Frontier days and westward movement as epitomised by Horace Greeley's 1865 editorial "Go West, young man!". It expressed Americans' belief in a boundless land of opportunities ready for the taking. There was a great need for able-bodied unattached young people to overcome the hardships of the land, the weather and hostile natives and to take the nation to the shores of the Pacific ocean.

...

When, by the 1890s, the land was finally pacified and settled from East to West, people began to look back on the good old Frontier days as the embodiment of what it meant to be America: leaving one's past behind to start from scratch, and succeeding by dedication, energy, resourcefulness and optimism. Consequently, for the following generations, geographic mobility has been equated with economic progress and upward social mobility – what *The Economist* described in July 2005 as "restlessness in the midst of plenty". As the story goes, since people often relocate to find better jobs, geographic mobility fosters economic mobility, upward mobility and social equality through the growth of an affluent middle-class.

But figures now show a different America emerging. The 2004 census showed that less than 14 percent of US residents had moved house – the lowest figure since the Census Bureau began collecting data in 1948, when the moving rate was 20 percent. By comparison, 11% of Britons moved (so much for the "young vs old continents" myth). And the movers are not going very far (19% changed states) nor are they climbing the social ladder – a mere 16% of moves were work-related. Social mobility has slowed down so much that, in 2006, *The Economist* wondered if the American Dream was still a valid concept. Reaganomics in the 80s and Neoconservatism in the early 21st century have widened the gap between the super-rich, the increasingly weakened middle-class and the poor.

Pronunciation

Listen and repeat.

pull [pʊl], **pool** [pu:l]

- foot/food, look/Luke, cook/goose, full/fool.
- Luke's goose was cooked when he pushed his foot in the food.

22 Chapter

Manifest Destiny

Language focus

Had + *V*-en *(le plus-que-parfait ou past perfect)*

• Il permet, en se situant d'emblée dans le passé, de parler d'événements ou d'états encore antérieurs à ce passé de référence :

*I landed in New York. I **had not eaten** for 24 hours.*

J'ai atterri à New York. Je n'avais pas mangé depuis 24 heures.

• Dans un texte littéraire, *had* + V-*en* permet de faire référence soit à l'origine de la situation narrée au preterit :

*She took him around Paris with a quiet expertise. He understood why when she told him she **had been living** near l'Étoile for 25 years.*

soit à l'évolution d'une situation entre son point de depart et le moment rapporté au preterit :

*When Ogami finally met Retsudo, he **had not forgotten** why he wanted his revenge.*

• De la même manière que le *present perfect*, il peut se combiner avec *be* + V-*ing*, avec les mêmes effets de sens (voir chapitre 16).

Wordbank

an alloting agent	*un chargé de distribution des terres*
to annex regions	*annexer des régions*
BIA (Bureau of Indian Affairs)	*Bureau des affaires indiennes*
a border state	*un État frontalier*
borderlands	*des terres frontalières*
to cede territory	*céder des territoires*
civil unrest	*l'agitation sociale*
to claim superiority	*revendiquer une supériorité*
a crumbling empire	*un empire qui s'effrite*
to dispatch troops	*envoyer des troupes*
a divine mission	*une mission divine*
to encroach upon	*empiéter sur*
to enslave	*réduire en esclavage*
to expand to the west	*s'étendre vers l'ouest*
a federal agent/policy	*un agent/une politique fédéral(e)*
a frontiersman	*un pionnier*
a forced march	*une marche forcée*
a frontier zone	*une zone frontalière*
"Go West, young man!"	*« Pars à l'ouest, jeune homme ! » (Horace Greeley)*

to hatch a theory	*donner naissance à une théorie*
hazardous terrain	*du terrain dangereux*
a heathen	*un païen*
an Indian reservation	*un réserve indienne*
the indigenous faith	*la foi du peuple indigène*
jurisdiction	*la juridiction*
to lead mankind	*être à la tête de l'humanité*
the Louisiana Purchase	*l'achat de la Louisiane*
a magnet for golddiggers	*un aimant pour les chercheurs d'or*
to move into new lands	*s'installer sur de nouvelles terres*
the northern boundary	*la frontière nord*
to nullify	*invalider*
to occupy territory	*occuper des territoires*
open conflict	*le conflit ouvert*
overland migration	*la migration par voie terrestre*
to pit themselves against each other	*se mesurer les uns aux autres*
to provoke discontent	*provoquer un mécontentement*
to raise a regiment	*lever un régiment*
to recognise a title deed	*accepter des titres de propriété*
to roll back the frontier	*faire reculer la frontière*
a settler	*un colon*
a sparsely-settled area	*une zone peu peuplée*
a swathe of land	*une étendue de terre*
tribal lands	*des terres tribales*
unavoidable	*inévitable*
to undergo turmoil	*subir des bouleversements*
a wagon trail	*une piste suivie par les convois de wagons*
in the wake of (the) pioneers	*à la suite des pionniers*
to wrestle land from	*arracher des terres à*

Translation

Translate the sentences into English.

1. Le peuple Lakota vivait dans les plaines du Dakota bien avant que le gouvernement américain ne crée le Bureau des affaires indiennes.

2. Bien qu'ils se soient installés dans le sud-ouest avant l'arrivée des colons espagnols, les Apaches furent persécutés ou réduits en esclavage par les Mexicains.

3. Le gouvernement américain avait envoyé des troupes à l'ouest avant que la Guerre de Sécession n'éclate en 1860.

4. La théorie de la Frontière qu'avait avancée Turner dans les années 1830 poussa de nombreux colons à s'installer à l'ouest après la Guerre de Sécession.

5. Crazy Horse et Sitting Bull étaient morts depuis lontemps quand Géronimo l'Apache finit par se rendre.

Read and answer

Read the article and then do activities A and B that follow.

The king of all trips

Apollo 11 was a lot of good things, including amazingly cool

I'm writing about the summer of 1969. Calm down, this is not about Woodstock. I would rather eat crushed glass than write about Woodstock. I remain irritated at people who swear they were there and in fact were drinking Cutty and water at Holiday Inns. Woodstock is stuck somewhere between myth, cliché, and the brown acid making the rounds there that was not altogether spectacularly wonderful. Like the rest of us, the event gets smaller as it gets older.

Not so the Apollo 11 flight to the moon and back, a few weeks earlier. Not when we put two men on the moon while a third orbited above and brought them all safely home. The moon mission made the thing at Max Yasgur's farm look tiny and self-absorbed, which it was, although many of us didn't realize it at the time. Herds of bloviators over the years have vastly inflated Woodstock's importance and meaning, which can be reduced to two words: "No Rain." Not so Apollo 11.

The success of Apollo 11 displayed American prowess to accomplish something extraordinarily difficult. It gave us bragging rights over the Soviets. But it had broader historical significance. It marked what turned out to be the apex of the best of American exceptionalism.

Some argue that the moon mission was but a brief respite from the deadly side of this exceptionalism, the war in Vietnam. They maintain the war subsumed the short, refulgent success of Apollo 11.

Nuts.

At no time since those days in July has the United States enjoyed the status it enjoyed during and after Apollo 11. The whole world stopped to watch. People from Montevideo to Moscow were held in suspended animation as they followed the mission. The Americans were leading mankind into space. God bless America. When was the last time you heard those words from abroad? And let us not mistake the global sympathy for the United States after the Sept. 11 attacks with admiration for the United States.

Journalists dislike, for good reason, to issue breathless, absolute statements. But I can find no greater drama in human history in such a compressed timeline - nine days - than Apollo 11. The dropping of the atom bomb on Hiroshima might have had a greater impact on the world today, but it wasn't drama. No one knew it was happening, so no one could watch it in real time. Apollo 11 is never dated. It transcended politics. There was a purity to the mission that secured its spot above the fray. It fused function and beauty. There was something very American about it, too. The mission was the product of our creativity, technical skills, and single-mindedness of purpose. A fractured country came together behind this effort. Name for me other efforts of such magnitude that have since brought us together. The human face of Apollo 11 was as much the guy in black frame glasses and a short-sleeve, no-iron, white shirt in Houston as it was Neil Armstrong. Apollo 11 was the triumph of the nerds and middle-class America.

...

. . .

And it was romantic. A young, charismatic American president had challenged the country at the beginning of that decade to put a man on the moon by the end of the decade.

[...] No one knew whether Armstrong and Buzz Aldrin would make it up from the lunar surface back to the command module skippered by Michael Collins orbiting above. No one knew if these guys would make it home at all. [...]

Today we still find yeasty pockets of conspiracy types who maintain the landing was a hoax by the government to fulfill Kennedy's challenge on time and beat the Soviets to boot. We do love our conspiracies.

The Observer was reveling in the joys of Army boot camp at Fort Dix, N.J., during the summer of 1969 and missed Woodstock. But my friendly drill instructor rousted us from bed in the middle of the night and ordered us to repair to the recreation room to watch the landing, 40 years ago tomorrow.

This was, to the best of my memory, the only thing he ever did that didn't hurt me. I don't know what was stranger – watching the landing itself on a grainy black and white TV or wondering if we were hallucinating.

Apollo 11 marked the height of an American exceptionalism that began with the concept of Manifest Destiny, hatched in the 1840s. This theory held that America had a special dispensation to expand to the Pacific at the expense of everyone and everything in its path. It grew over time to become a global sense of entitlement.

Ronald Reagan carried the standard of American exceptionalism, and nativists still crow about it today. Its dark side informed the belligerent and disastrous foreign policy of George W. Bush and Dick Cheney.

No one seems hot to return to the moon. The funds aren't there, for starters. We've got a trillion-dollar debt and are aiming at a trillion-dollar national health insurance plan while fighting two wars abroad.

Apollo 11 was, in my book, the coolest thing America has ever done in this kind of arena. It displayed this country's penchant for risk. It was an astonishing technical success and a profound triumph over fear.

Sam Allis, *The Boston Globe* (bostonglobe.com), 19/7/2009

A. Language

Find synonyms in paragraphs 3 to 7 of the article for the following: *showed off, to achieve, boasting, climax/summit, lethal aspect, period of relief, bright/radiant, nonsense, chronology, out of date, above the political battle, divided/broken, importance, geeks.*

B. Question

According to the columnist, why does Apollo 11's flight embody America's Manifest Destiny? (Answer in 200-250 words. Use information in the article but do not copy sentences directly: use your own words.)

Overview

Read a general overview of the subject.

From Monroe to Obama

Some historians have argued that Manifest Destiny is the driving force responsible for changing the face of American history. It is not tied to dates or even a period of time – Manifest Destiny is a philosophy, a set of beliefs and concepts that embraces American history as a whole.

We can trace its origin back to the Monroe Doctrine when President Monroe warned European countries in 1822 to "stay out of the Western Hemisphere" and established the US as the "protector of the Western Hemisphere". In 1845, Democratic leader John O'Sullivan's movement asserted Americans' "right to our manifest destiny to spread and possess the whole of the continent which Providence has given us for the development of the great experient of liberty and federative development of self-government entrusted to us". The phrase that he coined had a religious undertone and was aimed at giving a moral justification for America's claim to new territories. It became the rallying cry throughout the nation: it was the rightful destiny of the US to keep expanding for they had a right to any land they wanted. This idea certainly contributed to several wars (with Mexico in 1846 and the Sioux/Lakota tribes in 1873 after gold had been found in the Black Hills) and served to vindicate the great colonising journey that took settlers from the Mississippi to the Pacific.

Once the continent had been entirely settled and pacified, the Manifest Destiny doctrine took on a much wider meaning that would serve to justify US expansionism in Central America (Guam, Puerto Rico…) first with President Theodore Roosevelt's "Iron-fisted neighbor" policy and then across the world after World War II when the USA took the military, political and moral leadership of the free world against the Communist threat. After the fall of the Berlin Wall in 1989, America was the world's only "hyperpower", being to all intents and purposes the hub of international politics, economics and culture. As the only nation powerful enough to influence events anywhere in the world, the USA had become the "protector" of democracy, thus fulfilling its Manifest Destiny on a higher plane. But it lost part of its moral leadership when President George W. Bush launched the war against Iraq in 2003 which many believed was to serve a neoconservative vision of imperial America ruling the world and its resources. Since 2009, President Obama has been trying to mend fences with the Arab world, the USA's European partners, and the country that could be tomorrow's next hyperpower: China.

Pronunciation

Listen and repeat.

book [bʊk], **buck** [bʌk]

- stood/stud, hook/Huck, look/luck, rook/ruck.
- With luck, Huck could always hook the rook.

Chapter 23

Politics

Language focus

La traduction de depuis, il y a, pendant

• Il faut faire la distinction entre (1) la mesure et (2) le repérage d'un moment dans le passé.

1. La mesure :

– Durée = *for*

Nous avons mangé **pendant** trois heures.

*We were eating **for** three hours.*

Nous attendons **depuis** cinq minutes.

*We have been waiting **for** three minutes.*

On va rester (pendant) encore un an.

*We'll stay **for** another year.*

– Point = *since*

J'ai mal à la tête **depuis** hier. *I've had a headache **since** yesterday.*

2. Le repérage (*ago*) :

Je l'ai rencontré **il y a** deux ans. *I met him two years **ago**.*

• Notez la différence entre ces deux phrases :

*I'll be in Spain **during** the summer.* Je serai en Espagne pendant (une partie de) l'été.

*I'll be in Spain **for** the summer.* Je serai en Espagne **pendant** (toute) l'été.

Wordbank

the administration	*le gouvernement*
affirmative action	*la discrimination positive*
the approval ratings	*la cote de popularité*
the Bill of Rights	*les 10 premiers amendements à la Constitution*
to broker a deal	*négocier un accord entre deux partis*
a Congressman	*un élu du Congrès*
cronyism	*le favoritisme/le copinage en politique*
to cross the aisle	*changer de camp politique*
donkeys and elephants	*ânes et éléphants (symboles démocrates et républicains)*
an electoral campaign	*une campagne électorale*
executive privilege	*le privilège présidentiel*
a favourite son	*un candidat préféré souvent au niveau local*
a filibuster	*un obstructionniste*
a front runner	*celui qui arrive en tête dans les sondages*
the GOP (Grand Old Party)	*le parti républicain (terme des années 1870)*
the grassroots members/membership	*les adhérents/militants de la base*

the House of Representatives	*la Chambre des répresentants*
a key player	*un acteur majeur*
the mid term elections	*les élections de mi-mandat*
a narrow majority	*une courte majorité*
a national convention	*un congrès national (de parti politique)*
partisan politics	*la politique partisane*
a party caucus meeting	*une réunion du comité electoral d'un parti*
a party congress	*une conférence de parti*
a party treasurer	*un trésorier de parti*
pork, pork-barrelling	*le clientélisme, la distribution des subventions publiques*
a poll	*un sondage*
primaries	*les primaires*
a pro-choice activist	*un militant pour le droit à l'avortement*
a pro-life activist	*un militant anti-avortement*
the reins of power	*les rênes du pouvoir*
to remain in power	*rester au pouvoir*
to run for election	*être candidat à l'élection*
a sitting member	*un membre élu*
a slush fund	*une caisse noire*
a smear campaign	*une campagne de diffamation*
the Speaker	*le Président de la Chambre*
a spin doctor	*un consultant en communication*
the spoils system	*la redistribution de postes à la suite d'une élection*
to sponsor legislation	*proposer une législation*
a straw poll	*un sondage non-officiel*
Super Tuesday	*le mardi au cours duquel nombre d'États désignent leur candidat électif préféré*
to swear in	*prêter serment*
to swing voters	*faire changer d'opinion*
the floor of the house	*l'assemblée*
the political agenda	*le programme politique*
a think tank	*un groupe de réflexion*
to cast a ballot	*voter*

Translation

Translate the sentences into English.

1. Le clientélisme et le copinage existent depuis que les Pères Fondateurs ont conçu leur version de la démocratie il y a plus de deux siècles.

2. Il fait la course en tête depuis le début de la campagne éléctorale pour la Maison Blanche.

3. Il fut un membre de base du parti républicain au Texas pendant 40 ans.

4. Les sondages donnent le candidat local vainqueur aux élections de mi-mandat depuis quelques semaines.

5. Le trésorier du parti est victime d'une campagne de diffamation depuis qu'un élu du Congrès a révélé l'existence d'une caisse noire.

Read and answer

Read the article and then do activities A and B that follow.

Tea Party's rise could undercut mainstream GOP

WASHINGTON – The Tea Party movement is energizing elements of the Republican Party and fanning an anti-Washington fervor, but the biggest beneficiaries in the midterm elections, pollsters and political analysts say, could be the main target of their anger: Democrats. From North Carolina and Kentucky to Colorado and Nevada, candidates backed by Tea Party activists are making strong showings in primaries and opinion polls. Some of their campaigns, however, threaten to undercut GOP efforts to attract independents and moderates, prized voting factions in the general election.

"Republicans are definitely doing Democrats a favor if they nominate these Tea Party candidates," said Tom Jensen, director of Public Policy Polling, which has surveyed several of the states where such candidates are in play. "Even if these Tea Party candidates win in the primaries, things can look a lot worse in the general."

The anti-establishment candidates and their supporters insist they are simply voicing a widespread frustration with big government and big spending in Washington. Far from alienating Americans, Tea Party contenders will encourage conservatives to go to the polls in the midterm general election, when turnout is typically lower than in presidential elections, their supporters say. Nor is the GOP establishment ready to put a damper on the movement, which already has helped nominate libertarian-leaning Rand Paul in the Kentucky GOP primary for US Senate and tossed out veteran Senator Bob Bennett in Utah's GOP primary.

"These are Americans who are concerned about the government and spending and debt, so we ought to be able to find a way to be responsive to them," said Senator John Cornyn, chairman of the National Republican Senatorial Committee. "I don't consider them outliers or unwelcome."

Democrats fully expect to lose seats this fall, in part because of historical trends and in part because of a voter backlash against the Democrat-controlled government in Washington. And the majority party is experiencing infighting as well; incumbent Arkansas Senator Blanche Lincoln, for example, has been forced into a runoff against Bill Halter, the lieutenant governor whose candidacy has been backed by more liberal Democrats.

But Republicans are in a more vexing quandary, trying to channel the energy of the Tea Party movement while keeping its more controversial leaders from becoming the face of the GOP. Capitol Hill Republicans, for example, have distanced themselves from Paul's comments to MSNBC's Rachel Maddow that he would have sought to change in the 1964 Civil Rights Act one provision outlawing discrimination in certain businesses. Paul later said he would have voted for the act.

Republicans, however, are careful not to alienate the movement's rank and file.

"Tea Party people are people who are very concerned about the financial future of our country, and they certainly play a role," said Massachusetts GOP Senator Scott Brown, whose surprise victory in January was partly propelled by support from Tea Party and conservative activists. Brown added that he had not had time to listen to the comments made by Paul or other Tea Party-backed candidates. [...]

...

Tea Party defenders, however, call their candidates victims of both parties – Democrats seeking to taint GOP slates across the country with unfair caricatures and Republicans irritated that their hand-picked candidates aren't connecting with voters.

Angle is "the most vocal and consistent and authentic economic conservative in this race. That is going to be the message that resonates in the general election," said Michael Connolly of the Club for Growth, an antitax group that is running a TV ad for Angle.

Jesse Benton, Paul's campaign manager, said the Tea Party message – if articulated well – will bring in moderates and independents. "I think [Paul's] common-sense, reform-minded platform has tremendous appeal," Benton said. "You can express frustration, and express concerns, but make sure you're not just the angry guy yelling."

Susan Milligan, *The Boston Globe*, Globe30/6/2010

A. Language

Find synonyms in the title and paragraphs 1, 3 and 4 of the article for the following: *weaken/undermine, encouraging/stimulating* (two possible answers), *polling agencies, supported by, to woo, expressing discontent, candidates, the midterms, to discourage, are worried about.*

B. Question

What is the Tea Party Movement's impact on US politics? (Answer in 150-200 words. Use information in the article but do not copy sentences directly: use your own words.)

Translation

Translate the article into English.

Le mouvement Tea Party est voué à être éphémère

Où le mouvement des Tea Parties se place-t-il sur l'échiquier politique américain ?
Il est totalement sur la ligne des Républicains au plan fiscal et économique, et ce de façon assez radicale. Beaucoup de gens y partagent aussi des idées conservatrices au niveau religieux et social. Pour autant, ce n'est pas un mouvement que l'on peut classer dans un camp politique. D'ailleurs, 43 % des participants aux Tea Parties sont des indépendants, ceux là même qui ont soutenu Barack Obama aux élections présidentielles. De quoi faire taire les accusations de racisme que beaucoup profèrent à l'encontre de ce mouvement.

Quelles sont les revendications de ses membres ?
Ils s'opposent au renflouement des banques par l'État, à ses prises de participation dans certaines grandes entreprises pour leur venir en aide, et à la récente réforme de la santé. Mais derrière tout cela, ce que rejettent en bloc les Tea Parties, c'est le « Big Government », cette idée d'un gouvernement trop puissant, qu'ils voient se dessiner au travers de toutes ces décisions.

Olivier Faure, Reuters/Bryan Snyder (dans *L'Express* [lexpress.fr]), 15/4/2010

Overview

Read a general overview of the subject.

Personalities more than politics

Americans always seem to be electing someone, whether it be a judge, a mayor, a sheriff, a Congressman or a president. And yet, when it comes to political parties, they are not exactly spoiled for choice: there are only two of any importance and, from a European viewpoint, it is sometimes difficult to tell them apart. The Democratic Party (symbol: the donkey) may be said to be more to the left than Republican Party (also known as the Grand Old Party or GOP; symbol: the elephant) but nothing like as far left as any European socialist party. They monopolise the political arena for two reasons: firstly, the "first past the post" system disadvantages minority parties and, secondly, parties can spend as much as they like on election campaigns and there is no restriction on advertising, so any new candidate or party would have to be immensely wealthy to put up any sort of a fight with the established parties.

Being a Democrat generally means being more interventionist, more socially radical than a Republican, but party politics often play second fiddle to the importance of political personalities: voting for a particular person can be as important as voting for a party.

Members of the House of Representatives (the lower chamber) are normally elected every two years; members of the Senate every six years. Whereas the number of Representatives for each state depends on the state's population, there are two Senators per state. This means that the small states have a disproportionate level of power in the Senate where, unlike most other bicameral democracies, most of the power lies. The "2 Senators per state" system also tends to mean that ethnic and racial minorities are under-represented.

The President is not elected directly by universal suffrage. The election is the result of simultaneous state elections by an electoral college of electors chosen by voters at state "primaries". Since the procedure is not laid out in detail in the Constitution, each state has developed its own way of doing things. Such is the power invested in the President that the stakes are enormous for the political parties. Hence the millions of dollars that are spent on publicity and whistle-stop tours, the near-hysteria generated by winning or losing, and above all the ever-increasing personalisation of elections, leading to smear campaigns and the cult of personality, which can often get more votes than policies or politics.

Pronunciation

Listen and repeat.

gore [gɔː], **glue** [gluː]

- ford/food, morse/moose, spawn/spoon, ball/boon.
- The moose gored the Lord and glued him to his Ford.

24 Chapter

Religious diversity

Language focus

Les degrés de l'adjectif (comparatif, superlatif)

• Comparatif des adjectifs courts, (= les adjectifs d'une syllabe et les adjectifs de deux syllabes qui se terminent en *-y*, *-re*, *-le* ou *-ow*) :

*wide/wid**er**, big/bigg**er**, crazy/crazi**er***
***less** wide/big/crazy*

• Comparatif des adjectifs longs (= les autres adjectifs de 2 syllabes et les adjectifs de trois syllabes ou plus) :

***more** careful/pleasant/extraordinary*
***less** careful/pleasant/extraordinary*

• Complément introduit par *than* :

*He is tall**er**/**less** happy **than** me.*

• Superlatif des adjectifs courts :

*the wid**est**/biggest/craziest*

• Superlatif des adjectifs longs :

***the most** careful/pleasant/extraordinary*

Wordbank

agnostic	*agnostique*
to be born again	*renaître*
the Bible Belt	*la région du sud-est des États-Unis très éprise de protestantisme évangélique*
a bible thumper	*un évangéliste passionné*
a Catholic stronghold	*un bastion du catholicisme*
church attendance	*la fréquentation des églises*
a churchgoer	*quelqu'un qui fréquente l'église*
creationism	*le créationnisme*
the denomination	*la confession/la foi (de telle ou telle religion)*
a drive-in church	*une église dans laquelle on prie dans son véhicule*
the emergence of different creeds	*l'émergence de différentes croyances*
an evangelical Protestant church	*une église protestante évangélique*
a faith leader	*un leader religieux*
the faithful	*les fidèles*
fervor	*la ferveur, l'ardeur*
a fundamentalist Protestant	*un protestant fondamentaliste*
the Gospel	*l'Évangile*

a Jehovah's witness	*un témoin de Jéhovah*
Jewish	*juif*
a mainstream religion	*une grande religion*
a minister	*un pasteur*
a Muslim/Moslem	*un musulman*
the national religious profile	*le paysage religieux national*
the nones	*ceux qui ne se reconnaissent dans aucune religion*
a non-Judeo-Christian faith	*une foi non-judéo-chrétienne*
an offering	*une offrande*
an outdoor baptism	*un baptême en plein air*
a pastor	*un pasteur*
a place of worship	*un lieu de culte*
a prayer centre	*un centre de prière*
a preacher	*un prédicateur*
a priest	*un prêtre*
a public shrine	*un lieu saint public*
a Quaker	*un Quaker (*quake = *trembler)*
the rate of change	*la vitesse de changement*
the religious mosaic	*la mosaïque religieuse/des religions*
religious observance	*les observances religieuses*
religious practices	*les pratiques religieuses*
a scientologist	*un scientologue*
the secular boom	*la croissance du sécularisme*
a sin, a sinner	*un péché, un pécheur*
shared beliefs	*les croyances partagées*
to span a range of beliefs	*couvrir une gamme de croyances*
to switch beliefs	*changer de croyance*
televangelism	*le téléévangélisme*
the religious make-up of society	*la composition religieuse de la société*
the Seven Sisters	*les sept plus importantes églises protestantes américaines (Baptists, Congregationalists/Unitarians, Disciples of Christ, Episcopalians, Lutherans, Methodists, Presbyterians)*
an unaffiliated believer	*un croyant ne suivant aucune religion établie*

Translation

Translate the sentences into English.

1. C'est dans le sud-est des États-Unis que l'on trouve le plus d'évangélistes passionnés et de prédicateurs.

2. Les chrétiens de toutes confessions sont beaucoup plus nombreux que les bouddhistes et les musulmans aux États-Unis.

3. De plus en plus de fidèles changent de croyance devant la vitesse de développement d'une société de plus en plus multiculturelle.

4. Le paysage religieux est beaucoup moins varié en Europe qu'aux États-Unis.

5. Il y a moins de fidèles à la messe dans les lieux de cultes le dimanche.

Read and answer

Read the article and then do activities A and B that follow.

Religion in the High Court

If she's confirmed, court would have no Protestants

President Obama's nomination of Elena Kagan to the US Supreme Court represents a turning point in American religious history: If Kagan, who is Jewish, is confirmed, the high court will not have a single Protestant member. More than half of all Americans are Protestant, while less than one-quarter are Catholic and just 1.7 percent are Jewish, according to the US Religious Landscape Survey by the Pew Forum on Religion and Public Life. But, if Kagan is confirmed to the bench, the nation's highest court, dominated by Protestants for most of its history, will be made up of six Catholics and three Jews.

"This whole project of a Protestant America is really going under, and it's going under quickly," said Stephen Prothero, a professor of religion at Boston University and author of "God is Not One: The Eight Rival Religions that Run the World – and Why Their Differences Matter." Kagan's nomination, he said, "is an important moment of saying, 'Look, we've gone so far beyond the idea that this is a Protestant country that we can have a court with six Catholics and three Jews."

Martin E. Marty, professor emeritus at the University of Chicago Divinity School, said that these days, the question of whether there should be a distinctly Protestant voice on the court would elicit "a big yawn" from most mainline Protestants. "I was in an Episcopal church in Chicago on Sunday, and there were a lot of movers and shakers there, but we didn't sit around after and say, 'How can we get one of us on the Supreme Court?" he said.

Evangelical Protestants have been slow to embrace or to feel welcomed by elite law schools like Harvard and Yale that have become a veritable requirement for Supreme Court nominees. One reason for this, some scholars say, is an anti-intellectual strain within evangelicalism. "Evangelical Christianity has tended to be a populist religion that's strongly democratic, in urging people to read the Bible themselves," said Mark A. Noll, a history professor at the University of Notre Dame. "All these are traits that have positive sides, but not for intellectual preparation and education."

But Noll and others say this is changing. Like Catholics and Jews of the last century, evangelicals are increasingly realizing that they need intellectual credentials to acquire institutional power in America.

Influencing the high court is of special importance to evangelicals because of their opposition to abortion. […] .

A half-century ago, Catholics and Jews were the outsiders in the top echelons of the legal and political worlds. But barriers to their advancement have now largely disintegrated, as both groups have made significant strides in educational and professional achievement. "Education itself became important, with a kind of edge that was not present for most Protestant groups," Noll said.

Republican presidents, seeking Supreme Court nominees with strong educational credentials who oppose abortion rights, have in recent years turned repeatedly to Catholics. […]

…

...

Democratic presidents, seeking Supreme Court nominees who are reliably liberal, have several times nominated Jewish justices.

President Clinton appointed both of the court's current Jewish justices, Stephen Breyer and Ruth Bader Ginsburg.

Some scholars lament the lack of religious diversity on the court.

"We think through ethics and law in our lives, whether we are Supreme Court justices or not, in light of our backgrounds and religious commitments," Prothero said. "And I think it's a pity to have only two religious traditions represented on the court."

Lisa Wangsness, *The Boston Globe* (bostonglobe.com), 11/5/2010

A. Language

Find synonyms in paragraphs 1, 3, 4 and 5 of the article for the following: *a defining moment, 25%, in the position of judge, composed of, appointment, provoke nothing but indifference, influential people, to become part of/to join, pressing, are becoming aware, references, to gain.*

B. Question

To what extent can we say today's Supreme Court does not reflect the guiding principle of religious diversity in the US? (Answer in 150-200 words. Use information in the article but do not copy sentences directly: use your own words.)

Translation

Translate the article into English.

Religion : le doute de l'Oncle Sam

Polémiste brillant et drôle, le journaliste britannique Christopher Hitchens, installé à Washington, conquiert le public français avec *Dieu n'est pas grand. Comment la religion empoisonne tout* (Belfond). Regard d'un impie patenté sur l'Amérique croyante.

Votre livre est une provocation pour les 90% d'Américains qui disent avoir la foi...
Je ne crois pas à ce chiffre. Selon un récent sondage de l'institut Pew Research Center, seulement 50 % des Américains vont à l'église. Le nombre des athées est en pleine croissance.

L'idée que la religion tient la politique américaine serait donc fausse ?
De plus en plus. Malgré leur alliance, protestants de droite et catholiques réalisent qu'ils n'obtiendront jamais l'abolition de l'avortement. Plus récemment, nous avons assisté à une réaction outrée des familles de la middle class américaine contre l'enseignement du créationnisme dans les écoles. Elles craignent que ce rejet obtus de la science ne nuise à la réussite scolaire de leurs enfants et au prestige des États-Unis. Dans son discours inaugural, Barack Obama a fait appel à toutes les religions et « aux millions de non-croyants ». Cette reconnaissance de la légitimité du caractère séculier de la société américaine est une grande première.

Philippe Coste, *L'Express* (lexpress.fr), 13/3/2009

Overview

Read a general overview of the subject.

An amazing diversity

Religion has played an important role in American life since the Pilgrim Fathers, fleeing persecution in 17th century England, accosted on American shores bringing their Protestant puritanism with them. It could be said that their "Protestant work ethic" is the main reason why a small New World colony was able to turn into a superpower...

More than half of Americans these days call themselves Protestant, belonging to one or another of the mainline churches known as the "Seven Sisters", but there is no state religion although American presidents swear their oath on a bible. So many millions of copies of the bible are run off the presses every year that it is difficult to give exact figures, although some theological societies estimate that perhaps over 90% of American households possess at least one copy. This is certainly the case in the "Bible Belt", the expression used by H. L. Mencken in 1925 to denote certain parts of the southern US where religious fundamentalism was and still is very widespread. This is where you find the bible thumpers or bible bashers – believers and preachers who are often members of evangelical movements. It is also where most of the televangelists come from – the TV preachers who play such a large part in some Americans' lives.

The evangelical churches are an example of the amazing diversity of beliefs that make up the Christian community in the US, from the Quakers and Mormons of the north to the Baptists of the south. Many have used song as a means of praising God and spreading the Word, and several of the choirs formed to do this, whilst not a consumer product for export, have become a feature of concert circuits the world over. Other churches have become highly radical, like those that believe in creationism: the fact that they have managed to stop the teaching of the theory of evolution in some communities shows how much power they can wield.

You can see manifestations of Christian belief everywhere, from roadside hoardings with their "Jesus is coming" messages, to drive-in churches. Hotel bedrooms all have a bible and every community seems to have its place of worship, whether it be a community hall or a cathedral. But the country offers a mesh of different beliefs, mainstream religions and sects and, even though between half and three-quarters of Americans declare themselves to be Christian, Judaism and Islam are also very well represented across the religious spectrum.

Pronunciation

Listen and repeat.

hut [hʌt], **hurt** [hɜːt]

- bun/burn, fun/fern, duck/dirk, Sutton/certain.
- Bert killed the duck with his dirk near Sutton Ferns.

Chapter 25

The black community

Language focus

La morphologie des groupes adjectivaux

- Les groupes adjectivaux peuvent présenter un degré de complexité variable. Voici les principales possibilités d'expansion de l'adjectif :

a very ugly hat (adv. + adj.)	un chapeau très laid
a light grey shirt (adj. + adj.)	une chemise gris clair
a *navy-blue tie* (nom + adj.)	une cravate bleu marine

- On peut fabriquer un adjectif composé à partir de d'autres qualifications plus complexes :

a risk-free operation = an operation that is free of risks
une opération sans risque
easy-to-use software = software that is easy to use
un logiciel facile à utiliser
a user-friendly computer = a computer that is friendly to the user
un ordinateur convivial

Wordbank

to abolish slavery	*abolir l'esclavage*
the abolitionist movement	*le mouvement abolitionist*
to accede to the highest office	*accéder à office supréme*
to bar	*interdire*
the cause for black advancement	*la cause pour l'avancement de la population noire*
the black awakening	*le réveil de la population noire*
black liberation theologyy	*la théologie de la liberation des noirs*
the Black Panthers	*les Panthères noires*
black power	*le pouvoir noir*
black studies	*les études afro-américaines*
a bus boycott	*un boycott des bus*
civil disobedience	*la désobéissance civile*
the Civil Rights Act, 1964	*la loi sur les droits civiques, 1964*
civil rights reform	*la réforme des droits civiques*
the cotton belt	*la région de la culture du coton*
a cotton gin	*une égreneuse de coton*
a cotton/tobacco plantation	*une plantation de coton/tabac*
to cross racial barriers	*surmonter des préjugés raciaux*
a crusade against random lynching	*une croisade contre l'assassinat arbitraire*
desegregation	*la déségrégation*

emerging black literature	*la littérature noire émergente*
to enslave	*réduire en esclavage*
an epic event	*un événement épique*
equal voting rights	*les mêmes droits de vote*
a freed slave	*un esclave libéré*
a freedom march	*une marche pour la liberté*
a freedom rider	*un voyageur qui se battait contre la ségrégation dans les bus*
to gain acceptance	*gagner l'approbation*
a grassroots movement	*un mouvement des activistes de base*
indentured servants	*un domestique lié par contrat à son maître*
ingrained racial prejudice	*des préjugés raciaux profondément ancrés*
a labour shortage	*une carence de main d'œuvre*
the legacy of slavery	*l'héritage de l'esclavage*
NAACP (National Association for the Advancement of Colored People)	*L'Association nationale pour promouvoir les intérêts des personnes de couleur*
"picking up the gun"	*« en prenant le fusil » : une des philosophies des Panthères noires*
a plight	*une situation désespérée*
to quell violence	*réprimer la violence*
a race riot	*une émeute raciale*
the rural black belt	*les régions du sud-est des États-Unis où la déségrégation se révélait difficile*
segregationist practices	*des démarches ségrégationistes*
a self-evident truth	*une vérité qui va de soi*
separate but equal	*séparés mais égaux*
a sharecropper	*un métayer*
the slave trade	*le commerce des esclaves*
to spearhead a boycott	*mener un boycott*
a wave of sit-ins	*une vague d'occupations de lieux publics*
a whites/blacks-only facilities	*endroits réservés aux seuls blancs/noirs*

Translation

Translate the sentences into English.

1. Défendre le droit de vote pour tous n'était pas une activité sans danger dans les années 50 et 60.

2. Les associations de défense des droits civiques menèrent une croisade contre les assassinats arbitraires.

3. Le slogan des Panthères noires – "en prenant le fusil" – n'avait pas pour objectif de transformer les militants de la cause noire en fous de la gâchette.

4. Pam Grier fut un très beau symbole du réveil culturel de la communauté noire dans le cinéma américain des années 70.

5. De Rosa Parks à Martin Luther King, la lutte pour obtenir l'égalité des droits pour la population noire fut jalonnée d'événements marquants.

Read and answer

Read the article and then do activities A and B that follow.

Obama elected President as racial barrier falls

Barack Hussein Obama was elected the 44th president of the United States on Tuesday, sweeping away the last racial barrier in American politics with ease as the country chose him as its first black chief executive. The election of Mr. Obama amounted to a national catharsis – a repudiation of a historically unpopular Republican president and his economic and foreign policies, and an embrace of Mr. Obama's call for a change in the direction and the tone of the country. But it was just as much a strikingly symbolic moment in the evolution of the nation's fraught racial history, a breakthrough that would have seemed unthinkable just two years ago.

Mr. Obama, 47, a first-term senator from Illinois, defeated Senator John McCain of Arizona, 72, a former prisoner of war who was making his second bid for the presidency. To the very end, Mr. McCain's campaign was eclipsed by an opponent who was nothing short of a phenomenon, drawing huge crowds epitomized by the tens of thousands of people who turned out to hear Mr. Obama's victory speech in Grant Park in Chicago. [...]

"If there is anyone out there who still doubts that America is a place where all things are possible, who still wonders if the dream of our founders is alive in our time, who still questions the power of our democracy, tonight is your answer," said Mr. Obama, standing before a huge wooden lectern with a row of American flags at his back, casting his eyes to a crowd that stretched far into the Chicago night. "It's been a long time coming," the president-elect added, "but tonight, because of what we did on this date in this election at this defining moment, change has come to America."

Mr. McCain delivered his concession speech under clear skies on the lush lawn of the Arizona Biltmore, in Phoenix, where he and his wife had held their wedding reception. The crowd reacted with scattered boos as he offered his congratulations to Mr. Obama and saluted the historical significance of the moment. "This is a historic election, and I recognize the significance it has for African-Americans and for the special pride that must be theirs tonight," Mr. McCain said, adding, "We both realize that we have come a long way from the injustices that once stained our nation's reputation."

Not only did Mr. Obama capture the presidency, but he led his party to sharp gains in Congress. This puts Democrats in control of the House, the Senate and the White House for the first time since 1995, when Bill Clinton was in office.

The day shimmered with history as voters began lining up before dawn, hours before polls opened, to take part in the culmination of a campaign that over the course of two years commanded an extraordinary amount of attention from the American public.

As the returns became known, and Mr. Obama passed milestone after milestone – Ohio, Florida, Virginia, Pennsylvania, New Hampshire, Iowa and New Mexico – people rolled spontaneously into the streets to celebrate what many described, with perhaps overstated if understandable exhilaration, a new era in a country where just 143 years ago, Mr. Obama, as a black man, could have been owned as a slave. [...]

Mr. Obama and his expanded Democratic majority on Capitol Hill now face the task of governing the country through a difficult period: the likelihood of a deep and prolonged recession, and two wars. He took note of those circumstances in a speech ...

...

that was notable for its sobriety and its absence of the triumphalism that he might understandably have displayed on a night when he won an Electoral College landslide.

"The road ahead will be long, our climb will be steep," said Mr. Obama, his audience hushed and attentive, with some, including the Rev. Jesse Jackson, wiping tears from their eyes. "We may not get there in one year or even one term, but America, I have never been more hopeful than I am tonight that we will get there. I promise you, we as a people will get there." [...]

Initial signs were that Mr. Obama benefited from a huge turnout of voters, but particularly among blacks. That group made up 13 percent of the electorate, according to surveys of people leaving the polls, compared with 11 percent in 2006.

In North Carolina, Republicans said that the huge surge of African-Americans was one of the big factors that led to Senator Elizabeth Dole, a Republican, losing her re-election bid.

Mr. Obama also did strikingly well among Hispanic voters; Mr. McCain did worse among those voters than Mr. Bush did in 2004. That suggests the damage the Republican Party has suffered among those voters over four years in which Republicans have been at the forefront on the effort to crack down on illegal immigrants.

The election ended what by any definition was one of the most remarkable contests in American political history, drawing what was by every appearance unparalleled public interest.

Adam Nagourney, *The New York Times* (nytimes.com), 5/11/2008

A. Language

Find synonyms in paragraphs 1, 2, 6 and 7 of the article for the following: *eradicating, obstacle, rejection, highly-charged and full of conflict, a major advance, attempt* (n.) *to obtain, exemplified/typified, expresses doubts about, the climax, watershed, exaggerated, happiness.*

B. Questions

Why was Barack Obama's election a milestone in US history? (Answer in 200-250 words. Use information in the article but do not copy sentences directly: use your own words.)

Overview

Read a general overview of the subject.

The long path to freedom

The election of Barack Obama as President with his slogan "Yes, we can" must have seemed like a dream come true for many non-white Americans, particularly for the African-American commuunity.

Brought to the US from Africa and later from the Caribbean as slaves, by the 19th century African-Americans were the main labour force on the tobacco, rice and cotton plantations. Their rights were not addressed in the Constitution, much to the shame of many Northerners who began to abolish slavery in certain states in the early 1800s. But slaves were by now so essential to the economy and way of life of the southern States that abolitionism in the North sparked off the attempted secession of the Southern states, leading to the American Civil War. The final victory of the North meant that President Lincoln's 1863 Emancipation Proclamation took effect and slavery was abolished.

However, this by no means meant an end to racial prejudice, segregation and discrimination, much of which came from the attitude of some white Southerners (as manifest in organisations like the Klu Klux Klan) and from the fears generated by the influx of blacks moving from the south to urban areas like Chicago. Over a long period, civil rights organisations lobbyed Congress or used direct action and civil disobedience to demand equal rights for all US citizens. A Supreme Court ruling officially banned segregation in 1954, but many states were recalcitrant and, when Rosa Parks, a black activist, refused to give up her seat for a white passenger on an Alabama bus in 1955, it sparked off a chain of high-profile demonstrations, aided by black personalities such as Martin Luther King, culminating in the famous peaceful march on Washington in 1963 which produced the "I have a dream" speech. As a result, Civil Rights Acts were passed between 1964 and 1968 which banned racial discrimination of any sort.

Since then, there has been steady progress in the economic and political power obtained by the black community. There are black senators, black business leaders – and black talk-show hostess Oprah Winfrey is one of the richest women in the world. However, problems of poverty and crime within the community are still extremely serious. An African-American may be president of the USA, but he is president of a country in which his own ethnic group has the highest imprisonment rate of any ethnic group anywhere in the world.

Pronunciation

Listen and repeat.

short [ʃɔːt], **shirt** [ʃɜːt]

- lawn/learn, Paul/world, ward/word, corn/girl, spawn/work, talk/Turk.
- Paul met the Turk and the girl after work on the lawn.

26 Chapter

The Hispanic community

Language focus

Groupes adjectivaux complexes

• La langue anglaise permet de fabriquer des *compound adjectives* à partir d'éléments qui ne sont pas des adjectifs :

a hard-working boy (adv. ou adj. + participe présent)
un garçon qui travaille dur
a heart-breaking story (nom + participe présent)
une histoire qui fend le cœur
a blue-eyed girl (adj. + nom en *-ed*)
une fille aux yeux bleus
a broken-hearted boy (*participe passé* + nom en *-ed*)
un gamin au cœur brisé
a home-made cookie (nom + participe passé)
un biscuit fait maison

• Deux types de qualifiants présentent une morphologie particulière :

a five-dollar bill = a bill worth five dollars
un billet de cinq dollars
a thirty-year-old man = a man who is thirty years old
un homme de trente ans

Notez la disparition du *-s* du pluriel de *dollars* et *years* quand le groupe devient épithète du nom.

Wordbank

to abide by tradition	*respecter la tradition*
agricultural work	*les travaux agricoles*
an alien registration card	*une carte de séjour permanente*
Arizona SB 1070	*loi d'État faisant de l'immigration illégale une activité criminelle*
a bilingual ballot paper	*un bulletin de vote bilingue*
a border crossing post	*un poste frontière*
the border police	*la police des frontières*
a burgeoning political force	*une force politique en plein essor*
the butt of racism	*la cible du racisme*
the changing face of the USA	*le visage changeant des États-Unis*
a Chicano	*un Américain originaire du Mexique*
a close-knit group	*un groupe très soudé*

a Cuban	*un Cubain*
demographic clustering	*les regroupements démographiques*
divided loyalties	*un conflit de loyautés*
downtrodden	*opprimé*
dreams of upward mobility	*des rêves de promotion sociale*
an ethnic minority	*une minorité ethnique*
ethnic pride	*la fierté d'appartenir à une communauté*
family ties	*les liens familiaux*
the fastest-growing segment	*le segment qui croît le plus rapidement*
a foreign-born Latino/Hispanic	*un Latino né à l'étranger*
the Hispanic underclass	*les Hispaniques défavorisés*
hispanophobic	*hispanophobe*
the impoverished borderlands	*les terres frontalières appauvries*
to lack resident status	*ne pas avoir le statut de résident*
the language conflict	*le conflit linguistique*
a Latino/Latina	*un(e) homme/femme d'origine latino-américaine*
law-abiding	*respectueux de la loi*
a mixed neighborhood	*un quartier mixte*
to narrow the gap	*réduire l'écart*
a Puerto Rican	*un Portoricain*
the quota system	*le système de quotas*
a recruitment agent	*un agent recruteur*
to reshape American society	*reconfigurer la société américaine*
rootless	*sans racines*
to self-identify	*se définir*
a sharp rise	*une augmentation rapide*
south of the border	*au sud de la frontière*
Spanish-speaking	*hispanophone*
to stem the tide of illegal labour	*endiguer le flot de main-d'œuvre illégale*
straddling two worlds	*à cheval entre deux mondes*
stringent law enforcement	*l'application stricte de la loi*
the tools for integration	*les outils d'intégration*
a wetback	*un clandestin mexicain (référence à ceux qui traversaient le Rio Grande à la nage pour entrer au Texas)*

Translation

Translate the sentences into English.

1. Son grand père mexicain était un travailleur acharné qui réussit à subvenir aux besoins d'une famille de cinq enfants souriants aux yeux sombres et aux cheveux bouclés.

2. Ce film angoissant raconte l'histoire bouleversante d'un groupe soudé de « dos mouillés » qui tente de traverser la frontière.

3. Mon voisin portoricain regrette les bons petits plats cuisinés par sa mère à San Juan.

4. Clara eut le cœur brisé de devoir laisser sa famille derrière elle à Cuba.

5. Ce jeune immigré de 24 ans est un citoyen respectueux des lois et ambitieux.

Read and answer

Read the article and then do activities A and B that follow.

Young Latinos Get a Push for Education

Hispanics are the fastest growing segment of the US population, but are the least likely to get college degrees

WASHINGTON DC. Latinos are the fastest growing segment of the U.S. population but Latino students are the least likely to get college degrees. According to the Hispanic College Fund, that's mainly because of the lack of role models, poverty and being unprepared to navigate through the American educational system.

The nonprofit Hispanic College Fund (HCF) is working to change that by providing Latino youth with the information and tools they need to pursue a college degree in order to become more competitive in the 21st century economy.

University of Maryland freshman Karen Guzman has big plans for her future. "I'm actually trying to [get a] double degree in computer science and psychology, with a minor in Latin American studies." The 18-year-old says her dreams have become possible thanks to a scholarship from the Hispanic College Fund, which is dedicated to developing the next generation of Hispanic professionals.

The annual Hispanic Youth Symposium offers an opportunity for young Latinos to build networks and self-esteem. Guzman says she was inspired to pursue a college education three years ago after attending one of HCF's programs, a four-day Hispanic youth symposium.

"That was the first time I saw so many young Latinos like me saying, 'I'm here in college and you can do it,' because before that I didn't have that, I guess, role model to look up to," she says. "Everyone I knew was either dropping out or their plans were not to go to college."

Robert Arenas, Jr., attended a Hispanic youth symposium last summer where he heard from Latin professionals. Many young people who attend the Hispanic Youth Symposiums say they hope to return one day as successful professionals to inspire other kids. […] The 17-year-old is now a high school senior. His father says the symposium inspired his son and filled him with hope and determination. […]

Like many other Hispanic parents who immigrated to the United States, Robert Arenas, Sr. doesn't know much about the U.S. educational system. Yet, he says, he knows a college degree is essential if his son is to have a better future.

Latino high schoolers say they find the Hispanic College Fund's events informative, inspiring and entertaining.

"I want to see Robert, my son, like Ms. Sotomayor," he says, referring to the first Latina Supreme Court Justice. "So we say, 'Robert I'm working so hard, your Mom and myself, so you have to go to college. You have to go to the university, to get a degree in something. That's the only way you can reward us.'"

The Hispanic College Fund fills the gap for students like Robert and Karen – whose parents realize how important higher education is but are unable to guide them through the process. The fund was established six years ago to give young Latinos the information they need to apply for college and the self esteem to succeed once they get there.

…

Program founder George Cushman says many young Hispanics think they are not smart enough to go to college. […]"

Cushman believes motivating and helping Hispanic youth get college degrees is an investment in the future of both the students and the nation.

"In America, there's many people like me in their 50s and 60s. They are highly educated. They are the engineers, the doctors, the lawyers, the health care professionals, the teachers. They are all hitting the exit doors because it's time to retire soon," he says. "The largest fastest-growing student population to follow in our footsteps is Hispanic, but they're getting college degrees late.You can feel the vacuum forming. If we don't fix that, it's going to hurt the economy. It's going to hurt the security of the country."

Faiza Elmasry, *Voice of America News* (voanews.com), 30/3/2010

A. Language

Find synonyms in the first six paragraphs of the article for the following: *mostly, the absence, to go to college, yearly, a chance, self-respect, taking part in, to admire, leaving school before completing their education, gave enormous motivation to, resolve.*

B. Question

What is the purpose of the Hispanic College Fund? (Answer in 150-200 words. Use information in the article but do not copy sentences directly: use your own words.)

Translation

Translate the article into English.

La mosaïque américaine

Depuis le 15 mars, quelque 120 millions de questionnaires sont glissés dans les boîtes aux lettres des Américains : le recensement de la population, entrepris tous les dix ans, est de retour. Si le formulaire est d'un modèle unique, ceux appelés à le remplir témoignent de la diversité croissante de la société américaine. Et ils en sont fiers.

En 2000, pour la première fois, plusieurs réponses étaient possibles à la question suivante : « À quelle race appartient chacun des membres de votre famille ? » À l'époque, 7 millions de résidents avaient saisi l'occasion de proclamer leur identité multiraciale. Cette année, ils pourraient être deux fois plus nombreux. Et pour cause : le nombre de mariages mixtes a augmenté de 20 % en dix ans, au point qu'ils représentent 8 % des familles. A ce rythme, les « multiraciaux » pourraient avoir supplanté l'actuelle majorité blanche à l'horizon de 2050.

Les États-Unis compteraient environ 304 millions d'habitants. Selon une enquête réalisée en 2008, ils seraient :

• Blancs à 75 % (soit 199 millions) • Hispaniques et latino-américains à 15,4 %
• Noirs ou Afro-américains à 12,4 % (soit 37,6 millions) • Asiatiques à 4,4 % (13,4 millions).

Philippe Coste, *L'Express* (lexpress.fr), 16/3/2010

Overview

Read a general overview of the subject.

An influential minority

The labels are many and often confusing – Hispanics, Hispanic-Americans, Latinos (Latino includes non-Spanish speaking states such as Brazil), Latino-Americans... A fast growing minority community, Hispanics are a large demographic group in the USA and, out of the total population of the USA, Hispanics officially count over 44 million people, with the number expected to grow 3-fold by 2050. The population is concentrated along the US southern border and the Pacific and Atlantic seaboard states but with newcomers now spreading out across all states.

Most people of Hispanic origin are city-dwellers, living and working in urban areas, although today, many – often illegal – immigrants, are recruited into menial domestic and agricultural jobs. Mass immigration began in the 50s and 60s out of Mexico, Puerto Rico and Cuba.

Most people of Hispanic origin and Latinos are Catholic and it is estimated that perhaps one third of American Catholics are Latino. The first waves of immigrants seeking to survive have a tendency to clump together for mutual protection, whether they are undocumented aliens or green card holders. They are therefore only concerned with local political issues, but with time and people fanning out, mingling with other communities, marrying and having families, long-term issues are no longer just parochial. A high population, even if it is only a minority, means a lot of voters to be courted and a lot of political clout to be wielded. Since before the 1960s, Hispanic-American politicians have been flexing their muscles for both the GOP and the Democrats. The Latino vote is a swing one and no one party or presidential candidate may consider themselves automatically as the chosen representatives.

Increasing integration means Hispanics share many of the problems of other Americans. Unemployment, poverty, health-care problems and sub-prime foreclosures (with resulting evictions) have struck the black and Hispanic communities in particular.

All in all, Hispanic influence is growing in American culture with media and music aimed linguistically and culturally at this particular minority. Economically, they represent a big market, with often Hispanic-specific marketing and advertising. Poverty levels for Hispanics in general and Hispanic single mothers are high and although overall high school dropout rates have declined over the past years, the rate has been lower for whites and blacks than for Hispanics who in 2008 showed a dropout rate of 18%.

Pronunciation

Listen and repeat.

pull [pʊl], **pearl** [pɜːl]

- wool/whirl, hood/herd, stood/stirred, could/verb, wood/word.
- The shepherd stood in the wood, he neither stirred nor uttered a word.

Chapter 27

Health care

Language focus

Ordre des qualifiants devant le nom

• Les adjectifs dénotant des qualifications subjectives sont toujours les plus loin du nom, les plus objectives, près du nom. L'ordre, de gauche à droite est jugement, évaluation de l'âge, forme, couleur, matériau :

	opinion	âge	forme	couleur	origine	matériel	
a	*beautiful*	*young*			*Danish*		*girl*
a	*funny*		*little*	*green*			*man*
a	*small*		*square*			*metal*	*container*

• S'il est présent, le génitif sera placé le plus loin du nom :
Mary's strange little green hat

Wordbank

to appeal (against) a decision	*faire appel d'une décision*
available resources	*les ressources disponibles*
a beneficiary	*un assuré social*
the burden of health costs	*le fardeau des coûts de santé*
capitation	*les frais forfaitaires*
a cash allowance	*une allocation en espèces*
COLA (Cost Of Living Adjustment)	*la hausse indexée sur le coût de la vie*
a community/neighborhood health center	*un centre médical communautaire*
to contain costs	*maîtriser les coûts*
cutting-edge/state-of-the-art technology	*la technologie dernier cri*
a disabled person	*une personne non-valide*
emergency treatment	*les soins d'urgence*
an employer–provided scheme	*une couverture proposée par l'employeur*
to be entitled to welfare	*avoir le droit aux aides sociales*
an entitlement	*un droit*
expenditure	*les dépenses de santé*
family allowances	*les allocations familiales*
a family medical practitioner	*un médecin de famille*
a for-profit health care provider	*une enterprise qui fournit de soins (et qui doit rester rentable)*
go to med(ical) school	*faire des études de medicine*

health care	*les soins de santé*
health care benefits	*les prestations maladie*
a health consumer	*un consommateur de produits et services de santé*
health coverage	*l'assurance-maladie*
a health plan	*une couverture assurance-maladie*
a heavy cost to the taxpayer	*un coût lourd porté par le contribuable*
an insurance premium	*une prime d'assurance*
an intern	*un étudiant en médecine en fin d'études*
life expectancy	*l'espérance de vie*
means-tested	*lié à des conditions de ressources*
Medicaid	*l'assurance maladie pour revenus modestes*
a medical facility	*un centre medical*
Medicare	*l'assurance maladie pour personnes agées ou handicapées*
to obtain access to a doctor	*obtenir accès à un médecin*
a patchwork of protectection	*une protection inégale*
patient rights	*les droits des patients*
to pay into a pension scheme	*cotiser à un plan d'épargne retraite*
prescription drugs	*les médicaments sur ordonnance*
a primary care provider	*un fournisseur de soins de base*
to restrict costs	*restreindre les coûts*
rocketing costs	*des coûts qui montent en flèche*
runaway costs	*des coûts incontrôlables*
a serious ailment	*une maladie grave*
a staff shortage	*une carence de personnel*
an under-insured patient	*un patient sous-assuré*
an uninsured patient	*un patient sans couverture médicale*
a waiting list/room	*une liste/salle d'attente*
a welfare caseworker	*un travailleur social*

Translation

Translate the sentences into English.

1. L'administration démocrate a dénoncé les mesures draconniennes désastreuses qu'avait initiées le gouvernement Bush pour le système de santé américain.

2. Notre main d'œuvre est jeune, dynamique et hautement qualifiée, elle mérite une couverture sociale intéressante.

3. Les bénéficiaires de soins de santé de plus de 65 ans s'inquiètent du coût croissant des médicaments.

4. Le coût effroyablement lourd supporté par le contribuable peut signifier l'effondrement du système de santé.

5. Même si les prestations sociales sont liées aux conditions de ressources, le système de couverture sociale semble de plus en plus menacé.

Read and answer

Read the article and then do activities A and B that follow.

Health reform in America: Signed, sealed, delivered

Barack Obama **has transformed health reform from near death to fact. So how will Obamacare change America's health system?**

WASHINGTON DC. The Barack Obama who addressed Americans at near midnight on March 21st had every right to gloat. After a year in which his proposals for health reform were savaged by Republicans and leftists alike, and declared dead half a dozen times by everyone, he has somehow managed to get them over the finishing line.

The reform package is made up of two bills. One, a flawed and pork-laden version of health reform passed by the Senate before Christmas, has now been approved by the House; Mr Obama signed this on March 23rd. The other is a "reconciliation" bill meant to fix some of its flaws, and the House also passed this. Because this is a new bill, the Senate has to pass it too. It can do so under special "reconciliation" rules that require only 50 votes, not a filibuster-proof 60. As *The Economist* went to press, it looked set to do so.

What will it mean for America? The short answer is that the reforms will expand coverage dramatically, but at a heavy cost to the taxpayer. They will also do far too little to rein in the underlying drivers of America's roaring health inflation. Analysis by RAND, an independent think-tank, suggests that the reforms will actually increase America's overall health spending – public plus private – by about 2% by 2020, in comparison with a scenario of no reform. And that rate of spending was already unsustainable at a time when the baby-boomers are starting to retire in large numbers.

The heart of the new reform is a restructuring of America's flawed insurance market. Insurers now face tough new regulations forbidding such practices as dropping people with "pre-existing conditions" (real or trumped-up), or putting lifetime caps on coverage.

In return, though, the insurance industry will benefit from a big expansion of the country's private insurance market. Heavily regulated exchanges, or insurance marketplaces, would be set up so that consumers not covered by employer-provided plans today could shop for ones more easily. Insurers would be required to offer plans that meet minimum government requirements for health coverage, and to price them transparently.

Some 32m of the country's 49m or so uninsured (most of those left out of the new scheme are undocumented aliens) would, starting in 2014, be required to take out insurance. The working poor and uninsured earning up to $88,000 a year get subsidies on a sliding scale so that they can afford to buy coverage; the poorest of all will be added to the rolls of Medicaid, a health scheme for the indigent. It is this binding requirement on individuals that exercises conservatives most. [...]

If coverage is the new law's strong point, cost control is its weakness. That is not to say that most ordinary people will pay more for coverage, as critics of reform noisily insist. True, some of those forced to buy insurance will earn too much to qualify for subsidies, and so will be spending more than they do today – but, in return, they will ...

. . .

get insurance plans that offer more generous coverage than current basic plans. What is more, many other Americans may end up with lower premiums.

The vast majority of workers enjoy health insurance today through employer-provided schemes. RAND estimates that by 2019 the employer-provided system will benefit from 6m new (mostly healthy) customers, and that premiums for everyone in that system will drop by 2% versus business-as-usual. [...]

Sceptics abound. Yes, the approach succeeded when used by the Pentagon to decide which military bases to shut down. But an earlier version of this idea, known as MedPAC, flopped because Congress simply ignored even worthy ideas that proved politically inconvenient. And the new law carves out a ten-year exemption for hospitals – appalling, when one considers that runaway costs and misaligned incentives in hospitals lie at the very heart of the cost problem. [...]

All this points to the only certain thing about Obamacare: that this is just another episode in the long saga of health reform. Indeed, by adding tens of millions of people to an unreformed and unsustainably expensive health system, this reform makes it all the more urgent to tackle the question of cost.

On that, at least, left and right seem to agree. Paul Krugman, an economics professor at Princeton and a liberal booster of reform, wrote on the eve of the votes: "There is, as always, a tunnel at the end of the tunnel: we'll spend years if not decades fixing this thing." Robert Moffit of the Heritage Foundation, a conservative think-tank opposed to the effort, agrees, albeit in darker terms: "This marks the beginning of the next phase of this hundred years war."

The Economist (economist.com), 25/3/2010

A. Language

Find synonyms in the title and the first four paragraphs of the article for the following: *approved, to show great pleasure at his own success, severely criticised, imperfect, with specific details of who benefits from funding, to mend some of the system's weaknesses, to control/to curb, driving forces, total, false.*

B. Question

What are the strengths and weaknesses of President Obama's health reform? (Answer in 200-250 words. Use information in the article but do not copy sentences directly: use your own words.)

Overview

Read a general overview of the subject.

The price of health care

When one looks at the US health system, two seemingly contradictory facts stand out:

– the USA is the only wealthy industrialised nation without a universal public health care program ensuring that all citizens are covered;

– the US government spends more per citizen than almost any other nation on health care.

Obviously, a lot of money is going to waste somewhere. In fact, it has been calculated that the amount spent on publicly-funded health programs (principally Medicare and Medicaid) to help the elderly, the disabled, service veterans, children and the poor would be enough to fund a universal health care program if based on European-style public ownership of certain resources. But Americans have always shied away from public sector expansion, hence the expense of using private sector providers for public health programs.

Almost 60% of Americans are insured through their employers, a system that goes back to the 1940s when businesses, attempting to get around wartime wage controls, began to compete for labour by offering health insurance. Private insurers entered the market, taking over from the Blue Cross, a non-profit organisation that had been offering health care insurance since the 1920s.

Since insurance provided by employers involves sizeable employee contributions, this can be quite a chunk out of one's paypacket. Worse still, if you are in poor health, it will cost you more because of the "relative risk" to the insurer. The financial burden of health insurance is so great for some people that it is estimated to be the cause of 50% of personal bankruptcies. About 47 million Americans have no health insurance. They either pay for everything out of their own pocket or fall back on charity organisations or public programs. Of the 100,000 deaths every year as the result of the lack of medical care, many of these can be attributed to the patients' financial situation.

The first attempt in recent years to reform the health care system was undertaken under the aegis of First Lady Hillary Clinton in 1993. It failed to get sufficient support and fell by the wayside. More recently, in 2010, the Patient Protection and Affordable Care Act was passed. It intends to reduce the number of uninsured by introducing a requirement for people to purchase health insurance and by imposing conditions on insurers so as to limit abuses. According to President Obama, this will give small businesses and uninsured Americans "a chance to choose an affordable health care plan in a competitive market".

...

Pronunciation

Listen and repeat.

debt [det], **dirt** [dɜːt]

• wed/word, best/worst, bed/bird, head/herd, ten/turn.
• For Ben and his herd, going west meant the worst.

28 Chapter

Poverty

Language focus

Les causatives

• Ces structures impliquent deux protagonistes : un qui fait l'action, l'autre qui provoque l'action. *Make* implique une relation forte :

*John **made** Jane leave.*	John a fait partir Jane.
*Onions **make** me cry a lot.*	Les oignons me font pleurer.

L'incitateur peut ne pas être explicite :

*Jane was **made** to leave.*	On a fait partir Jane.

• *Have*, contrairement à *make*, n'implique pas de pression de la part de l'incitateur ; la relation entre les protagonistes peut être contractuelle ou informelle :

*I **had** him repair my car.*	Je lui ai fait réparer ma voiture.
*I **had** my car repaired.*	J'ai fait réparer ma voiture.

• Il existe également de nombreux autres verbes causatifs par leur sens même :

*I **got** him to quit smoking.*	Je l'ai amené à arrêter de fumer.

Wordbank

a bag lady	*une clocharde*
the bare necessities	*le strict minimum*
the basic needs	*les besoins de base*
to be left out	*être exclu*
a beggar	*un mendiant*
the brink of poverty	*le seuil de la pauvreté*
broke	*fauché*
a charity	*une œuvre caritative*
chronic poverty	*la pauvreté chronique*
consistent poverty	*la pauvreté constante*
dire straits	*une situation désespérée*
to dispossess	*déposséder*
to eke out a living	*vivoter*
to be eligible for	*remplir les conditions pour*
to be evicted	*être mis à la porte*
a food bank	*une banque alimentaire*
food pantries/shelves	*œuvres de dons alimentaires*
food stamps	*les bons alimentaires*
to foreclose	*saisir (un bien)*
hand-outs	*des aides, des aumônes*

hand-me-down clothes	*des vêtements d'occasion*
hard times	*des temps difficiles*
to hock/pawn	*mettre en gage, mettre au clou*
homeless	*sans domicile fixe*
to hit a rough patch	*traverser une passe difficile*
inherited poverty	*pauvre de père en fils*
to live below the poverty line	*vivre sous le seuil de pauvreté*
to live from hand to mouth	*vivre au jour le jour*
to live on the streets	*vivre dans la rue*
to live on welfare	*vivre de l'aide sociale*
a low-income household	*un ménage à faibles revenus*
to make ends meet	*joindre les deux bouts*
the needy	*les nécessiteux*
a night shelter	*un abri de nuit*
to panhandle	*mendier*
penniless	*sans un sou*
the poverty line	*le seuil de pauvreté*
poverty-stricken/-ridden	*frappé/accablé par la pauvreté*
the poverty trap	*le cercle vicieux de la pauvreté*
the ranks of the poor	*la population pauvre*
relief	*les allocations*
to slip into poverty	*tomber dans la pauvreté*
a soup kitchen	*la soupe populaire*
a squat	*une occupation illégale*
to starve (to death)	*mourir de faim, être affamé*
to throw into hardship	*jeter dans la misère*
an under-nourished child	*un enfant sous-alimenté*
a vagrant	*un SDF*
vagrancy	*le vagabondage*

Translation

Translate the sentences into English.

1. Voir un de ses amis proches devenir SDF l'a amené à donner de la nourriture et un coup de main à la banque alimentaire de son quartier.

2. Dans la morale puritaine, se retrouver dans une situation désespérée fait partie des aléas de l'existence qui forcent l'individu à dépasser ses limites pour s'en sortir.

3. La banque a fait saisir tous les biens des Bauer parce que l'argent de Jack est arrivé 24 heures trop tard.

4. On lui a fait mettre ses meubles en gage pour payer ses dettes.

5. La perte de son emploi lui a fait quitter la ville et placer les enfants chez leurs grand-parents.

Read and answer

Read the article and then do activities A and B that follow.

The Big Apple is hungry

NEW YORK. Barbara Waas used to be a book-keeper for a small brokerage firm. Since October she has been relying on the Holy Apostles soup kitchen for food. The Rev. Elizabeth Maxwell, who presides there, first observed a steep increase in people looking for help a year ago. Her church is now feeding 1,250 people a day, more than ever before. There are lots of new faces. Ninety-three percent of emergency food sites have seen an increase in first-time users of their services. According to the Food Bank for New York City, an estimated 1.3m New Yorkers now rely on soup kitchens (which provide hot meals) and food pantries (which give away food). The number of people having trouble paying for food has increased 60%, to 3.3m, since 2003.

New Yorkers with children are among the most vulnerable to food poverty. Almost half of all New York City households with children have difficulty affording enough food. A staggering one in five of the city's children, 397,000 small people, rely on soup kitchens – up 48% since 2004.

Some food programmes are struggling to meet the growing need. In 2008 many ran out of food, and some were forced to turn people away or reduce their opening hours. Fortunately, 2009 was a little easier. The soaring demand at soup kitchens and food pantries last year was counterbalanced by increased participation in the food-stamps programme and a surge in funds to alleviate hunger via the federal recovery and farm bills, according to a recent report by the New York City Coalition Against Hunger. This meant that fewer people had to be turned away last year. Some 1.6m New Yorkers were receiving food stamps.

That report had a title that was also a warning: "NYC Hunger Catastrophe Avoided (For Now)". Holy Apostles has seen its donations fall. But the number of people needing emergency food is expected to grow in 2010, just as kitchens and pantries are again finding it harder to raise money for their services. A surprising number of New Yorkers are vulnerable: almost 20% would not be able to afford food if they lost their jobs. The Food Bank's main office is just steps away from some of the firms who were given federal bail-outs. Áine Duggan of the Food Bank says: "We're the only bank on Wall Street you can trust."

The Economist (economist.com), 14/1/2010

A. Language

Find synonyms in the first three paragraphs of the article for the following: *accountant, counting on, sharp, supply, having the financial means to pay for, stunning, are having difficulties, lacked food, skyrocketing, to reduce.*

B. Questions

Answer each of the following questions in 50 words. Use information in the article to answer but do not copy sentences directly: use your own words.

1. What are the difficulties faced by food programs in New York?

2. What can account for the rising number of people looking for help?

Translation

Translate the article into English.

Nouveaux pauvres américains

Et si on oubliait Wall Street et ses riches, pour parler des « nouveaux pauvres » ? Aux États-Unis, les médias, formules chocs à l'appui (« L'Amérique de l'ombre », « Nos transparents voisins »...), se préoccupent de plus en plus de l'émergence d'une vaste pauvreté.

Une récente étude du Centre du marché du travail de Northeastern University, constate que le décile inférieur de la population active, où le revenu familial n'excède pas les 12 500 dollars annuels, a connu au dernier trimestre 2009 un taux de chômage de 30,8 % – supérieur de 5 points au taux constaté au pic de la Grande Dépression, dans les années 1930. Le décile précédent, situé entre 12 500 et 20 000 dollars par an, enregistre un chômage de 19,1 %.

Ces chiffres sont de deux à trois fois supérieurs à la moyenne nationale. Ces 20 % de la population active étant également les plus concernés par le travail à temps partiel non volontaire, c'est une personne active sur deux qui est affectée par le sous-emploi. Pour mémoire, ces données ne comptent pas les millions d'indigents qui ont renoncé depuis longtemps à chercher un travail.

L'Amérique a évité une dépression, et les mesures de soutien à l'économie adoptées par l'administration Obama y ont contribué, écrivent les rapporteurs du Centre du marché du travail, mais « une véritable dépression de l'emploi touche ceux qui se situent au bas de la répartition des revenus, et une profonde récession prévaut dans les catégories situées au milieu de l'échelle ». Ce sont ces catégories-là, et non les plus pauvres, auxquelles l'administration entend consacrer le gros de son soutien. C'est parmi elles que l'on retrouve ceux qui font appel à une aide sociale pour la première fois : les tickets d'alimentation, par exemple, dont la distribution croît rapidement ; ou encore l'aide au chauffage, demandée par 5,7 millions de foyers américains il y a deux ans, et par 8,8 millions cet hiver - une hausse de 54 %. [...]

Quand ils perdent leur travail, la quasi-totalité des salariés perdent également très vite leur assurance-maladie... quand ils en détenaient une (ce qui était le cas de ceux dont l'emploi n'était pas précaire). Leurs indemnités de chômage, elles, se situent d'un État à l'autre entre 1 400 et 2 600 dollars maximum par mois, quel qu'ait été leur précédent salaire. Après six à neuf mois, ils en sont donc également privés. Aucune prise en charge de la « longue durée » n'existe.

Sylvain Cypel, *Le Monde* (lemonde.fr), 2/3/2010

Overview

Read a general overview of the subject.

Living on the bread line

Today's US poverty line for a single person is $10,830, and $22,050 for a four-person family. The line differs according to the number of people and incomes in a family. The mathematical/monetary threshold formula was defined in the mid-sixties and measures the cost of basic alimentary necessities multiplied by three. Despite widely varying urban and rural geography and widely differing rates of employment and family patterns, the poverty line remains the same for all fifty states. Figuring among the least well-off are the southern states such as Mississippi, Arkansas and Alabama.

The US is not a "welfare state" but, when applying for help such as food programs and medical care, the same formula is applied to the poor from New York to Los Angeles. Poverty is of a cyclical nature and obviously linked to economic recessions and downturns. For example, following the 1929 slump, millions found themselves without homes, jobs or revenue and with the recent sub-prime crisis and its consequences, the scourge has been on the upturn again. The poverty rate in the US in 2008 was just over 13% – approximately 40 million people – with just over 23% of Hispanics and almost 30% of the black population being officially poor.

Statistics show that almost 10% of the over-65s were on the breadline in 2008, but children are among the hardest hit by the problem: 19% of the under-18s live in poverty, notably children from one-parent families. With poverty comes malnutrition, low self-esteem and learning difficulties at school, if indeed poor children do go to school. In turn, poor school results mean menial jobs with low salaries.

Minorities are particularly hard-hit, but some sociologists point out that poor neighbourhoods can act like a shackle: being born in a poor neighbourhood can remain a lifetime bane preventing socially-upward mobility. In 2009, more than half of black children and young adults aged 9 to 24 were growing up in areas where poverty reaches levels of 20%. If poverty and its supposed causes may be measurable then it is perhaps up to the legislator to take steps to counteract that poverty. However the US has not always hailed a welfare-for-all system. Some have argued for the "workfare" system wherein, in exchange for public assistance, the recipient will do some community work. Some even argue that poor people are to blame for their own predicament, and that immigrants – legal or illegal – should receive no anti-poverty or welfare help whatsoever.

Pronunciation

Listen and repeat.

girl [gɜːl], **goal** [gəʊl]

- fern/phone, learn/lone, burn/bone, burst/boast, flirt/float.
- The hollow girls burned their shirts and took an oath.

Chapter 29

Education

Language focus

Les résultatives

- Les structures les plus fréquentes sont les suivantes :

    He kicked the door shut.

    Il a fermé la porte d'un coup de pied.

    I worried myself sick.

    Je me suis rendu malade à force de m'inquiéter.
- D'autres constructions permettent d'exprimer le résultat obtenu :

    I talked her into buying that dress.

    Je l'ai convaincue d'acheter cette robe./Je lui ai fait acheter cette robe en lui parlant.

Wordbank

academic achievement	*la réussite scolaire*
academic expectations	*les attentes scolaires*
an achiever, a super-achiever	*un élève brillant*
an accrediting agency	*une agence d'accréditation*
a boarding school	*un internat*
bullying	*la brutalité (entre élèves)*
to bus to school	*transporter à l'école par bus*
to cater for special needs	*s'occuper d'enfants ayant des problèmes de scolarité*
a charter school	*une école recevant des fonds publics mais avec une gestion pédagogique autonome*
a class period	*le temps consacré au cours (de 30, 60 ou 90 mn)*
a college board	*un conseil d'établissement*
a community school	*une école pour élèves en difficulté*
a core class	*une matière principale*
a deadline	*une date-butoir*
a dormitory	*un dortoir*
an elective	*un cours facultatif*
elementary school	*l'école primaire (*grades *1 à 6/8)*
enrol(l)ment	*l'inscription*
first grade	*la première année de l'école primaire*
free meals	*les repas gratuits pour élèves de familles modestes*
a freshman	*un élève en première année de* high school
a gifted student	*un élève doué*
to get good grades	*obtenir de bonnes notes*

grade school	*l'école primaire*
a high school diploma	*un diplôme délivré en fin de lycée*
the high school prom	*le bal de fin d'année*
an honors class	*un cours exigeant pour les meilleurs élèves*
an impoverished inner-city school	*une école défavorisée dans un quartier difficile*
kindergarten	*la première année d'école*
middle school, junior high	*les* grades *6/7 à 8/9*
a (university) prep(aratory) school	*une école privée mais aussi une école préparant spécifiquement pour l'entrée en université*
a principal	*un chef d'établissement*
the pupil teacher ratio	*le rapport élève/enseignant*
the PTA (Parent-Teacher Association)	*l'association regroupant les parents d'élèves et les enseignants*
a schedule	*un emploi du temps*
compulsory school attendance	*la scolarisation obligatoire*
the school board	*le conseil d'établissement*
a school counsel(l)or	*un CPE (conseiller pédagogique d'éducation)*
a school district	*un secteur scolaire*
to seek accreditation	*demander l'agrément ministériel*
senior high school	*l'école secondaire (*grades *10 à 12)*
a special high school	*une école spécialisée pour élèves en difficulté*
a study room/hall	*une salle d'étude*
a superintendent	*un inspecteur*
a turnaround school	*une école passant d'échec à succès*
tuition-free studies	*des études gratuites*

Translation

Translate the sentences into English.

1. Certains élèves se rendent malades à force de travailler pour intégrer une des huit universités les plus prestigieuses.

2. Le professeur d'EPS a forcé certains élèves en difficulté à arrêter de brutaliser les élèves plus brillants.

3. Le conseiller d'éducation a renvoyé chez lui l'élève qui avait fermé la porte de son bureau d'un coup de pied.

4. À force d'arguments, l'inspecteur a persuadé les enseignants de cette école en difficulté de revoir leurs objectifs à la hausse.

5. Le chef d'établissement a réussi à convaincre cette élève douée mais un peu désinvolte de suivre le cours de spécialité en Maths en flattant son ego.

Read and answer

Read the article and then do activities A and B that follow.

Schools reform: The next test

CHICAGO. Health reform was supposed to be the crowning achievement of Barack Obama's first year as president. Instead it has riled Republicans, alienated leftists and exhausted everyone else. However, on March 15th Mr Obama presented Congress with a plan that ought to have a greater chance of support: reforming No Child Left Behind (NCLB), America's main federal education programme. Everyone agrees that America's public schools are floundering, and NCLB is widely considered to have failed.

NCLB, enacted in 2002, transformed education policy. It gave the federal government a crucial role in education, forcing states to set standards and hold their schools accountable for meeting them. Schools that failed to make progress would face financial sanctions. All students were to be proficient in reading and maths by 2014. George Bush championed the law; Congress supported it wholeheartedly.

The deadline for proficiency now looks comical. The broad support for NCLB has shattered. Parents and teachers complain that the law encourages "teaching to the test". Perfectly decent schools have been labelled failures. Students in bad schools supposedly may transfer elsewhere; few have. Most important, many states have set alarmingly low standards. Now some dissenters even doubt the reform movement's guiding principles of accountability and choice. Diane Ravitch, an influential and prominent scholar who once praised NCLB, says that it has produced no real gains. The emphasis on maths and reading has crowded out other subjects. An accompanying push for charter (independent, government-funded) schools has had mixed results at best. One study found that 83% deliver results that are either the same as, or worse than, those of the public schools.

Arne Duncan, Mr Obama's education secretary, likes to say that the new plan is about "getting accountability right". [...] A state could no longer set a low bar for achievement. By 2015 states would be required to adopt stringent new standards and tests for English and maths, with a goal of being "college- and career-ready" by 2020. (In a boost for the president, the National Governors Association presented a draft of standards last week.) Schools would be judged not by snapshots of performance but by whether students progress over time. Mr Obama would reward schools that show the most improvement and require intervention for those that show the least. For the vast majority of schools, however, states and districts would be left alone to meet their targets. On top of these main reforms Mr Obama offers a thick layer of grants for favoured initiatives, such as merit pay and expanding the school year.

Chester Finn of the conservative Fordham Institute, praises the plan as "tight about the ends and loose on the means", helping to set goals but giving states more flexibility to meet them. Even so the path to reauthorisation remains treacherous. Some states have already come out against the push for new standards. John Kline, the top Republican on the House education committee, worries about too much federal intrusion. Tim Knowles, of the University of Chicago's Urban Education Institute, worries about too little, leaving mediocre schools with not enough incentive to improve.

The Economist (economist.com), 18/3/2010

...

A. Language

1. Find synonyms in the first three paragraphs of the article for the following: *the major success, has annoyed, has antagonised and made unfriendly, are struggling (to meet objectives), that were unable to get better results, supported the legislation, (time) limit, efficient, have been described as, may change schools, responsibility, leading academic, disappointing results.*

2. Find antonyms in the last two paragraphs of the article for the following: *lax, punish, for very few schools, thin, criticises, rigidity, excellent.*

B. Questions

Answer each of the following questions in 50 words. Use information in the article to answer but do not copy sentences directly: use your own words.

1. What were the objectives of former President Bush's "No child left behind" program?

2. To what extent has the program been a failure?

3. How does President Obama plan to reform the school system?

Translation

Translate the article into English.

L'école à la maison

L'éducation à domicile – *home schooling* – est en passe de devenir, en tout cas pour la classe moyenne intellectuelle, un choix parmi d'autres lorsqu'il s'agit de décider de l'éducation de ses enfants. En l'absence de statistiques officielles récentes, les estimations vont de 800 000 à 2 millions d'enfants concernés. Mais une chose est sûre : le phénomène gagne, et ces familles qui choisissent de faire faire l'école buissonnière à leurs enfants échappent aux classifications qui prévalaient au moment de ce nouveau type d'éducation, il y a vingt ou trente ans. […]

« Les parents, bien sûr, ne parlent que de l'intérêt de l'enfant, mais c'est bien de choix d'adultes qu'il s'agit », tempère Mitchell Stevens, sociologue à l'université de New York. « Le *home schooling* permet à certaines femmes actives, ayant fait des études, de résoudre le dilemme entre mener une carrière professionnelle et s'occuper de leurs enfants. » Enseigner à ses enfants, ce n'est pas être une mère au foyer ordinaire. « D'ailleurs, beaucoup de ces mères développent de petites entreprises en relation avec l'enseignement à domicile (matériel pédagogique, magazines….). »

La révolution Internet est aussi passée par là : elle met tous les contenus d'enseignement à disposition de chaque foyer, « surtout, elle donne une tonalité high-tech au home schooling », note Patrick Farenga.

Si le *home schooling* remporte un tel succès, c'est parce qu'il est tout sauf une révolution du système éducatif américain. « Notre système est décentralisé, rappelle Mitchell Stevens. Le secteur privé y est considérable, le rôle des parents, y compris à l'école, est très important. » Bref, ces parents ne font que pousser plus loin la logique d'un système américain qui leur donne déjà beaucoup de pouvoirs.

Dominique Audibert, *Le Point* (lepoint.fr) 17/1/2007

Overview

Read a general overview of the subject.

From nursery school to a high school diploma

The US education system is managed largely through state and local education authorities, rather than by the federal government – the 10th Amendment makes it clear that education is not dependent on a central state system. The Federal Secretary for Education intervenes essentially on a budgetary level or for certain specialised programmes. Each state has a Secretary of Education with a Commissioner of Education whose job it is, together with the State Board of Education, to decide on policy and teacher accreditation. Responsibility then fans out to the school boards at district level and it is here that budgets are decided, programmes voted in or out, teachers and staff recruited and Superintendents hired. Although states and local school districts are responsible for running their schools, they do have to respect federal laws such as the 2001 Elementary and Secondary Education Act (called the "No Child Left Behind Act") aimed at improving performance for underachievers.

Children may start school as early as three in a nursery school before moving on to a kindergarten at age five. At age six they go to their first official graded year at primary school (also sometimes referred to as grade school, the term "grade" being used to mean either school year or mark). A wide spread of schools – public schools, faith schools, private schools… – offers primary schooling from age eleven (or 6th grade).

From primary school, at age eleven or twelve, young Americans will go on to high school, itself divided into two cycles – junior and senior high. The school day at high school is divided into periods of 45 minutes or double periods of 90 minutes and children are also encouraged and advised to take part in extra-curricular activities after school. 12th grade is at age 17 and it is at this age that teenagers obtain their high school diploma. However, since programs are decided at local level, varying from one state to the next, the high school diploma is not a national diploma and does not therefore act as an automatic passport to higher education. There are, at secondary school level, a certain number of fee-paying private schools called "prep schools" preparing "preppies" for university entrance.

American teachers are not government employees and pay scales vary between states. Teachers apply for jobs on an individual basis after obtaining their university and teaching qualifications and are recruited by the school board after interview. Their contracts may be terminated by the board.

Pronunciation

Listen and repeat.

ox [ɒks], **oaks** [əʊks]

- got/goat, rob/robe, sock/soak, block/bloke, rod/road.
- Tom did not goad John with a poker in Oxford.

30 Chapter

Higher education

Language focus

L'expression du révolu : used to/would

• L'anglais dispose de deux opérateurs verbaux qui expriment l'idée du révolu.

• *Used to* remplace le preterit simple lorsque la phrase ne comporte pas d'autre élément permettant d'ancrer l'action dans un passé révolu ; c'est une forme très marquée, qui a souvent un effet de sens nostalgique, mélancolique :

There ***used to be*** *a pub here.*
Autrefois, il y avait un pub ici.

Cette forme ne doit pas être confondue avec *be used to* + V-*ing* qui exprime l'habitude, présente ou passée, selon le temps de *be* :

I am ***used to*** *drink****ing*** *a lot of coffee.*
J'ai l'habitude de boire beaucoup de café.

• Pour dire une action répétée dans le passé, on peut utiliser *would* :

When I was a child, I ***would pretend*** *I was a superhero.*
Quand j'étais petit, je faisais semblant d'être un super-héros.

Wordbank

a credit	*un crédit*
the GMAT	*le test subi avant l'entrée en MBA*
an accredited establishment	*un établissement agréé*
to admit to a university	*accepter en université*
the alumni	*les anciens étudiants*
an associate degree	*un diplôme de deux ans*
a bachelor's (degree)	*une licence (diplôme accordé après trois ans)*
a college	*un collège ou une faculté*
a college education	*des études de niveau universitaire*
a community/junior college	*un établissement, souvent local, proposant des cours, souvent spécialisés, de deux ans*
a counsel(l)or	*un conseiller*
the course load	*la charge de cours*
the dean	*le doyen*
a doctoral student	*un doctorant*
to drop a course	*laisser tomber un cours*
to drop out	*arrêter ses études*
to excel at one's studies	*briller dans ses cours*
the faculty	*le corps enseignant*

to flunk *(fam.)*	*échouer*
a fraternity	*un club pour étudiants*
a freshman	*un étudiant de première année*
a gifted student	*un étudiant doué*
grad(uate) school	*les études post licence*
the grade scale	*l'échelle des notes*
an instructor	*un chargé de cours*
the Ivy League	*les huit plus prestigieuses universités (Brown, Columbia, Cornell, Dartmouth, Harvard, Princeton, Pennsylvania, Yale)*
law school	*la faculté de droit*
a lecture hall	*un amphithéâtre*
major	*discipline/cours principal*
a masters/master's (degree)	*maîtrise, diplôme post licence en un ou deux ans*
MBA (Masters degree in Business Administration)	*maîtrise en adminisration d'entreprise*
med(ical) school	*la faculté de médecine*
mid term exams	*les examens subis avant fin semestre*
minor	*discipline/cours secondaire*
a peer group	*un groupe de pairs*
a post-graduate course	*un cursus/un stage après la licence*
the prerequisite level	*le niveau pré-requis*
a proctor	*un surveillant*
the SAT (Scholastic Aptitude Test)	*l'examen à réussir pour faire des études universitaires*
a scholarship	*une bourse*
a sophomore	*un étudiant de deuxième année*
a sorority	*un club pour étudiantes*
a term paper	*une dissertation à rendre pendant le semestre*
a transcript of grades	*un relevé de notes*
an undergraduate	*un étudiant non-diplômé*
vocational studies	*des études professionnelles*
to work one's way through college	*travailler pour payer ses études*

Translation

Translate the sentences into English.

1. Lorsqu'il était étudiant en doctorat à Harvard, Langdon allait nager une heure tous les soirs avant de travailler à la bibliothèque universitaire.

2. Les étudiants de première année doivent s'habituer à une charge de travail plus lourde s'ils veulent briller dans leur spécialité.

3. Si tu as l'habitude de faire la fête un soir sur deux, tu vas rater tes exams de fin d'année.

4. Les anciens étudiants les plus âgés constatent avec regret que les choses ne sont plus ce qu'elles étaient dans les facs.

5. Au lycée, Tom pensait qu'il devrait travailler pour payer ses études, c'est pourquoi il lisait régulièrement les petites annonces pour trouver des petits boulots.

Read and answer

Read the article and then do activities A and B that follow.

Five myths about college admissions

This spring, more than 3 million students will graduate from America's high schools, and more than 2 million of them will head off to college in the fall. At the top colleges, competition has been increasingly fierce, leaving many high school seniors licking their wounds and wondering what they did "wrong". But do selective colleges and universities do a good job of identifying the best and brightest? And is the concern about who gets into the best colleges justified?

1. Admissions officers have figured out how to reward merit above wealth and connections. A 2004 Century Foundation study found that at the most selective universities and colleges, 74 percent of students come from the richest quarter of the population, while just 3 percent come from the bottom quarter. Rich kids can't possibly be 25 times as likely to be smart as poor kids, so wealth and connections must still matter. Leading schools have two main admissions policies that favor wealthy students. The more glaring of these is legacy preferences – an admissions boost for the children of alumni. Legacy preferences increase a student's chances of admission by, on average, 20 percentage points over non-legacies. Schools use such preferences on the theory that they increase donations from alumni, but new research by Chad Coffman questions that premise. Those universities that have abandoned legacy preferences – or never used them – have plenty of alumni donors. [...]

Less obvious is the role of the SAT, which was, when it was introduced in 1926, supposed to help identify talented students from across all schools and backgrounds. Instead, it seems to amplify the advantages enjoyed by the most privileged students. New research by Georgetown University's Anthony Carnevale and Jeff Strohl finds that the most disadvantaged applicants (those who, among other characteristics, are black, attend public schools with high poverty rates, come from low-income families and have parents who are high school dropouts) score, on average, 784 points lower on the SAT than the most advantaged students (those who, among other things, are white, attend private schools and have wealthy, highly educated parents). This gap is equivalent to about two-thirds of the test's total score range. If the SAT were a 100-yard dash, advantaged kids would start off 65 yards ahead before the race even began.

2. Disadvantages based on race are still the biggest obstacle to getting into college. More than race, it's class: The effects of racial discrimination are increasingly dwarfed by the impact of socioeconomic status. Take that 784-point difference in SAT scores between the most advantaged and the most disadvantaged students. All other things being equal, the researchers found that there was a 56-point difference between black and white students. Most of the rest of the gap was the result of socioeconomic factors. To truly even the playing field, the system would therefore need to provide a lot of affirmative action to economically disadvantaged students who beat the odds and a little bit of affirmative action based on race.

Yet colleges and universities today do the opposite: They provide substantial preferences based on race and virtually none based on class. According to researchers William Bowen, Martin Kurzweil and Eugene Tobin, at highly selective institutions, ...

for students within a given SAT range, being a member of an underrepresented minority increases one's chance of admission by 28 percentage points. [...]

3. Generous financial aid policies are the key to boosting socioeconomic diversity.
In response to the growing scarcity of poor and working-class students on campus, roughly 100 universities and colleges have boosted financial aid in the past several years. But these programs have not been enough to change the socioeconomic profile of these schools' student bodies. At the University of North Carolina at Chapel Hill, for example, a generous financial aid program, the Carolina Covenant, was instituted in 2004. Under its terms, low-income students are not required to take out loans as part of their financial aid packages. [...]

4. Selective colleges are too expensive and aren't worth the investment.
A selective institution with a large endowment may indeed be worth the money. The least selective colleges spend about $12,000 per student, compared with $92,000 per student at the most selective schools. Put another way, at the wealthiest 10 percent of institutions, students pay, on average, just 20 cents in fees for every dollar the school spends on them, while at the poorest 10 percent of institutions, students pay 78 cents for every dollar spent on them.

Furthermore, selective colleges are quite a bit better at retention: If a more selective school and a less selective school enroll two equally qualified students, the more selective school is much more likely to graduate its student. Future earnings are, on average, 45 percent higher for students who graduated from more selective institutions than for those from less selective ones, and the difference in earnings is widest among low-income students. And according to research by Thomas Dye, 54 percent of America's top 4,325 corporate leaders are graduates of just 12 institutions.

5. With more students going to college, we're closer to the goal of equal opportunity.
The good news is that students are going to college at a higher rate than ever before; the bad news is that stratification is increasing at colleges and universities. Much as urban elementary and secondary schools saw white, affluent parents flee to suburban schools in the 1970s and 1980s, less selective colleges are now experiencing white flight. According to Carnevale and Strohl, white student representation declined from 79 percent to 58 percent at less selective and noncompetitive institutions between 1994 and 2006, while black student representation soared from 11 percent to 28 percent. American higher education is in danger of quickly becoming both separate and unequal.

Richard D. Kahlenberg, *The Washington Post* (washingtonpost.com), 23/5/2010

A. Language

Find synonyms in section 1 of the article for the following: *intelligent, obvious/flagrant, heritage, former students, have given up, spot gifted high school graduates, across the board, the least fortunate, discrepancy.*

B. Questions

Answer each of the following questions in 50 words. Use your own words.

1. Why does the writer question the Scolastic Assessment Test?

2. What is the biggest obstacle to college education?

3. Does the rising number of students mean that equal opportunities are guaranteed?

Overview

Read a general overview of the subject.

Making the right choice

The oldest institution of higher learning in the USA is Harvard, founded in 1636 by Englishman John Harvard, but it was the Morill Land Grant Act of 1862, granting each state the land on which to found higher education institutions, which really set the ball rolling. Today there are over 2,600 accredited universities and colleges although, if the non-accredited ones are included, the total number is around the 4,000 mark. Accreditation is by government-approved agencies that ensure the maintenance of a certain number of standards and objectives. The most highly-renowned universities are the eight Ivy League universities on the east coast, but only about 200 of the thousands of institutions of further education are actually universities: there are thousands of private "junior colleges" or public "community colleges" which offer two-year courses. The term "college" is also applied to liberal arts colleges where students study for a BA over a four-year period.

With such widely varying high school curricula in the USA, students wishing to enrol in further education are required to take pre-admission assessment tests such as SAT or ACT (often criticised as unfitting for those about to embark on intricate subjects over a long period of time) or GMAT, which is for admission to business schools' MBA programs. Some universities have their own highly-selective entrance criteria. Once enrolled, the first-year student is called a freshman. He or she then goes on to be a sophomore, a junior and finally a senior student.

The USA counts 18.6 million college undergraduates and graduates who all have to pay for their studies. They work their way through college by taking out loans, getting jobs, finding grants, using personal savings, obtaining scholarships, and of course being helped by their parents. Grants are restricted to less than half the student population, and vary from $2,200 for community college to $7,000 for private universities. Students from deprived backgrounds may benefit from Pell Grants after means testing, and a lucky few top students and highly gifted athletes may benefit from free tuition – "full-ride" scholarships. Over the past few years, fees have risen more notably in public institutions than private ones and, in a community college, a student without a grant may pay as much as $5,000. In an in-state public university, fees may be in the order of $18,000; a private university, $37,000; and it will cost you $50,000 a year to enter a Harvard undergraduate programme.

Pronunciation

Listen and repeat.

chalk [tʃɔːk], **choke** [tʃəʊk]

- ball/bowl, court/coat, mourn/moan, corn/cone, forks/folks.
- Walk to the door, choke that awful ghost and phone home to your folks.

Chapter 31

Foreign policy

Language focus

Le prétérit modal

• Il s'agit d'emplois du prétérit qui ne renvoient pas au passé temporel. Ils apparaissent dans les systèmes hypothétiques (voir chapitre 42) et un certain nombre d'autres structures :

I wish/If only we ***had*** *more money in the bank.*
Si seulement on avait un peu plus d'argent à la banque.
It's high time we ***left****.*
Il est grand temps que nous partions.
You ***had*** *better come back tomorrow.*
Tu ferais mieux de revenir demain.

Wordbank

the aftermath	*les conséquences*
an ambassador	*un ambassadeur*
an arms control treaty	*un traité de limitation des armes*
the balance of power	*l'équilibre du pouvoir*
belligerency	*la belligérance*
a bulwark	*un rempart*
the Cold War	*la Guerre froide*
to contain	*endiguer*
the diplomatic corps	*le corps diplomatique*
the domino theory	*la théorie des dominos*
a dove	*une colombe*
an executive agreement	*un accord, avec effet de loi, entre le président des États-Unis et un autre pays*
eyeball to eyeball	*nez à nez, face à face*
the Far East	*l'Extrême-Orient*
a foreign policy hearing	*une audition de politique étrangère*
a geo-political power shift	*un transfert de pouvoirs*
glasnost	*glasnost (la transparence)*
hard bargaining	*les négociations difficiles*
a hawk	*un faucon*
to win the hearts and minds	*gagner les cœurs et les esprits*
the Iron Curtain	*le rideau de fer*
the joint chiefs of staff	*les chefs d'état major des forces américaines*

a long-range missile	*un missile à longue portée*
the Middle East	*le Moyen-Orient*
military procurement	*l'approvisionnement en matériel militaire*
most-favoured nation status	*le statut de nation la plus favorisée (commerce)*
a plenipotentiary	*un ministre plénipotentiaire*
the national export initiative	*le plan d'exportation (2010)*
an open door trade policy	*une politique d'ouverture commerciale*
the Peace Corps	*volontariat de coopération et d'aide*
political fallout	*les retombées politiques*
the road map for peace	*la « feuille de route » vers la paix*
SALT (Strategic Arms Limitation Talks)	*négociations sur la limitation des armes stratégiques*
to scale down a commitment	*réduire un engagement*
a seasoned decision-maker	*un décideur expérimenté*
the Secretary of State	*le Ministre des Affaires étrangères*
the Senate Foreign Relations Committee	*la Commission des affaires étrangères du Sénat*
to shape foreign policy	*définir la politique étrangère*
"speak softly and carry a big stick"	*parler gentiment en montrant une grosse matraque*
a stand-off	*une impasse*
START (Strategic Arms Reduction Treaty)	*traité sur la réduction des armes stratégiques*
the State Department	*le ministère des Affaires étrangères*
a stealth bomber	*un bombardier furtif*
a superpower	*une superpuissance*
a taut relationship	*des rapports tendus*
a test ban treaty	*traité d'interdiction d'essais nucléaires*
a thawing relationship	*des rapports qui se dégèlent*
the Truman doctrine	*la politique anti-soviétique de 1947 qui soutenait l'Europe*
warfare	*la guerre*
weapons of mass destruction	*les armes de destruction massive*

Translation

Translate the sentences into English.

1. La ministre des Affaires étrangères souhaitent que les relations avec les pays arabes deviennent moins tendues.

2. Il est grand temps que les super puissances s'accordent sur une feuille de route pour garantir la paix au proche-orient.

3. Si les rapports avec la Russie se dégelaient davantage, ces deux puissances pourraient s'entendre sur un traité de limitation des armes plus intéressant dans le long terme.

4. Les colombes du Congrès feraient mieux de se souvenir de la devise de Teddy Roosevelt selon lequel il vaut mieux « parler gentiment en montrant une grosse matraque ».

5. Le Ministère des Affaires étrangères préférerait que le Sénat ne vote pas une réduction du budget pour le volontariat à l'aide et à la coopération.

Read and answer

Read the article and then do activities A and B that follow.

US foreign policy: Speaking too softly

Relations between America and China may chill over a meeting with the Dalai Lama

NEW YORK. It is bound to be a controversial meeting. The Dalai Lama, Tibet's spiritual leader, goes to Washington, DC, this week and will sit down with President Barack Obama for the first time on Thursday February 18th. American presidents have long been happy to meet the Tibetan leader and to tolerate subsequent angry huffing from China, not least as a means of responding to public concern over human rights without doing anything serious to jeopardise trade or other ties with Beijing.

But in Mr Obama's case, with China increasingly assertive internationally and the American president perceived in many quarters as cautious, even timid, in foreign policy, the encounter with the Dalai Lama has assumed extra significance. Mr Obama will be studied closely. Human-rights activists will listen with care to the language that the American president uses, straining to hear whether he goes further than merely suggesting more dialogue between Tibetans and the Chinese leadership. Might the president dare to deliver real criticism of repression and human-rights abuses in Tibet?

Kenneth Roth, the head of Human Rights Watch, an activist group in New York, offers a mixed assessment of Mr Obama's foreign policy so far in its treatment of human rights. He suggests that no other recent American leader has taken such care with his rhetoric, judging how it is received by the rest of the world. But substantial steps too rarely follow Mr Obama's fine words. The president's speeches – as in Cairo last year – have helped to set a conciliatory tone for American foreign policy, and to reassure Muslims and others that America is not determined to seek confrontation for the sake of it. Thoughtful comments to African leaders, urging the continent to develop strong and democratic institutions, have also been well received. But Mr Roth sees little evidence of a leader who is prepared then to press reluctant regimes, as for example did Ronald Reagan (and before him, Jimmy Carter) in pushing the Soviet Union to sign up to an international commitment, the Helsinki Final Act, which promoted individual rights.

Mr Obama's foreign-policy approach of seeking engagement with opponents such as Iran, in an effort to establish dialogue and more effective diplomatic channels, has made it harder for him to beat the human-rights drum loudly. But by failing to speak up about repression, the American leader risks being perceived as weak. His muted reaction to the rigged presidential elections in Iran and the violent repression that followed (and continues) has seemed deferential. His eagerness to "reset" relations with Russia, for example by scrapping a planned anti-missile defence shield in eastern Europe, has coincided with near total silence over the murders of journalists and the clamping down on democracy in that country. It is unclear, in either case, that biting his tongue has brought any gains from the respective regimes.

Particularly troubling has been America's attitude to China and human rights. After Hillary Clinton's first visit to China as secretary of state, in February 2009, she announced that concern over human rights should not "interfere" with getting co-ope-

...

ration on other issues such as climate change and the global economy. Human-rights defenders were deflated. Mr Obama then avoided meeting the Dalai Lama when he visited America in September and postponed a scheduled meeting in October, to avoid upsetting the government in China ahead of a presidential visit. During Mr Obama's subsequent visit to China, he made few and limited comments on human rights. The Chinese government responded by becoming more assertive. It helped to scupper a deal at the Copenhagen summit on climate change in December and snubbed the American president by sending a deputy minister to a crucial meeting. China has generally proven to be increasingly unwilling to co-operate with America, for example over United Nations sanctions against Iran.

The administration, however, may now be toughening up. American rhetoric over Iran has become firmer. On Monday Mrs Clinton warned that a military dictatorship was emerging in Tehran. Relations with China, too, have become frostier, for example over a long-planned (and routine) decision by the American government to sell weapons to Taiwan. Mrs Clinton has also spoken up more forcefully about the need for internet freedom in China, in the wake of sophisticated cyber-attacks on Google that many believe had Chinese government fingerprints on them. This week's meeting with the Dalai Lama is thus a moment to demonstrate that Mr Obama is ready both to signal his concern for human rights and that his foreign-policy is becoming more assertive.

The Economist (economist.com), 15/2/2010

A. Language

1. Find synonyms in the first three paragraphs of the article for the following words and expressions: *contentious, reacting, worries/fears, to put at risk, more and more, confident/self-assured, wary, political speaking, significant measures, pacifying/friendly, to squeeze/to force, championed.*

2. Find antonyms in paragraphs 3, 4 and 5 of the article for the following: *negligible/insignificant, is willing/keen to, which denied rights, loud/outspoken, establishing, losses, to initiate/promote/reach an agreement, welcomed the president.*

B. Question

What does the EU blame President Obama's foreign policy for? (Answer in 150-200 words. Use information in the article but do not copy sentences directly: use your own words.)

Overview

Read a general overview of the subject.

The changing focus of policy

The USA is often reproached for interfering in the affairs of other countries, but prior to the country's 1917 engagement in WWI, its key philosophy had been isolationist: non-engagement in Europe. Since WWII, which saw it fighting on every front, the USA has been present on every continent and, just after the end of the Second World War in 1947, the Marshall Plan was instituted, an economic programme set up to help get Europe on the move.

1947 was also when the USA – through the Truman Doctrine – became engaged in helping countries resist communism. As the cold war and the "iron curtain" divided Europe east from west, this Doctrine was behind the successful Berlin airlift in 1948 and, although it did not stop the 1949 victory of communist forces over nationalist forces in China, it did manage containment of communism in Europe. During the post-war period, the USA focused on slowing Soviet expansion. Nuclear deterrence through "mutual assured destruction" was the emphasis during the cold war years but America and the Soviet Union did engage in SALT, later START (Strategic Arms Limitation/Reduction Talks). 1983 brought with it the Strategic Defense Initiative projects, an expensive program designed to protect the US from incoming missiles through satellite-based stations. It is argued that the economic cost of a program to counter the SDI was a major cause of the collapse of the Soviet Union.

After the fall of the Berlin Wall in 1989 and the subsequent collapse of the Eastern Bloc, America's foreign policy has changed focus. Attempts to find a solution to tension in the Middle East have been ongoing for many years, together with military intervention in cases of perceived threats (the Gulf wars of 1991 and 2003). Although America's war on terrorism seems to be its greatest concern and cause for debate not only in the USA but abroad, foreign policy is no longer a simple question of going to war or imposing sanctions. America and the rest of the world have been economically challenged by the powerhouse of China and a growing number of emerging countries, constituting an economic threat to trading blocs of which the USA is a member.

That economic tension will remain a challenge for an America moving out of recession, and politically, eyes will continue to be turned to the Middle and Far East.

Pronunciation

Listen and repeat.

pull [pʊl], **pole** [pəʊl]

- bull/bowl, could/code, room/roam, hooks/hoax, crook/croak.
- I'll be in his good books if I load the boat with Coke.

32 Chapter

Security issues

Language focus

Modalité d'énoncé vs modalité d'énonciation

• Les auxiliaires de modalité servent à exprimer la position que le locuteur prend par rapport à ce qu'il dit. Cette prise de position peut être de deux types différents.

1. La modalité de phrase

• Le locuteur évalue les chances de réalisation de l'événement. Ce type de modalité peut être également exprimé par des adverbes :

*I **must have lost** my keys./I have probably lost my keys.*
J'ai très probablement perdu mes clés.
*She **may be** Australian./Perhaps she's Australian.*
Elle est peut-être australienne.

2. La modalité de sujet

• Elle exprime une relation spécifique entre le locuteur et le sujet :

*You **may go** to the party.*	Tu as la permission d'aller à la fête.
*This athlete **can run** very fast.*	Cet athlète a la capacité de courir très vite.

Wordbank

an aircraft carrier	*un porte-avions*
asset freezing	*le gel d'avoirs financiers*
the Attorney General	*le Procureur général*
a biological weapons threat	*une menace d'attaque biologique*
bio-security	*la sécurité biologique*
to botch an attempt	*bâcler une tentative*
a charge	*un chef d'inculpation*
a coastguard	*un garde-côte*
counterfeit currency	*des devises contrefaites*
the customs	*la douane*
cyber-fraud	*la fraude informatique*
data sharing	*le partage de données*
a dirty bomb	*une bombe sale*
an electricity grid	*un réseau éléctrique*
an emergency response	*un secours d'urgence*
enhanced security	*la sécurité améliorée*
a financial meltdown	*un effondrement économique*

flooding	*les inondations*
forensic science	*la médecine légale*
to ground an airplane	*interdire de vol*
hacking	*le piratage informatique*
to hedge against risks	*se protéger contre des risques*
to hijack	*détourner*
human trafficking	*le trafic de personnes*
an informer	*un informateur, un indicateur*
law enforcement	*l'application de la loi*
a mastermind	*un cerveau*
a maverick scientist	*un scientifique renégat*
a mole	*un agent infiltré, une taupe*
to monitor	*surveiller*
the most wanted persons	*les personnes les plus recherchées*
a plot	*un complot*
to prosecute	*poursuivre*
a reward	*une récompense*
a ringleader	*un meneur*
a roadside bomb	*une bombe placée en bord de route*
a rogue state	*un État voyou*
to screen	*examiner*
a search warrant	*un mandat de perquisition*
smuggling	*faire de la contrebande*
to spread infectious diseases	*répandre des maladies infectieuses*
a spy in the sky	*un satellite espion*
to storm	*donner l'assaut*
a SWAT (Special Weapons And Tactics) team	*une équipe d'intervention de la police*
a task force	*un groupe d'intervention spécialisée*
to take into custody	*mettre en état d'arrestation*
to thwart an attempt	*déjouer une tentative*
an underground link	*un lien clandestin*
an underground network	*un réseau clandestin*

Translation

Translate the sentences into English.

1. N'importe quel virus mortel comme la peste ou la grippe peut mettre en danger la sécurité sanitaire du pays.

2. Il se pourrait que les satellites espions surveillent les faits et gestes de chaque citoyen américain.

3. Je suis sûr que l'équipe d'assaut de la police de L.A. a arrêté ce réseau clandestin de pirates informatiques.

4. Il est possible que le meneur de ce complot terroriste ait infiltré les garde-côtes américains.

5. L'agent des douanes nous a laissé partir en nous disant : « Vous pouvez y aller, vous n'êtes pas parmi les personnes recherchées. »

Read and answer

Read the article and then do activities A and B that follow.

Many Homeland Security initiatives are called flops

A high-tech "virtual fence" to catch illegal border-crossers. Next-generation nuclear detectors at ports. Tamper-proof driver's licenses in every state. These were signature Bush administration initiatives to protect the country against terrorism and secure its borders. All have been proven to be flops, according to government and outside experts, and expensive ones at that.

The Department of Homeland Security paid defense contractor Boeing Co. $1.1 billion to build what is sometimes called the virtual border fence. But the system of radars and cameras can't consistently tell terrorists from tumbleweed, according to the Government Accountability Office. In March, Homeland Security Secretary Janet Napolitano froze funding on the project.

In February, she overhauled plans to install so-called Advanced Spectroscopic Portal radiation detectors to screen cargo at ports. The units were prone to false alarms and hadn't proved themselves in testing, according to the accountability office. Developed by defense contractor Raytheon under a $1.2-billion program, the $822,000 detectors will now be relegated to a secondary screening role.

Last May, the Transportation Security Administration removed 37 explosive trace detection machines – or "puffers" – that had been deployed at airports to screen airline passengers at a total cost of $30 million. The machines had maintenance problems and didn't work consistently.

"DHS was pushing technology pretty hard under the Bush administration, and we were willing to risk failure because of the risks," said Stewart Baker, the former Homeland Security policy chief and author of a forthcoming memoir, "Skating on Stilts." "I'd put all of those things in the category of course corrections based on new data, perhaps made easier because this administration had not started the projects and so it could declare them failures without taking blame for the failure."

Napolitano aides say they don't blame their predecessors, who were under intense pressure to prevent another terrorist attack, for attempting fixes that ultimately didn't pan out. But outside analysts say the failures were the predictable result of an agency with too little experience at making major purchases and of contractors peddling untested products. "Before they did the puffers, everybody told them it wasn't going to work," said Richard Roth, an aviation security expert with CTI Consulting in Maryland. "The only guy that said it was going to work was the lobbyist for the company."

Corporations "have figured out that a whole lot of money has been budgeted for homeland security and counter-terrorism, and they're really eager to market all sorts of gigantic technological solutions," said Charles Faddis, a former CIA officer and author of "Willful Neglect: The Dangerous Illusion of Homeland Security." "We end up in a situation where there's all sorts of very straightforward things that we don't do, because there's no money to be made in it," he said. For example, Faddis said, the government should make greater use of explosive-sniffing dogs at airports and should counter vehicle bombs

...

by requiring simple steps at industrial plants that store dangerous chemicals. Napolitano told Congress recently that she supports expanding the use of bomb-sniffing dogs.

The Department of Homeland Security is hampered by a shortage of procurement officials experienced in buying complicated systems, said Rick "Ozzie" Nelson, a homeland security specialist at the Center for Strategic and International Studies, a think tank.

The department says it has been hiring more experts to better evaluate contract proposals and oversee projects. The virtual fence, radiation detectors and the puffer machines each had something in common, the accountability office says: All three technologies were selected before having been proven to work. Sometimes that's a reasonable way to deploy new security measures, said Brian Jenkins of the Rand Corp., who has advised the government on homeland security measures. [...] Still, he said, the Homeland Security Department is overly reliant on technology. "We are constantly searching for a silver bullet. We think that can solve all problems with superior technology," he said. "I don't think that's true."

Ken Dilanian, Washington Bureau, *Chicago Tribune* (chicagotribune.com), 14/5/2010

A. Language

Find synonyms in paragraphs 1, 3, 4, 5, 6 and 9 of the article for the following: *undocumented immigrants, that cannot be forged, independent consultants, changed (in order to improve), inspect/check, occasionally broke down, facilitated, without being held accountable, trying solutions, finally, has been taking on, to assess, sensible, a miracle solution.*

B. Question

To what extent has President George W. Bush's homeland security policy proved ineffective? (Answer in 150-200 words. Use your own words.)

Translation

Translate the article into English.

Washington et les mesures de sécurité dans les aéroports

Le renforcement de la sécurité dans les aéroports implique de nombreuses mesures, a affirmé vendredi à Tolède la secrétaire américaine à la Sécurité intérieure des États-Unis. Pour elle, leur uniformisation n'est pas souhaitable. « En fait, nous ne souhaitons pas l'utilisation de mesures identiques, car alors les terroristes sauraient quoi affronter et s'emploieraient à les déjouer », a expliqué Janet Napolitano lors d'un point de presse au lendemain d'une réunion avec ses homologues de l'Union européenne.

Les scanners corporels sont « un outil », mais « il doit y avoir une combinaison d'autres mesures », a-t-elle soutenu. « Les pays décident seuls de la combinaison de ces mesures », a-t-elle insisté, se défendant de vouloir imposer quoi que ce soit aux Européens. « Les média se sont focalisés sur les scanners corporels, mais la réunion avec mes homologues européens était centrée sur la nécessité d'augmenter la collecte des informations sur les gens qui voyagent en avion et leur partage », a-t-elle précisé.

AFP (dans *Le Point* [lepoint.fr]), 22/1/2010

Overview

Read a general overview of the subject.

The domestic legacy of 9/11

On September 11, 2001, millions of Americans suddenly realised that they were the target of such hate that their safety at home could no longer be guaranteed. The general feeling of immunity which had previously spurred the country to engage its armed forces abroad vanished to give way to a new sense of vulnerability. Such painful awareness was met with intense patriotic fervour.

Two days later, the White House identified the culprits as members of an Islamic fundamentalist terrorist group based in Afghanistan but with terrorist cells throughout the world. US Attorney General John Ashcroft went to Congress with a list of recommended changes in the legislation to fight terrorism both at home and abroad. Some of these security measures had long been opposed by members of Congress as infringing the rights of Americans, but the 9-11 attacks had swept away all previous objections: the American people's patriotic fervour and fears about their safety had to be met by an equally powerful response. The Senate quickly passed the "USA Patriot" Act (Uniting and Strengthening America by Providing Appropriate Tools Required to Intercept and Obstruct Terrorism).

The Patriot Act expanded the definition of terrorism – formerly used to target rogue states and international terrorist organisations – to "domestic terrorism" enabling the removal of most of the restrictions on telephone bugging, e-mail surveillance and investigations into medical, financial and other records. The "war on terror" seemed to be putting an end to many basic liberties but it was supported by a nation in shock.

The US Department of Homeland Security (DHS) was established in 2002. It was a massive reorganisation of 22 previously separate agencies into one unit with five basic aims:

– preventing terrorist attacks by improving domestic intelligence while preserving civil liberties;
– reducing the country's vulnerability to terrorism by improving and protecting vital infrastructures;
– preparing to react and recover from an attack or from natural or man-made disasters;
– sustaining homeland security consistent with American values and regulations;
– restoring lost US leadership abroad to win back the hearts and minds for democracy.

Even though President Obama urged his fellow Americans to start looking beyond the scars of 9-11 during the 2008 presidential campaign, one cannot but wonder how Americans are managing to come to terms with the 9-11 trauma in a land where citizens seem to have lost a good deal of their freedom.

Pronunciation

Listen and repeat.

grew [gruː], **grow** [grəʊ]

- soup/soap, rule/role, cool/coal, boon/bone, boot/boat, moon/moan.
- Joan moaned and swooned under the full moon in June.

Chapter 33

The Commonwealth

Language focus

May, might, can, could

• *May* exprime la possibilité ou la permission :

*You **may go** out tonight.* (modalité de phrase)
Tu peux sortir ce soir.
*He **may not be** happy about this situation.* (modalité de sujet)
Il se peut que cette situation lui déplaise.

• *Might*, la forme prétérit de *may*, ne peut exprimer qu'une possibilité à laquelle on croit encore moins qu'avec *may* :

*She **might be** British.* (modalité de phrase)
Il se pourrait qu'elle soit britannique.

• Les sens de *can* sont la capacité/l'incapacité ou la permission/l'interdiction (formes affirmative et négative), ou encore l'improbabilité (forme négative uniquement) :

*He **can speak** Chinese.* (modalité de sujet)
*You **can go out** tonight.* (modalité de sujet)
*He looks about 25 but he **can't be** more than 15.* (modalité de phrase)

• Contrairement à *can*, *could* peut exprimer la possibilité à la forme affirmative :

*He **could be** away at the moment.* (modalité de phrase)
Il se peut qu'il soit absent en ce moment.

Comme modalité de sujet, il signifie la capacité au passé :

*She **could swim** for several hours.* (modalité de sujet)
Elle était capable de nager pendant des heures.

Wordbank

to achieve self-government	*accéder à l'indépendance*
allegiance to the crown	*l'allégeance à la couronne*
in arrears	*redevable d'arriérés*
to attend the summit	*assister au sommet*
the bargaining table	*la table des négociations*
a clash	*un affrontement*
a commitment	*un engagement*
the Commonwealth Summer Games	*les Jeux d'été du Commonwealth*
dependency	*un état dépendant*
a dominion	*un État souverain dans l'Empire*
economic ties	*des liens économiques*
to expel a country	*exclure un pays*

formerly	*anciennement*
the Fourth World	*le quart-monde*
free association	*l'association libre*
a go-between	*un intermédiaire*
to hamper	*entraver*
a Head of State	*un chef d'État*
a highlight	*un temps fort*
historical links	*des liens historiques*
to hold together	*maintenir la cohésion (entre)*
a host country	*un pays d'accueil*
a membership	*une appartenance*
non-binding	*non-obligatoire*
a parliamentary democracy	*une démocratie parlementaire*
a relief program	*un programme de secours*
a round of talks	*une série de pourparlers*
a running budget	*un budget d'exploitation*
scattered over the world	*dispersé à travers le monde*
to set down/out principles	*établir des principes*
a shared goal	*un objectif commun*
a stand-off	*une impasse*
the Statute of Westminster 1931	*décret qui reconnaissait le droit à l'autonomie*
the subscription dues	*les droits d'appartenance*
to suspend a member	*suspendre un membre*
sustainable development	*le développement durable*
the symbolic head	*le chef symbolique*
voluntary	*sur la base du volontariat*
a war grave	*un tombeau militaire*
to shed the ties	*se débarasser des liens*
to shake off	*se libérer de*
the body politic	*le corps politique*
the Third World	*le tiers-monde*
the overthrow	*le renversement*
the World Bank	*la Banque mondiale*

Translation

Translate the sentences into English.

1. Il est possible que les chefs d'États africains n'assistent pas au sommet qui se tiendra à Canberra.

2. Il se pourrait que les pays membres du Commonwealth se retrouvent dans une impasse sans pouvoir dégager d'objectifs communs.

3. La Reine d'Angleterre peut se déplacer dans n'importe quel pays membre du Commonwealth dont elle est le chef symbolique.

4. Le Commonwealth peut exclure un pays de la table des négociations pour le forcer à se libérer du joug de la dictature militaire.

5. Le Canada va être le pays d'accueil d'une série de pourparlers portant sur les liens économiques entre nord et sud.

Read and answer

Read the article and then do activities A and B that follow.

The Commonwealth: Wider still and weaker?

PORT OF SPAIN, Trinidad. Britain's empire, in the sense of overseas territories under United Kingdom sovereignty, has shrunk and shrunk: it now consists of just 14 islands, rocks and barely inhabited strips of land, the biggest of them in Antarctica. Meanwhile, the body that emerged from the empire 60 years ago, the Commonwealth, risks the opposite: growing so large, loose and floppy that it merges with the rest of humanity.

Its 53 countries already represent a fifth of earth's land area and nearly a third of the human race; their leaders, or most of them, were due to converge in Trinidad on November 27th – with many of their staff staying on two cruise ships, looming over Port of Spain's waterfront. Just over half the Commonwealth's 2 billion people are Indian; but awkwardly, a poll of seven Commonwealth countries, including India, found that only a third of respondents could name something the body did.

In several ways, this will be a bigger summit than ever. It will be joined by Ban Ki-moon, the UN secretary-general; and also, for a day, France's president, Nicolas Sarkozy, as well as Denmark's prime minister. All see the meeting as a useful precursor to the Copenhagen deliberation on climate change. The states present in Trinidad range from flat, vulnerable islands to powerful carbon-belching economies. And in yet another fading of an already faint contour, the Trinidad summit is expected to admit Rwanda, the first member with a colonial culture (inherited from Belgium) that is more Francophone than Anglophone. The old restriction to ex-British territories was broken in 1995, when ex-Portuguese Mozambique gained entry.

Welcoming a French-speaking African state to the Commonwealth is a much bigger landmark. Anglo-French rivalry has overshadowed the continent until very recent times. (For example, Rwanda's genocide and civil strife might have met a firmer response if the French- and English-speaking worlds had put up a united front, instead of seeming to compete by proxy.) But once the Anglo-French divide is transcended, the question of what defines the Commonwealth becomes still harder.

To concentrate minds, leaders arriving in the Caribbean will be presented with two reports, both of which are remarkably blunt, considering that one was funded in part by the Commonwealth's small Secretariat, and the other came from the Royal Commonwealth Society, the largest of the NGOs that promote the club. Both reports suggest that the group must acquire more bite, as a promoter of democracy and human rights, or else it might as well shut up. Not that the Commonwealth is entirely toothless. It has a patchy record of suspending or forcing the withdrawal of members that grossly violate its ideals of electoral democracy and racial equality. And there is a mild incentive for virtue: the joyous welcome afforded to countries that gain readmission after a period of isolation (as happened to South Africa after apartheid or Pakistan when democracy returned). [...]

One report, "Democracy in the Commonwealth", reflects the passion of people who can tell good democratic systems from bad. One of its authors is Asma Jahangir, a Pakistani human-rights campaigner who has faced death threats, and in 2007,

...

house arrest. The report is presented by Amartya Sen, a Nobel laureate who wants the Commonwealth to stand for something subtler than ballots and voting booths. It should urge reasoned debate and "governance by discussion" in domestic and global affairs, as preached by the philosopher John Stuart Mill. [...]

If that study is scathing about democracy in the Commonwealth, the other one, "Common What?", is pretty frank about the club itself. Drawing on polls, focus groups and web chats involving tens of thousands of people, it found that the Commonwealth was more popular among poorer states than richer ones, but misunderstood everywhere. Only about a third of Australians or Canadians would be "sorry" or "appalled" if their country quit the club, though two-thirds of Indians and Malaysians would feel that way.

The Economist (economist.com), 26/11/2009

A. Language

Find synonyms in the first five paragraphs of the article for the following: *has dwindled, is made up of, scarcely, blends with, gather, embarrassingly, 33% of the people questioned, producing high amounts of carbon dioxide, vanishing, has clouded/darkened/spoiled, stood united, to focus, direct/straightforward, impotent/powerless, encouragement.*

B. Questions

Answer each of the following questions in 50 words. Use your own words.

1. What is the Commonwealth? 2. Why is Rwanda's application a landmark? 3. What is the agenda of the Commonwealth summit?

Explain the following quotation in 100 words: "Both reports suggest that the group (the Commonwealth) must acquire more bite, as a promoter of democracy and human rights, or else it might as well shut up."

Translation

Translate the article into English.

Des soldats du Commonwealth tombés en 1916 ont enfin leur sépulture en France

Avec une salve de fusils d'assaut et la sonnerie aux morts, le premier des 250 soldats du Commonwealth tombés au combat en 1916 à Fromelles (Nord-Pas-de-Calais) et exhumés l'an dernier de fosses communes, a été réinhumé samedi avec les honneurs militaires. Salués par des anciens combattants français, des fantassins et des fusiliers australiens ont porté le cercueil jusqu'à sa sépulture au cours d'une cérémonie à laquelle assistaient plus de 200 personnes.

« Nous sommes rassemblés pour rendre les honneurs à ceux des nôtres qui sont tombés ici [...], une génération perdue » de jeunes volontaires fauchés sur le champ de bataille de la première guerre mondiale, a déclaré le ministre australien des Anciens combattants, Alan Griffin. [...] Recouvert samedi matin par une fine couche de neige, le nouveau cimetière militaire de Fromelles a été édifié non loin du champ où les corps des soldats du Commonwealth avaient été enterrés et où ils ont été retrouvés en 2008 grâce à la persévérance d'un chercheur australien. [...]

AFP (dans *Le Point* [lepoint.fr]), 30/1/2010

Overview

Read a general overview of the subject.

From Empire to Commonwealth to... ?

As from the late 1880s, British politicians realised that the British Empire could not go on forever in the same way: the power structure had to change so that the colonies would be considered as partners, not as conquered nations. When this led inevitably to independence, it was however to no one's advantage to break the commercial ties which underpinned the fragile ex-colonial economies. So the Commonwealth gradually came into being, an organisation now comprising 54 nations, almost all of them former British colonies. The aims – outlined in the 1971 Singapore Declaration – are wide-ranging and ambitious to say the least. The Commonwealth officially aims to promote world peace, free trade and equality, and to combat discrimination, poverty, ignorance and disease.

A cynic would say that leaders of the member countries see the real purpose of the Commonwealth as guaranteeing a market for their country's goods and giving them as individuals a couple of all-expenses-paid 5-star holidays every year at the Commonwealth Conference and the Commonwealth Games. Even if one takes a less cynical approach, it is hard to see how the Commonwealth has any role to play in a world dominated by other, more powerful associations like the European Union, OPEC, the World Trade Organisation, the International Monetary Fund, NATO and the United Nations... some of which also have Commonwealth countries as members even though there may sometimes be a conflict of interests. At the same time, many of the Commonwealth's aims overlap those of UNESCO, meaning that some countries in the world are funding UNESCO programs to further world peace, equality and so on, and funding Commonwealth programs that do exactly the same...

Even if there is no real commercial or humanitarian justification for the existence of the Commonwealth in today's global economy, there are emotional ties between Britain and its former colonies which many think can bear fruit in times of political crisis, although this was patently not true in the case of South Africa under apartheid or present-day Zimbabwe. Commonwealth loyalties do not seem to be as strong as racial or tribal ones... However, respect for the Queen is surprisingly strong in many Commonwealth countries, even those which do not recognise her as Head of State, and it is her personality that has, to some degree, been responsible for the continuance of the Commonwealth over the past 50 years. The big question is: what will happen when she is no longer there to smooth over the deep cracks in the brickwork?

Pronunciation

Listen and repeat.

a boat [ə'bəʊt], **about** [ə'baʊt]

- tone/town, know/now, goat/gout, hole/howl, drone/drown.
- The old goat drowned in a water-hole near town.

34 Chapter

Australia

Language focus

Shall *et* will

• *Shall* et *will* combinent souvent les deux types de modalité en même temps. *Shall* exprime une prédiction ou un fort engagement :

*We **shall** overcome.* Nous vaincrons.

• En anglais britannique, *shall* apparaît fréquemment dans les questions à la première personne :

***Shall** I open the window?* Veux-tu que j'ouvre la fenêtre ?

• *Will* sert à exprimer un simple futur (voir chapitre 44), mais aussi une quasi-certitude :

*A letter from Japan? That **will** be Harakumi!*

Une letter du Japon ? C'est certainement Harakumi !

• Quand la modalité du sujet est très marquée, *will* renvoie à la volonté du sujet, aux formes négatives et interrogatives :

"***Will** you do this for me?*" "*No, I **won't**.*"

– Tu veux bien faire ça pour moi ? – Non, je refuse.

• Enfin, *will* sert à exprimer une caractéristique du sujet :

*He **will** do things like that!*

C'est bien typique de lui, de faire une chose pareille.

Wordbank

the Ashes	*un trophée de cricket âprement convoité*
a bicameral parliament	*un parlement à deux chambres*
the bush	*les zones sauvages de l'Australie*
a bush fire	*un feu de brousse*
a bushranger	*une personne qui se réfugie dans le* bush
cattle breeding	*l'élevage de bétail*
claimant processing	*le traitement des demandes (d'asile)*
to clear for pasture	*débroussailler avant pâturage*
commodity exports	*les exportations de matières premières*
convict transportation	*la déportation de détenus*
down-under *(UK, fam.)*	*l'Australie*
drought	*la sécheresse*
equal powers	*des pouvoirs égaux*
exponential growth	*la croisssance exponentielle*
far-reaching powers	*des pouvoirs importants*
the federal parliament	*le parlement fédéral*

the flying doctor service	*le service de médecine volant*
the gold rush	*la ruée vers l'or*
the Governor-General	*le représentant de la monarchie britannique*
grazing land	*le pâturage*
a harsh climate	*un climat dur*
a health check	*un examen médical*
indigenous folkore	*les traditions populaires des indigènes*
to land	*débarquer*
Medicare	*l'accès aux soins hospitaliers gratuits et un remboursement partiel de frais de médecin*
mistreatment	*le mauvais traitement*
national general elections	*les élections législatives nationales*
the outback	*les régions intérieures (désertiques) du continent*
an Ozzie *(fam.)*	*un Australien*
a penal colony	*une colonie pénitentiaire, un bagne*
reserve powers	*des pouvoirs réservés*
a road-train	*un camion articulé multi-remorques*
a self-governing territory	*un territoire autonome*
sheep farming	*l'élevage de moutons*
a sheep shearer	*un tondeur de moutons*
a sheep station	*un élevage de moutons*
a shipload of settlers	*un navire rempli de colons*
to sight land	*apercevoir la terre*
the southern cross/constellation	*la croix du sud (symbole sur le drapeau)*
a state government	*un gouvernement d'état*
a stock drover	*un conducteur de bestiaux*
a swagman	*un ouvrier agricole itinérant*
a territorial claim	*une revendication territoriale*
urban sprawl	*l'étalement des zones urbaines*
the wilderness	*les étendues sauvages*
a written constitution	*une constitution rédigée*
an open-cast mine	*une mine à ciel ouvert*

Translation

Translate the sentences into English.

1. Boire de la bière blonde fade et glacée en regardant le cricket, c'est bien typique d'un Australien!

2. Le nouveau gouvernement s'engage à prendre en compte les revendications territoriales des aborigènes.

3. Les nouveaux immigrants ne veulent plus aller s'installer dans les régions désertiques en plein milieu du continent.

4. Les tisseurs de rêves aborigènes ont prédit que l'Australie remporterait le trophée de cricket contre l'Angleterre trois années de rang.

5. S'il travaille cet été dans un élevage de moutons, il essaiera de devenir le meilleur tondeur de l'équipe.

Read and answer

Read the article and then do activities A and B that follow.

Let Aboriginal communities have a say over intervention

This week marks the third anniversary of the Northern Territory intervention. On Monday night, the Senate passed legislation to partially restore racial discrimination protections and modify aspects of the intervention, including income management. In doing so, it made profound changes to the Australian social security system, which will impact upon poor and socially excluded Australians across the country, black and white.

The intervention was announced on June 21, 2007 by the Howard government. Without consultation, radical changes were made to the daily lives of Aboriginal people in Northern Territory communities. While few denied the urgent need to act, many were shocked and angered at the failure to engage communities in developing solutions.

Indeed, the independent Northern Territory Emergency Response (NTER) Review reported in 2008 that "one of the impacts of the NTER was to fracture an already tenuous relationship with government". On its election in late 2007, the Rudd government committed to "resetting" the relationship with indigenous Australians. Hopes were high that this would entail a significant re-think of the intervention, and lead to its transition into a sustainable community development strategy. Instead, the intervention has continued as a highly bureaucratic, blunt, and inefficient response to complex social issues. The partial reinstatement of racial discrimination protections is a significant improvement on the previous situation but it comes almost a year after the government's original deadline. Further, many intervention measures remain beyond legal challenge, including the compulsory five-year leases over land.

While some improvements have been made, the Rudd government's approach maintains some of the most coercive aspects of the Howard intervention model. This includes extraordinary government powers to vary and terminate funding agreements and control the management and assets of Aboriginal service organisations. More than $2 billion has now been spent over the three years of the intervention. The new income management scheme alone has a $350 million price tag in the Northern Territory. The lack of positive results shows all too clearly that top-down approaches that do not engage communities in addressing the problems they face will have limited, if any, positive effect.

A recent report by the NT Children's Commissioner revealed a system chronically under-funded and in crisis, with 1,200 matters not investigated within the required time frame last year. The federal government's own NTER monitoring report published this week shows that confirmed incidences of child abuse have more than doubled and domestic violence incidents increased by 75 per cent. While these figures may be due in part to increased police and reporting, the evidence suggests that violence and abuse have not reduced as a result of the intervention, despite this being its rationale. […]

The *Little Children are Sacred Report* made 97 recommendations to protect children from abuse and address the urgent social issues being faced by communities.

"The thrust of our recommendations," Patricia Anderson and Rex Wild wrote, "is for there to be consultation with, and ownership by the communities, of those solutions."

...

These included concrete proposals to both respond to and prevent child abuse and neglect, to strengthen child sexual abuse crisis services, expand parenting and family support services and develop programs to reduce the risk of victims becoming perpetrators.

Recognising that poverty, alcohol and drug abuse, housing shortages and unemployment are all key risk factors for child abuse and neglect, Anderson and Wild's recommendations were broad in vision and scope.

They ranged from investing in child and adolescent mental health services and family support services in communities, reforming education programs to improve attendance (with smaller classes and flexibility in timing of the school year) and consulting with communities to develop individual community alcohol management plans.

Jacqueline Phillips, *The Sydney Morning Herald* (smh.com.au), 22/6/2010

A. Language

Find synonyms in the first four paragraphs of the article for the following: *will have weighty consequences for, drastic, flimsy/insubstantial, expectations, bring about/cause, restoration, advance, former, mandatory, forceful, possessions, facing the issues.*

B. Question

What does Jacqueline Phillips blame the NTER for? (Answer in 200-250 words. Use information in the article but do not copy sentences directly: use your own words.)

Translation

Translate the article into English.

L'Australie porte sa première femme à la tête du gouvernement

L'Australie a porté jeudi 24 juin pour la première fois une femme à la tête du gouvernement, Julia Gillard, après l'éviction surprise au sein du parti travailliste de Kevin Rudd dont la popularité s'était récemment délitée. Julia Gillard, une ancienne avocate de 48 ans à l'accent australien bien marqué, a remporté les voix des parlementaires travaillistes rassemblés pour désigner un successeur à Kevin Rudd.

Julia Gillard, qui assumait depuis 2007 les fonctions de vice-Premier ministre, a prêté serment jeudi lors d'une cérémonie organisée quelques heures seulement après ce « putsch » au sein du parti travailliste, dont Kevin Rudd avait récemment abandonné la direction.

« J'ai demandé à mes collègues d'apporter un changement en termes de leadership, car je crois qu'un bon gouvernement était en train de s'égarer », a-t-elle dit. « Je n'allais pas demeurer les bras croisés ».

« Je me sens très honorée », a-t-elle déclaré à la presse à sa sortie du Parlement à Canberra. Elle a toutefois admis qu'elle n'avait « pas été élue par le peuple australien » et qu'elle demanderait « dans les prochains mois au gouverneur général de convoquer des élections de façon à ce que les Australiens puissent exercer leur droit originel et choisir leur Premier ministre ».

Le Nouvel Observateur (nouvelobs.com), 24/6/2010

Overview

Read a general overview of the subject.

Beach barbecues and... opera

Although the Dutch had charted much of the west of the Australian continent in the 17th century, the English were the first to settle there. Colonisation began in 1788, after Captain Cook had mapped the east coast in 1770. Britain gradually claimed the whole of Australia as its own, founding six separate colonies which gained considerable autonomy over the years and were then federated and finally transformed into a nation state in 1931. It was not however until the Australia Act of 1986 that all legal ties between Britain and Australia were finally severed – with the exception of the maintenance of the British monarch as Head of State. This may seem like a curious anomaly to some, but 30% of Australians are of British origin and have a strong sentimental attachment for the "old country", although Australians' lifestyle now more closely resembles that of the USA than of Britain: Australians may play cricket and drive on the left, but they also surf and have beach barbecues.

The early settlers, many of whom were convicts transported there to penal colonies, soon came into contact with the indigenous inhabitants, the Aborigines, who had been there for thousands of years. Although there were no massacres or wars (unlike what happened in the Americas), it was considered at the time that Aborigines had no natural rights to the land or its resources, so the colonists were given legal title. Some Aborigines became educated and successful, but many were excluded from society and became an underclass, turning to drink and to crime. It was not until the late 20th century that measures were taken to better their situation. Between 1999 and 2008, following the fashion of *mea culpa* statements from political and religious leaders all over the world apologising for past behaviour, Australia admitted it had mistreated the Aboriginal population and set about trying to repair the damage.

Up until about the 1970s, Australia's image had been that of a country of opportunity – an attractive prospect for people seeking a good standard of living in a hot climate, but it was thought to be lacking any sort of refinement. Europeans would go there to see the unique wildlife, the outback and the bush, but very few people could name an Australian writer, actor or singer. Things have changed a lot since then. The completion of the Sydney Opera House in 1973 was a symbolic event, marking the beginning of Australia's cultural coming of age.

Pronunciation

Listen and repeat.

cow [kaʊ], **car** [kɑː]

- stout/start, out/art, mouse/mars, bowed/barred, doubts/darts.
- He bowed to the bard in the bar and they started drinking stout.

Chapter 35

Canada

Language focus

Would, wouldn't, should, shouldn't

• *Would* (le prétérit de *will*) est essentiellement un modal du sujet. Il exprime soit une caractéristique du sujet ; c'est le *would* dit fréquentatif qu'on trouve dans des récits au passé. Dans les phrases négatives et interrogatives, il renvoie à la volonté du sujet :

Would you do that for me? — Tu veux bien faire ça pour moi ?

• *Should*, la forme prétérit de *shall*, n'a jamais de sens passé. Le prétérit y est toujours modal. Quand *should* exprime une modalité de phrase, il exprime une quasi-certitude, plus faible que *must* :

It shouldn't be too difficult to find him.
Cela ne devrait pas être trop difficile pour le trouver.

• En tant que modalité du sujet, *should* exprime un conseil, une obligation atténuée sur le mode condescendant :

You should be more careful with him. You shouldn't drive so fast.

Wordbank

an ABM (Automatic Bank Machine) *(Can.)*	*un distributeur de billets*
aboriginal/indigenous culture	*la culture indienne/indigène*
an accretion of provinces and territories	*une juxtaposition/un amalgame de provinces et de territoires*
Canada (*Kanata* en Iroquois)	*un village, une communauté*
the (Canada) Constitution Act 1982	*Loi d'Indépendance du Canada*
Canada Day	*Jour de la Fête nationale (1er juillet 1867)*
a Canuck *(fam.)*	*un Canadien*
colonisation	*la colonisation*
a colony	*une colonie*
The Commissioner of Official Languages	*le Haut Commissaire aux affaires linguistiques*
a constitutional monarchy	*une monarchie consitutionnelle*
core French/English (teaching)	*l'enseignement des bases du français/de l'anglais (= un cours spécialisé comme un cours de langue vivante en France)*
a dominion	*territoire, colonie*
ESL/FSL (English/French as a Second Language)	*l'enseignement de l'anglais/du français comme seconde langue*
to establish a settlement	*fonder une colonie/un village*

the executive/legislative/judicial branch	*le pouvoir exécutif/parlementaire/judiciaire*
a federation of provinces	*une fédération de provinces*
a First Nation reserve	*une réserve indienne*
the French-speaking minority	*la minorité linguistique francophone*
the 49th parallel	*la frontière États-Unis/Canada (le long du 49e parallèle)*
a French settlement	*une colonie/un territoire français(e)*
to go north of 60 *(Can.)*	*monter vers l'Arctique*
the Governor General of Canada	*le gouverneur général du Canada*
immersion French/English	*l'enseignement en immersion (= toutes les matières sont enseignées dans la langue cible)*
the lieutenant governor	*le lieutenant-gouverneur*
a loonie, a toonie/doubloon *(Can.)*	*une pièce d'un dollar, une pièce de deux dollars*
the lower tiers of government	*les strates/niveaux inférieures des administrations (au niveau des provinces, territoires, municipalités)*
a mountie	*un agent de la police montée* (Royal Canadian Mounted Police)
a noun of indigenous origin	*un mot d'origine indienne (ex : canoe, maple, tobacco)*
official bilingualism	*le bilinguisme officiel/d'État*
The Official Language Act	*la loi sur les langues nationales*
a settler	*un colon*
a trade/trading outpost	*un comptoir de commerce*
a trader	*un marchand*
a (fur) trapper	*un trappeur/chasseur (de peaux)*
unicameral legislation	*le pouvoir législatif à une seule chambre/monocaméral*
unilingual	*monolingue*

Translation

Translate the sentences into English.

1. La politique officielle sur le bi-culturalisme au Canada devrait inspirer les pays européens, notamment en matière d'enseignement des langues.

2. Au XVIIe siècle, les habitants appelaient la région située entre le fleuve Saint-Laurent et les Grands Lacs, la Nouvelle-France.

3. Si tu veux faire ton doctorat sur la vie dans les réserves indiennes du Canada, tu devrais commencer à apprendre une des langues indigènes comme le cree ou l'algonquin.

4. Tu veux bien m'expliquer en quoi le Canada est une démocratie parlementaire ? Quand j'étais enfant, mon oncle québécois n'arrêtait pas de me dire que c'était la Reine d'Angleterre le chef d'État.

5. Les touristes européens, peu habitués aux grands espaces, ne devraient pas s'aventurer seuls dans les forêts au printemps... il y a trop d'ours affamés !

Read and answer

Read the article and then do activities A and B that follow.

Quebec to amend controversial language law

PQ says possibility of allowing some francophone and immigrant students to attend English-language schools could "recreate a storm"

The Quebec government is creating a breach in the province's controversial language law that, under strict conditions, could eventually allow certain francophone and immigrant students to attend English-language public schools.

A bill was tabled on Wednesday to comply with last fall's Supreme Court of Canada ruling that struck down provisions in the language law that prevented francophone and immigrant students - mainly from wealthy families - who attended private, non-subsidized, English-language schools from becoming eligible to transfer to English-language public schools. The bill proposes that such students may be admitted to English-language public schools after being assessed according to a grid and a point system defined by the Ministry of Education. It would make the transfer difficult but not impossible, according to Minister of Education Michelle Courchesne. "We aren't saying it will be impossible," she said. "We are saying that we are tightening the rules to the maximum to ensure the spirit of the French Language Charter and our laws that state that in Quebec teaching is conducted in French."

According to the Parti Québécois, the Liberal government may regret having opened up a debate that could focus attention on the survival of the French language in Quebec and upset the province's social and linguistic peace. "I believe an historic error has been committed that threatens to recreate a storm in our social climate," PQ language critic Pierre Curzi told reporters. [...] "The prominence of the French language may not be negotiable but it is now up for sale. [...] All this does is make it a little more expensive to buy a right. You have just created two classes of citizens." [...] Ms. Courchesne rejected the accusations, insisting that each request will be carefully examined to ensure that the language law was not being circumvented. "The bill does not allow for anyone to buy a constitutional right," she said.

According to the bill, if a student follows what is called a "genuine educational pathway" that proves an "authentic commitment" to being educated in English, then he or she may satisfy the requirements and reach the 15 points needed to be admitted to an English-language public school. Students will be evaluated based on a set of criteria defined by ministry officials. In their assessment, for instance, officials will allocate points based on how long a student has continuously attended a private English-language school. They will also examine the family's genuine desire to be part of the English minority, as well as the language of education of the parents or the motivation behind the decision to attend English-language schools. Under the bill, private schools will be prohibited from deliberately admitting students with the intent of circumventing the language law's restrictive provisions.

One of those restrictions requires children from immigrant and francophone families to attend French-language schools. The exception is that, if one of the two parents, or one of their children, attended an English-language school in Canada, the family is exempted from the bill's education restrictions.

...

...

However, until 2002 some wealthy francophone and immigrant parents who did not have English schooling in Canada bypassed the law by sending their children to non-subsidized, private, English-language schools, at an estimated cost of $6,000 to $12,000 a year. These were called "bridging schools" because after only a single year in a private school, a student, as well as all brothers and sisters, could then enroll in the English-language public school system as provided by the language law.

In 2002, the National Assembly unanimously adopted a Parti Québécois government bill that plugged the loophole and eliminated "bridging schools." That law was struck down last October by the Supreme Court, sending the government back to the drawing board. [...]

Rhéal Séguin, *The Globe and Mail* (theglobeandmail.com), 2/6/2010

A. Language

1. Find synonyms in paragraphs 3 and 4 of the article for the following: *a mistake has been made, to trigger social unrest again, was not being sidestepped, sincere/honest, meet the expectations, assessed, award, intentionally, evading/getting around.*

2. Find antonyms in the first three paragraphs of the article for the following: *lenient, prohibit, to go against/to break (the law), that enabled them to be entitled to, are relaxing, may wish they had opened up, restore the peace.*

B. Questions

Answer each of the following questions in 50 words. Use information in the article to answer but do not copy sentences directly: use your own words.

1. Describe Quebec's language law.

2. What does the government plan to do?

3. What do the government's critics blame it for?

Translation

Translate the article into English.

Les séparatistes du Québec devant les libéraux, selon un sondage

OTTAWA. Les séparatistes francophones de la province canadienne du Québec gardent un net avantage sur les libéraux au pouvoir et auraient une bonne chance d'obtenir la majorité au parlement régional si des élections avaient lieu aujourd'hui, selon un sondage.

Ce sondage Léger réalisé pour les journaux *Le Devoir* et *The Gazette* crédite les libéraux de 30 % d'opinions favorables, soit un point de moins qu'il y a un mois. Le Parti québécois (PQ), qui prône l'indépendance de la province, gagne un point avec un taux de satisfaction de 41 %.

Les libéraux ont remporté les élections provinciales de décembre 2008 mais ont été affaiblis depuis lors par des allégations de scandales et de corruption. Plus de 75 % des sondés se sont déclarés mécontents du gouvernement.

Reuters (dans *Le Nouvel Observateur* [nouvelobs.com]), 14/5/2010

Overview

Read a general overview of the subject.

Multiculturalism : the key to national identity

Ever since Canada's adoption of multiculturalism in 1971, supporters and critics have debated its impact on the integration of immigrants and visible or religious minorities. Supporters contend that multiculturalism removes barriers to immigrants' participation in Canadian life, and leads by the same token to a stronger sense of belonging. Critics argue that multiculturalism worsens the ghettoisation and balkanisation of the social fabric, by encouraging members of ethnic groups to keep to themselves, thus emphasising ethnic differences rather than their shared rights or common identity as Canadian citizens.

According to recent polls, 85% of Canadians believe multiculturalism is beneficial to their country. Not only do Canadians view immigrants and demographic diversity as basic features of their own Canadian identity, but they are also uninclined to believe that immigrants are prone to crime.

In terms of political integration, immigrants in Canada are more likely to become naturalised and more likely to actually participate in the political process as voters, party members or even candidates running for political office than in any other country. For example, the percentage of foreign-born Canadian members of the federal Parliament is 13%, compared with only 2% in the USA.

In terms of social integration, the children of immigrants have better educational results and prospects in Canada than in any other Western democracy. According to an OECD report in 2006, second-generation immigrants in Canada outperform children of non-immigrant parents, even when they come from disadvantaged backgrounds.

In terms of cultural integration, surveys show the absence of minority ghettos in Canada; mixed ethnic neighbourhoods prevail, and are the first step to integration. Compared to other countries, Canada has been less affected by the global surge in anti-Muslim feelings: according to a survey led by Focus Canada in 2006, 83% of Canadians agree that Muslims make a positive contribution to Canada.

All in all, Canada seems to do better than other countries on the integration of immigrants and minorities. This runs counter to the general feeling of failure in Europe where a liberal country like The Netherlands has pulled back from the generous multicultural policies implemented in the eighties to give way to much more coercive "civic integration" policies which look increasingly like a return to assimilation. Even Britain, which had unrolled the welcome mat in the early 2000s, has come up with a citizenship test and is currently considering a points-based system.

Pronunciation

Listen and repeat.

high [haɪ], **how** [haʊ]

- pride/proud, bind/bound, rise/rouse, sprite/sprout.
- He likes how she cooks brussels sprouts.

36 Chapter

New Zealand

Language focus

Must, have to, have got to

• *Must* exprime une obligation morale (= interne) et *have to* exprime soit une obligation morale soit une obligation imposée (= externe). Avec *must*, l'énonciateur cautionne cette obligation morale, pas forcément avec have to. *Have got to* remplace souvent *must*, surtout dans la langue parlée :

*We've **got to**/we **have to**/we really **must** go now.* (obligation « interne »)
Nous sommes obligés de partir maintenant.
*I **have to** wear a tie at the office.* (obligation « externe »)
Je dois porter la cravate au bureau.

• Attention aux formes négatives :

*You **mustn't** park here.* (= interdiction)
Il est interdit de se garer ici.
You **don't have to** *park here.* (= absence d'obligation)
Tu n'es pas obligé de te garer ici.

• L'absence d'obligation peut aussi être exprimée par *don't need to (US, UK)* ou *needn't (UK).*

Wordbank

AANZFTA	*le bloc commercial ASEAN + Australie + la Nouvelle-Zélande*
an active volcano	*un volcan actif*
anti-nuclear policy	*la politique anti-nucléaire*
ANZAC day	*journée du souvenir des combattants de la première Guerre mondiale*
an awesome landscape	*un paysage impressionnant*
cattle breeding	*l'élevage de bétail*
to chart	*établir des cartes*
collective wage negotiation	*les négociations salariales collectives*
a Crown health enterprise	*un établissement hospitalier autonome*
a cultural mix	*un mélange culturel*
the district health board	*le fournisseur régional de services de santé*
the economic hub	*le centre économique névralgique*
ethnic conflict	*le conflit ethnique*
female suffrage	*le suffrage féminin*
the food-processing industry	*l'industrie agro-alimentaire*
a government transfer	*une allocation*

a haka	*une danse guerrière traditionnelle*
a healthcare supplier	*un fournisseur de soins médicaux*
the House of Representatives	*la Chambre des députés*
a kiwi	*un kiwi (oiseau ou fruit), un néo-zélandais non-maori (fam.)*
laid-back	*décontracté*
the legal minimim wage	*le salaire minimum légal*
a lush countryside	*une campagne luxuriante*
the mainstay of the economy	*le pilier de l'économie*
a Maori	*un Maori*
means testing	*une enquête de ressources*
an outlying island	*une île au large*
outspokenness	*le franc-parler*
a poverty-associated disease	*une maladie associée à la pauvreté*
the quality of life	*la qualité de vie*
relocation costs	*les frais de déménagement*
Royal Assent	*l'assentiment royal*
a self-governing island dependency	*une île souveraine associée*
silver fern	*la fougère argentée symbole de la Nouvelle-Zélande*
a skilled migrant	*un immigrant qualifié*
social legislation	*la législation sociale*
a spiralling health budget	*la montée en flèche des coûts de santé*
the student loan entitlement	*le droit aux prêts étudiants*
subsidised healthcare	*les soins médicaux subventionnés*
turmoil	*l'agitation*
unicameral	*unicaméral*
a whaler	*un baleinier*
a widely-scattered landmass	*des terres très éparpillées*
to wipe out	*éradiquer*
a work permit	*un permis de travail*

Translation

Translate the sentences into English.

1. La Nouvelle-Zélande doit continuer à donner facilement des permis de travail aux travailleurs très qualifiés pour garantir la croissance économique.

2. Tu ne dois pas réduire la Nouvelle-Zélande à la fougère argentée et à la danse traditionelle des All Blacks : c'est avant tout un centre économique important pour la zone Pacifique.

3. Tu n'as pas besoin de t'inquiéter au sujet des frais de déménagement, c'est ton futur employeur qui doit les prendre en charge.

4. Il faut que le gouvernement maîtrise la montée en flèche des coûts de santé pour préserver le système des soins subventionnés.

5. Les néo-zélandais blancs doivent respecter les coutumes maoris pour ne pas créer de conflits ethniques.

Read and answer

Read the article and then do activities A and B that follow.

All Black great joins race row

A second All Black legend has thrown fuel on the rugby racism fire by claiming Pacific players need things explained with "simple concepts". Twenty-one test veteran Bernie Fraser's outburst followed Andy Haden's claim that the success of the Crusaders Super 14 franchise was based on their selection of "three darkies, no more". Fiji-born Fraser said yesterday: "In terms of Pacific Islanders, if you have too many of them, what they need are simple concepts." He said his conclusions were based on his experience of coaching Fijians. "If you say something to them they all nod, typical because they're shy they say 'yes, yes, yes' - then they go away and do something totally different. It's a fact."

Race Relations Commissioner Joris de Bres also entered the fray last night and said the episode was more evidence rugby was mired in a racist past. Canterbury and New Zealand Rugby Union officials have strenuously denied the quota allegations. [...]

Haden last night offered a qualified apology for his comments. "I apologise if anyone was offended by my use of the term 'darkies' - it wasn't made with the intention of offending anyone." But he blamed "PC types" for the criticism he was receiving. "My crime appears to be my age."

All Black and Samoa legend Michael Jones has spoken of his personal offence at Haden's use of the word "darkie". "It's certainly not a word that should be thrown out on national TV. I think it's totally disrespectful, and a slap in the face." But Fraser said he had no problems with Haden's use of such language. "I don't have any problem with the term 'darkie' being used. I mean, Christ, when I was playing I was the biggest racist out," he said. "I regard myself as a coconut and I call every other Polynesian a coconut." He blamed the furore created by Haden's comments on over-sensitivity. "I think we are so bloody PC now it's bloody disgraceful."

Fraser said he heard about a racial quota [...] He said it was a winning strategy, but stressed the ethnicity rule shouldn't be absolute, pointing to Hurricanes flanker – and law and commerce graduate – Victor Vito.

"If I was a coach with a quota system I wouldn't put him in that category because look, he is a super-sharp dude."

Fraser said there was unlikely to be any hard evidence to support allegations of racial quotas. "You'd be mad to put that in writing, wouldn't you? You'd have the race relations people hunting you."

De Bres last night drew parallels with the "darkies" incident and the overdue apology to Maori players over non-selection for tours to apartheid-era South Africa. "Codes like rugby union are still needing to move from the 20th to the 21st century – and that business of the apology was evidence of that," he said.

Rugby had been at the forefront of promoting Maori and Polynesian players, De Bres said, but the management of the game was monochromatic. "They need to open up their decision-making to a more diverse community – they've got to engage more. If they open this up, the culture will change."

New Zealand Rugby Union chief executive Steve Tew said last night he would not enter into "a public slanging match with the race relations conciliator". Tew conceded

...

...

the NZRU board wasn't especially diverse. He said the All Black squad named today would be more reflective of New Zealand society. And he said the "vast majority" of people involved in rugby were "decent, fair-minded and balanced" but there would be "rednecks" on the margins.

Carolyne Meng-Yee & Matt Nippert, *The New Zealand Herald* (nzherald.co.nz), 30/5/2010

A. Language

Find synonyms in paragraphs 1, 2 and 7 of the article for the following: *former star of the New Zealand rugby team, has made worse, asserting, explosion/attack, allegation, joined the battle, was tarnished with, vigorously/forcefully, concrete proof.*

B. Question

What is the race row over the All Blacks about? (Answer in 100-150 words. Use information in the article but do not copy sentences directly: use your own words.)

Translation

Translate the article into English.

Le prince William acclamé en Nouvelle-Zélande

Le prince William a été acclamé, lundi 18 janvier, par plusieurs milliers de personnes en Nouvelle-Zélande, où il effectue sa première visite officielle à l'étranger au nom de la reine Elizabeth II.

Arrivé dimanche, le prince, âgé de 27 ans et deuxième dans l'ordre de succession au trône d'Angleterre, a inauguré le nouveau bâtiment de la Cour suprême à Wellington.

Il a été acclamé par 3.000 à 4.000 personnes lors de son arrivée, drapé dans un costume d'apparat maori orné de plumes, tandis qu'un groupe de « guerriers » torse nu l'a accueilli par un célèbre Haka maori.

« William, nous t'aimons », lui a lancé une femme dans la foule.

Une autre, revêtue du drapeau néo-zélandais, a estimé que le petit-fils de la reine était un exemple pour la jeunesse. « J'apprécie le fait que c'est un modèle pour mes enfants. Il est animé de compassion, pas comme toutes ces rock stars », a déclaré Sue Reid.

« Tu ressembles exactement à ta mère, Lady Diana », lui a crié une autre admiratrice. Le prince William a ensuite pris un bain de foule, multipliant les poignées de main et remerciant le public pour son enthousiasme.

Un petit groupe de manifestants républicains a toutefois déroulé une banderole: « Le temps de la République est venu », sur le passage du prince mais sans perturber sa visite.

La Nouvelle-Zélande est une monarchie constitutionnelle, dont le chef de l'État, aux fonctions essentiellement honorifiques, est la reine d'Angleterre Elizabeth II représentée à Wellington par un gouverneur général.

Le Nouvel Observateur (nouvelobs.com), 18/1/2010

Overview

Read a general overview of the subject.

Protecting the environment and protecting people

Present-day New Zealand could well be mistaken for a sort of paradise. You have only to look at the international league tables concerning quality of life, happiness, life expectancy, political freedom and so on, and you will find New Zealand in the top ten in most categories. It has long been forward-looking in its social policies. For example, it was the first country to give women the vote (1893) and one of the first to adopt old age pensions (1898). Those who applaud New Zealand's social achievements also tend to admire the country's ecologically-aware "nuclear-free" image – none too popular with the USA. However, New Zealand's recent economic recovery, due largely to free market policies operated along lines that would have been applauded by Reagan and Thatcher, is an embarrassing slap in the face for those who unthinkingly place environmental concerns and monetarism at opposite ends of the political spectrum. Recent policies have brought New Zealand into the limelight: tourism is on the increase, unemployment is at an all-time low, and, because of its amazing and varied scenery, more and more big-budget movies (such as *Lord of the Rings)* are being filmed there.

The nation has a strong attachment to Maori culture. Even Kiwis (New Zealanders of European origin) seem to accept this as part of the natural order. Logically, such an attachment seems disproportionate given that 73% of the population is of European descent and, after all, the Maoris only arrived in New Zealand some 400 years before the Europeans, so they have no claim to a "First Nation" status. Why then has the haka become part of the All Blacks' pre-match ritual? Why has Maori been an official language since 1987 even though only 4% of the population speak it? Is New Zealand just jumping on the ethnic bandwagon that brings in the tourist dollars or is it guilt over something in the past? Unlike the Aborigines of Australia, the Maoris signed a treaty with Britain about land rights and sovereignty (the Treaty of Waitangi in 1840). However, violations of the treaty by both settlers and Maoris led to the Land Wars of 1845-72, after which a great deal of Maori land was confiscated, provoking long-lasting resentment on the part of the Maoris. Could it be that the highlighting of Maori culture is a way for Kiwis to clear their consciences?

Pronunciation

Listen and repeat.

heart [hɑːt], **height** [haɪt]

- cart/kite, bark/bike, calm/fine, tart/tight, martyr/mitre.
- Mike left his mark on Bart's kite.

Chapter 37

Ireland

Language focus

Les propositions relatives

- Les pronoms relatifs sujets :

*the man **who/that** lives next door*	l'homme **qui** vit dans la maison à côté
*the car **which/that** is parked outside my house*	la voiture **qui** est garé devant chez moi

- Les pronoms relatifs compléments (COD et COI) :

*the man **ø/that/who(m)** you admire*	l'homme **que** tu admires
*the car **ø/that/which** I bought*	la voiture **que** j'ai achetée
the girl ***ø/that/who(m)** you were talking to.*	la fille **à qui** tu parlais.

- La traduction de « dont » (possession) :

the girl whose dress is blue — la fille dont la robe est bleue

the car whose colour is so strange / the colour of which is so strange

la voiture dont la couleur est si bizarre

Wordbank

an absentee landowner	*un propriétaire absentéiste*
an asylum seeker	*un demandeur d'asile*
bloodshed	*l'effusion de sang*
a bubble	*une bulle*
the Celtic Tiger	*le Tigre celtique (référence aux tigres asiatiques, économies à haute performance)*
the Celtic/Irish revival	*la renaissance culturelle irlandaise à la fin du XIXe siècle*
a coffin ship	*un navire cercueil (référence aux navires qui coulaient avec leurs passagers, des émigrants)*
Dail Eireann	*le parlement irlandais*
the Easter/1916 rising	*le soulèvement de Pâques*
an economic rescue package	*un plan de sauvetage économique*
economically strapped	*en difficulté économique*
Eire	*nom du pays adopté dans la constitution de 1937*
the Emerald Isle	*l'île d'Émeraude*
Fianna Fail	*un parti politique (fondé en 1926)*
Fine Gael	*un parti politique (fondé en 1933)*
GAA (Gaelic Athletic Association	*association pour la promotion de jeux irlandais*
the Garda	*la police irlandaise*

the housing construction boom	*l'essor du marché immobilier*
hurling	*le* hurling *(jeu de crosse)*
industrial development	*le développement industiel*
the Irish brogue	*l'accent irlandais*
an itinerant population	*une population itinérante*
a landlord	*un propriétaire terrien*
a leaving certificate	*un certificat de fin d'études secondaires*
a membership	*une appartenance*
NAMA (National Asset Management Agency	*agence établie à la suite de la crise financière de 2009/2010*
partition	*la division du pays (1921)*
the potato blight	*le mildiou de la pomme de terre*
public spending cuts	*les réductions de dépenses publiques*
a rack rent	*un loyer exorbitant*
rags-to-riches	*de la misère à la richesse*
a settlement	*une installation*
the shamrock	*le trèfle*
Sinn Fein	*un parti politique (fondé en 1905)*
a stalemate	*un point mort*
a staple food	*une nourriture de base*
stout	*la bière brune*
a strained relationship	*des rapports tendus*
the Taoiseach	*le Premier ministre*
a TD (Teachta Dála)	*un député*
the 26 counties	*les 26 comtés, référence à la composition de la république*
the tricolour	*le drapeau irlandais*
an underlying economic problem	*un problème économique sous-jacent*
an uprising	*un soulèvement*
a wave of emigration	*une vague d'émigration*

Translation

Translate the sentences into English.

1. William Butler Yeats est l'écrivain irlandais de langue anglaise qui a initié la renaissance culturelle irlandaise à la fin du XIXe siècle.

2. La maladie qui a condamné une partie de la population à la famine au milieu du XIXe siècle est le mildiou de la pomme de terre.

3. L'accent irlandais qu'on peut entendre dans un pub au fin fond du Donegal est très différent de l'anglais de la BBC.

4. Quelques propriétaires terriens dont les cultures furent ravagées par le mildiou passèrent de la richesse à la misère en un clin d'œil.

5. Le drapeau irlandais – dont les 3 couleurs sont le vert, le blanc et l'orange – symbolise la fierté de tout un peuple.

Read and answer

Read the article and then do activities A and B that follow.

Lenihan hails Yes vote as a rejection of 'junk politics'

The resounding Yes to Lisbon was hailed by Finance Minister Brian Lenihan as an emphatic rejection of the "junk politics" of the far left who want Ireland to descend into a bunker of economic isolationism.

Mr Lenihan said that passing the second referendum on the treaty was an important first step towards economic recovery, but he warned that tougher decisions lay ahead. Obviously relieved at the endorsement of Lisbon, Mr Lenihan insisted that the Government would not engage in any celebratory parties. "I am very grateful to the Irish people for the vote we have received today. That is a collective decision of the Irish people, not a decision of the Government," he said.

But Mr Lenihan also sounded a word of caution about the challenges that lay ahead. "We are in a very difficult place and that is precisely why people have voted Yes; because they know that our markets, our economic future, lies with the other European countries," he said.

He rejected claims by No campaigners, including Richard Boyd Barrett, that the referendum had been presented by the Government as a job-creation programme. "That is simply not correct. We are going to get jobs by being competitive, by selling our goods and services to other countries, by attracting visitors to our own country. That's real economics."

"What I saw in this debate is a growing realisation among the people that junk economics and junk politics from far-left politicians are not going to solve any of our problems," he declared.

He suggested that what he found on the doorsteps during his canvass was a realistic assessment among the electorate that our best interests are bound up in Europe. "It wasn't about fear, it was about where we belong. A Yes vote was a positive vote which says that the Irish people are engaging with Europe, working on the problems together, working on our banking problems with the help of the Commission of the European Central Bank and, above all, on our job creation problems, our markets, and how we can get economic growth going again," he said. "We can't retreat into economic nationalism or economic isolationism, and that's been the subtext of some of the far-left opposition to this treaty. They wanted a bunker established in Ireland which would not solve Ireland's problems, and I think everyone recognised this during the campaign," he added. "We are in a very difficult economic position and this Yes vote is a very essential first step towards recovery," Mr Lenihan said. But he stressed there were other steps that had to be taken. "We, as a government, take no pleasure from this. But we are doing what is right for this country and I'm delighted that the people of Ireland have seen where Ireland's future lies. That is what's good about this result. It will inspire confidence in Ireland all over Europe."

Mr Lenihan said his view was that the Yes vote was grounded in a new realism. "A great deal of realism entered this debate. The Irish people have always known that their economic destiny is bound up with Europe and, when the recession developed since the last referendum, people recognised that."

...

...

Mr Lenihan said he had not felt free to say it during the campaign, but as Finance Minister he was meeting an emerging hostility in European circles. "They wanted to know whether or not Ireland was interested in working with other countries," he said.

Jerome Reilly, *Sunday Independent* (independent.ie), 4/10/2009

A. Language

Find synonyms in paragraphs 3 to 7 of the article for the following: *a warning, the difficulties looming ahead, depends on, a growing awareness, worthless/useless, election campaign, hidden agenda, underlined, was based on.*

B. Question

How does the Irish Finance Minister justify the government's support for the Lisbon European treaty? (Answer in 100-150 words. Use information in the article but do not copy sentences directly: use your own words.)

Translation

Translate the article into English.

Invitation historique de la reine d'Angleterre en Irlande

LONDRES. Le Premier ministre irlandais, Brian Cowen, a invité la reine Elizabeth II à se rendre en visite en République d'Irlande en estimant que l'amélioration des relations bilatérales avait ouvert la voie pour un premier déplacement d'un monarque britannique dans le sud de l'île Emeraude.

La République d'Irlande, qui comprend les 26 comtés du sud de l'île, fut reconnue par la Grande-Bretagne le 6 décembre 1921. Mais le Sinn Fein et l'IRA refusèrent le rattachement des six comtés d'Ulster au Royaume-Uni, d'où de sanglantes violences communautaires entre protestants pro-britanniques et catholiques républicains qui firent 3.600 morts dans les trente dernières années du XXe siècle.

Ces violences ont pris fin aux termes des accords du 10 avril 1998 prévoyant un partage du pouvoir entre les deux communautés d'Irlande du Nord.

« Il n'existe plus aujourd'hui d'obstacles [...] à des visites de courtoisie normales entre des États voisins et amis par le biais de leurs chefs d'État », a expliqué le Premier ministre irlandais à la télévision d'État RTE après avoir rencontré à Londres son homologue britannique, David Cameron.

« Je pense que ce serait un heureux développement », a dit Cowen à propos d'une visite de la reine. « Il est temps aujourd'hui d'aller de l'avant dans nos relations. »

Selon Cowen, cette visite pourrait intervenir avant l'expiration, fin 2011, du mandat de la présidente irlandaise Mary McAleese.

À Londres, une source proche du palais de Buckingham a fait savoir que les projets de déplacement de la reine ne faisaient pas l'objet de commentaires à l'avance.

Reuters (dans *Le Nouvel Observateur* [nouvelobs.com]), 24/6/2010

Overview

Read a general overview of the subject.

The Celtic Tiger

Ireland lies on the north-western rim of Euro-27. Although the Romans appear not to have invaded it, the Vikings landed in the 9th century followed by The Normans and successive waves of English and Scottish colonists (Plantation), in the 16th and 17th centuries, who were to put Ireland under English commercial, economic and political dominion until the 20th century. If today's population is 4.4m, it is estimated that millions have emigrated over the past two centuries giving Ireland its own Diaspora. Indeed, when the country's staple food, the potato, suffered blight in the mid 19th century, perhaps 1 million died on the spot, and 1 million fled by sea, most notably to England and America – a flight that was to have lasting repercussions on future generations. Ireland was shaken by insurrection and revolution until partition in 1921. Following division came civil war and the birth of the Irish Free State, the 26 counties becoming a republic in 1949.

Today's Eire is a parliamentary democracy with a president whose powers are limited, and although just under 170km separates Dublin from Belfast, politicians did not visit each other until 1965. With the Belfast agreement of 1998 came a change in the constitution stipulating that Irish national unity could only be achieved with the consent of people both north and south and, in 2007, the N.I. Assembly met with its executive in the presence of governments both British and Irish.

The tourist industry is one of the key elements of the Irish economy, generating billions of euros per annum, with thousands of SMEs depending on it. However, fiscal incentives combined with low wages, an educationally-mature strata of young labour, EU help, and investment in learning led to two decades of the "Celtic Tiger". From exporting agricultural produce, the country was to become one of Europe's major software service initiators.

The country went through a boom between the mid-nineties and the beginning of the economic crisis of 2008-2009. As a result of that crisis, from a boom, the economy contracted, leading the government to take a series of austerity measures under NAMA, including wage freezes, and civil service cutbacks.

There is no official religion nor is the president a defender of any faith, but the Catholic Church has traditionally been very strong in Eire. Abortion is illegal and divorce has only been possible since the referendum of 1995.

Pronunciation

Listen and repeat.

by [baɪ], **boy** [bɔɪ]

- tile/toil, kind/coined, giant/joint, pint/point, isle/oil, vice/voice.
- The kind giant toiled for a pint on the Island of Vice.

38 Chapter

South Africa

Language focus

La traduction de ce qui/ce que

- Avec *what* (= ce qui/ce que), on annonce quelque chose qui vient après :
  ***What** makes me happy is knowing that she is safe.*
  Ce qui me rend heureux, c'est de savoir qu'elle est en sécurité.
  ***What** I like best is pasta.*
  Ce que je préfère, c'est les pâtes.
- Avec *which* (= ce qui), on reprend une proposition qui se trouve avant dans le texte :
  *She is safe, **which** makes me happy.*
  Elle est en sécurité, **ce qui** me rend heureux.
- Le verbe qui suit *which* est toujours à la 3e personne du singulier.

Wordbank

the advent of democracy	*l'avènement de la démocratie*
affirmative action	*la discrimination positive*
an Afrikaner	*un afrikaner (sud-africain blanc d'origine néerlandaise)*
AIDS	*le SIDA*
the ANC (African National Congress)	*le parti politique majoritaire*
apartheid	*l'apartheid (la politique de ségrégation)*
the black middle class	*la classe moyenne noire*
blood diamonds	*les diamants sales*
a Boer	*un pionnier-agriculteur d'origine néérlandaise*
a breakaway state	*un État dissident*
to bribe	*soudoyer*
coal-generated power	*l'énergie à base de charbon*
commodities	*les matières premières*
to curb crime	*freiner le crime*
a deep-rooted belief	*une croyance profondément enracinée*
a diamond mine	*une mine de diamants*
to empower	*habiliter*
the energy crunch	*la crise énergétique*
a goldseam	*un filon d'or*
Grade "R"	*la première année de scolarisation*
the Great Trek	*la Grande marche 1835-1843 (migration de Boers vers l'est face à l'expansionnisme des Britanniques)*
a township	*(à l'origine) ville/village réservé(e) aux « non blancs »*

grinding poverty	*la misère noire*
the health train	*le « train de la santé » qui dispense soins et formation dans les régions éloignées*
the highveld, the lowveld	*la terre herbeuse*
the homeland	*la terre natale*
a housing voucher	*une subvention pour construction immobilière*
the illiteracy rate	*le taux d'analphabétisation*
land issues	*des problèmes de foncier*
land reform	*la réforme agraire*
the legacy of apartheid	*l'héritage de l'apartheid*
Matric(ulation)	*la dernière année de scolarisation secondaire (*Grade 12*)*
the mining industry	*l'industrie minière*
the natural resources	*les ressources naturelles*
the National Legislature	*le parlement sud-africain*
a power shortage	*carences énergétiques*
the rainbow nation	*la nation arc-en-ciel*
the rand	*le rand (monnaie sud-africaine)*
a shack	*une cabane*
a shantytown	*un bidonville*
a shortage of skilled labour	*un manque de main d'œuvre qualifiée*
to stave off	*retarder*
a Technikon	*un établissement technologique supérieur*
a vuvuzela	*une corne bruyante*
whites/blacks only	*zones pour seuls blancs/noirs*
white, coloured, black	*les trois catégories raciales reconnues par les gouvernements ségrégationistes*
wrongdoing	*des méfaits*

Translation

Translate the sentences into English.

1. La fin de l'apartheid a permis à la classe moyenne noire de se développer, ce qui est vital à la fois pour la démocratie et l'économie.

2. Ce qui permet d'espérer de nets progrès pour le pays, ce sont ses immenses richesses naturelles.

3. Ce que le monde entier a fini par condamner, c'est l'apartheid, qui était basé sur la ségrégation raciale.

4. Ce qui inquiète les touristes étrangers, c'est le fort taux de criminalité dans les grandes villes du pays.

5. Ce qui rend la nation arc-en-ciel si fascinante, c'est le mélange d'espaces urbains ultra-modernes et de majestueux paysages.

Read and answer

Read the article and then do activities A and B that follow.

South Africa: When the whistle blows

South Africans can be proud about hosting the World Cup. Less so about the state of their nation

Ke nako! It is time! On June 11th the opening match of the football World Cup takes place at Soccer City near Soweto, a sprawling black township outside Johannesburg. For the past four years South Africa has been preparing to host the world's greatest sporting event after the Olympics – the first African nation to do so in the tournament's 80-year history. Sceptics said South Africa would never make it. But, billions of dollars and much heartache later, it is ready. With ten spectacular new or upgraded stadiums, as many new or revamped airports, hundreds of kilometres of expanded highways and city streets, and the continent's first high-speed train up and running (just), South Africa is rightly proud of its achievement.

And not only in preparing for the World Cup. South Africa boasts private companies, banks, financial markets and auditing standards that are as good as any, anywhere. It is Africa's largest economy (and the world's 24th-biggest), accounting for 40% of sub-Saharan Africa's total GDP. It is also by far the most sophisticated, open and democratic country in the region, with one of the most progressive constitutions anywhere. It is the only African member of the G20 and has just been nominated for a (second) two-year seat on the Security Council, the UN's decision-making body, starting in January. The country is leader of a continent that has weathered the financial crisis surprisingly well, thanks largely to its fabulous mineral wealth. In some African countries attitudes have slowly begun to shift away from the backing of "big men" towards a more accountable sort of democracy.

Yet South Africa struggles, for all that. […] The threats and flaws it must overcome would make even the bravest reformer quail: rampant corruption and patronage throughout the public sector; the world's highest unemployment rate, with more than one in three out of work; one in eight of the population infected with HIV/AIDS; public hospitals described as "death traps" by their own health minister; 80% of schools deemed dysfunctional; terrible drug and alcohol abuse; crumbling infrastructure; lethal roads. Thanks to black-empowerment policies, a small new black middle class has emerged, yet more than 40% of the population still lives on less than $2 a day. Tragically, since the end of apartheid inequality in South Africa has grown.

The African National Congress and its leader, South Africa's president, Jacob Zuma, did not create this mess, but they will have to sort it out. Just 16 years ago the ANC inherited a country that was virtually bankrupt, riven with racial hostility and wracked by poverty. Although there have certainly been improvements, those living without jobs in shoddy homes in poor black townships need more. Many of the young are getting desperate. Violent protests are spreading.

More than ever the country needs strong political leadership. After one year in office, the polygamous, ever-charming Mr Zuma is doing better than many critics had feared. He has been making all the right noises on things like corruption, crime, poverty and

...

...

education. But as the coming attacks from within his own faction-ridden party mount, he seems to lack vision and drive. He needs to show he can get things done. Some wonder whether he will even be able complete his five-year mandate. As the anthems draw to a close and the players take their positions to start football's great tournament, South Africa can allow itself a moment of satisfaction. But a daunting amount of work lies ahead.

The Economist (economist.com), 3/6/2010

A. Language

Find synonyms in paragraphs 1, 2, 3 and 5 of the article for the following: *untidy and tentacular, to accommodate/to welcome, improved, is proud to have, representing, the support of major economic players, flinch/shake, uncontrolled, nepotism and partiality, estimated inefficient, delegating power to the black community, to be short of ideas and energy, a discouraging workload.*

B. Question

What are the strengths and weaknesses of South Africa? (Answer in 200-250 words. Use information in the article but do not copy sentences directly: use your own words.)

Translation

Translate the article into English.

Vingt ans après Mandela, la misère perdure en Afrique du Sud

Vingt ans après la libération de Nelson Mandela, l'Afrique du Sud connaît une vie démocratique intense, mais une grande partie de la population est toujours plongée dans la misère.

La libération de l'icone de la lutte anti-apartheid le 11 février 1990, au terme de 27 ans d'emprisonnement, avait débouché sur la tenue historique d'élections multiraciales en 1994 et l'élection du premier président noir d'Afrique du Sud, permettant au pays d'accéder au rang de démocratie. [...]

Mais vingt ans après ce jour historique de février 1990, beaucoup de noirs sud-africains continuent de vivre dans une extrême pauvreté dans des bidonvilles sordides. [...]

Le taux officiel de chômage se situe tout juste en dessous de 25 %, mais serait en fait plus élevé selon les analystes. [...]

Au moins 34 % des 50 millions de Sud-Africains vivent avec moins de deux dollars par jour, selon la Banque mondiale.

Après avoir connu une période de croissance record, l'économie sud-africaine, plombée par la crise économique mondiale, est entrée en récession au début de l'année 2009.

Même si le pays est aujourd'hui sorti de la récession, les analystes prévoient une croissance à la traîne des autres pays émergents. Seule une restructuration importante, selon eux, pourrait renverser la tendance.

Reuters (dans *Le Point* [lepoint.fr]), 9/2/2010

Overview

Read a general overview of the subject.

Apartheid and after

On paper, because of its climate and resources, the "Rainbow Nation" of South Africa seems like a wonderful place to live. It certainly *was* wonderful for white South Africans under apartheid, a concept of racial separation that had its roots in the desire of white settlers for dominance over the native black population. Laws passed after the Second World War separated the population into three groups: whites, blacks and coloureds (which included those of Asian descent). Inter-racial marriage was forbidden and access to certain jobs was restricted to whites. In 1951, the Bantu Authorities Act created "homelands" to which every African was assigned: they were to become citizens of the homelands and were no longer considered citizens of South Africa. Henceforward, in order to travel in and out of white areas, they had to carry passes. Then, in 1953 and 1960 came even harsher measures, imposing strict penalties for any dissent and finally establishing martial law. After a revolt at Sharpeville in 1960, which left many dead, activists – including Nelson Mandela – began a sort of guerilla war against the government.

Mandela was imprisoned in 1964 but the activities of his party, the ANC (African National Congress) continued and voices of protest from personalities like Desmond Tutu, the black Archishop of Cape Town, were heard all over the world. Eventually, trade sanctions and overall exclusion from the international community forced South Africa into realising that apartheid had to end. Mandela was released and the ANC came to power in 1994 after the first ever universal elections in South Africa.

Since then, it has to be said that not everything has gone swimmingly. The ANC was left with an economy that had suffered from years of trade sanctions that had prevented goods from being exported. Measures have been introduced to boost production and employment, but a lot needs to be done. Prosperity is still concentrated in the four main cities and, outside these urban areas, there is massive poverty. In fact, since 1994, poverty and unemployment levels have increased among the black population despite the rise of the black middle class. Crime levels have not been reduced either: South Africa has the highest murder rate in the world. There are also doubts surrounding the policies of the ANC: some fear that the country might lapse into the racism of Zimbabwe or the tribalism of Rwanda, instead of showing to the rest of the world that post-apartheid South Africa can govern itself as well as any Western democracy.

Pronunciation

Listen and repeat.

rate [reɪt], **right** [raɪt]

- fate/fight, race/rice, paint/pint, bait/bite, today/to die, late/light.
- You'll be right as rain after a pint of ale!

Chapter 39

India

Language focus

Les questions indirectes

• À la différence du français, l'ordre des mots dans les questions indirectes est *toujours* celui des affirmations, pas des questions directes :

Who is that beautiful girl? Who is she? (questions directes)
Qui est cette belle fille ? Qui est-elle ?
I wonder who that beautiful girl is. I wonder who she is. (questions indirectes)
Je me demande qui est celle belle fille. Je me demande qui elle est.
What does that word mean? What does it mean? (questions directes)
Que veut dire ce mot ? Que veut-il dire ?
Tell me what that word means. Tell me what it means. (questions indirectes)
Dis-moi ce que ce mot veut dire. Dis-moi ce qu'il veut dire.

Wordbank

Bollywood	*l'industrie du film basée à Mumbai (étymologie : Bombay + Hollywood)*
bond labour, debt bondage	*l'asservissement en remboursement de dette*
buffer food stocks	*des réserves de nourriture en cas d'urgence*
the caste system	*le système des castes*
child labour	*la main d'œuvre infantile*
the child literacy rate	*le taux d'alphabétisation infantile*
the child survival rate	*le taux de survie infantile*
the craft industry	*l'artisanat*
the dalit community	*les sans-caste, les intouchables*
to deny opportunites	*refuser des opportunités*
to die of starvation	*mourir de faim*
Diwali	*Diwali, le festival de lumière*
drought	*la sécheresse*
an earthquake	*un tremblement de terre*
an emerging market	*un marché émergent*
famine	*la famine*
a fast-growing economy	*une économie en croissance rapide*
flooding	*l'inondation*
foodgrain production	*la production de céréales*
gender-based discrimination	*la discrimination sexuelle*

the green revolution	*la révolution verte (de nouvelles pratiques agricoles à partir de 1995)*
a harvest	*une moisson*
high-scale urbanisation	*l'urbanisation intense*
insidious	*insidieux*
the landless poor	*les pauvres sans terres*
to look down on	*mépriser*
micro-credit/-loans	*le micro-crédit*
outsourcing	*la délocalisation*
patriarchal traditions	*la culture patriarcale*
populous	*populeux*
the prevalence of disease	*la fréquence des maladies*
the livelihood	*le gagne-pain*
sati, suttee	*sati (la pratique interdite de l'immolation funéraire)*
a slum area	*une zone insalubre*
a slum dweller	*l'habitant d'un taudis*
software engineering	*l'ingénierie logicielle*
street children	*les enfants des rues*
a sullied well	*un puits souillé*
undernourishment	*la sous-alimentation*
universal food entitlements	*les droits alimentaires universels*
the untouchables	*les intouchables*
the urban poor	*les démunis des villes*
the urban water supply	*l'approvisionnement en eau par le service des eaux*

Translation

Translate the sentences into English.

1. Je me demande où se trouvent les studios de Bollywood.

2. Le professeur d'histoire nous a expliqué comment le système des castes fonctionne en Inde.

3. On peut se demander pourquoi l'ONU n'interdit pas le travail des enfants dans le monde entier.

4. L'expert nous a démontré comment et pourquoi la discrimination sexuelle menacerait à moyen terme le taux de natalité en Inde.

5. Lors de notre court séjour à Calcutta avec les Simmons, notre guide nous montra comment les habitants les plus démunis survivent au jour le jour.

Read and answer

Read the article and then do activities A and B that follow.

The Indian census and caste: Caste in doubt

The perilous arithmetic of positive discrimination

DELHI. Sixty years after India's constitution banned caste discrimination, Hinduism's millennia-old hierarchy retains a tight grip. Lonely-hearts ads in the newspapers are classified by caste and sub-caste. Brahmins, at the top, dominate many professions. There are still hundreds of "honour killings" by which families avenge inter-caste marriages and liaisons. Caste discrimination is still drearily evident in the wretched lives of dalits, formerly "untouchables", who remain India's poorest and least educated people. It is not surprising, then, that India is considering the inclusion of caste in its ten-yearly census, the next of which is due in 2011.

The proposal has caused a storm of controversy. India has not counted caste in its census since 1931. Many argue that its inclusion would buttress a system that independent India's first leaders railed against. The Congress party, which led the independence struggle, struck caste from government forms and has resisted calls for a nationwide caste count.

However, now heading a coalition government, Congress needs the support of smaller parties, including a number of caste-based groups that have sprung up in recent years, to push through important legislation. A system of affirmative action has given caste greater potency. In 1990 "reservations" in government jobs and university places for dalits were extended to a group of castes slightly higher-up the pecking order, the "Other Backward Classes" (OBCs). Reservations are based on data from the 1931 census. Caste politicians are not alone in arguing that this makes a nonsense of the system.

Counting caste in the census, however, would be difficult, or even impossible. Besides the four main varna, or castes, India has uncounted thousands of sub-castes, few of which census officials will recognise. More worryingly, the count would surely lead to a flood of demands for more reservations; already, the government is battling quota demands from non-OBC castes, Muslims and Christian converts from Hinduism – and a call for reservations to be extended to India's private sector.

Six decades of reservations have done little to better the lot of low-caste Indians. But recent economic growth has been more transformative. As millions have moved to urban areas in search of work, they have left the rigid social groupings of their villages for the relative anonymity of cities, and swapped hereditary trades for jobs in which family background is largely immaterial. Many Indians are becoming caste-blind, and marrying across caste lines. Anidhrudda, a 30-year-old software engineer in Kolkata (Calcutta), says his inter-caste marriage was no big deal. But even he concedes there are limits. If he had married a dalit, he says, "my family would not have been able to face society."

The Economist (economist.com), 10/6/2010

A. Language

Find synonyms in the first three paragraphs of the article for the following: *prohibited, take revenge on, love affairs, obvious, has stirred up, reinforce/strengthen, leading, have emerged/mushroomed, power.*

B. Questions

Answer each of the following questions in 50 words. Use information in the article to answer but do not copy sentences directly: use your own words.

1. Is the caste system still alive in India?

2. Why is the 2011 census a controversial issue?

3. To what extent has affirmative action been positive for the country?

Translation

Translate the article into English.

L'Inde aurait été touchée de toutes façons par le ralentissement

Jean-Joseph Boillot, économiste membre du CEPII, revient sur la situation économique du pays. Dans quelle situation économique le parti vainqueur trouvera-t-il le pays ?

On ne peut pas parler de véritable crise de l'économie indienne puisqu'il n'y a pas de mouvement de panique économique et financière. Pour l'instant il s'agit plutôt d'un fort, très fort ralentissement puisqu'on passe de 9 % à 4-5 %. L'ampleur du choc est lié à la conjugaison du cycle domestique et de la crise global. D'une part, au niveau strictement interne, l'Inde est en effet dans une situation « post exubérance ». Entre 2002 et 2009, le PIB du pays croissait au rythme insoutenable de 9 % avec une inflation salariale importante et une économie d'endettement comme ailleurs. [...]

En trois plans de stimulation budgétaire et monétaire, il a ainsi dépensé au quelques mois l'équivalent de 6 points de PIB. Les mesures ont été relativement efficaces pour soutenir la consommation, notamment celle des classes populaires, celles qui font les élections dans ce pays. Mais inversement, il a aussi contribué à creuser considérablement le déficit du pays. On peut parler d'un véritable dérapage fiscal. Le gouvernement, qui prendra le pouvoir, trouvera des caisses vide. Compte tenu d'un déficit extérieur qui se creuse rapidement et d'échéances financières majeures prévues en 2009, il n'est évidemment pas exclu que l'Inde doive faire appel au Fonds monétaire international si la crise internationale restait forte, si le résultat des élections était fortement instable et enfin si la mousson était exécrable. Mais on en n'est pas encore là. Comme le dit un proverbe indien : « La liane plie mais ne rompt pas ».

Adeline Haverland, *L'Expansion* (lexpansion.com), 17/4/2010

Overview

Read a general overview of the subject.

Rags and riches

India was famously known as the Jewel in the Crown – the most valuable of all the lands that made up the British Empire. It was both a supplier of cheap raw materials (like cotton for the mills of Northern England) and a captive market for British goods. When it came under the rule of the British crown in 1859, India was a vast country with a recorded history dating back over 2,000 years, a rigid caste and class system, a highly complex mix of religions and beliefs, and a culture that could rival any other in sophistication. Had it not been for India's fierce and never-ending internal conflict, it is unlikely that Britain could ever have done any more than trade with it. But instead, it subjugated India for nearly a hundred years. It is unfashionable these days to see any positive aspects in 19th century colonialism, but it is interesting to note two major effects of such a long period of "cultural proximity": (1) there is a solid parliamentary democracy in India and (2) curry is top of the favourite food list in Britain (ahead of fish and chips).

Probably one of the biggest mistakes Britain ever made in its colonial affairs was the partition of India when it became independent in 1947. The creation of the Moslem state of Pakistan caused massive migration – and massacres – and left the subcontinent irreversibly divided. It also led to an influx of Indian and Pakistani immigrants into Britain, which has created its own problems in the long run.

For a long period after independence, India was ruled by socialist governments with protectionist policies which, instead of boosting the national economy, led to corruption and stagnation. With a change to free-market policies in the early 1990s, India now has one of the fastest-growing economies in the world. This has been helped by the establishment of Banglalore as a vibrant centre for high-tech industries.

At the same time, there is still widespread poverty. Westerners arriving for the first time in cities like Calcutta or Delhi are taken aback by the sheer number of beggars and by the shocking contrast between the blocks of luxury apartments that are rising every day and the appalling living conditions in the nearby slums. But this is nothing new; India has always had these extreme contrasts, and not all of them can be resolved overnight by Western-style solutions.

Pronunciation

Listen and repeat.

grade [greɪd], **greed** [gri:d]

- shape/sheep, hate/heat, great/greet, whale/wheel, mail/meal, maid/meat.
- The maid hates baked meat but loves cakes made from wheat.

40 Chapter

Languages

Language focus

Expressions de la cause et de la conséquence

• La langue anglaise dispose de différents outils pour exprimer ces relations (des conjonctions, des prépositions, des adverbes…) :

He came here ***because*** *he wanted to win.* (parce que)
Since/as *it was late, they decided to stay.* (puisque)
In view of/Given/Owing to/Because of *the strike, they…* (à cause de)
He killed her ***out of*** *jealousy.* (par)
There was a strike. ***Consequently,/Therefore/That's why*** *he couldn't leave* (c'est pourquoi)

• Les constructions correlatives :

He is ***so*** *hard-working* ***that*** *he hardly ever goes out.*
Il est si assidu qu'il ne sort presque jamais.
They made ***such*** *noise* ***that*** *the neighbours came over.*
Ils ont fait un tel vacarme que les voisins sont venus.
Don't be ***so*** *stupid* ***as to*** *believe him.*
Ne sois pas assez idiot pour le croire.

Wordbank

an associate official language	*une langue officielle associée*
basic communication skills	*les compétences de base en communication*
a borrowing	*un emprunt*
casual language	*la langue décontractée/informelle*
cockney	*un argot londonien dérivé du milieu du crime (cf. le verlan)*
a driving force	*un moteur*
an economic steamroller	*un rouleau compresseur économique*
the English language industry	*l'industrie de la langue anglaise*
English language requirements	*des pré-requis en langue anglaise*
the English market	*le marché de l'enseignement de l'anglais*
estuary English *(pej.)*	*la façon de parler des classes ouvrières de l'est de Londres (estuaire de la Tamise)*
the first/native language	*la première langue*
fluency	*la maîtrise*
the focal point	*le point de convergence*
Globish	*nom donné à une sorte d'anglais simplifié, « neutre » (cf. pidgin)*

to hanker after the past	*rêver du passé*
the language barrier	*la barrière de la langue*
leading-edge technology	*la technologie de pointe*
to lose grip	*perdre prise*
a mother tongue	*une langue maternelle*
a native speaker	*un locuteur natif*
an official language	*une langue officielle*
a pattern of communication	*un type de communication*
pidgin	*une langue simplifiée utilisée entre deux personnes qui ne sont pas des locuteurs natifs*
the pitch, the tone	*le ton*
the population flow	*le flux migratoire*
a range of accents	*une gamme/un éventail d'accents*
RP (Received Pronounciation)	*la prononciation standard de l'anglais britannique*
a shortage of teachers	*un manque d'enseignants*
Singlish/Spanglish/etc.	*un anglais (parlé à Singapour/aux États-Unis par des hispanophones…) ponctué par des erreurs volontaires ou des mots étrangers*
a speech habit	*une habitude de parler*
sprinkled with	*saupoudré de*
Standard (American) English	*l'anglais standard (américain)*
to standardise	*normaliser*
the supremacy of English	*la suprématie de l'anglais*
a talking point	*un sujet de discussion*
trade-driven	*dont le moteur est le commerce*
a turning point	*un tournant*
up-to-date	*à jour*
widespread	*étendu*
a working language	*une langue de travail*

Translation

Translate the sentences into English.

1. Ne pensez pas qu'il soit si à l'aise en anglais qu'il puisse faire le discours inaugural à l'assemblée générale.

2. Comme l'anglais est la langue de travail dans le secteur des services, l'industrie de l'enseignement des langues est en plein essor.

3. Je n'ai rien compris à ce qu'il disait car il parle l'anglais de Singapour.

4. Grâce à l'anglais simplifié que tout le monde peut comprendre, la barrière de la langue n'empêche plus de découvrir le monde à sa guise.

5. La maîtrise de l'anglais est obligatoire dans le secteur des technologies de pointe, c'est pourquoi tous les jeunes diplômés doivent améliorer leurs compétences linguistiques.

Read and answer

Read the article and then do activities A and B that follow.

Globish and its discontents

Globish occurs in the news almost every day, in different guises. The news that Obama has authorised the hunting down and elimination of the al-Qaeda mastermind, Anwar al-Awlaki, highlights this Most Wanted Man's mastery of the internet, English, and international propaganda skills. Anwar al-Awlaki posts his jihadist sermons on the internet, using both Arabic and English. He is also said to namecheck US rappers and reach out, rhetorically, to potential Muslim sympathisers in the west. To me, this is a classic example of contemporary Globish, the part-linguistic and part-cultural use of Anglo-American resources. Once again, words (intrinsically neutral) acquire an explosive connotation in conjunction with current events.

I've always known that the English language is a hot-button issue, and two recent posts here [lien] and here [lien] only confirm that. Nor, by the way, does the English language have a monopoly of public, cultural anxiety. French, German, Russian and Spanish speakers will express linguistic-cum-cultural fears. Language is a lightning conductor for one's attitude to the state of the world, and the sense that everything is going to hell in a handcart. […]

But I also detect – without much difficulty, because it's so explicit – something else: a geopolitical class division between some elite US and UK Anglo-English mother-tongue users and some possibly less privileged non-native English users. For the latter, the idea of "Globish" is so obvious, and so much part of their everyday experience, it causes virtually no comment. It's a lingua franca they are accustomed to, across a wide spectrum of usage. For the former, it is a silly, slick, almost meaningless term that does not answer to experience and seems to threaten the sovereignty of British and American Standard English.

A few clarifications: what Globish is NOT. It is not Basic English, or Esperanto. I part company with Jean-Paul Nerriere on his vocabulary of 1,500 words. For me, Globish describes the use of English (at varying levels of expertise) in situations where the local language fails to work for outsiders. Also: it is NOT a pidgin. That's a specific kind of language formed by the linguistically dispossessed (slaves on the Middle Passage, for instance, or South Sea islanders cut off from other cultural influences), and pidgins lead inexorably to creoles (as in the Caribbean). Globish is neither a pidgin nor a creole.

And it's not a dialect. […] For me, "Globish" is, as I say above, part-linguistic, and part-cultural. It's a phenomenon that derives its inspiration from Anglo-American language and culture, but it now has a momentum that is independent of both US and UK.

One final correction: Globish may be, as I contend, a global phenomenon, but, like Latin before it, is vulnerable to change and decay. It won't be global forever.

The Guardian (guardian.co.uk), 12/4/2010

A. Language

Find synonyms in paragraphs 2, 3 and 4 of the article for the following: *a very sensitive matter, an indicator, going to rack and ruin, comes under severe criticism, common language, a broad variety, dominance, know-how, foreigners, isolated from.*

B. Questions

Answer each of the following questions in 50 words. Use information in the article to answer but do not copy sentences directly: use your own words.

1. What is globish?

2. What is the difference between pidgin, creole and Basic English?

Explain the following quotation in 100 words: "Globish occurs in the news almost every day in different guises."

Translation

Translate the article into English.

Bush, Schwarzenegger et Cantona au panthéon du charabia de langue anglaise

L'ancien président américain George W. Bush a remporté haut la main un sondage publié mercredi sur les pires exemples de charabia dans la langue de Shakespeare, devant Arnold Schwarzenegger ou Eric Cantona et ses célèbres sardines.

M. Bush, dont les nombreuses perles sont entrées dans la légende, a été plébiscité par les 4.000 personnes interrogées sur internet par la « Campagne pour un anglais simple » *(Plain English Campaign)*, un groupe de pression britannique.

Il s'est imposé avec cette phrase mémorable, prononcée à Washington en 2004 : « Nos ennemis innovent, ils sont pleins de ressources. Nous aussi. Ils n'arrêtent jamais de réfléchir à de nouveaux moyens de nuire à notre pays et nos compatriotes. Nous non plus ».

L'ancien acteur devenu gouverneur de Californie, Arnold Schwarzenegger, se hisse à la deuxième place avec ce point de vue énigmatique, exprimé lors d'une campagne électorale en 2003 : « Je pense que le mariage gay devrait être entre un homme et une femme ».

L'ancien footballeur français Eric Cantona, qui a fait les beaux jours du club de Manchester United, décroche la 8e marche pour sa désormais célèbre métaphore des mouettes lors d'une conférence de presse en 1995, immortalisée dans le dernier film de Ken Loach *Looking for Eric* : « Quand les mouettes suivent un chalutier, c'est parce qu'elles pensent que des sardines seront jetées à la mer ».

George W. Bush place une deuxième « busherie » dans les dix premières places (9e), avec une pensée datant de 2001 : « Je sais ce que je pense. Je continuerai à dire clairement ce que je pense et ce que je pense – je pense que ce que je pense est juste ».

AFP (dans *Le Point* [lepoint.fr]), 9/9/2009

Overview

Read a general overview of the subject.

From Received Pronunciation to Estuary English

To criticise the way people speak is as difficult as to criticise their clothes or their hair-style, because one's choice of words and one's accent reflect one's personality and one's origins. Origins include not only a geographical region, but also social background and education. Because of present-day mobility, accents have become less easy to identify but, thirty years ago, an Englishman had only to open his mouth and you could tell not only where he came from, but which class he belonged to and sometimes which school he went to!

In early 20th century Britain, the non-regional accent of ladies and gentlemen (i.e. that of the upper and upper-middle classes) served also as a model for educators. As from 1917, a standardised version of this neutral accent came to be known as RP (Received Pronunciation). Wikipedia will tell you – erroneously – that RP is also known as Oxford or Cambridge English. This is not true: the accents of the two universities were regarded at the time as affectations. On the other hand, RP did become "the BBC accent" for decades and remained the accepted norm until the early 1960s, although some diphthongs (notably the one in "no" or "boat") changed slightly over the years, getting less nasal and more "rounded".

Then, between 1960 and 1990 came a succession of people and fashions that were to change things: the angry young men (working- or middle-class authors like John Osborne and Alan Sillitoe), the Beatles (with Liverpool accents), working-class heroes (like Michael Caine the Cockney actor and Arthur Scargill the Yorkshire trade unionist), Australian soap operas like *Neighbours*, Princess Diana (with a laid-back Sloane Square accent that sounded more "ordinary" than the clipped vowels of her noble forebears and was part-way towards becoming Estuary English [see below]), and golden boys (brash young stock exchange traders with more money than class). They all contributed to what some would call the "dumbing-down" of English by pulling RP off its pedestal. Nowadays, in a celebrity culture where the voices of footballers and rock stars are listened to and imitated more often than those of academics or aristocrats, it is hardly surprising that RP is no longer as desirable as it was. It is gradually being replaced by "Estuary English", an approximation of the working class accent of the Thames Estuary area, and an accent which even the upper classes are adopting as a means of appearing less posh.

Pronunciation

Listen and repeat.

break [breɪk], **brick** [brɪk]

- pain/pin, pail/pill, stakes/sticks, take/tick, quake/quick, sake/sick.
- Mick Drake was sick so he took a pill to stop the pain.

Chapter 41

The future of work

Language focus

Some, any, no

• *Some* s'emploie dans les affirmations pour dire une certaine quantité ou un certain nombre qu'on ne précise pas :

I'd love ***some*** *tea.*

Some *people say that cloning is dangerous.*

• Dans une interrogative, son emploi suppose qu'on sait que l'objet existe :

Do you have ***some*** *change ?*

As-tu de la monnaie ?

• Dans le même contexte, *any* voudrait dire qu'on doute de son existence :

Do you have ***any*** *change ?*

Par hasard, tu n'aurais pas de la monnaie ?

• *Any* dans les phrases affirmatives a un sens qualitatif :

You can take ***any*** *cookie you like.* (n'importe lequel)

• *Any* remplace *some* dans les phrases négatives :

I don't have ***any*** *change.*

• Mais *any* n'est pas intrinsèquement négatif. Le seul quantifieur qui a cette propriété est *no* : *I have* ***no*** *desire to go there.*

Wordbank

the allocation of space	*l'attribution d'espace*
to apply for a job	*postuler à un emploi*
an applicant, a candidate	*un candidat*
a letter of application	*une lettre de candidature*
a blue-collar worker	*un col bleu*
the corporate culture	*la culture d'entreprise*
the digital divide	*la fracture numérique*
to downsize	*réduire les effectifs*
economic recovery	*la reprise économique*
education and training	*l'éducation et la formation*
a forecast	*une prévision*
a freelance	*un travailleur indépendant*
grey workers	*les travailleurs âgés, les seniors*
an incentive	*un encouragement*
a job for life	*un poste pour la vie*
a job hunt	*une recherche d'emploi*

job mobility	*la mobilité professionnelle*
job security	*la sécurité de l'emploi*
a jobseeker	*un demandeur d'emploi*
the labour market	*le marché du travail*
to land a job	*décrocher un emploi*
to lay off	*licencier*
a micro-business	*une micro-entreprise*
off-shoring	*délocaliser*
outsourcing	*externaliser*
peer-to-peer	*entre collègues*
a pink-collar worker	*quelqu'un qui fait un métier traditionnellement c onsidéré comme réservé aux femmes*
a pitfall	*un piège*
to have a portfolio career	*cumuler plusieurs emplois/fonctions*
a retiree	*un retraité*
self-employed	*indépendant*
a skill	*une compétence*
the speed of change	*la vitesse du changement*
a start-up	*une start-up, une nouvelle entreprise*
a steel collar	*un col d'acier, un robot*
to streamline	*dégraisser*
to tackle the crisis	*s'attaquer à la crise*
to take on	*embaucher*
teleworking	*le télétravail*
a tertiary industry	*une industrie tertiaire*
the turnover	*la rotation d'effectifs ; le chiffre d'affaires*
to unleash (the) potential	*libérer le potentiel*
to upsize	*augmenter les effectifs*
a white-collar worker	*un col blanc*
to work from home	*travailler de chez soi*
a work-life balance	*un équilibre travail-vie personnelle*
the workplace	*le lieu de travail*

Translation

Translate the sentences into English.

1. Les travailleurs âgés n'ont aucune envie de faire des heures supplémentaires.

2. Y aura-t-il de nouvelles offres d'emplois dans notre société d'ici Noël ? J'en doute.

3. Parce qu'il n'y a ni crèche ni assez de postes à temps partiel, des femmes très qualifiées doivent interrompre leur carrière.

4. Le directeur des ressources humaines a décidé de ne pas embaucher d'autres employés de bureau dans le service comptabilité.

5. Il y a des patrons qui pensent que la façon la plus rapide de gonfler leurs bénéfices est de dégraisser les effectifs.

Read and answer

Read the article and then do activities A and B that follow.

Training young people: Another brick in the wall

The growing popularity of apprenticeships

The Acacia Hair and Beauty Salon in Worcester Park, a suburb in south-west London, is looking for an apprentice. The owner wants someone hardworking, reliable and honest to wash hair, launder towels and gowns, mix hair dyes and make cups of coffee for her well-coiffed clientele. After two years' training, her apprentice will qualify as a hair stylist, with a certificate to boot.

The economic downturn has seen a revival in the fortunes of the apprenticeship. As apprentices, young people learn a trade or craft directly from an employer, sometimes spending a day a week or so at college. The National Apprenticeship Service, which now has responsibility for trainee hairdressers, aspiring bricklayers and the like, reports that the number of apprentices more than doubled over the decade to 2007 and has risen sharply in the months since then for which data are available. In 2002 barely a quarter of those who started an apprenticeship completed it; by 2008 the figure had risen to 64%. It is possible now to begin one of more than 190 different careers as an apprentice, including accountancy, business administration, textiles and veterinary nursing.

In the good times, such opportunities were overlooked by ambitious youngsters who aspired to a university place. Now they are grateful for what they can get. Unfortunately that isn't very much. Politicians wring their hands at the number of young people not in education, employment or training, and Labour has promised every school-leaver some sort of job or training or place at college. Yet the number of apprenticeships advertised through the national service is painfully low.

A recent search for vacancies in "retail and commercial enterprise" – a category spanning careers from logistics to manicure, for example – turned up just over 1,000 opportunities across England. Another for apprenticeships in "engineering and manufacturing technologies" garnered fewer than 2,000 vacancies.

Firms need encouragement to offer more places. A survey of English employers by IFF Research, published last month by the Commission for Employment and Skills, a quango, found that more than 90% of them were aware of apprenticeships but just 8% offered them, and typically only 4% at any given time.

Then there is the tricky question of who gets to say whether an apprentice has learned his stuff. Those who attend colleges must pass basic exams; others whose learning has taken place entirely on the job are visited by inspectors.

Alison Wolf of King's College London argues that the government is wasting cash paying external observers to issue certificates that "workplace learning" has occurred; it used to be taken for granted that completing an apprenticeship meant that something had been learned. And assessing skills does not come cheap: the state pays £6,500 for an outside body to provide a certificate saying that an apprentice hairdresser is qualified to do the job, and £9,000 to certify an engineer's training.

Despite all this, the government wants 20% of school leavers to become apprentices by 2020. That will be tough without incentives to encourage employers to provide

...

…

the opportunities. These days they are required to pay their apprentices the minimum wage, along with teaching them. Yet apprenticeships – even with the certificates that signify their completion – may be the best way forward for young people keener on a job than a degree.

The Economist (economist.com), 31/3/2010

A. Language

Find synonyms in the article for the following: *industrious, dependable, slump, finished, neglected/ignored, chances, thankful, bemoan, gathered/collected, has learned his trade.*

B. Question

What can account for the growing popularity of apprenticeship in the UK? (Answer in 200 words. Use information in the article but do not copy sentences directly: use your own words.)

Translation

Translate the article into English.

Les métiers verts peuvent-ils sauver l'emploi?

Bâtiment, ingénierie, transport, agriculture… Le secteur de l'emploi n'échappe pas au tournant vert. En décembre 2009, l'Ademe, l'Agence de l'environnement et de la Maîtrise de l'énergie, a évalué la croissance de l'emploi dans les activités écologiques à 3 % par rapport à 2008. À titre de comparaison, la moyenne des autres industries était d'environ 0,9 %. Le tournant pris par la France et l'Europe en matière de développement durable va générer des centaines de milliers d'emplois dans les dix ans à venir. On va assister à la création de nouveaux métiers comme dans l'ingénierie ou les travaux publics mais également au 'verdissement' de postes existants déjà comme dans les transports, l'énergie ou le bâtiment », assure Marie-Claire Carrère-Gée, présidente du Conseil dorientation pour l'Emploi (COE). Si tous les secteurs de l'économie seront directement ou indirectement touchés par cette évolution, une dizaine de domaines prometteurs, à l'instar de l'énergie, de l'eau, des transports ou de l'électricité sont particulièrement suivis.

Si d'une manière générale, le virage vert a été très bien accueilli par les entreprises, certaines sociétés ont plus de mal à l'adopter. En effet, dans les petites structures, s'adapter aux techniques vertes est bien plus lourd que dans les multinationales. Suivre des formations, changer le matériel pour le mettre aux normes, s'adapter aux nouvelles normes, tout cela nécessite d'importants investissements. Si les sous-traitants ou les petits artisans peinent à prendre le virage de l'économie verte, on peut craindre que les grosses entreprises qui les emploient cassent les contrats et que les emplois disparaissent.

Caroline Politi, *L'Express* (lexpress.fr), 2/4/2010

Overview

Read a general overview of the subject.

New occupations in a world of new technology

For many white-collar workers, the line between office and home is already becoming blurred – teleworking has brought the office into the home – and for blue-collar workers too, technology is creating new patterns of work. Many blue-collar jobs are changing radically or are disappearing as previously undreamt-of gadgets and professions emerge alongside the globalisation of markets and communications. For everyone, handheld mobile communications systems already mean that one is never out of calling distance from one's colleagues, clients or superiors. And the world of work is set to change even more radically over the coming years, especially as advances in electronics and AI (Artificial Intelligence) increase in pace.

From about 2011, huge numbers of baby boomers will be reaching retirement age. Of course, many will be kept on by their employers because of their experience (and despite any physical drawbacks) or will even start up their own new ventures. For those who do retire, the problem will be posed as to who, if anybody, will take their place. It might be someone from the Hispanic or Asian minorities – the fastest-growing group in the US working population. It might be a woman, for women, although underpaid, will become more numerous on payrolls and on the executive ladder.

It might of course be a steel-collar worker: a robot – already present in automobile assembly plants. With the coming of robotics that incorporate AI, certain tasks will be undertaken only by robots, notably dangerous maintenance missions or routine pharmaceutical laboratory tasks. This will increase productivity and lower manufacturing costs, and at the same time generate a need for a new category of human worker: someone who is technologically aware, IT-savvy, and highly skilled in programming and engineering. This in turn will mean that employees will be obliged to become more flexible in their attitudes to the tasks they carry out. Moreover, continuing globalisation will mean new attitudes towards transport and logistics, perhaps leading to more products being made under licence in an effort to bring down energy-related costs.

The recent economic crisis has severely shaken Western industry and few employment patterns or companies will emerge unscathed. Experts point out that the crisis and its continuing effects will oblige employers to take more account of the human aspects of work and rethink human resource management. One of the trends will almost certainly be the "greening" of products and producers' images, in both industry and agriculture, a trend that will spawn a whole host of occupations.

Pronunciation

Listen and repeat.

tell [tel], **tail** [teɪl]

- let/late, fell/fail, when/wane, test/taste, shed/shade, edge/age, pen/pain.
- The men failed to fell the tree as their strength waned in the shade.

42 Chapter

Women at work

Language focus

Les systèmes hypothétiques

Les trois systèmes *(= the three conditionals)* sont analogues à ceux du français.

1. Le potentiel *(= the first conditional)*, qui renvoie à une évolution **plausible** d'une situation réelle :

    If I win (présent), *I will buy a new car* (*will* + V).
    Si je gagne, j'achèterai un une nouvelle voiture.

2. L'irréel présent *(= the second conditional)*, qui renvoie à une hypothèse ; il est **peu probable** que l'hypothèse se réalise :

    If I won (prétérit), *I would buy a castle* (*would* + V).
    Si je gagnais, j'achèterais un château.

3. L'irréel passé *(= the third conditional)*, hypothèse rhétorique, qui est **irréalisable** :

    If I had won (*had* + V-*en* [= *plus-que-parfait*]), *I would have bought* (*would have* + V-*en*) a castle.
    Si j'avais gagné, j'aurais acheté un château.

Wordbank

abusive practices	*les pratiques abusives*
to assess	*jauger, évaluer*
to award	*attribuer à, discerner, donner*
to be aware of	*être conscient de*
to benefit from	*profiter de*
to bridge a gap	*rapprocher des points de vue opposés*
to campaign against	*faire campagne contre*
to champion	*prendre fait et cause pour*
the crux of the problem	*le cœur du problème*
to curtail	*écourter, raccourcir*
to disadvantage women	*désavantager les femmes*
an egalitarian society	*une société égalitaire*
to encounter/clear hurdles	*rencontrer/franchir des obstacles*
to ensure	*assurer, garantir*
equal pay	*un salaire égal*
equality of opportunity	*l'égalité des chances*
female corporate leaders	*les femmes chefs d'entreprise*
a female-friendly environment	*un contexte favorable aux femmes*
the glass ceiling	*la discrimination invisible*

to grant rights	*accorder des droits*
to hail	*saluer, acclamer*
to harass	*harceler*
an imbalance	*un déséquilibre*
to impede career advancement	*freiner la progression professionnelle*
to implement	*mettre en œuvre*
litigation	*un litige*
a male-dominated business	*un secteur dirigé par les hommes*
the male-female issue	*les problèmes hommes-femmes*
the male preserve	*le pré carré des hommes*
meaningful	*significatif*
a partnership	*un partenariat*
to pave the way	*ouvrir la voie*
to phase in a female quota	*introduire progressivement un quota de femmes*
a pitfall	*un piège, une embûche*
power	*le pouvoir*
a pressure group	*un groupe de pression*
to raise a problem	*soulever un problème*
to rank	*classer, figurer, compter parmi*
regardless of gender	*sans tenir compte du sexe*
the rule of law	*l'autorité de la loi*
to seek promotion	*demander/chercher à avoir une promotion*
to seek redress for	*demander réparation pour*
to safeguard	*sauvegarder, protéger*
to seize leadership opportunities	*saisir les occasions de prendre les rênes*
the share of female directors	*la proportion de femmes aux postes de direction*
a significant improvement	*une amélioration considérable*
to strengthen	*renforcer*
a telephone helpline	*une aide téléphonique*
to be trapped	*être piégé*
vulnerable	*vulnérable*
a watchdog	*une agence de veille/surveillance*

Translation

Translate the sentences into English.

1. Si les entreprises aménagent les conditions de travail, la discrimination invisible disparaîtra.

2. Si elle avait souffert de la mysogynie de ses collègues masculins, elle aurait contacté un comité de défense des droits des femmes.

3. Si l'entreprise respectait les droits des femmes, elle donnerait à tous ses employés les mêmes avantages.

4. Si le gouvernement veut promouvoir la parité, il devra mettre en œuvre des mesures pour combler l'écart salarial.

5. Si l'égalité des chances était une réalité, certaines femmes ne seraient pas obligées de démissionner pour élever leurs enfants.

Read and answer

Read the article and then do activities A and B that follow.

Women and work: we did it!

The rich world's quiet revolution: women are gradually taking over the workplace

At a time when the world is short of causes for celebration, here is a candidate: within the next few months women will cross the 50% threshold and become the majority of the American workforce. Women already make up the majority of university graduates in the OECD countries and the majority of professional workers in several rich countries, including the United States. Women run many of the world's great companies, from PepsiCo in America to Areva in France.

Women's economic empowerment is arguably the biggest social change of our times. Just a generation ago, women were largely confined to repetitive, menial jobs. They were routinely subjected to casual sexism and were expected to abandon their careers when they married and had children. Today they are running some of the organisations that once treated them as second-class citizens. Millions of women have been given more control over their own lives. And millions of brains have been put to more productive use. Societies that try to resist this trend – most notably the Arab countries, but also Japan and some southern European countries – will pay a heavy price in the form of wasted talent and frustrated citizens.

This revolution has been achieved with only a modicum of friction. Men have, by and large, welcomed women's invasion of the workplace. Yet even the most positive changes can be incomplete or unsatisfactory. This particular advance comes with two stings. The first is that women are still under-represented at the top of companies. Only 2% of the bosses of America's largest companies and 5% of their peers in Britain are women. They are also paid significantly less than men on average. The second is that juggling work and child-rearing is difficult. Middle-class couples routinely complain that they have too little time for their children. But the biggest losers are poor children – particularly in places like America and Britain that have combined high levels of female participation in the labour force with a reluctance to spend public money on child care.

These two problems are closely related. Many women feel they have to choose between their children and their careers. Women who prosper in high-pressure companies during their 20s drop out in dramatic numbers in their 30s and then find it almost impossible to regain their earlier momentum. Less-skilled women are trapped in poorly paid jobs with hand-to-mouth child-care arrangements. Motherhood, not sexism, is the issue: in America, childless women earn almost as much as men, but mothers earn significantly less. And those mothers' relative poverty also disadvantages their children.

Demand for female brains is helping to alleviate some of these problems. Even if some of the new theories about warm-hearted women making inherently superior workers are bunk, several trends favour the more educated sex, including the "war for talent" and the growing flexibility of the workplace. Law firms, consultancies and banks are rethinking their "up or out" promotion systems because they are losing so many able women. More than 90% of companies in Germany and Sweden allow flexible working. And new technology is making it easier to redesign work in all sorts of family-friendly ways.

...

...

Women have certainly performed better over the past decade than men. In the European Union women have filled 6m of the 8m new jobs created since 2000. In America three out of four people thrown out of work since the "mancession" began have been male. And the shift towards women is likely to continue: by 2011 there will be 2.6m more female than male university students in America.

The Economist (economist.com), *30/12/2009*

A. Language

FInd synonyms in the title, subtitle and paragraphs 1 and 2 of the article for the following: *we won, seizing control, an applicant, labour force, manage, access to power, were submitted to, occasional, to give up, inferior, to withstand, foot the bill.*

B. Questions

Answer each question in approximately 50 words.

1. Explain what "women's economic empowerment" consists of.

2. To what extent is such progress still limited?

3. Why and how will companies improve their female employees' working conditions?

Translation

Translate the article into English.

Les mâles féministes

Commençons par oublier les détails qui fâchent - ces agaçantes tâches ménagères qui retombent à 80 % sur le dos de la gent féminine ou ces congés parentaux, dont les mâles ne sont que 1 % à voir l'intérêt.

En cette année de célébration des 40 ans du Mouvement de libération des femmes, alors que ces dames s'écharpent sur le retour des couches lavables et des mères au foyer – avec la philosophe Elisabeth Badinter dans le rôle de l'incendiaire – et qu'à droite comme à gauche on dénonce les timides avancées de la parité, il fallait bien se pencher sur l'autre versant de la question : les hommes. Combien sont-ils à penser que l'égalité des sexes n'est pas un vain mot ? [...]

Loin des banderoles, des hommes bousculent aussi les codes au quotidien. Certains aménagent leurs horaires de travail pour rentrer plus tôt le soir. Le modèle du jeune papa avec porte-bébé se démocratise. Au pays du très macho Berlusconi, un dénommé Fiorenzo Bresciani a même eu l'outrecuidance de créer l'Association italienne des hommes au foyer, en 2002.

Plus près de nous, Michel Morvan discute depuis deux ans recettes de cuisine et droits des femmes sur son blog au titre très années 1950 : L'Homme au foyer. Ce Breton de 37 ans, cadre culturel, a l'intention de jouer les *Desperate Housewives* avec ses deux enfants « pendant quatre ou cinq ans », pour que son épouse puisse mener sa carrière tambour battant.

Claire Chartier & Margaux Duquesne, *L'Express* (lexpress.fr), 5/6/2010

Overview

Read a general overview of the subject.

Equal or not? The fight goes on...

British women were given the same voting rights as men in 1928 and American women were allowed to vote under certain conditions in 1920. But the right to vote is only one aspect of women's empowerment. Social progress is closely linked to early schooling both for boys and for girls. However, schooling is an expensive process in numerous parts of the world, especially in the poverty-stricken world of the developing countries. Often, very large families have to make a choice between sending children to school, keeping them at home or sending them to work in the fields or a factory. It is feared that the present financial crisis, by pushing poor countries into further hardship, could have a negative impact on their provision of children's schooling. It is difficult to estimate with certainty, but it is thought that up to 66% of the world's illiterate may be women, 85 million of them young women. Africa and Asia both have high rates of illiteracy for young women. Inadequate schooling at early age leads in turn to lower numbers entering higher education, forcing women to remain in menial or low-skilled jobs where they may be exploited and subject to harassment.

Very few top jobs in developing countries are open to women. It is only recently that women, after hard-fought battles, have been able to occupy positions of importance in affluent countries. Even then, when women *do* work, the issues of pay and equal opportunities for promotion have to be addressed, for women in jobs similar to men's do not always receive the same pay or have the same prospects. In affluent western countries, campaigns to get more women into business and politics have put forward political parity and affirmative action as ways to achieve this. There are, however, some very notable examples of women obtaining key governmental posts in countries both developed and developing.

Violence against women is still rife whether it be in the home or in the theatre of war where women are routinely humiliated. Human trafficking, prostitution and slavery continue to be widespread.

The 1948 Universal Declaration of Human Rights calls for women to be given equal rights to men, and, in 1979, the UN General Assembly adopted the Convention on the Elimination of all forms of Discrimination Against Women. However, despite these advances, the situation remains bleak for many millions and the struggle for gender equality and equal opportunities is far from over.

Pronunciation

Listen and repeat.

bay [beɪ], **beer** [bɪə]

- pay/peer, ray/rear, day/deer, gay/gear, rail/real, clay/clear.
- Dear Ray had to pay for his peers' beers that day!

Chapter 43

The ageing population

Language focus

L'expression du souhait et du regret

Pour dire le souhait et le regret, on utilise le verbe *wish* (souhaiter) ou l'expression *if only* (= si seulement), suivi de l'une de deux structures.

1. Le prétérit, pour exprimer un souhait pour le présent ou pour l'avenir :

    *I wish I **had** a new computer.*
    J'aimerais tellement avoir un ordinateur neuf.
    *If only we **were lying** on a beach somewhere!*
    Si seulement on était étendus sur une plage quelque part !

Attention ! Ne pas confondre :

    I wish he could speak English! (= Il ne sait pas parler anglais.)
    I wish he would speak English! (= Il sait parler anglais, mais il ne veut pas.)

2. Le plus-que-parfait, pour exprimer un regret :

    *I wish he **had been** there.*
    J'aurais aimé qu'il soit là.
    *If only you **hadn't lied** to me.*
    Je regrette que tu m'aies menti.

Wordbank

an acute illness	*une maladie grave*
acute pain	*la douleur aigüe*
affordable health care	*les soins médicaux abordables*
the aged	*les personnes âgées*
an age group	*une tranche d'âge*
aging, ageing	*le viellissement*
average life expectancy	*l'espérance de vie en moyenne*
a baby boom/bust	*un taux de naissance à la hausse/baisse*
a burden	*un fardeau*
a carer	*un accompagnateur-soignant*
cell death/regeneration	*la mort/regénération de cellules*
of childbearing age	*en âge d'avoir des enfants*
chronic pain	*la douleur chronique*
current forecasts	*les prévisions actuelles*
day care	*les soins de jour*

the death rate	*le taux de mortalité*
dementia	*la démence*
the dependency ratio	*le rapport dépendants/valides*
a disease	*une maladie*
to downsize needs	*créer moins de besoins*
the retirement age	*l'âge de la retraite*
the fertiilty rate	*le taux de fécondité*
frail	*frêle*
grey spending power	*le pouvoir d'achat des seniors*
the grey market	*le marché des seniors*
a life span	*une durée de vie*
a livelihood	*un gagne-pain*
lively	*vibrant*
long-term care	*les soins de longue durée*
the average age	*l'âge moyen*
the median age	*l'âge médian*
a medical breakthrough	*une percée médicale*
a minder	*un accompagnateur*
the mortality rate	*le taux de mortalité*
a nursing home	*une maison de repos*
a retirement home	*une maison de retraité*
the onset of a disease	*le commencement d'une maladie*
a pension fund	*un fonds de retraite*
to pension off	*mettre à la retraite*
a physical impairment	*une diminution des facultés physiques*
the growth rate	*taux de croissance*
a retirement savings plan	*un plan de retraite*
retirement/sheltered housing	*le logement pour les personnes âgées*
self-directed support	*le soutien auto-géré*
a senior citizen	*un senior*
a shrinking population	*une population en baisse*
spending patterns, consumer habits	*des habitudes de consommation*
the threshold of old age	*le seuil de la vieillesse*

Translation

Translate the sentences into English.

1. J'aimerais vraiment que l'âge de la retraite ne soit pas repoussé à 70 ans !

2. Si seulement les progrès de la médecine permettaient d'allonger la durée de la vie sans souffrir ou tomber malade.

3. Les retraités aimeraient que le gouvernement plafonne les prix dans les maisons de retraite, mais c'est malheureusement impossible.

4. Les différents acteurs sociaux et politiques aimeraient que les entreprises françaises arrêtent d'envoyer à la retraite des employés expérimentés avant l'âge de 60 ans.

5. Miss Murple aurait aimé que l'accompagnateur de sa vieille tante soit au courant des conséquences de sa maladie.

Read and answer

Read the article and then do activities A and B that follow.

The grey vote: Meet the grandparents

Old people go to the polls in droves, but often need government help the least

Ageing societies put their electioneering politicians in a bind. Being seen to represent youth, the future and the prospect of change is generally a good thing. At the same time, policies must be crafted with the teeming grey vote in mind. The result is often a dissonance between a party's brand and its actual product.

New Labour, as the name suggests, made a fetish of youth; Tony Blair went out of his way to speak of Britain as a "young country". Many of its most expensive innovations, though, such as free television licences for the elderly and the broader strategy to fight pensioner poverty, were in fact aimed at old people.

Something similar is true of the Conservatives now. David Cameron, their leader, trades on his youth as much as Gordon Brown, the prime minister, burnishes his middle-class social background. But there are many Tory policies that are either aimed at old people directly (such as his promise to peg the state pension to earnings, a pledge also made by the government) or benefit them disproportionately (such as the two-year freeze on local council tax, the bane of those on fixed incomes).

It is easy to see why political parties are keen on oldsters. To start with, there are more of them all the time as baby-boomers hit retirement. The median age in Britain rose from 34 in 1971 to 39 in 2004, and is expected to hit 43 in 2031. There are 17m people over the age of 55, and, thanks to improvements in health care, the very old are growing particularly fast. Age UK, a pressure group for the elderly, is running a campaign during the election under the slogan "our power is our number".

The ultimate power of older folk, however, stems from their propensity to vote. A survey published by Age UK on April 5th showed that eight out of ten over-55s said they would definitely vote in the coming general election. That is 13.4 million votes, or half the total turnout at the last two general elections. Only half of 18- to 24-year-olds said they were certain to vote. And grey voters are strategically scattered across the country. In research conducted for the pressure group by De Montfort University, over-55s were expected to account for the majority of votes cast in 94 marginal constituencies.

The grey vote leans Tory. Those between 55 and 64 prefer Mr Cameron's party over Mr Brown's by a margin of 12 points, which grows to 26 points among the over-65s. This is an historic pattern, but it may also owe something to Mr Brown's personal unpopularity among some of the elderly. As chancellor of the exchequer for ten years, his efforts to improve the lot of poor pensioners often saw him claw funds from more prosperous ones. Many have not forgiven him for a paltry increase in the basic state pension in 2000, or for removing a tax relief enjoyed by private pension funds three years earlier.

Still, Mr Brown may be right to question whether doing more for the elderly as a group is a sensible idea. Many of them remain poor, it is true, and even those who are not may have serious anxieties about the affordability of social care. But the elderly as a whole are better off than their children are likely to be. Baby-boomers have done well out of the welfare state.

...

…

In a recent book, "The Pinch", David Willetts, a cerebral shadow cabinet member with a special interest in generational politics, estimates that the over-65s own £2.3 trillion of Britain's £6.7 trillion in personal wealth and those aged between 45 and 64 £3.5 trillion. Younger adults have more limited prospects of a decent occupational pension or housing nest-egg and will work far longer than their parents.

Some older voters, perhaps moved by their offspring's inability to buy their own home, recognise this. The Age UK survey shows that 71% of over-55s think there is too much emphasis on youth in politics, but only 50% agree that politicians actually "put the needs of younger people before those of older people". Many politicians (and Mr Cameron more than most) try to exude youth while designing policy for the old; they should try doing the opposite.

The Economist (economist.com), 8/4/2010

A. Language

Find synonyms in the first six paragraphs of the article for the following: *put someone in trouble, meanwhile, exploits, polishes, the curse, stop working, average, old people, disposition, trend, improve the living conditions.*

B. Question

Explain the final sentence in 200 words: "Many politicians try to exude youth while designing policy for the old; they should be doing the opposite." (Use information in the article but do not copy sentences directly: use your own words.)

Translation

Translate the article into English.

2010 : le pari sur les seniors

Le gouvernement a décidé de frapper fort pour que les 50 ans et plus ne se retrouvent pas sur le carreau. Les cartes sont distribuées mais la partie est loin d'être gagnée. […]

Après des années de dispositifs incitatifs encadrant le travail des seniors, le gouvernement a franchi une étape supplémentaire en passant aux sanctions. […]

Pas de révolution grise à l'horizon, non, mais un début de prise de conscience et des négociations qui se sont multipliées fin 2009 dans les entreprises. Chez Frères Blanc, un groupe de restauration de 1 800 personnes, la DRH Sophie Chabot le dit tout net : « J'ai vu arriver le décret et j'ai souhaité anticiper les choses avant d'être au pied du mur. » En termes de gestion des seniors, le terrain était vierge. Elle a mis en place des bilans de compétences, instauré une politique de tutorat et organisé des formations au management et à l'oenologie. Pour les 10 % de salariés de plus de 45 ans de son groupe, il y a eu un avant et un après décret. Les mentalités semblent ainsi changer doucement mais sûrement.

L'Express (lexpress.fr), 15/4/2010

Overview

Read a general overview of the subject.

The cost of growing old

Fertility rates are declining worldwide and life expectancy is on the increase. The number of over 65s in the USA – just 35 million in 2000, increasing to 40 million in 2010 – is expected to hit 72 million in 2030. These are striking figures for a total population of 307 million (in 2009).

An older population may be enriching for society through its experience of life – and by providing a useful niche market – but it may also be looked on as a population at risk both for itself and society. First, the health problem: although the over-65s may, thanks to medical advances, be in a position to fend for themselves for quite a while, this will be less and less true as they reach their 70s and beyond (a projected 6.5% of the population in 2020). Also, in a country where the notion of "welfare state" does not exist, people have mostly to pay their own way. In normal economic circumstances this would mean revenue filtering back from private pension schemes but the recent crisis has meant that income has dropped and real estate investments have not always turned out as they were expected, sometimes even becoming negative equity. In 2007, the income of American senior citizens was as follows: 87% depended on social security, 52% on the return on their investments, 28% on private pensions, and 25% on private earnings. The last figure is set to rise with more people being obliged to find some sort of paid activity. Many Americans would like to put off retirement, even going so far as attending careers fairs for senior citizens!

Poverty is an increasing problem and there has been a dramatic rise over recent years in the number of older Americans being helped by the social security administration's "supplemental security income" program (which provides food stamps), by housing aid and by Medicaid.

For the legislator, an ageing population means solutions have to be found for the financing of health care networks and long-term care when the baby-boom generation reaches 65 (between 2011 and 2030) because ageing brings physical problems and chronic diseases – muscular and cardio-vascular problems, arthritis... Nor will the USA escape the increasing rates of neuro-degenerative diseases which are predicted for the world's population. However, some pundits predict that the increasing numbers of elderly people will in fact turn out to be a boon to the economy by stimulating medical and pharmaceutical research.

Pronunciation

Listen and repeat.

tease [tɪːz], **tears** [tɪəz]

- fee/fear, be/beer, weed/weird, knee/near, see/seer, pea/pier, cheese/cheers.
- The beer you see is dear but you can have it free.

44 Chapter

The press

Language focus

L'expression du futur

- *Will.* Réaction à une situation ou à une condition :
  *If I **will buy** a castle.*
  (on sonne à la porte) ***I'll go** and see who it is.*
- *Be going to.* Prévision d'après des indices ou certitude forte :
  *The floor is slippery, you**'re going to** fall.*
  Le sol est glissant, tu vas tomber.
- Présent + *be* + V-*ing*. Un projet :
  ***I'm seeing** John this afternoon.*
  Je vois John cet après-midi.
- Présent simple. Ce qui est prévu, indépendamment du locuteur :
  *His plane **lands** at 10:30.*
  L'avion atterrit à 10h30.
- *Will* + *be* + V-*ing* et *will have* + V-*en*. Projection dans l'avenir (on s'y voit déjà) :
  *This time next week, **I'll be sunbathing** in Florida.*
  À cette heure-ci la semaine prochaine, je serai en train de bronzer en Floride.
  *This time next week, **I'll have finished** the painting.*
  À cette heure-ci la semaine prochaine, j'aurai terminé la peinture.

Wordbank

to break the news	*annoncer la nouvelle*
to broadcast	*diffuser*
a broadsheet, a quality paper	*un quotidien de qualité*
the circulation	*le tirage*
a column	*une chronique*
a columnist	*un chroniqueur*
a copy	*un exemplaire*
current events	*l'actualité*
a daily newspaper	*un (journal) quotidien*
an editor	*un rédacteur en chef*
an editorial, a leader, a leading article	*un éditorial*
a feature	*un reportage spécial*
the Fourth Estate	*le quatrième pouvoir*
a hatchet job	*un lynchage médiatique*
a (banner) headline	*un gros titre, une manchette*

to hit/make the front page(s)/ the headlines	*faire la une/les gros titres*
an in-depth analysis	*une analyse détaillée*
to indulge in sensationalism	*se complaire dans la recherche du sensationnel*
information	*l'information, les renseignements*
to infringe on	*empiéter sur*
to investigate	*enquêter*
investigative journalism	*le journalisme d'investigation*
an issue	*un numéro*
journalese	*le jargon journalistique*
to libel	*diffamer*
to make a splash	*faire des vagues*
media hype	*le battage médiatique*
a medium, the media	*un média, les médias*
the news *(n. sing.)*	*les infos, les nouvelles*
news coverage	*la couverture médiatique*
a news item	*une info*
a newspaperman, a newsman/woman, a journalist	*un journaliste*
a piece of news	*une nouvelle*
a publisher	*un éditeur*
to pull to pieces	*éreinter*
a report	*un reportage*
a review	*une critique (livre, film, spectacle…)*
a scoop	*une exclusivité*
to sensitise public opinion	*sensibiliser l'opinion publique*
to spread a message	*faire passer un message*
to be sued for libel	*être poursuivi en diffamation*
a Sunday paper	*une édition dominicale*
a tabloid	*un quotidien populaire*
a target audience	*un public cible*
a weekly/monthly magazine	*un magazine hebdomadaire/mensuel*

Translation

Translate the sentences into English.

1. Si le rédacteur en chef publie cette exclusivité, nous allons vendre deux fois plus d'exemplaires.

2. Ce nouveau scandale à caractère sexuel va faire la une dans la presse populaire.

3. Cet homme politique de premier plan va attaquer notre éditeur en justice.

4. Demain matin au petit matin le monde entier lira notre compte-rendu du mariage de ces deux vedettes d'Hollywood.

5. Le comité éditorial se réunit à 20 heures pour décider des gros titres, et le journal est imprimé à 3 heures du matin.

Read and answer

Read the article and then do activities A and B that follow.

American newspapers: Not dead yet

Newspapers have cut their way out of crisis. More radical surgery will be needed

Whatever happened to the death of newspapers? A year ago the end seemed near. The recession threatened to remove the advertising and readers that had not already fled to the internet. Newspapers like the *San Francisco Chronicle* were chronicling their own doom. America's Federal Trade Commission launched a round of talks about how to save newspapers. Should they become charitable corporations? Should the state subsidise them? It will hold another meeting on June 15th. But the discussions now seem out of date.

In much of the world there is little sign of crisis. German and Brazilian papers shrugged off the recession. Even American newspapers, which inhabit the most troubled corner of the global industry, have not only survived but often returned to profit. Not the 20% profit margins that were routine a few years ago, but profit all the same.

It has not been much fun. Many papers stayed afloat by pushing journalists overboard. The American Society of News Editors reckons that 13,500 newsroom jobs have gone since 2007. Readers are paying more for slimmer products. Some papers even had the nerve to refuse delivery to distant suburbs. Yet these desperate measures have proved the right ones and, sadly for many journalists, they can be pushed further.

Newspapers are becoming more balanced businesses, with a healthier mix of revenues from readers and advertisers. American papers have long been highly unusual in their reliance on ads. Fully 87% of their revenues came from advertising in 2008, according to the OECD. In Japan the proportion is 35%. Not surprisingly, Japanese newspapers are much more stable.

The whirlwind that swept through newsrooms harmed everybody, but much of the damage has been concentrated in areas where newspapers are least distinctive. Car and film reviewers have gone. So have science and general business reporters. Foreign bureaus have been savagely pruned. Newspapers are less complete as a result. But completeness is no longer a virtue in the newspaper business. [...]

The problem with such newspapers is that, although they do much that is excellent, they do little that is distinctive enough for people to pay for it. *The Los Angeles Times*'s foreign reporting is extremely good. But it is hard to argue that it is better than the stuff supplied by *The New York Times* or foreign papers – sources to which the residents of Los Angeles now have unfettered, largely free access via their laptops and iPhones. Similarly, it has never been clear why each major newspaper needs its own car reviewer: a Corolla is a Corolla, whether it is driven in Albuquerque or Atlanta. And by extension, it is not clear why presidential candidates or sport teams require huge journalistic entourages. Papers should concentrate on what they do best, which means, in many cases, local news and sport. If the rest is bought in from wire services or national outfits, readers are unlikely to complain – as long as there is enough competition between those larger providers to keep up standards (and thanks to the internet there probably is now). Specialisation generally means higher quality.

...

...

It is grim to forecast still more writers losing their jobs. But whether newspapers are thrown onto doorsteps or distributed digitally, they need to deliver something that is distinctive. New technologies like Apple's iPad only make this more true. The mere acquisition of a smooth block of metal and glass does not magically persuade people that they should start paying for news. They will pay for news if they think it has value. Newspapers need to focus relentlessly on that.

The Economist (economist.com), 10/6/2010

A. Language

Find synonyms in paragraphs 1, 2, 3 and 5 of the article for the following: *escaped to, their death, a succession of, rode out the storm of, by getting rid of, faraway, have turned out to be, unfortunately, drastically downsized.*

B. Question

According to *The Economist*, how has the US press coped with the crisis and what are its prospects? (Answer in 200-250 words: use your own words.)

Translation

Translate the article into English.

Google revoit en profondeur sa stratégie autour de Google News

Google veut faire la paix avec les éditeurs de presse. Certains d'entre-eux accusent en effet le géant américain de piller sans vergogne leurs contenus à travers Google News

En tête de la fronde, News Corp., le groupe de Rupert Murdoch, qui contrôle notamment *The Wall Street Journal*, le *Times*, *The Sun*, la chaîne de télé Fox News...

En guise de contre-attaque, ce dernier a plusieurs envisagé d'empêcher l'indexation de ses sites par le moteur Google afin de valoriser ses contenus, notamment les contenus payants. « Cela nous coûte beaucoup d'argent de présenter de bons journaux avec des contenus de qualité », a fait valoir le magnat. [...]

Le moteur, qui explique vouloir simplement organiser au mieux l'information mondiale au profit des internautes, a néanmoins mis de l'eau dans son vin. En décembre dernier, il annonce l'option First Click Free qui permet de « limiter le nombre d'accès gratuits à cinq par internaute et par jour via Google et Google News ». Histoire de mettre en avant la consultation payante d'articles supplémentaires. [...]

Aujourd'hui, Google [...] proposerait, selon une information de la presse italienne, un nouveau service baptisé NewsPass [qui] rendrait payants des articles déjà référencés par le moteur. [...]

Autre innovation, officielle cette fois, la possibilité laissée aux éditeurs de décider ou non de faire remonter leurs articles dans Google News. [...]

Suffisant pour calmer les éditeurs de presse ? La question reste posée. Mais il faut néanmoins rappeler que si Google News récupère du contenu de presse, il renvoie systématiquement vers le site de la source. D'où un levier d'audience non négligeable.

Olivier Chicheportiche, ZDNet.fr (dans *L'Express* [lexpress.fr]), 21/6/2010

Overview

Read a general overview of the subject.

Democracy and the decline of the traditional media

In August 2006, *The Economist*'s leading article "Who killed the newspaper?" mourned the impending death of the press, and the potential threat to quality information. Four months later, *Time* magazine's first issue of 2008 marvelled at the way in which Web 2.0, the name now given to the second generation of web development and design, has enabled amateurs "to fill in the vacuum created by everything the old media chose to ignore".

This radical shift from the traditional news industry to digital web-based information resources could mean a more democratic access to quality information. This is the view of the French scientist Joel de Rosnay, who maintains that people are making the most of the Internet's empowerment tools in order to change from the the top-down method of traditional media (whereby the few inform the many), to the people-to-people approach of the web's data-sharing community.

The internet's most recent killer applications have done exactly this: the former system by which a small number of people designed the news for the masses – on radio, TV and in the press – has become a "many-to-many" system that enables internet users to post and share fresh information instantly through journals, blogs, e-mails, chatrooms, newsgroups and sites like twitter.com.

Internet gives access to a land of digital information and knowledge in unlimited abundance. Podcasts and P2P TV are now challenging radio and TV networks while citizen journalists and bloggers can now hold the corporate world and politicians directly to account, something the press has sometimes been reluctant to do for fear they could be sued for libel. *The Economist* has predicted that non-profit groups might also combine the work of these "professional amateurs" with that of professional journalists, to develop investigative journalism online.

Although the user-generated content of Wikipedia and of blogs has been accused of dumbing down both traditional journalism and academic knowledge, Joel de Rosney asserts that the Internet has already generated the tools necessary to assess the quality of the content posted online. Smart programs and search engines can already channel the information to groups of specialised pro-amateur editors in charge of guaranteeing its reliability. We may well have moved from mass media to media for the masses, into the era of the "smart mobs" heralded by Harold Rheingold, who predicted in 2002 that online communities would pave the way to the next social revolution.

Pronunciation

Listen and repeat.

dear [dɪə], **dare** [deə]

cheer/chair, peer/pear, here/hair, tear *(= larme)*/tear *(= déchirer, déchirure)*, ear/air.
I hear, my dear, that you're scared of comparing these pairs of spears.

Chapter 45

Television

Language focus

Les petites et les grandes quantités

- Les emplois des quantifieurs *much, many, few* et *little* sont déterminés par le caractère dénombrable ou indénombrable du nom qu'ils déterminent.
- *A lot of* et *lots of* sont utilisés plus fréquemment à l'oral qu'à l'écrit et peuvent qualifier un nom dénombrable ou indénombrable.
- *Many* et *much* sont préférés pour les phrases interrogatives ou négatives.
- Au comparatif, *few* donne *fewer* (moins de) et *little* donne *less* (moins de).

dénombrables	indénombrables
a few (quelques)	*a little* (un peu de)
few (un faible nombre de)	*little* (une faible quantité de)
many (beaucoup de)	*much* (beaucoup de)
lots of, a lot of (beaucoup de)	*lots of, a lot of* (beaucoup de)

Wordbank

an aerial	*antenne*
to air an issue	*présenter un problème*
an anchorman, an anchorwoman	*un présentateur, une présentatrice*
audience measurement	*le calcul du taux d'écoute*
to broadcast	*émettre*
the box	*la télé*
cable television	*la télévision par câble*
to broadcast live	*transmettre en direct*
a commercial	*un spot publicitaire*
the control room	*la régie*
a couch potato	*un accro de la télévision*
the crew	*l'équipe*
digital television	*la télévision numérique*
a discussion programme	*une émission de débat*
glued to the box	*collé à la télé*
the goggle box	*la télé*
a hand-held screen	*un écran portable*
the highlights	*les meilleurs moments*
to host a programme	*présenter une émission*
in-car television	*la télévision en voiture*

to jam a broadcast/programme	*brouiller une émission*
lighting	*l'éclairage*
the linkman/presenter	*présentateur*
a link-up	*une émission en duplex*
a live broadcast	*une émission en direct*
a long-running show	*une émission diffusée depuis longtemps*
a newsflash	*un flash info*
the newsroom	*la salle de rédaction*
a panel(l)ist	*un invité (jeu télévisé)*
a pay channel	*une chaîne payante*
a phone-in show	*une émission d'échanges par téléphone*
prime time	*l'heure de grande écoute*
a quizmaster	*un animateur d'émission de jeu*
the (viewer) ratings	*le taux d'écoute*
to reach viewers	*atteindre des téléspectateurs*
to regulate	*contrôler*
the remote (control)	*la télécommande*
the screen	*l'écran*
a sitcom (= situation comedy)	*une série comique*
a slant	*un point de vue*
a soap (opera)	*un feuilleton*
state-controlled television	*la télévision contrôlée par l'État*
to subscribe	*s'abonner*
the tube	*la télé*
television advertising	*la publicité à la télévision*
an awards ceremony	*une remise de récompenses*
coverage	*la couverture*
a viewer	*un téléspectateur*
the weather forecast	*la météo*

Translation

Translate the sentences into English.

1. Peu d'adultes passent moins de deux heures par jour collés à leur écran de télévision.

2. De nombreux téléspectateurs préfèrent désormais les chaînes payantes pour pouvoir choisir parmi un grand choix d'émissions.

3. Qu'ils se passent à Dallas ou dans un quartier de Marseille, les feuilletons télé plaisent à beaucoup de personnes d'âges et de milieux différents.

4. Que ce soit en Grande-Bretagne ou en France, les chaînes publiques proposent quelques émissions et documentaires très intéressants.

5. Je regarde peu la publicité à la télévision, il y en a beaucoup trop.

Read and answer

Read the article and then do activities A and B that follow.

The great survivor

TV has coped well with technological change. Other media can learn from it

Newspapers are dying; the music industry is still yelping about iTunes; book publishers think they are next. Yet one bit of old media seems to be doing rather well. In the final quarter of 2009 the average American spent almost 37 hours a week watching television. Earlier this year 116m of them saw the Super Bowl – a record for a single programme. Far from being cowed by new media, TV is colonising it. Shows like "American Idol" and "Britain's Got Talent" draw huge audiences partly because people are constantly messaging and tweeting about them, and discussing them on Facebook.

Advertising wobbled during the recession, shaking the free-to-air broadcasters that depend on it. But cable and satellite TV breezed through. Pay-television subscriptions grew by more than 2m in America last year. The explosive growth of cable and satellite TV in India explains how that country has gone from two channels in the early 1990s to more than 600 today. Pay-TV bosses scarcely acknowledge the existence of viewers who do not subscribe to multichannel TV, talking only of people who have "yet to choose" a provider. This is not merely bluster. As our special report this week explains, once people start paying for greater television choice, they rarely stop.

It helps that TV is an inherently lazy form of entertainment. The much-repeated prediction that people will cancel their pay-TV subscriptions and piece together an evening's worth of entertainment from free broadcasts and the internet "assumes that people are willing to work three times harder to get the same thing", observes Mike Fries of Liberty Global, a cable giant. Laziness also mitigates the threat from piracy. Although many programmes are no more than three or four mouse clicks away, that still sounds too much like work for most of us. And television-watching is a more sociable activity than it may appear. People like to watch programmes when everybody else is watching them. Give them devices that allow them to record and play back programmes easily, and they will still watch live TV at least four-fifths of the time.

Yet these natural advantages alone are not enough to ensure television's survival. The internet threatens TV just as much as it does other media businesses, and for similar reasons. It competes for advertising, offering firms a more measurable and precise way of reaching consumers. Technology also threatens to fracture television into individual programmes, just as it has ruinously broken music albums into individual tracks. TV has endured because it has responded better to such threats than other media businesses.

One of the lessons from TV is to accept change and get ahead of it. Broadcasters' initial response to the appearance of programmes online was similar to the music industry's reaction to file-sharing: call in the lawyers. But television firms soon banded together to develop alternatives to piracy. Websites like Hulu, a joint venture of the American broadcasters ABC, Fox and NBC, have drawn eyeballs away from illicit sources. Gradually it has become clear that these websites pose a threat to the TV business in themselves, and that they are not bringing in as much advertising money as might be expected (which is similar to the problem faced by the newspaper business). So television is changing tack again.

...

With impressive speed, TV firms are now building online subscription-video services. The trendiest model is authentication: prove that you subscribe to pay-television and you can watch all the channels that you have paid for on any device. Such "TV Everywhere" services are beginning to appear in America and Canada. It is likely that Hulu will become a "freemium" service – mostly free, but with some shows hidden behind a paywall. The move from an ad-supported model to a mixture of subscriptions and advertising is tricky, but logical. It shows that it is not enough to embrace technological change. Businesses must also work out how to build digital offerings that do not cause their analogue ones to collapse.

Television has domesticated other disruptive technologies. Ten years ago digital video recorders like TiVo promised to transform the way people watched TV. The devices made it easy to record programmes and play them back, zooming through ads. The TV networks responded by running advertisements that work at high speed. Cable and satellite companies built cheap digital video recorders into set-top boxes and charged viewers extra for them. In effect, money flowed back to the television business. In Britain those boxes will soon be deployed to deliver targeted advertising, enabling the living-room television to compete with the internet.

That box might appear to be sitting in the corner of the living room, not doing much. In fact, it is constantly evolving. If there is one media business with a chance of completing the perilous journey to the digital future looking as healthy as it did when it set off, it is television.

The Economist (economist.com), 29/4/2010

A. Language

Find synonyms in the first five paragraphs of the article for the following: *complaining about, afraid of, attract, was unstable/fell a little, was unharmed/unaffected, boom, hype, seldom, naturally, forecast, organise, to divide, has resisted, trying a different approach.*

B. Question

What can explain the fact that TV has survived the digitization of the mass-media? (Answer in 200-250 words. Use information in the article but do not copy sentences directly: use your own words.)

Overview

Read a general overview of the subject.

One in every living-room...

With practically 1 set per inhabitant, the USA has hundreds of TV channels, many local and regional. The major conglomerates are ABC, CBS, Fox and NBC, founded in 1943, 1986, 1949 and 1939 respectively. These companies were spin-offs from ventures in the communications and entertainment sectors – radio channels, film companies or utilities.

The programmes they show tend to be made by independent production companies, which are then often networked to local channels and reach a very wide target audience.

…

Cable television, born in 1948 as a local experiment to help viewers living in areas where they could not receive broadcasts, is also very popular and counts 65 million subscribers. Other favourites include CNN, the Atlanta-based, round-the-clock news network which began operations in 1980. With religion of such importance in the USA it is also not surprising that many Americans watch their favourite televangelist from their homes. And of course the political importance of TV cannot be underestimated, with reporters always on the lookout for the sound bite that betrays or beefs up a politician's words.

The USA has no official state or government TV. Public television exists in the form of PBS (Public Service Broadcasting), thanks to federal help, public donations and foundations. It makes programmes of high quality, notably educational and cultural programmes.

The Federal Communications Commission regulates television, not as a government censorship agency, but with a brief to ensure that Americans have a safe and unimpeded access to all types of communications services and that no commercial group should hold a broadcasting monopoly.

Reaching the target audience and capturing market share is of utmost importance to the programme-makers. Competition for audience ratings is intense and each network vies with the others to produce the most successful programmes, notably sit-coms and soap operas (originally financed by soap-making companies, hence the name). Advertising (by programme sponsors) interrupts programmes regularly especially at "prime time" when viewer numbers are at their highest and advertising at its most expensive… TV advertising generates billions of dollars, so much so that it is argued that TV could not continue to exist without it: advertising is in a sense a guarantor of television independence. 2010's televised Super Bowl is reported to have generated $215 million and was watched by 95 million people.

American TV is often blamed for many ills but, in 2009, Americans watched on average 153 hours of TV per month from their homes, with the over-65s watching as much as 207 hours per month.

Pronunciation

Listen and repeat.

cell [sel], **stairs** [steəz]

- shed/shared, merry/Mary, dead/dared, ferry/fairy, fled/flared, bled/blared.
- Mary and Ken shared many merry moments on the ferry.

46 Chapter

Social networks

Language focus

Les modalités au passé

• La modalité de phrase est un jugement que porte le locuteur sur un événement. Pour marquer que l'événement sur lequel elle porte est passé, on utilise un modal + *have* + V-*en* (le participe passé) :

You ***could/might/would have*** *been injured.* Tu aurais pu être/Tu aurais été blessé.

You ***should/must have known*** *it would happen.* Tu aurais dû savoir que cela se passerait.

• Pour exprimer certaines modalités de sujet au passé ; on n'utilise pas de modaux, mais des équivalents :

had to (obligation) *didn't have to* (absence d'obligation)

was not allowed/supposed to (interdiction) *was able to* (capacité réalisée)

• Notez le sens de la modalité de sujet au passé de *could* (capacité non réalisée) et *couldn't* (absence de permission ou de capacité). Comparez avec *was able to* :

Peter ***could*** *swim but he* ***couldn't*** *swim across the river.*

Peter savait nager mais il n'était pas capable de traverser la rivière à la nage.

Jane ***was able to*** *swim across the river.*

Jane réussit à traverser la rivière à la nage.

Wordbank

bandwith	*la bande passante*
broadband access	*l'ADSL*
to broadcast a message widely	*diffuser un message largement*
to browse	*flâner, surfer sur le net*
a browser	*un navigateur internet*
BBS (Bulletin Board System)	*le système de bulletins électroniques*
to build relationships	*tisser des liens*
computer-mediated social interaction	*les relations sociales facilitées par l'internet*
online community services	*les services publics en ligne*
an online dating service	*une agence matrimoniale en ligne*
a cybernaut, an internaut, an internet-user	*un internaute*
to customise one's startpage	*personnaliser sa page d'accueil*
cyberspace	*le cyber-espace*
a database	*une base de données*
datatheft	*le vol de données*
a dotcom	*une société sur internet*
to download	*télécharger (vers son ordinateur)*

e-activism, electronic advocacy, cyberactivism, e-campaigning	*l'activisme sur internet*
an e-mail bomb, mass e-mailings	*le mail-bombing/ bombarderie (québécois)*
e-mail, an email	*le courrier électronique, un courriel*
file encryption	*le cryptage des données*
a generic template	*un format standard*
a homepage, a startpage	*une page d'accueil*
a hotline	*un service d'assistance technique par téléphone*
an IAP (internet access provider)	*un fournisseur d'accès*
the information highway	*l'inforoute, l'autoroute de l'information*
an IRC chatroom	*un salon de bavardage en direct*
instant messaging	*la messagerie instantanée*
to interact over the internet	*entrer en relation par internet*
an invasion of privacy	*une atteinte à la vie privée*
to join a network	*rejoindre un réseau*
a list of contacts	*une liste de contacts*
to log off/on	*se déconnecter/se connecter*
a newsgroup	*un forum de discussion*
to post a message	*afficher un message*
an online social network	*un réseau social en ligne*
to purge undesirables	*éliminer les indésirables de son profil*
P2P (peer-to-peer)	*poste à poste*
a recommendation system	*un système de cooptation*
a search engine	*un moteur de recherche*
social networking tools	*des applications pour réseaux sociaux*
to surf the web	*surfer sur la toile*
to upload	*télécharger (à partir de son ordinateur)*
a toolkit	*une boîte à outils*
user-generated content	*du contenu créé par l'internaute*
Web 2.0	*le web interactif*
Web 3.0	*le web autonome personnalisé*
a web portal	*un portail internet*

Translation

Translate the sentences into English.

1. Le fournisseur d'accès aurait pu nous prévenir que nos boîtes mels sont contrôlées régulièrement.

2. Pour te protéger du vol de données, tu as dû changer le codage de tes fichiers confidentiels.

3. Il y a quelques semaines il ne savait même pas ce qu'était Internet et ce soir il a réussi à personnaliser sa page d'accueil tout seul !

4. Tu aurais dû rejoindre le réseau en ligne des anciens élèves de l'université pour décrocher un entretien d'embauche plus vite.

5. Malgré une demi-heure au téléphone, le technicien de l'assistance technique n'a pu m'aider à récupérer ma liste de contacts.

Read and answer

Read the article and then do activities A and B that follow.

Deliberative democracy: Ancient Athens online

Democracy is about discussion, not just voting

Reflection and representation are not an easy fit. For an individual voter, being well-informed about every twist of public policy is an irrational use of time. But leaving a self-selecting elite of wonks and careerists in charge of policy-making is unappealing. In ancient Athens, which invented both democracy and the dilemma, a machine called a kleroterion picked a random 500 people to make policy from the 50,000-odd polity. The jury excluded women and slaves and the decisions it reached were sometimes dodgy (condemning Socrates was probably a mistake). But the approach is returning in a modern guise, under the label of "deliberative democracy".

A leading practitioner is James Fishkin of Stanford University. He starts by canvassing views from a large sample of people. Then a smaller subset (normally around 300-strong) receives briefing materials from the opposing advocacy groups. Moderators lead small group discussions which then draw up questions for experts and policy-makers. If the samples are statistically representative, that should, so goes the theory, give a credible picture of what the entire population would think, were it as well-informed.

Such polls have covered aboriginal rights in Australia and traffic jams in La Plata. A Chinese jury is looking at land rights. In Fujisawa in Japan a poll on local-government planning will start in August.

Discussions and briefing often lead to a shift away from populist viewpoints. In a recent poll in Britain support for making party manifesto promises legally binding plunged from 41% to 18%. In recession-hit Michigan a discussion raised support for bigger taxes (from 27% to 45% for income tax, for example). By contrast, support for cuts in corporate taxes rocketed 27 points to 67%: the more people thought about the issue, the more they wanted a better business environment and a lower deficit. But some results are discomfiting (at least for those with this newspaper's views). A pan-European poll in October 2007 found that support for European Union membership for Turkey and Ukraine fell by a fifth as the discussion progressed.

Deliberation counts for something, with a statistically significant shift in opinion on three out of four questions, and the biggest changes coming from those whose gains in knowledge are the greatest. The internet means that the discussion no longer needs to be face-to-face, though it involves fixes to ensure a statistically fair proportion of the unwebbed population is included. But being online can cut costs by as much as 90%. Mr Fishkin recalls that the first America-wide deliberative poll, in 1996, required airline sponsorship to fly participants to the venue in Austin, Texas.

Trademarking the methodology of a deliberative poll (as Mr Fishkin has done) may be a form of quality control. Even so the polls risk remaining an interesting gimmick, rather than a substitute for the messy business of elections, referendums and media campaigns: unless, that is, their conclusions have real bite.

But some signs suggest this is happening. In 2007 the Panhellenic Socialist Movement (Pasok), then in opposition, used deliberative polling to select its mayoral candidate for the Athenian district of Marousi (in the real election, he lost). Traditionalists looked

...

in vain for the kleroterion, however: a personal computer drew the sample instead. In 2005 the local authorities in Zeguo, China, used the technique to apportion a 40m yuan ($5.9m) infrastructure budget. In 2008 the approach was extended to the township's entire kitty. On May 10th the Central Party School, a hatchery for Beijing's top cadres, will start a pow-wow on the theory and practice of deliberative democracy. In a country where rulers are edgy about the masses getting too much power, the carefully channelled discussions of a deliberative poll could prove a useful safety valve.

The Economist (economist.com), 6/5/2010

A. Language

1. Find synonyms in the the first two paragraphs of the article for the following: *unexpected development, illogical, high-flyers, unattractive, chose, without any plan or pattern, a bit doubtful, a modern look/appearance, collecting opinions, trustworthy.*

2. Find antonyms in the last four paragraphs of the article for the following: *opposition to, skyrocketed, encouraging, ignorance, not at a real meeting, clean, quiet/confident.*

B. Question

To what extent can online deliberative polls benefit democracy? (Answer in 200-250 words. Use information in the article but do not copy sentences directly: use your own words.)

Translation

Translate the article into English.

Les réseaux sociaux, outils de recrutement ?

Près de 30 millions de d'inscrits sur le réseau social professionnel Viadeo, lancé en 2004, dont 3,5 en France ; plus de 70 millions sur Linkedin dans le monde, dont la version française, lancée l'an dernier, en compte près de 2 millions... Ces réseaux professionnels en ligne sont en pleine croissance, mais ceux-ci sont-ils vraiment utiles pour les candidats et les recruteurs ? Tel est l'objet d'une étude du site de recrutement Regionsjob.com, portant sur plus de 2 200 candidats, âgés de 18 à 60 ans, et sur 157 responsables des ressources humaines, présentée vendredi 18 juin.

Les sites de recherche d'emploi, utilisés par 97 % des candidats, demeurent les principaux supports de recherche, devant les candidatures spontanées (71 %). Ils sont 36 % à déclarer utiliser les réseaux sociaux dans leur recherche d'emploi. « Les réseaux sociaux servent à prolonger le réseau personnel. Ceux qui utilisent les réseaux sociaux sont également plus actifs sur les autres plates-formes de recrutement », souligne Flavien Chantrel, chargé de projet Web communautaire de RegionsJob. Alors qu'un candidat utilise en moyenne quatre modes de recherche différents, les utilisateurs de réseaux sociaux en utilisent 4,8. Du point de vue des recruteurs, l'outil de prédilection demeure largement le site d'emploi (88 %), devant les candidatures spontanées (80 %) et le site des ressources humaines de l'entreprise (61 %). Représentant 47 % des réponses, les réseaux sociaux arrivent au même niveau que les cabinets de recrutement.

Le Monde (lemonde.fr), 21/6/2010

Overview

Read a general overview of the subject.

Web 2.0

The Internet is a network of networks, the world's largest interconnected group of computer networks. And, since the larger a network gets, the more information it can provide, the Internet was branded in the early nineties "The Information (super) Highway" by US Vice-President Al Gore. The Internet, rebranded "cyberspace"» in 1984 by sci-fi writer William Gibson, has been hailed as the greatest revolution in human knowledge since Gutenberg's printing press in the 15th century.

Yet, it has taken more than the last two decades to shape today's state-of-the-art information technology medium. The Internet's history goes as far back as the early sixties when UCLA Professor Kleiner put forward the "packet-switching information flow" in 1961 and the first network experiment was conducted in 1965 at the MIT with Larry Roberts using packet-switching technology to get two computers to exchange data. The first e-mail programmes were written by Arpanet scientist Tomlinson in 1972 and the first Arpanet international connections took place in 1973 between academics in London and Norway. Ten years later, Transmission Control Protocol/Internet Protocol (TCP/IP) became the standard for Internet computers.

The watershed came in 1989 when Tim Berners-Lee, then a scientist at CERN, came up with a groundbreaking way of distributing information: the hypertext link which enables users to connect from one page to another via HTML links. This graphic interface was much more user-friendly and accounts for the advent of the "surf the web" era in the mid-nineties. The White House opened its website in 1994 while the first dot.coms were established. At the same time came spamming and the Netscape Navigator, a browser to make surfing through cyberspace easier by the use of keywords. In 1996, there were already 45 million Internet users. Three years later it had soared to 150 million and "E-commerce" became the new buzz word as Internet shopping started spreading like wildfire, triggering off the first "dotcom bubble" of Internet start-ups. The birth of Google in 1998, the creation of MySpace.com and Napster in 1999 (an application making it possible to swap music freely over the Net), threats of viruses that replicate themselves through a user's email address book, the birth of Wikipedia in 2001… all these paved the way to the web as we know it today. In 2009, there are approximately 100 million websites for more than a billion users and the Internet, originally based on webpages, has moved into "people-to-people" Web 2.0's era.

Pronunciation

Listen and repeat.

dew [djuː], **duel** [djʊəl]

- cue/cure, stewed/steward, few/fewer.
- The steward will be cured if he eats fewer stews.

Chapter 47

Net privacy

Language focus

Each, every, all, the whole

• *Each* et *every* (suivis d'un nom dénombrable singulier) correspondent au quantifieur français « chaque ». On choisira *each* quand on veut singulariser :

Each day is a new day.	Chaque jour est un jour nouveau.

• *Every* comporte une nuance totalisante supplémentaire :

Every day is different.	Chaque jour est différent. (= Tous les jours partagent une même propriété, celle d'être différent des autres.)

• *All* renvoie directement à la totalité, dénombrable ou non :

all the books; all of you	tous les livres; vous tous
all Scots; all the money	tous les Écossais; tout/la totalité de l'argent

• L'adjectif *whole* se construit toujours avec un nom dénombrable singulier et renvoie à la totalité, l'intégralité :

the whole world	le monde entier

Wordbank

to activate a virus	*activer un virus*
an antiviral program	*un programme antivirus*
a back door	*une porte de sécurité secrète*
to break/hack into a computer	*pénétrer un système par effraction*
to cause malfunctions	*provoquer des dysfonctionnements*
to clog a system	*encombrer un système*
a clone	*une copie*
to compile detailed user profiles	*compiler des profils d'internautes détaillés*
computer piracy/hacking/pirating	*le piratage informatique*
computer security	*la sécurité informatique*
confidential data	*des données privées*
to crack a code/a password	*trouver la clé/le mot de passe*
data integrity	*la sécurité des données*
to delete, to erase	*effacer*
digital inquisition	*l'inquisition numérique*
to duplicate itself	*se reproduire*
encryption	*le codage*
to eradicate a virus	*éliminer/extirper un virus*
to escape detection	*échapper à la surveillance/au contrôle*
a firewall	*un pare-feu*

a foolproof system	*un système à toute épreuve*
a hacker	*un pirate informatique*
to harbo(u)r a virus	*abriter un virus*
to invade citizens' privacy	*envahir la vie privée des citoyens*
to lie dormant	*être en sommeil*
to monitor the people's lives	*contrôler la vie des gens*
P3P (Platform for Privacy Preferences Project) recommandations	*conseils pour établir un profil sécurisé*
potential misuses	*des abus potentiels*
to purge the memory	*purger la mémoire*
restricted access files	*des fichiers sécurisés*
the right to privacy	*le respect de la vie privée*
a rogue program	*un programme infectieux*
to scan a disk	*examiner un disque*
a self-replicating mechanism	*un mécanisme d'autoreproduction*
to share personal information	*transmettre des données confidentielles*
to shut off a program	*fermer un programme*
to slow operations	*ralentir les opérations*
a soft bomb	*un programme destructeur*
to spawn tons of spam	*engendrer des tonnes de pourriels*
spyware	*un logiciel espion*
to be stricken by a virus	*être atteint d'un virus*
system check software	*un logiciel de contrôle de système*
to tamper with	*trafiquer*
to track net users	*suivre les internautes à la trace*
a Trojan horse	*un cheval de Troie*
unauthorised entry	*une effraction*
an unwanted intruder	*un intrus indésirable*
violations of privacy	*des atteintes à la vie privée*
a virus-ridden file	*un fichier bourré de virus*

Translation

Translate the sentences into English.

1. Chaque pirate informatique veut laisser une trace en piratant par exemple un système aussi protégé que les sites gouvernementaux américains.

2. Tous les ordinateurs aujourd'hui sont livrés avec anti-virus et pare-feu .

3. Chaque utilisateur d'Internet est bien conscient qu'il doit varier ses mots de passe.

4. Le réseau tout entier peut être infecté en 24 heures à cause du mécanisme d'autoreproduction de ce virus.

5. Un cheval de Troie qui est en sommeil sur votre disque dur peut transférer toutes vos données confidentielles et privées vers des sites commerciaux ou pire...

Read and answer

Read the article and then do activities A and B that follow.

Facebook, Google and privacy: Dicing with data

In the space of a week two of the best-known internet companies have found themselves in a pickle over privacy. Facebook faces criticism for making more information about its users available by default. Meanwhile Google has been castigated by a bevy of privacy regulators for inadvertently collecting data from unsecured Wi-Fi networks in people's homes as part of a project to capture images of streets around the world.

Although the two cases are distinct, they have revived fears that online privacy is being trampled underfoot as internet behemoths race to grab as much data as possible. And they have provoked calls for tougher action by regulators and governments to prevent web firms from abusing the mountains of personal data they now hold. Danah Boyd, a social-networking expert, has even argued that Facebook, with its hordes of members around the world, is now so embedded in people's lives that it should be regulated as a utility.

The firms have fought back. Facebook claims that most of its users are comfortable with the changes it has introduced, including one that lets it share detailed customer data with some external sites. It has blamed the furore on media hysteria; only a few privacy activists have publicly committed "Facebook suicide" by closing their accounts. As for Google, it has apologised for its "mistake" and says that leaders of its Street View project knew nothing about the software that allowed its roving vehicles to capture snippets of e-mails.

At its most extreme, the attack on Facebook and Google makes little sense. Treating them as utilities seems excessive, for two reasons. They are not essential services that enjoy a local or national monopoly; people who feel their privacy is being violated are free to hop to other web services (remember AltaVista and MySpace?), though many sites deliberately make it hard for them to take their data with them. A second reason to tread carefully is that strict regulation could stifle the rapid innovation in business models that has thrived on the internet. Instead, officials should concentrate on enforcing existing privacy rules – something they seem reassuringly keen to do. Canada's privacy commissioner, Jennifer Stoddart, has given warning that her organisation may take action against Facebook for violating a deal reached last year requiring the network to seek users' permission before sharing their data.

However, even if, like this newspaper, you both distrust government intervention and believe the world has gained from the sharing of information on the web, there are plainly real grounds for concern. For instance, Google claims it discovered that its software had been accidentally recording private information for several years only after privacy officials in Germany demanded that it come clean about the data being collected. That is a stunning admission from a technology giant – and privacy watchdogs are right to investigate that.

Facebook's problem is more fundamental. True, the social network has some of the most extensive privacy controls on the web, but these have now become so complex – and are tweaked so often – that even privacy experts find them bamboozling. The company also has a powerful incentive to push people into revealing more information. Facebook generates most of its revenue from targeted advertisements based on users' demography and interests, so the more data users share publicly the more money it

...

...

can mint from ads. It may well be betting that users are now so hooked that they are unlikely to revolt against a gradual loosening of privacy safeguards.

The worst thing is Facebook's underlying prejudice against privacy. Sign up and it assumes you want to share as much data as possible; if not, you have to change the settings, which can be a fiddly business. The presumption should be exactly the opposite: the default should be tight privacy controls, which users may then loosen if they choose. If Facebook fails to simplify and improve its privacy policy, it will justly risk the wrath of regulators – and many more Facebook suicides.

The Economist (economist.com), 20/5/2010

A. Language

1. Find synonyms in the first six paragraphs of the article for the following: *have found themelves in a mess/jam, criticised, a huge group of, watchdogs concerned with privacy, accidentally, vulnerable, part and parcel of, a public service, easily accept. moving from place to place, bits, twisted, misleading.*

2. Find antonyms in paragraphs 2, 3 and 4 of the article for the following: *allayed, revered, midgets, to let go of, gentler, is rather logical, protected, to act recklessly, to stimulate, flouting, reluctant.*

B. Questions

Answer each of the following questions in 50 words. Use your own words.

1. What have Facebook and Google been accused of?

2. Why do such attacks "make little sense" according to *The Economist*?

3. What are the main issues net users should focus on?

Translation

Translate the article into English.

Vie privée sur le Net : premier succès pour la CNIL

Il est loin le temps où l'Internet fleurait bon son petit côté libertaire. Sous la pression conjuguée des États (la lutte contre le terrorisme a toujours bon dos) et de la réalité économique (il faut bien rémunérer des services «gratuits»), les géants de la Toile captent, conservent et vendent de plus en plus de données relatives à la vie privée des utilisateurs.

La CNIL vient de remporter un succès dans la défense de ces derniers. Le 26 mai, la Commission nationale de l'informatique et des libertés a adressé *«une mise en demeure»* à Google pour l'obliger à livrer des données collectées pour son programme *StreetView*. [...]

Il a fallu à Google un énorme travail de collecte pour monter le programme. C'est l'objet de « StreetView» : des *Google cars* – voitures de Google équipées de neuf caméras et de scanners – sillonnent les villes du monde entier, repèrent les bornes et photographient les rues : les États-Unis ont été scannés, le Japon, une grande partie de l'Australie et de l'Europe, dont la France. Les visages et les plaques d'immatriculation sont floutées et le résultat est mis gracieusement en ligne sur Google Maps.

Le Monde (lemonde.fr), 17/6/2010

Overview

Read a general overview of the subject.

How much do you want them to know?

With 500 millions of Facebook users sharing detailed accounts of their humdrum lives, our very notion of privacy – the definition of what should be considered as appropriate or not to post online – is being challenged by social networking websites.

What appeals so much to Internet users is the mix of networking tools that enables them to meet online with family and friends. It is only logical that our online profile should reflect our behaviour and tastes offline – to build up what Facebook founder Mark Zuckerberg has labelled a "social graph". If you add that Facebook's geolocation services are able to spot each user by means of his mobile phone and that Google's StreetView cars picking up data from users' computers have fuelled the debate about the protection of personal details and confidential data online, no wonder networking sites' privacy policies are under increasingly wary public scrutiny and under pressure to make sites much safer for users. Privacy campaigners have attacked Google Earth for its assault on our right to privacy while some Facebook users have badgered the site into providing simpler privacy settings by threatening to remove their profiles.

Each and every individual connected to the interactive web can capture and share information. The challenge posed to web providers, decision-makers and users is how to manage that ever-increasing flow of data – in other words, where is the line to be drawn between public and private spheres?

Because technological advance has moved the boundaries much farther than our laws and social standards were prepared to, the "privacy bar" must be reset. So far, critics have mostly voiced concern over the potential damage to one's reputation through the public exposure of past personal information – the damning snapshot of you completely plastered at a New Year's Eve party – and data theft (of confidential information such as your credit card number). A dystopian view of Web 2.0's potential misuse of personal profiles predicts the advent of "Big Sister"'s digital inquisition to control our lives through the capture and storage of our online details, but such exaggeration sounds rather unrealistic.

There is no denying that some hackers and an army of marketing experts may be using search engines to track our online footprint for their own agenda but users should bear in mind first and foremost that it's really up to them to decide what they want to keep private.

Pronunciation

Listen and repeat.

The "-s" ending

- the witch's switches, her niece's pieces, Ann's plans, the nurse's purses.
- My friend spends a lot while your friends spend little.

48 Chapter

The consumer society

Language focus

Place de l'adverbe dans la phrase

• Les adverbes, beaucoup plus nombreux et fréquents en anglais qu'en français, signalent l'opinion du locuteur ; ils occupent des positions variables en fonction de leur contribution sémantique.

1. Adverbes de modalité (ex : *maybe, perhaps, probably, possibly…)* :

***Maybe** she doesn't like wine.*	Peut-être n'aime-t-elle pas le vin.
*She **probably** doesn't like beer.*	Elle n'aime probablement pas la bière.

2. Adverbes de fréquence (ex : *often, rarely…*) :

*She **often** goes to the movies.*	Elle va souvent au cinema.
*He is **rarely** late.*	Il est rarement en retard.

3. Adverbes de manière (ex : *quickly, badly*) :

*He speaks German **fluently**.*	Il parle allemand couramment.

4. Adverbes semi-négatifs (ex : *hardly, barely, scarcely…)* :

*She **barely** knows a word of French.*	Elle connaît à peine trois mots de français.

Wordbank

an age group	*une tranche d'âge*
an aisle	*une allée de magasin*
an all-inclusive price	*un prix TTC*
the average propensity to consume (APC)	*la propension moyenne à consommer*
base point pricing	*le prix de base théorique*
behavioural patterns	*des modèles de comportement*
a budding/promising market	*un marché prometteur*
buyers and sellers	*acheteurs et vendeurs*
the buying decision	*la décision d'achat*
the central shopping area	*les commerces du centre ville*
a competitive price	*un prix concurrentiel*
commodities	*les marchandises, les denrées, les produits*
consumer behaviour	*le comportement des consommateurs*
consumer goods	*les biens de consommation*
consumer habits	*les habitudes des consommateurs*
the consumer society	*la société de consommation*
the cost price	*le prix coûtant*
a customer	*un client*
a department store	*un grand magasin*

a department	*un rayon*
a discount, a rebate	*un rabais, une ristourne*
a display rack/stand	*un présentoir*
disposable income	*le revenu disponible*
the domestic/home market	*le marché intérieur*
down-/mid-/up-market	*bas, milieu, haut de gamme*
downscale, upscale	*bas de gamme, haut de gamme*
durable goods	*des biens d'équipement*
edibles, foodstuffs	*les denrées alimentaires*
family income, income per household	*le revenu par ménage*
a fast-growing/growth market	*un marché en pleine croissance*
the foreign markets	*les marchés étrangers*
goods and services	*les biens et les services*
household consumption	*la consommation des ménages*
an impulse buy/purchase	*un achat d'impulsion*
manufactured goods	*les produits manufacturés*
market mechanisms	*la loi du marché*
market segmentation	*la segmentation du marché*
niche shops	*les boutiques spécialisées*
a price war	*une guerre des prix*
price-cutting	*la baisse des prix*
purchasing/spending power	*le pouvoir d'achat*
to reach a broad section of consumers	*atteindre un large segment de consommateurs*
to segment a market	*segmenter un marché*
a shop assistant, a sales clerk *(US)*	*un vendeur*
a shop window	*une vitrine*
a shopping arcade	*une galerie marchande*
a shopping mall	*un centre commercial*
to slash prices	*sacrifier les prix*
a staple good	*une denrée de première nécessité*
supply and demand	*l'offre et la demande*
to target a market	*cibler un marché*

Translation

Translate the sentences into English.

1. À peine une société a-t-elle lancé un nouveau produit que ses concurrents sortent d'autres modèles.

2. Les denrées de première nécessité ne sont pas vraiment des produits qui éveillent l'intérêt des consommateurs.

3. Acheteurs et vendeurs sont rarement d'accord sur le prix de vente d'une voiture.

4. Il est probable que le marché naissant du livre numérique explosera d'ici dix ans avec l'arrivée d'une nouvelle génération de lecteurs.

5. Les denrées alimentaires comme les produits laitiers ou les fruits s'accommodent mal des transports longue distance.

Read and answer

Read the article and then do activities A and B that follow.

America's shoppers: The retailers' dilemma

NEW YORK. The mood of executives at retail firms normally moves in lockstep with that of their customers. But in America the news on May 25th that consumer confidence had reached its highest level in two years left them oddly subdued. Consumer spending per person, which fell for two years in a row for the first time since the Depression last year and the year before, has been rising again in recent months. But as retail executives place orders for the crucial end-of-year rush, they are anxiously debating how strong and lasting the consumer's revival will be. [...]

Although profits were up at Wal-Mart, sales at its American stores fell by 1.4% compared with a year earlier. "More than ever, our customers are living pay cheque to pay cheque," says Tom Schoewe, its chief financial officer. "I'm worried," admits the boss of another large retail chain, privately. "Things seem a little rougher now than in the first quarter." The effect of the government stimulus is running out and consumers' finances remain stretched, he confides. The International Council of Shopping Centres, a trade group, recently trimmed its sales projections for May.

Everyone agrees that American consumers are more cheerful than they were last year. A new survey by Deloitte, a consultancy, found that nearly two-thirds of them say their financial situation is as good as or better than it was a year ago, and that accordingly they plan to spend the same as last year or more. "Retailers should be encouraged by consumers' tone as they plan for the critical fall and winter selling seasons," says Stacy Janiak, who heads Deloitte's retail practice in America. [...]

The typical customer "still has a lot of fear in her heart, and she is still being very cautious," says Michael Silverstein, a consultant and co-author of "Women Want More", which argues that women control the lion's share of household spending. "She had over-consumed before the recession. At the bottom of the recession, she had nothing unworn, nothing new. This spring, she looked at her closet, her kitchen, said, 'Goddamit, I still have a job', and decided to loosen the purse strings."

This might explain the recent sharp increase in spending on lingerie, dresses, coats and even the higher sales at Home Depot, given that women, Mr Silverstein argues with dogged consistency, tend to initiate redecorating sprees. Loosening the purse strings did not mean abandoning the frugality that was the clearest consumer trend during the recession. [...]

"The assumption that when the recession was over consumers would return to where they were has already been disproved," says Paul Leinwand, a consultant at Booz & Company. Retailers are investing heavily to track consumers' behaviour in an attempt to work out what they might want to buy and how much they are willing to pay.

In general, retailers have learned to focus far more on lowering prices, and in particular to stock a larger proportion of products at the low end of the price range. Saks has been especially astute at this, not least by increasing significantly the share of goods on its shelves that carry its own label. This has been a trend across the retail industry in the past two years, and no one expects it to be reversed now that consumer sentiment is starting to improve. On the contrary, the proportion of private-label sales may well continue to rise to levels long seen in Europe.

...

. . .

Nor does anyone expect any reversal of another trend: consumers have been buying through a growing number of channels, from department stores to discount warehouses to the internet, often going online first to hunt for the best prices. All of the leading retailers have tried to spruce up their online act during the downturn, but few have done as well as start-ups such as Gilt Groupe, which uses social networking to carry out discounted sales of designer-label clothes and homeware, and luxury holidays.

The Economist (economist.com), 27/5/2010

A. Language

1. Find synonyms in the title and paragraphs 1, 2 and 5 of the article for the following: *a quandary, matches, had peaked, strangely, increased, incentive, scaled down, obstinate, bouts of excessive spending.*

2. Find antonyms in paragraphs 3, 4 and 5 of the article for the following: *wholesalers, deterred, unimportant, reckless, finish, the least obvious.*

B. Questions

1. What is the dilemma US retailers are currently facing? (Answer in 200 words. Use information in the article but do not copy sentences directly: use your own words.)

2. Explain the following quotation in 100 words: "The typical customer [...] had over-consumed before the recession. At the bottom of the recession, she had nothing unworn, nothing new. This spring she looked at her closet, her kitchen [...] and decided to loosen the purse strings."

Translation

Translate the article into English.

Les Français bien dans leur vie

Heureux ? La majorité des Français se sentent bien dans leur vie quotidienne et tout particulièrement à travers les moments d'échanges et de convivialité avec les autres. Tel est le premier constat de l'étude « Les Français, la santé et le bien-être », réalisée par l'Ifop pour Philips et présentée ce mardi 22 juin. Pour 61 % d'entre eux, être bien dans sa tête est le visa indispensable pour le bien-être, alors que quatre Français sur cinq estiment le développement durable et la protection de l'environnement essentiels à leur bonheur. Côté équipement ménager, la tendance est à la simplicité : la télévision se place en tête des exigences, talonnée par la chaîne hi-fi et le mixeur. Les équipements high-tech arrivent loin derrière.

Sur le plan de la santé, on se fait beaucoup plus de souci qu'avant, avec le sentiment diffus que les conditions sanitaires se sont dégradées ces dernières années. [...]

Quant au regard que l'on porte sur l'avenir, il est plutôt morose. Le vieillissement de la population devient une préoccupation majeure. Un Français sur deux pense que l'exposition aux risques sanitaires sera plus élevée dans les prochaines années.

Betty Mamane, *L'Express* (lexpress.fr), 22/6/2010

Overview

Read a general overview of the subject.

The pursuit of happiness and profit

Because of the emergence of the American-style consumer society in the western world after World War II, commerce has gradually become the key issue around which the whole world revolves. The global trade of goods and services has turned into a global cut-throat competition and spawned its own transnational culture in which the world's younger generations have been immersed from their very birth. As Andrew Marr put it in his *History of Modern Britain* (2007): "The British had become a nation of shoppers".

To meet consumer demand, manufacturers and service providers have implemented all sorts of means to boost mass consumption: market segmentation (to target each and every potential buyer), market research (to analyse customers' patterns of behaviour), marketing (to organise the creation and launch of new products) and promotion (policies to woo customers). Fierce competition is said to be good for both sellers and buyers because, in order to generate profit, companies are forced to keep innovating: customers demand attractive, state-of-the-art products at a reasonable price. Products improve in quality and variety (which benefits the consumer), the market booms, prices fall and the consumer benefits again.

In our consumer society, happiness and well-being are equated with the amount of products and services we can buy; they are a function of our spending power which is usually associated with a certain social status. Our shopping sprees at the local mall are also ego trips where branded goods cater to our every whim, our changes of mood, the way we want to appear to others. Our needs for status, our response to peer pressure or our desire for self-development all come into play when we "shop until we drop" as we attempt to enhance our image to match the perception we have of ourselves.

As American-born marketing has always been based on behavioural studies, manufacturers and the advertisers they hire are well aware that the key to profit lies in making the right appeal: how, for example, can one cajole buyers into purchasing the latest "green" car?

Our society has moved from one based on a specific set of shared historical values and references to a transnational universe of brands that are supposed to embody our innermost dreams, ideals and beliefs. Unfortunately, it has also encouraged excessive materialism and individualism by reducing the pursuit of happiness to the never-ending quest for instant gratification.

Pronunciation

Listen and repeat.

The "-ed" ending

- play/played, paint/painted, walk/walked.
- He played while she rested; you danced while I waited.

Chapter 49

Brands

Language focus

La traduction de « on »

• Selon le référent qu'on souhaite sous-entendre derrière « on », on choisira l'une des formulations ci-dessous.

• Le passif, si l'agent est complètement inconnu ou sans importance :

On dit qu'il est très riche. *He **is said** to be very rich.*

• *One*, dans les phrases générales, les proverbes :

On n'est jamais assez prudent. ***One** can't be too careful.*

• *People* ou *they* = les gens :

Les gens ont tendance à croire ce qu'ils voient à la télévision.

***People** tend to believe what they see on TV.*

• *You*, quand le locuteur veut s'exclure :

Chez vous, en Grande-Bretagne, on boit beaucoup de thé.

*In Great-Britain, **you** drink a lot of tea.*

• *We*, quand le locuteur veut s'inclure au contraire :

Chez nous, on aime le bon vin.

*Here, **we** like good wine.*

Wordbank

to blur/tarnish the brand image	*brouiller/ternir l'image de marque*
a brand	*une marque*
brand awareness	*la notoriété d'une marque*
the brand image	*l'image de marque*
a brand life cycle	*le cycle de vie d'une marque*
brand loyalty	*la fidélité à une marque*
brand managing, branding policy	*la politique de la marque*
a brand manager	*un chef de produit*
brand switching	*changer de marque*
branding	*l'invention d'une marque*
to build a brand name	*se faire un nom en tant que marque*
to cater for/to consumer demand	*satisfaire la demande des consommateurs*
a consumer goods brand	*une marque de produit de consommation*
cost-effective	*d'un bon rapport qualité prix*
counterfeiting	*la contrefaçon*
cutting-edge	*à la pointe du progrès*
a discount	*une ristourne*

fashion products	*les articles de mode*
a flop	*un échec*
to go global	*se mondialiser*
a hard-core user	*utilisateur inconditionnel*
to identify with a brand	*s'identifier à une marque*
a label	*une étiquette*
a leading brand	*une grande marque*
a loss leader	*un produit d'appel*
to market a brand	*commercialiser une marque*
market penetration	*la pénétration d'un marché*
a no-brand product	*un produit libre*
an own-label brand	*une marque de distributeur*
the packaging	*le conditionnement*
the packing	*l'emballage*
product capabilities	*les capacités d'un produit*
a product lifecyle (PLC)	*le cycle de vie d'un produit*
product profitability	*le rendement d'un produit*
a product range/line/mix	*une gamme de produits*
the rankings of brands	*le classement des marques*
a rebate	*un rabais*
the resilience of a brand	*la résistance d'une marque*
to revive a brand	*relancer une marque*
a star/flagship product	*un produit vedette*
state-of-the-art	*dernier cri*
a sub-brand	*une sous-marque*
to take on/to break into new markets	*mettre le pied sur de nouveaux marchés*
to tap foreign markets	*exploiter des marchés étrangers*
to be top of the pile/shelf	*être en tête des marques*
a top-selling brand	*une marque qui se vend bien*
a trademark	*une marque déposée*

Translation

Translate the sentences into English.

1. On dit de ce jeune chef de projet qu'il est très ambitieux.

2. Cette marque d'équipement électrique a la réputation d'être une marque de qualité.

3. Les gens disent que la fidélité à une marque dépend surtout du rapport qualité-prix.

4. Quand on travaille dans le marketing on s'intéresse à tout ce qui est susceptible de stimuler l'appétit des consommateurs.

5. On a pensé à tort dans les années 90 que l'avènement d'Internet sonnerait la fin de la publicité dans les médias traditionnels.

Read and answer

Read the article and then do activities A and B that follow.

Saving Chevrolet Means Sending 'Chevy' to Dump

On Tuesday, G.M. sent a memo to Chevrolet employees at its Detroit headquarters, promoting the importance of "consistency" for the brand, which was the nation's best-selling line of cars and trucks for more than half a century after World War II.

And one way to present a consistent brand message, the memo suggested, is to stop saying "Chevy," though the word is one of the world's best-known, longest-lived product nicknames.

"We'd ask that whether you're talking to a dealer, reviewing dealer advertising, or speaking with friends and family, that you communicate our brand as Chevrolet moving forward," said the memo, which was signed by Alan Batey, vice president for Chevrolet sales and service, and Jim Campbell, the G.M. division's vice president for marketing.

"When you look at the most recognized brands throughout the world, such as Coke or Apple for instance, one of the things they all focus on is the consistency of their branding," the memo said. "Why is this consistency so important? The more consistent a brand becomes, the more prominent and recognizable it is with the consumer."

Although the memo cites Coke, it does not note that Coke is shorthand for Coca-Cola – or that Apple is not commonly used in reference to its products, which are known simply as iPads, iPhones and MacBooks.

One expert on branding said G.M.'s effort ran counter to a trend in which corporate names had become more casual. The consultant, Paul Worthington, head of strategy for Wolff Olins, a brand consulting company, noted that FedEx had replaced Federal Express, KFC had supplanted Kentucky Fried Chicken and "even RadioShack has evolved into the Shack."

Regardless, if Chevrolet plans to put the Chevy genie back in the bottle, the task could prove harder than climbing out of bankruptcy.

As of Wednesday night, the word Chevy appeared dozens of times on Chevrolet's Web site, chevrolet.com, including a banner on the home page that said, "Over 1,000 people a day switch to Chevy." One of the dropdown menus was "Experience Chevy." On Facebook, brand pages include Chevy Camaro, Chevy Silverado and Team Chevy. […]

And what about rolling back the popular culture references to Chevy? Elton John, Bob Seger, Mötley Crüe and the Beastie Boys have all sung about Chevy, and hip-hop artists rap about "Chevy Ridin' High" or "Ridin' in My Chevy."

There are also a good many auto enthusiasts who have "Chevy" tattooed onto various body parts. Some probably have a Chevy II or two tucked in their garages.

"It's a 'Vette, it's a Caddy, it's a Chevy," said Dick Guldstrand, a long-time racer who has been inducted into the Corvette Hall of Fame. He noted that the brand was named for Louis Chevrolet, a race driver of the early 20th century.

"Once it became an American icon, America took it away from G.M.," said Mr. Guldstrand, 83. "They made it a Chevy. You're doing a disservice to all the people by telling them not to call it a Chevy."

In 2006, Chevrolet updated a series of popular commercials with the tagline "Baseball, hot dogs, apple pie and Chevrolet," which noted how the brand was woven into the fabric of American culture.

...

...

The commercial juxtaposed imagery of past baseball greats with modern ones. And at the end, the narrator says, "Apparently, baseball's changed a little over the years, but not America's love of the game – or love for Chevy." [...]

Mr. Worthington, the branding expert, said Chevrolet seemed unclear what the brand stood for. "So what it would appear they are trying to do, by centralizing to a single formal name, is to try to get some focus as to what that brand stands for, and get that out into the marketplace, which makes a lot of sense."

Ultimately, he said, consumers "will call you whatever they want to call you."

Richard S. Chang, *The New York Times* (nytimes.com), 9/6/2010

A. Language

Find synonyms in the first four paragraphs of the article for the following: *main office, championing, the country's favourite range, coherent, pet names, an agent for a car manufacturer, concentrate on, brand management.*

B. Questions

1. What are the strengths and weaknesses of Chevrolet's new brand management? (Answer in 150-200 words. Use your own words.)

2. Explain the following quotation in 100 words: "Once it became an American icon, America took it away from GM. They made it a Chevy. You're doing a dissservice to all the people by telling them not to call it a Chevy."

Translation

Translate the article into English.

Ekyog, la marque qui monte

Ekyog est une histoire de couple. Nathalie (36 ans) et Louis-Marie Vautier (37 ans) ont eu le flair de se lancer dans le prêt-à-porter écologique dès 2004, à un moment où l'on parlait encore peu des questions d'environnement.

Quel est l'engagement écologique d'Ekyog ?

Le respect de la marque tant pour les hommes que pour la planète est irréprochable. « Nous ne travaillons que des matières qui ont un faible impact sur l'environnement » explique Louis-Marie Vautier. « Il s'agit principalement de coton certifié bio, de laine biologique et de tencel (matière issue du bois). La seule matière synthétique que nous tolérons est le polyester recyclé. »

Vigilant sur les matières premières, Ekyog respecte également un strict cahier des charges à chacune des étapes de transformation, qu'il s'agisse des teintures (garanties non nocives) ou des conditions de travail des ouvriers. Non content de se plier aux exigences des certificateurs, le couple réalise même des audits réguliers dans ses usines partenaires afin d'être sûr de respecter ses engagements. Enfin, par mesure d'économie d'énergie, les vêtements sont – dans la mesure du possible – fabriqués là où pousse la matière première.

Géraldine Dormoy, *L'Express* (lexpress.fr), 22/6/2010

Overview

Read a general overview of the subject.

Describing the product or the consumer?

In our mass-production and mass-consumption global economy, the brand is what links the product to the producer in terms of market-positioning and segmentation, and what enables the consumer to identify the product, to associate it with a certain image and equate it with a certain lifestyle or certain values. Hence the widespread opinion that a reputable brand means good value for money. However, with the arrival of television in almost every household in the 60s and the spread of the Internet since the 90s, successful branding means that, by favouring a certain brand, the customer is making a statement about his or her personal values and beliefs. Whereas the original purpose of branding was simply to identify the product, it now identifies its consumer too.

The increasing presence of branded goods in every walk of life reflects our culture's obsession with the display of wealth through status symbols: what you buy shows your station in society and your spending power. This was particularly true in the 80s when Reaganomics and Thatcherism were promoting free enterprise; no stigma was attached to success and material wealth. But then brands started meaning more than wealth or success. Benetton, for example, championed human rights in its ads, believing its brand could symbolise the values and beliefs of both its chairman and its customers. Interestingly, it went into partnership with Renault to produce the Twingo Benetton in the 1990s. At the time, Renault's slogan (created for the launch of the Twingo), *Renault, des voitures à vivre,* epitomised the "lifestyle brand" and Benetton identified the Twingo driver as having more or less the same profile as the Benetton wearer: "a free spirit, a non-conformist, an individualist who is socially aware and has a cosmopolitan vision".

Both companies realised that consumers no longer define themselves in terms of the traditional categories of nationality, region, ethnicity, class or religion. In a world of globalisation which is ill-defined and unstructured, we are undergoing what the concept-makers have called a "post-modern identity crisis". No longer do mainstream values in the USA and the UK reflect those of the white, Anglo-Saxon, Protestant middle-class; nowadays people tend to define themselves by their style of clothing and furnishings, their choice of car, what they eat and drink, and how they spend their leisure time. The world of brands has been turned upside down: it is no longer about endowing products with virtual virtues, it's all about asserting "I'm here" to the rest of a six-billion-people global village.

Pronunciation

Listen and repeat.

Reading dates

• 4/5/1990 *(UK)* • 1/6/2009 *(US)* • 2054 • 13th April.
• Wednesday 12th August.

50 Chapter

Advertising

Language focus

Expressions du but et du moyen

• Les expressions les plus courantes du but et du moyen sont des subordonnées ou des groupes prépositionnels :

He came here	*in order to win.*	pour gagner.
	for everyone to see him.	pour que tout le monde le voie.
	so that she would/may/might see him.	pour qu'elle le voie.
	with a view to winning.	dans le but de gagner.
He succeeded	*by working hard.*	en travaillant dur.
	thanks to a stroke of luck.	grâce à un coup de chance.

Wordbank

to advertise	*faire de la publicité pour*
an advertisement/advert/ad	*une publicité*
an advertiser	*un publiciste*
advertising	*la publicité*
an advertising blitz	*un matraquage publicitaire*
an advertising budget	*un budget publicitaire*
an advertising claim	*un argument publicitaire*
an advertising medium	*un support publicitaire*
advertising space	*de l'espace publicitaire*
to analyse market demand	*analyser les besoins du marché*
a billboard, a hoarding	*un panneau publicitaire*
a brand image campaign	*une campagne d'image*
to brighten (up) an ad	*égayer une publicité*
a captive/loyal customer	*un client captif/fidèle*
a cluster analysis	*une analyse par segment*
cluster sampling	*l'échantillonnage par segment*
a commercial	*un spot publicitaire à la télévision*
comparative advertising	*la publicité comparative*
to conduct market research	*procéder à l'analyse de marché*
to conduct/carry out a survey	*mener une enquête*
consumer appeal	*l'attrait pour le consommateur*
to convey a message	*véhiculer un message*
a cross section	*un échantillon représentatif*

to endorse a product	*faire de la réclame pour une marque*
to get across a message	*faire passer un message*
to influence a buying trend	*influencer une tendance d'achat*
a jingle	*un jingle, une mélodie publicitaire*
to launch a campaign	*lancer une campagne*
a mailing	*un publipostage*
market forces	*les tendances du marché*
the market forecast	*les prévisions du marché*
a media plan	*un plan média*
misleading advertising	*la publicité mensongère/trompeuse*
an opinion poll	*une enquête par sondage*
to plan a campaign	*concevoir une campagne*
to play down	*minimiser un défaut*
to play on an appeal	*jouer sur un axe psychologique*
to praise/to brag about a product	*vanter les mérites d'un produit*
to push a product	*faire vendre un produit*
a random sampling	*un échantillon aléatoire*
the reach of a campaign	*la couverture publicitaire*
research findings	*les résultats d'une étude de marché*
to set a new trend	*lancer une nouvelle tendance*
a show, an exhibition	*un salon*
to talk viewers into buying	*convaincre les téléspectateurs d'acheter*
a teaser campaign	*une campagne de provocation*
a trendsetter	*un créateur de tendances*
to woo/seduce/attract prospects	*séduire/attirer les acheteurs potentiels*

Translation

Translate the sentences into English.

1. Le fabricant de jouets va procéder à l'analyse du marché chez les garçons de 6 à 10 ans avant de lancer sa nouvelle gamme de robots.

2. Ce grand constructeur automobile a investi des millions d'euros en spots télé pour présenter son tout nouveau modèle de 4X4.

3. Grâce à cette vedette de cinéma qui a fait de la réclame pour notre société de cosmétiques, nos bénéfices ont explosé à la fin des années 90.

4. Il est facile de séduire les consommateurs en jouant sur les axes psychologiques du plaisir, de la peur ou du sexe.

5. Les publicistes de Madison Avenue ont engagé le dernier des grands groupes de rock pour cette campagne publicitaire dans le but évident d'attirer les nostalgiques des années 60.

Read and answer

Read the article and then do activities A and B that follow.

Charity as advertising: Give and take

Will Pepsi profit by enlisting the public in its philanthropic efforts?

NEW YORK. The 107m Americans who tuned in to watch the Super Bowl on February 7th did not see any advertisements for Pepsi. Instead of spending $20m on a handful of 30-second spots, the firm decided to give that amount away. Under the slogan "Refresh Everything", the Pepsi Refresh campaign asks the public to vote online for charities and community groups to receive grants ranging from $5,000 to $250,000. A few days before the game its arch-rival, Coca-Cola, was also bitten by a charitable bug. It promised to give $1 to the Boys & Girls Clubs of America every time someone watched its Super Bowl ads on its Facebook page, up to a maximum of $250,000.

Pepsi Refresh is probably the most prominent example so far of "cause marketing" – trying to win customers by ostentatiously doing good. Other recent examples include Chase Community Giving, in which small charities competed to win $5m in donations from JPMorgan Chase, and American Express and NBC Universal's "Shine A Light" programme, which awarded a grant of $100,000 to a small business chosen through its website.

Marketing people say consumers are increasingly trying to do good as they spend. Research in 2008 by Cone, a brand consultancy, found that 79% of consumers would switch to a brand associated with a good cause, up from 66% in 1993, and that 38% have bought a product associated with a cause, compared with 20% in 1993. Rather than try to make products that can be marketed as ethical in their own right, such as "fair trade" goods, firms are increasingly trying to take an ordinary product and boost its moral credentials with what one marketing guru calls "embedded generosity". The fad for online competitions to award the handouts also appeals to another trend, so-called "slacktivism", whereby people are turning to the internet to give their consciences a boost without doing anything more onerous than clicking a mouse a few times.

The strategy seems to be working, judging by the proliferation of articles (such as this one) noting Pepsi's campaign. JPMorgan Chase claims its campaign was not marketing, but simply an attempt to manage its existing corporate philanthropy more imaginatively. If so, its marketing staff are missing a trick, given that around 2m people signed up to vote on Facebook, many of whom were not existing Chase customers. Moreover, the favourable headlines generated by Chase's $5m outlay contrasted strikingly with the grudging reaction to Goldman Sachs's launch around the same time of a $500m campaign to support small businesses.

Although the public likes online popularity contests, they can have unintended consequences. Chase, for example, caused a fuss by excluding a pro-life group and an outfit that wants to legalise cannabis from its competition. Moreover, many firms see virtue in tying themselves to a particular cause. Ten firms, including Gap, Apple and most recently Nike, have deals with (RED), a scheme fronted by Bono, a rock star, to raise money to fight AIDS. It has raised $140m so far, despite fears that, as Susan Smith Ellis, its boss, puts it, "it would be just a big launch on Oprah then never heard of again." Equally, Pepsi's efforts to promote healthy lifestyles while selling healthier products and Coca-

...

...

> Cola's various initiatives to protect water supplies in developing countries are critical to the pair's future. Refreshing everything, in contrast, is a more nebulous goal.
>
> *The Economist* (economist.com), 11/2/2010

A. Language

Find synonyms in the first four paragraphs of the article for the following: *switched on the TV, donations, main competitor, pledged, the most visible/the leading, conspicuously/extravagantly, can be sold, qualifications, passing trend, are not aware of the bigger picture, investment/expenditure.*

B. Questions

Answer each of the following questions in 50 words. Use information in the article to answer but do not copy sentences directly: use your own words.

1. What is "cause marketing"?

2. Is such advertising policy effective?

3. Can doing good backfire on profit-making companies?

Translation

Translate the article into English.

La publicité en 3D relief s'installe sur les écrans de cinéma

« Jaune, Jaune ! » Un bonbon M&M's rouge crie en cherchant son compagnon coloré. Tout à coup, sa main sort de l'écran de cinéma et vient cueillir Jaune, comme s'il était assis dans la salle. Puis une pluie de bonbons virtuels tombe sur l'assistance. Peut-être découvrirez-vous le nouveau spot publicitaire de cette marque en 3D relief avec ces effets de jaillissement de l'image lors d'une prochaine sortie dans les salles obscures.

La première marque à avoir dégainé en France est Haribo. Conseillée par l'agence KR Media, elle a sorti son spot à l'été 2009. Mais a surtout profité du formidable succès d'Avatar. Le « 40 secondes » a fait mouche, parfois plus que le long métrage de James Cameron. Nombre de téléspectateurs ont évoqué l'envol des bonbons gélifiés dans la salle presque à portée de main ou de bouche. Devant l'intérêt suscité par cette expérience, d'autres annonceurs se sont mis au travail, pour élaborer leur propre spot en 3D. Et les sorties de *Shrek 4* le 30 juin et de *Toy Story 3* le 14 juillet leur fournissent une plate-forme de lancement idéale. [...]

Même limité à un laps de temps de 30 ou 40 secondes, et peut-être surtout à cause de cette concision, l'exercice est loin d'être simple pour les agences et les producteurs. Gang Films, qui a produit le spot Carte Noire, l'a appris à ses dépens. Le tournage et la postproduction de la publicité pour la marque de café ont joué les prolongations, et il est devenu évident, au cours de la préparation, que l'effet relief fonctionne mieux lorsque le plan est large et le fond blanc. Un point important pour une marque qui flirte avec le côté sombre du breuvage. Finalement, l'héroïne du spot se retrouve dans un loft aux murs blancs.

Laurence Girard, *Le Monde* (lemonde.fr), 24/6/2010

Overview

Read a general overview of the subject.

From Big Ad, with love...

Promotion refers to all the means and techniques used to encourage consumers to make a purchase, and the most visible feature of companies' promotional mix is advertising.

Unlike "publicity" which was coined from the French *publicité* in 1791 to describe the process of "making something known" in any field, "advertising" has been mostly applied to commerce since it appeared in 1826. Advertising is alleged to provide useful information to consumers – by making them aware such or such a product or service is now available – but it usually seeks to persuade prospective buyers to buy the product advertised, regardless of demand or of the customer's actual needs.

It began in America, principally on New York's Madison Avenue, and is closely connected to behavioural studies that inspired marketing theories. Advertisements play upon consumers' psychological needs, dreams and motivations. They appeal to different facets of each consumer's personality: the need for security, the desire for prestige and recognition or the craving for novelty. To get the right message across to each target group, advertisers rely on market and sociological studies to detect or set new trends and so be able to project the image that will attract the most customers. In our youth-obsessed, ego-driven Western culture, most ads and commercials picture young, healthy, sexy, attractive actor-models who are supposed to represent the average man- and woman-in-the-street.

For decades, the main mass media used for advertising were television, radio, the press and billboards. Television reaches the largest number of people but TV commercials come at a high cost, which has deterred many companies from paying through the nose for TV ads.

Advertising moved into another era when the Internet's information highway became a worldwide phenomenon in the late nineties. Web 2.0's interactive tools and interconnectedness have kept making it easier to target the right ad to each net user. The increasing shift of advertising budgets to the Internet now threatens the press because loss of advertising revenue has led to job-cuts even in the best papers. However, experts at Morgan Stanley have recently pointed out that the amount of attention paid to ads on TV and in other media outperforms that paid to online customised ads using highly-detailed user profiles as a basis. But, if tomorrow's high-tech wizards can come up with a TV system that delivers ads of the same type as profile-based online display advertising, this could be the adman's dream – and maybe a nightmare for others.

Pronunciation

Listen and repeat.

Stress in compound words

- **book**shop, **bus** stop, **sun**glasses, **super**market, **travel** agent.
- **hand**-made shoes, **second**-hand clothes, an **old**-fashioned clock, a **bad**-tempered man.

Chapter 51

Sport

Language focus

La traduction de « dont »

- La traduction de « dont » dépend de ce que le pronom recouvre.
  1. Possession (voir aussi chapitre 37) :
     L'homme **dont** la voiture a été volée est mon père.
     *The man **whose** car was stolen is my father.*
  2. Complement de verbe (voir aussi chapitre 37) :
     Celui **dont** tu parles est mon frère.
     *The man **ø/that/whom** you're talking about is my brother.*
     Le livre dont tu te sers est le mien.
     *The book **ø/that/which** you're using is mine.*
  4. Le partitif :
     J'ai vu les suspects, dont quelques-uns ont déjà fait de la prison.
     *I've seen the suspects, some **of whom** have already been in prison.*
     J'ai lu ses livres, **dont** la plupart sont bons.
     *I've read his books, most **of which** are good.*

Wordbank

the agony of defeat	*les affres de la défaite*
an all-round sportsman	*un sportif accompli*
the attendance	*le public*
to attract a large following	*attirer de nombreux supporters*
to be awarded a medal	*se voir décerner une médaille*
to battle for the lead	*se battre pour prendre la tête*
to compete with	*rivaliser avec*
a competitor	*un concurrent*
a contender	*un prétendant au titre*
a contest	*une rencontre, un combat*
a contestant, an opponent	*un adversaire*
a daily workout	*un entraînement quotidien*
to defeat, a defeat	*battre, une défaite*
to draw applause	*provoquer les applaudissements*
to draw crowds	*attirer les foules*
to draw up the rules	*établir le règlement*
drug-enhanced performances	*les performances améliorées grâce au dopage*
to field a team	*aligner une équipe*

to fight tooth and nail	*se battre avec acharnement*
fitness	*la forme physique*
the home/visiting team	*l'équipe locale/visiteuse*
hooliganism	*le vandalisme*
to increase muscle bulk	*développer la masse musculaire*
an indoor event	*une rencontre en salle*
to join the professional ranks	*rejoindre les rangs des professionnels*
to lay down the rules	*fixer les règles*
to lead the pack	*mener le peloton*
to be outclassed	*être dominé*
the pitch, the ground	*le terrain*
to push oneself to the limits	*aller au bout de ses forces*
to put out a challenge	*lancer un défi*
a referee, to referee	*un arbitre, arbitrer*
refereeing	*l'arbitrage*
the runner-up	*le second*
a scout	*un recruteur*
to set/smash a world record	*établir/pulvériser un record du monde*
to sign a contract	*signer un contrat*
sportsmanship	*la sportivité*
the stadium	*le stade*
the stands	*les tribunes*
a stirring performance	*une performance enthousiasmante*
strenuous exercise	*l'effort soutenu*
to suffer a defeat	*subir une défaite*
a team mate	*un équipier/coéquipier*
to be in top shape/form	*être au meilleur de sa forme*
a track meet	*une rencontre d'athlétisme*
to use steroids	*prendre des stéroïdes*
to vie with one another	*se mesurer*
a winning streak	*une série de matchs gagnants*
a work-out program(me)	*un programme de (re)mise en forme*
a world record holder	*le détenteur d'un record du monde*

Translation

Translate the sentences into English.

1. Le concurrent dont vous parlez a été un prétendant à la victoire jusqu'au bout de cette épreuve indécise.

2. Pour redorer son blason, le président est allé faire du sport avec quelques grands sportifs, dont certains ont été champions du monde.

3. Le programme quotidien de remise en forme que tu suis avec enthousiasme pourrait te causer de sérieux problèmes articulaires dans le moyen terme.

4. Cette grande société de BTP parraine de nombreux événements sportifs, dont certains attirent le gratin de la société.

5. Ce coureur de 800 mètres kenyan dont le record du monde vient juste d'être homologué, sera le premier à descendre sous les 1 minute 40.

Read and answer

Read the article and then do activities A and B that follow.

Golden glow

VANCOUVER. Canadians used to think of themselves as being quiet, modest and unassertive. No longer. After their athletes topped the medals table with 14 golds at the winter Olympic games, some 100,000 flag-waving locals took to the streets of Vancouver and the nearby ski resort of Whistler, deliriously singing the national anthem. The crowning triumph had come with victory over the United States in the men's ice-hockey final. Even though this mood of brash patriotism had been building steadily both before and during the games, it took outsiders and even some Canadians by surprise.

The Vancouver Olympics got off to a dreadful start. Early on the opening day, a Georgian athlete, Nodar Kumaritashvili, was killed during a practice run when his luge flipped over, throwing him into a steel pole and raising questions about the track's safety. Foreign journalists pounced on a series of glitches. The Olympic torch did not burn properly during the opening ceremony, an ice-making machine broke down as did several buses, and unseasonably mild weather caused events to be postponed. Visitors to Vancouver were frustrated that the outdoor Olympic flame was cordoned off behind a chain-link fence (it was quickly opened up). "The worst games ever," wrote a columnist in *The Guardian*, a British newspaper, much to the annoyance of Canadians.

They weren't. And they got better and better, especially for home fans. At the previous two Olympics held on their soil, Canadians had failed to win a single gold medal. Their success this time stemmed from a programme to finance athletes' preparation and training, called "Own the Podium" and organised by the Canadian Olympic Committee five years ago. It had a budget of C$117m ($104m), raised from government and business, and it worked – although the Americans finished first in the overall medal count.

This hard-nosed approach irritated some foreign athletes, who had less chance to practise at the facilities than did their Canadian rivals. The jingoistic mood may have added to the pressure on Canadian athletes, but Canadian success created an infectious public enthusiasm for the games on the streets of Vancouver, which impressed visiting officials from the 2012 London Olympics.

Canadian success also inspired an outpouring of national pride that is unusual in a fissiparous country often seemingly racked by self-doubt. Whether the games have succeeded in rebranding Canada as a modern, youthful sporting power, as some of the organisers apparently hoped, remains to be seen.

Now the bills will fall due. Last year Vancouver city council bailed out the developers building the Olympic village, because the softening of the property market made it hard to sell flats there. The Canadian Olympic Committee faces a $22m shortfall for "Own the Podium", and the federal government has declined to stump up more. Two decades ago 50% of Canadian adults took part in sport of some kind. Now the figure is only 30%, and obesity rates are rising. Perhaps Canada was just renting the podium.

The Economist (economist.com), 4/3/2010

A. Language

Find synonyms in paragraphs 2, 4 and 5 of the article for the following: *exposed, things that went wrong, stopped working, quite warm weather, delayed, annoyed, chauvinism, contagious, flood, potentially divided, torn apart by, refreshing the image of, has yet to be proved.*

B. Question

To what extent were the Vancouver Olympics a success story? (Answer in 100-150 words. Use information in the article but do not copy sentences directly: use your own words.)

Translation

Translate the article into English.

La Coupe du monde, une aliénation planétaire

Fabien Ollier est directeur de la revue *Quel sport.*

Vous comparez le sport en général, le football en particulier, à une aliénation planétaire. **Que vous inspire la Coupe du monde ?**

Fabien Ollier : Il suffit de se plonger dans l'histoire des Coupes du monde pour en extraire la longue infamie politique et la stratégie d'aliénation planétaire. Le Mondial sud-africain ne fait d'ailleurs pas exception à la règle. L'expression du capital le plus prédateur est à l'œuvre : les multinationales partenaires de la FIFA et diverses organisations mafieuses se sont déjà abattues sur l'Afrique du Sud pour en tirer les plus gros bénéfices possibles. Un certain nombre de journalistes qui ont travaillé en profondeur sur le système FIFA ont mis en évidence le mode de fonctionnement plutôt crapuleux de l'organisation. Ce n'est un secret pour personne aujourd'hui. De plus, il y a une certaine indécence à faire croire que la population profitera de cette manne financière. Le nettoyage des quartiers pauvres, l'expulsion des habitants, la rénovation luxueuse de certains townships ont été contrôlés par des « gangs » qui n'ont pas l'habitude de reverser les bénéfices. Avec la majorité de la population vivant avec moins de 2 euros par jour, cet étalage de richesse est pour le moins contestable.

Votre thèse réfute l'idée du football ou du sport en général comme simple reflet de la société avec son lot de violences.

[…] À mon sens, il n'est pas seulement le reflet, le football est également producteur de violences sociales, générateur de violences nouvelles. Il impose un modèle de darwinisme social. Cela tient à sa structure même : le football est organisé en logique de compétition et d'affrontement. Jouer ce spectacle par des acteurs surpayés devant des smicards et des chômeurs est aussi une forme de violence. Une logique contradictoire se fait d'ailleurs jour. D'un côté, les supporters ont conscience du fait que les sportifs gagnent des sommes folles par rapport au néant qu'ils produisent mais de l'autre côté, dans une soif d'identification liée à leur propre misère, il y a une impossibilité à ne pas « *rêver* » devant cette marchandise vivante qui démontre que l'on peut se hisser au sommet de l'échelle.

Le Monde (lemonde.fr), 10/6/2010

Overview

Read a general overview of the subject.

Sport and politics

In Ancient Greece the Olympiads served the double purpose of boosting physical training for war while preserving a truce between cities. Since then, sport and politics have often been intertwined because of political and nationalistic undercurrents whenever sporting prowess has been put to the test. For example, the French created jousting tournaments in the Middle Ages to assert their knights' superiority and, later, Anglo-French negotiations went downhill after Francis I defeated Henry VIII in a wrestling match…

The Olympic Games in the 20th century were repeatedly tarnished by boycotts, counter-boycotts and political gestures. In the thirties, during the rise of fascism and nazism, the Italians and Germans paraded their sportsmen and women in massive events to underscore a political message. This worked for the Italians who achieved world-wide acclaim for their double victory in the 1934 and 1938 World Cups, and the Germans impressed the world with the Berlin stadium and the opening ceremony of the 1936 Olympics. But the public humiliation for Hitler and his regime of Jesse Owens's four splendid gold medals also made the headlines across the world.

In 1968, at the height of the civil rights movement in the USA, black American sprinter Tommy Smith and other US medal winners gave the Black Power salute by raising a clenched black-gloved fist at the awards ceremony at the Mexico Olympics.

The worst nightmare took place at the 1972 Munich Olympics when Palestinian terrorists attacked the Olympic village and killed several Israeli athletes. Then, in 1976, the Montreal Olympics saw boycotts from several Commonwealth countries because the IOC had banned South Africa for its apartheid policies.

In 1980, the United States pulled out of the games because of the Soviet invasion of Afghanistan, which the US condemned. But their decision to boycott the Games backfired as the Moscow Games proved to be a popular success with athletes. And the Soviets got their own back by boycotting the 1984 Olympics in Los Angeles.

The Los Angeles games marked the end of an era and the beginning of another. An amateur sporting event that had been run up to then by international organisations based on the original British model gave way to an event in which international corporations invested millions of dollars for advertising purposes. The LA "Coca-Cola games" heralded the role of big business in sport, which may mean, for better or for worse, less politics for the sake of more profit.

Pronunciation

Listen and repeat.

Stress in longer words

- unfor**get**table, edu**ca**tion, mu**si**cian, deco**ra**tion, ar**tis**tic, scien**ti**fic, eco**no**mic, popu**la**tion
- **pub**lic/pub**li**city, **pho**tograph/pho**to**graphy, **ci**vilise/civili**sa**tion.

52 Chapter

Entertainment

Language focus

Chassé-croisé et modulation

• Le chassé-croisé consiste à faire permuter deux éléments de sens :

He swam across the river.

Il traversa la rivière à la nage

He kicked the door open.

Il ouvrit la porte d'un coup de pied

• La modulation est un changement de point de vue nécessaire lorsqu'on passe d'une langue à l'autre, parce que celles-ci ne représentent pas les choses de la même manière :

Description spatiale :

Don't shout down the street. Ne crie pas de l'autre bout de la rue.

Abstrait/concret :

seat belt ceinture de sécurité

Affirmation/négation :

Remember the guide! N'oubliez pas le guide !

Inversion du point de vue :

Lost Property Office Bureau des objets trouvés.

Partie/tout : *I've had the children under my feet all day.*

J'ai eu les enfants collés à moi toute la journée.

Wordbank

an award-winning play	*une pièce de théâtre à succès*
BAFTA	the British Academy of Film and Television
the BBFC	the British Board of Film Censors
a billboard	*un panneau d'affichage*
a blockbuster	*un succès retentissant*
the box office	*le guichet*
a box office success	*un film/pièce à succès*
a boxing/wrestling ring	*ring de boxe/catch*
butterflies, stage fright	*le trac*
the cast (of a movie)	*la distribution (d'un film)*
censorship	*la censure*
a crooner	*un chanteur de charme*
a director	*un metteur en scène*
to download a film	*télécharger un film*
a feature film	*un long métrage*

the FCC	the Federal Communications Commission
the film rights	*les droits d'adaptation pour le cinéma*
the flicks, the pictures *(UK, fam.)*	*le ciné*
a flop	*un bide*
the (football) pools (UK)	*le loto sportif*
the gambling industry	*l'industrie du pari*
the Grammy Awards	*les récompenses dans l'industrie de la musique*
to rent a video	*louer une vidéo*
horse/dog racing	*les courses de chevaux/lévriers*
the majors	*les grands studios*
the movie moguls	*les grands patrons*
a movie theater (US)	*un cinéma*
the MPAA	the Motion Picture Association of America
a multiplex	*un complexe de salles de cinéma*
a music academy	*un conservatoire de musique*
an occasional moviegoer	*un amateur occasionnel*
on-board entertainment	*un divertissement dans l'avion, voiture, train…*
a one-armed bandit	*un bandit manchot*
the orchestra pit	*la fosse d'orchestre*
a pirated edition	*une copie piratée*
a producer	*un producteur*
the props	*les accessoires*
to release	*sortir (un film, disque, CD…)*
a sample	*un échantillon*
to screen a movie	*projeter un film*
a silent movie	*un film muet*
a slasher movie *(fam.)*	*un film d'horreur violent*
a slot/fruit machine	*une machine à sous*
a space opera	*un film de science fiction à effets spectaculaires*
the takings	*la recette*
Tinseltown *(fam.)*	*Hollywood*
top of the bill	*le haut de l'affiche*
a soundbite	*une petite phrase*

Translation

Translate the sentences into English.

1. Le chanteur de charme devint un acteur célèbre capable d'incarner un dur qui ouvre les portes à coups de pied et gagne les cœurs à coups de poing.

2. Cette actrice traversa toute la salle en courant pour aller recevoir l'Oscar pour son rôle dans *Running Girl.*

3. Le metteur en scène a obligé ses acteurs à traverser la rivière à la nage et à grimper les collines en rampant dans son dernier film de guerre à gros budget.

4. L'industrie du cinéma est de plus en plus menacée par les téléchargements illégaux.

5. Les milliards dépensés pour amuser les humains seraient peut-être mieux investis dans des projets humanitaires sérieux.

Read and answer

Read the article and then do activities A and B that follow.

The worldwide cinema boom: The box office strikes back

Once incidental to Hollywood's fortunes, cinema is now the fastest-growing and most innovative part of the film business

Summer begins on May 7th, at least according to Hollywood's calendar. On that day "Iron Man 2" is due to be released in American and Asian cinemas (it appeared a week earlier in Europe, to take advantage of the May Day holiday). Like many modern blockbusters, the film trades on nostalgia. It is based on a comic-book series that began in the 1960s and even features a Russian baddie. This is appropriate, given the state of the film business. Technological progress and changes in tastes mean that Hollywood depends more and more on the old-fashioned practice of showing films in cinemas.

Film exhibition was until recently a humdrum business. The formula for success was simple: sell lots of tickets at the same price, then funnel punters past salty popcorn and fizzy drinks. Cinemas keep about half the price of a ticket and up to 90% of the money spent at concession stands. For film-makers, showing movies in cinemas was important not so much in its own right but as a means of drawing attention to a product, the most profitable incarnations of which would appear later. The real money was in home entertainment, especially sales of DVDs.

But now the pendulum is swinging back towards the box office. In 2009 global box-office revenues increased by 7.6%, but total revenue for the biggest Hollywood studios fell by 4.3%, "due to the collapse of consumer spending on DVDs", according to Bernstein, a research firm.

Since 2005 North American box-office receipts have risen by 20% (see chart). Ticket sales grew strongly during the recession, as people sought a cheapish night out, and have not slowed. Box Office Mojo, which tracks films, estimates that box-office receipts this year are running at 6% above last year's level. Elsewhere cinema is healthier still. Ticket sales outside America and Canada have risen by 35% since 2005 and are now worth about two-thirds of the global total. A boom in multiplexes – that is, cinemas with at least eight screens – is unlocking latent demand. In 2006 Russians made a total of 89.5m visits to the cinema. Last year they made 132.3m. This is especially surprising in a country where the number of young people is falling. [ ]

What is driving the cinema boom? The most obvious answer, for consumers, is the rise of three-dimensional films. Audiences have flocked to films like "Avatar", a vaguely ecological fantasy, and "Alice in Wonderland". In North America 3-D films drove almost all the growth in box-office receipts last year. Although the premium that cinemas charge for 3-D films has risen steeply from as little as $1 per ticket to $3 or more, consumers have not balked. "We still don't know how much they are willing to pay," says David Passman, chief executive of Carmike, a cinema chain.

More important, though less visible, is the digitisation of cinema. The number of screens served by digital projectors worldwide rose from about 3,000 to 16,400 between 2006 and 2009, according to Screen Digest, a research firm. That primed the explosion in 3-D films: it is hard, though not impossible, to project a 3-D image using …

old-fashioned film. Digitisation has made it easier for multiplex owners to shuffle films around screens to cope with surges in demand. And satellite distribution is making it easier and cheaper for films to open simultaneously around the world. [...]

The response to 3-D films and IMAX proves [...] cinema is evolving from a commodity into a business that sells differentiated products at varied prices. The example of India suggests that there is room for further differentiation. Multiplexes are rising in many Indian cities: Mumbai alone has added more than 75 screens in the past five years, says Anil Arjun, chief executive of Reliance MediaWorks. They appeal to, and are priced for, India's aspirant middle class. Fame, a cinema chain, charges an average of 141 rupees ($3.15) per ticket, in a country where daily income per person is just 120 rupees. Some cinemas have replaced rows of seats with widely spaced reclining chairs, with tray tables and waiter service. This model appears to be spreading to the West. Carmike has opened a cinema in Tennessee that serves alcohol and food, to great success. The draw seems to be not just comfortable seats, but the absence of teenagers.

Film-makers are adapting to these changes. India's new cinemas have given rise to "multiplex films", focused on the concerns of affluent youngsters and with somewhat less singing and dancing than in standard Bollywood fare. Elsewhere the rise of 3-D and the super-sizing of screens are leading studios to focus on visual spectaculars. "French table dramas do not look much better on IMAX," notes Julian Stanford, who manages that company's business in Europe and Africa. The growth of screens outside America also favours big action films: an explosion is an explosion, regardless of language.

The loser, as so often, is grown-up drama. In the past two years the big studios have shut or run down "specialty" divisions like Focus Features and Miramax (the latter may yet return, in a much depleted state, to Bob and Harvey Weinstein, who founded it). Fans of such films are out of luck. They should certainly steer clear of cinemas this summer.

The Economist (economist.com), 6/5/2010

A. Language

Find synonyms in paragraphs 2, 3, 6, 7 and 8 of the article for the following: *ordinary/ mundane, to lead customers, the trend is reversing, equipped with, at the same time, to be expanding, adjusting, have caused the arrival of, without paying attention to, adult.*

B. Question

What are the reasons for the world cinema boom? (Answer in 200-250 words. Use information in the article but do not copy sentences directly: use your own words.)

Overview

Read a general overview of the subject.

Hollywood and after

A lot of early research into moving pictures was done in both the USA and Europe. Edison started his cinema studios in New Jersey in 1893 and the Lumière brothers produced their first film in Lyon in 1895. And yet it is Hollywood in California that is the undisputed movie capital of the world, with its white lettering picked out against the hillside. And it is here that the US movie business has become a global industry, even though movie finance has been driven by investment companies and banks situated on the east coast.

There are many reasons that pushed the nascent movie industry to set up in west coast California, including simply the weather! Early studios were built to let in the light through the roof and even designed to be moved in line with the sun. Also, little time was wasted because of bad weather when shooting outdoors in California, so equipment costs were amortised quickly.

The first moving pictures were silent – not very much bigger than a modern credit card – and they were to remain silent and in black and white until the first "talkie", *The Jazz Singer,* was released by Warner Brothers in 1927. Even though the Great Depression was to blight America, the 1930s saw the beginning of Hollywood's Golden Age. It was the beginning of the modern entertainment industry, growing up in an environment where financing was relatively easy to come by. At that time, fewer than 10 studios, each with their own exclusive stable of actors, competing with each other in technological innovation and creativity, produced almost 95% of the moviegoers' fare and, although television has since put paid to the golden age with millions of American homes having permanent access to onscreen entertainment, people are still fascinated by stars of the silver screen, and world-renowned A-list bankable actors are able to reap in millions of dollars for their work.

However, the movie theater no longer has the appeal of yesteryear. People no longer need to be together to be entertained and, with increasingly sophisticated technology, the vehicles of entertainment have moved on: the big bulky TV set has been replaced by the lightweight flat screen; you can watch a movie or a DVD of your favourite soap in your car; and you can load images and sound – whether a box-office blockbuster or the latest shoot-em-up video game – onto your portable computer.

Pronunciation

Listen and repeat.

Pronouncing short words (a, of, or)

- a cup of tea, a glass of milk, a piece of ham, a jar of jam.
- salad or rice, heads or tails, sink or swim.

Chapter 53

Going green

Language focus

Les exclamations

• Sur un nom, avec *What* + groupe nominal (attention au caractère dénombrable ou non du nom) :

What a *beautiful flower!*	Quelle fleur magnifique !
What ø *gorgeous weather!*	Quel temps splendide !
What ø *lovely clothes!*	Quels beaux vêtements !

• Sur un adjectif ou un adverbe, *How* + adjectif/adverbe. Attention à l'ordre des mots :

How tall *that player is!*	Comme ce joueur est grand !
How fast *he can run!*	Comme il court vite !

Wordbank

an awareness-building campaign	*une campagne de sensibilisation*
to cause a public outcry	*déclencher un tollé général*
to change one's habits	*changer ses habitudes*
to comply with/abide by environmental laws	*respecter les lois anti-pollution*
conservation, preservation	*la sauvegarde, la protection*
a conservationist	*un protecteur de l'environnement*
an eco-defender	*un défenseur de la nature*
an eco-fair	*une foire écologique*
eco-friendly, environmentally-friendly	*sans danger pour l'environnement*
an eco-labelling scheme	*un système d'étiquetage écologique*
an eco-warrior	*un écologiste activiste*
ecologically-minded	*soucieux de l'environnement*
the eco-movement, the green movement	*le mouvement écologique*
eco-tourism	*le tourisme écologique*
to engage in environmentally-sound practices	*adopter des pratiques sensées sur le plan écologique*
an environmental fund	*un budget pour l'environnement*
environmental policies	*les politiques de l'environnement*
an environmentalist	*un écologiste*
to go green	*se convertir à l'écologie*
green activism	*le militantisme écologique*
a green bill	*un projet de loi écologique*
a green brand	*une marque écologique*

to be green-minded	*penser écologique*
green power	*le pouvoir des écologistes*
a green product	*un éco-produit*
the green revolution	*la révolution écologique*
a green sentiment	*un état d'esprit écologique*
a green voter	*un électeur écologiste*
harmless, non-toxic	*sain, inoffensif*
to make someone aware of	*sensibiliser qqn à*
to monitor pollution	*surveiller la pollution*
a nature reserve	*une réserve naturelle*
public awareness	*la prise de conscience collective*
to set off alarm bells	*tirer la sonnette d'alarme*
substitutes	*des produits de remplacement*
ungreen	*non écologique*
a watchdog agency	*un organisme de surveillance*
to cut down on energy costs	*réduire les coûts énergétiques*
to cut the energy bill	*réduire la facture énergétique*
the depletion of resources	*la diminution, l'épuisement des ressources*
an electrical power capacity	*une capacité à produire de l'électricité*
energy, power	*l'énergie*
energy conservation	*la maîtrise de l'énergie*
energy consumption	*la consommation d'énergie*
the energy crisis	*la crise de l'énergie*
energy efficiency	*l'économie d'énergie*
to become energy-efficient	*faire des économies d'énergie*
energy requirements	*les besoins énergétiques*
energy-producing facilities	*les équipements énergétiques*

Translation

Translate the sentences into English.

1. Qu'elles sont rouges ces tomates ! Je crois fermement au développement de l'agriculture biologique, j'en prends deux kilos !

2. Qu'elles sont laides ces éoliennes sur la lande de Cornouailles, je préfère les champs de panneaux solaires d'Almeria.

3. Comme nous avons eu raison de sensibiliser les jeunes aux défis liés au réchauffement climatique ! Nous aurions dû commencer plus tôt.

4. Comme les gens changent vite d'avis ! Il y a 10 ans, le jeune cadre dynamique rêvait d'une voiture de sport alors qu'aujourd'hui ils veulent tous une voiture électrique.

5. Quelle idée magnifique ! Interdisons définitivement l'utilisation de la voiture dans les zones urbaines pour réduire à la fois la facture énergétique et l'empreinte carbone.

Read and answer

Read the article and then do activities A and B that follow.

Organic Farms as Subdivision Amenities

SOUTH BURLINGTON, Vt. – The bewildered Iowan who converted his farm into a ballpark in "Field of Dreams" in 1989 might reverse the move today. From Vermont to central California, developers are creating subdivisions around organic farms to attract buyers. If you plant it, these developers believe, they will buy. Increasingly, subdivisions, usually master-planned developments at which buyers buy home sites or raw land, have been treating farms as an amenity. "There are currently at least 200 projects that include agriculture as a key community component," said Ed McMahon, a senior fellow with the Urban Land Institute. [...]

"Open space improves the return for a developer," Mr. McMahon said. "We have 16,000 subdivisions around golf courses, where developers found they could charge a lot premium of 25 to 50 percent over comparable tract subdivision. But most people who live on golf courses do not play golf." The latest variation on this is blending in working agriculture, Mr. McMahon said. Living with a farm, he noted, can bring a buyer permanent views, wholesome activities for children, access to walking and riding trails and inclusion in an epicurean club.

Here in South Burlington, David Scheuer, a developer, runs a firm called Retrovest that specializes in pedestrian-friendly subdivisions. He is adapting the Prairie Crossing model with a 220-acre project called South Village, where he eventually hopes to sell 334 homes at prices of $200,000 to nearly $700,000. A 16-acre segment of the property, which was not previously used for farming, is now producing lettuce, garlic and other crops, which are harvested for sale to homeowners and others from the area who have joined a local community-supported agriculture group. "Agriculture can be the caboose on the train," Mr. Scheuer said, "and housing can be the engine." Once he is selling 20 homes a year, he said, he hopes to pay the salary of a full-time farmer.

At the 220-home Serenbe project near Atlanta's airport, the cachet of local produce has been added to retiree-friendly businesses, including galleries, a bed-and-breakfast and three restaurants. Steve Nygren, an Atlanta restaurant impresario, started the project on his 900-acre farm. "We preserved forest and pasture, and there were 20 acres left for an organic farm, and we also have a large wildflower meadow," Mr. Nygren said. "We've set up the design so 90 percent of the houses back up to one of those natural amenities. We are selling our lots at a premium that's probably three times what the raw lot is."

Mr. Nygren has focused Serenbe's second phase on "edible landscaping," he said. "At street corners there are blueberry bushes, fig bushes, peach trees and spotted apple trees."

And in more rural areas, developers are buying big tracts of ranchland and selling small lots to buyers. David Hamilton, a principal in Qroe Farm Preservation Development, is pursuing this approach at the sprawling Bundoran Farm subdivision outside Charlottesville, Va. "We go through a mapping process to see functional agricultural units, if they are good for apples or cattle or whatever, then see where they go together."

Qroe (pronounced "crow") leases some of the land to cattle ranchers and orchard managers. A buyer of a home site hires a builder from a developer-approved list. Qroe

...

is marketing lots of under four acres for less than $400,000, Mr. Hamilton said. "You're buying two acres but access to 2,000 acres," he said.

Grady Lewis, a Virginia native who closed on his 2.67-acre lot in 2007 and moved into his 1,800-square-foot house at Bundoran with his wife, Diane, this spring, responded to Qroe's idea of preserving "rural quality."

When all the house lots have been sold, the rental income from the farmers, which currently goes to the developer, will go to the homeowners' association. "Beyond it being great to see 300 head of Angus scattered across the acres," Mr. Lewis said, "it's a cash-flow issue."

Alec Appelbaum, *The New York Times* (nytimes.com), 1/7/2009

A. Language

Find synonyms in paragraphs 1, 2 and 4 of the article for the following: *stunned, transformed, make a U-turn, to woo customers, undeveloped/untouched, the profit, healthy, the additional appeal, facilities for people's enjoyment.*

B. Questions

Answer each of the following questions in 50 words. Use information in the article to answer but do not copy sentences directly: use your own words.

1. What are subdivision amenities?

2. What can explain the success of farming amenities?

3. To what extent has the growing interest in environmental concerns been changing the trend in land development?

Translation

Translate the article into English.

Qu'attendent les Français d'une maison innovante ?

Pour la majorité des Français, une maison innovante est une maison écolo. Interrogés sur les critères d'une maison innovante par le Baromètre Union des Maisons Françaises (UMF) et l'institut de sondage CSA en mars dernier, les Français ont cité « spontanément une dizaine d'innovations, toutes liées à l'écologie ». En tête des réponses : le recours à l'énergie solaire pour 37 % des sondés, suivi par la maison écologique à l'usage (31 %) et l'utilisation des énergies renouvelables (20 %). Loin derrière le peloton de tête et « dans un mouchoir de poche » arrivent les critères tels que l'isolation (14 %), la maîtrise des dépenses énergétiques (14 %), la maison en bois (13 %) et enfin le système de chauffage écologique (13 %).

La maîtrise de l'énergie reste une préoccupation majeure. Questionnés sur « ce à quoi ils ne renonceraient pas dans leur projet de construction d'une maison en cas de restriction budgétaire », les Français ont répondu pour plus d'un tiers (37 %) la « maîtrise de l'énergie ».

Le Nouvel Observateur (nouvelobs.com), 26/4/2010

Overview

Read a general overview of the subject.

Green activism

With the growing awareness of the ever more dilapidated state of some areas of the planet has come growing activism. From the anti-war and anti-nuclear stance of the sixties and seventies, activism has evolved into more complex structures. Each decade seems to have been centred on one issue, be it nuclear weapons, the nuclear arms race, chemicals military and civil, acid rain, greenhouse gases, global warming… Now these problems are seen not as single issues but as part of a wider eco-political issue.

One of the first groups to come to public notice was the Greenpeace movement. With its easily-recognisable, rainbow-coloured mother ship, it scours the planet bringing attention to issues from whale-hunting to high-voltage power lines. On the seas, its *modus operandi* includes slowing down, interrupting and halting vessels by means of dinghies launched from its own craft. Members have scaled nuclear power-plant cooling towers and chained themselves to trees… Other movements propose even more radical stances, some fringing on the brutal and the confrontational, sabotaging crops in the process.

With passing years green activism has become more politically mainstream. Political parties once very swift to lambast green movements as being political agitators have now integrated the green platform into their political campaigns. Protecting the environment has now become a duty for governments, who have set up numerous bodies to monitor and protect land, sea and air.

Four major conferences – Stockholm, Rio, Johannesburg and Kyoto – have brought nations together in an attempt to hammer out solutions to the problems of reduced biodiversity, global warming, greenhouse gases and sustainable development.

Citizens are more and more active in the fight to protect the environment. Multinationals, often pointed out as being destroyers of nature, are now careful to include the green aspects of their business in their marketing and communication campaigns. High-profile show business and sports personalities are also enlisted by organisations in the fight to make the planet a better place to live, or, at least, to slow down our approach to the brink of eco-doom. Many ad hoc associations are also formed to stop specific projects like mining that would remove a mountain top or to protect Alpine flowers. Schoolteachers are inculcating the protection of nature in children, and adults on an individual basis are involved in activities from refuse sorting to buying green gift vouchers for friends. Everyone seems to have become a friend of the earth…

Pronunciation

Listen and repeat.

They sound the same!

- pets enter/pet centre, ice-cream/ I scream, known aim/no name, under age/under rage, after eight/after rate.

54 Chapter

Environmental concerns

Language focus

Les noms composés

• Les noms composés anglais s'écrivent soit en deux mots, reliés ou non par un tiret, soit en un seul. Un nom composé crée un nouveau « type » : *a teapot* est un type de *pot* particulier, reconnaissable ; *a laptop computer* est un ordinateur d'un genre particulier ; *a beer glass* est un verre à bière, qui peut contenir autre chose.
• Dans certains cas, on ne peut pas fabriquer un nom composé : un groupe extrait d'un ensemble (*a bunch of flowers*), une partie d'un tout (*the page of a book, a piece of soap*).
• Pour certaines structures de noms composés, la question du choix entre nom composé et groupe nominal *of* ne se pose pas :
a close-up (un plan rapproché) *a breakthrough* (une découverte majeure)

Wordbank

acid rain(s)	*les pluies acides*
air pollution	*la pollution atmosphérique*
to breathe in	*inhaler, respirer*
CFCs	*les chlorofluorocarbones*
chemicals	*les produits chimiques*
to choke	*s'étouffer*
climatic forecasts	*les prévisions climatiques*
climatic/climate change	*le changement climatique*
CO_2 emissions	*les émissions de carbone*
a danger zone	*une zone dangereuse*
dangerous materials	*des substances dangereuses*
domestic/household waste	*les ordures ménagères*
drought	*la sécheresse*
to dump waste	*déverser des déchets*
a dust bowl	*un désert de poussière*
an earthquake	*un tremblement de terre*
an ecological catastrophe	*une catastrophe écologique*
environmental damage	*les dégâts écologiques*
environmental degradation	*la dégradation de l'environnement*
an environmental threat	*une menace écologique*
exhaust fumes	*les gaz d'échappement*
an eyesore	*une horreur dans le paysage*
fumes	*des vapeurs, des émanations*

garbage, refuse, rubbish, trash, waste	*les déchets, les ordures*
a garbage/rubbish dump	*une décharge*
gas-guzzling	*qui consomme beaucoup de carburant*
to generate a climate	*produire un climat*
global warming	*le réchauffement climatique*
the greenhouse effect	*l'effet de serre*
greenhouse gases	*les gaz à effet de serre*
harmful	*toxique*
HFCs	*les hydrofluorocarbones*
a hurricane	*un ouragan*
industrial waste	*les déchets industriels*
a landfill site	*un site d'enfouissement*
noise pollution	*la pollution sonore*
an oil slick	*une nappe de pétrole*
an oilspill, a black tide	*une marée noire*
the ozone layer	*la couche d'ozone*
ozone-friendly	*sans danger pour la couche d'ozone*
pesticides	*les pesticides*
phosphates	*les engrais phospatés*
plastics	*les matières plastiques*
a pollutant	*un polluant*
to pollute	*polluer*
a polluter	*un pollueur*
the range of temperature	*l'écart de températures*
a record high/low	*un record de chaleur/froid*
rising sea levels	*la montée du niveau des mers*
seasonal variations	*les variations saisonnières*
to shape the climate	*déterminer le climat*
sludge	*les boues*
to threaten natural species	*menacer les espèces naturelles*
a tidal wave	*un raz-de-marée*
to upset the natural balance	*bouleverser l'équilibre naturel*
urban sprawl	*l'extension spectaculaire de la ville*
water wastage	*le gaspillage de l'eau*

Translation

Translate the sentences into English.

1. L'Outback australien est un désert de poussière pour l'agriculteur et une zone dangereuse pour le touriste.

2. Plus nous relâchons de gaz à effet de serre dans l'atmosphere, plus la couche d'ozone s'amenuise.

3. Entre les raz de marée, le niveau des eaux qui monte et les tempêtes, il y a de quoi s'interroger sur le réchauffement climatique.

4. Cette décharge illégale est une horreur dans le paysage paisible de la campagne provençale.

5. L'expansion ininterrompue de l'espace urbain menace de bouleverser l'équilibre naturel.

Read and answer

Read the article and then do activities A and B that follow.

Climate science: Spin, science and climate change

Climate-change legislation, dormant for six months, is showing signs of life again in Washington, DC. This week senators and industrial groups have been discussing a compromise bill to introduce mandatory controls on carbon. Yet although green activists around the world have been waiting for 20 years for American action, nobody is cheering. Even if discussion ever turns into legislation, it will be a pale shadow of what was once hoped for.

The mess at Copenhagen is one reason. So much effort went into the event, with so little result. The recession is another. However much bosses may care about the planet, they usually mind more about their bottom line, and when times are hard they are unwilling to incur new costs. The bilious argument over American health care has not helped: this is not a good time for any bill that needs bipartisan support. Even the northern hemisphere's cold winter has hurt. When two feet of snow lies on the ground, the threat from warming seems far off. But climate science is also responsible. A series of controversies over the past year have provided heavy ammunition to those who doubt the seriousness of the problem.

Three questions arise from this. How bad is the science? Should policy be changed? And what can be done to ensure such confusion does not happen again? Behind all three lies a common story. The problem lies not with the science itself, but with the way the science has been used by politicians to imply certainty when, as often with science, no certainty exists.

When governments started thinking seriously about climate change they took the sensible step of establishing, in 1989, the Intergovernmental Panel on Climate Change. It was designed to get scientists to work out what was happening to the climate, and to get governments to sign off on the scientists' conclusions. It has done the job of basic science pretty well. There have been occasional complaints both that it has overstated the extent of the problem, and that it has understated it. Its reports trawl through all recent climate science. The wide range of the outcomes it predicts – from a mildly warming global temperature increase of 1.1°C by the end of the century to a hellish 6.4°C – illustrate the uncertainties it is dealing with.

But the ambiguities of science sit uncomfortably with the demands of politics. Politicians, and the voters who elect them, are more comfortable with certainty. So "six months to save the planet" is more likely to garner support than "there is a high probability – though not by any means a certainty – that serious climate change could damage the biosphere, depending on levels of economic growth, population growth and innovation." Politics, like journalism, tends to simplify and exaggerate. [...]

As our briefing explains in detail, most research supports the idea that warming is man-made. Sources of doubt that have seemed plausible in the past, such as a mismatch between temperatures measured by satellites and temperatures measured at the surface, and doubts about the additional warming that can be put down to water vapour, have been in large part resolved, though more work is needed. If records of temperature across the past 1,000 years are not reliable, it matters little to the overall story. If there ...

...

are problems with the warming as measured by weather stations on land, there are also more reliable data from ships and satellites.

Plenty of uncertainty remains; but that argues for, not against, action. If it were known that global warming would be limited to 2°C, the world might decide to live with that. But the range of possible outcomes is huge, with catastrophe one possibility, and the costs of averting climate change are comparatively small. Just as a householder pays a small premium to protect himself against disaster, the world should do the same.

The Economist (economist.com), 18/3/2010

A. Language

Find synonyms in paragaphs 1, 2, 3, 4 and 6 of the article for the following: *inactive, compulsory, eco-warriors, was invested in, to sustain costs, angry row, a long way away, to guarantee, reasonable, to calculate, has exaggerated, has underestimated, a discrepancy, can be explained by.*

B. Question

To what extent have climate scientists been used by politicians? (Answer in 200 words. Use information in the article but do not copy sentences directly: use your own words.)

Translation

Translate the article into English.

Les Français convaincus du réchauffement climatique

Un sondage Ipsos indique qu'une forte majorité de Français croiraient au réchauffement climatique et le considéreraient comme scientifiquement prouvé.

84 % des Français croient « tout à fait » (40 %) ou « plutôt » à la réalité du réchauffement climatique, selon une étude Ipsos réalisée auprès d'un échantillon de 1003 personnes. Avec l'âge, le doute se fait toutefois plus fort: seuls 74 % des plus de 55 ans estiment que le réchauffement climatique est avéré.

Pour ceux qui croient à l'existence du phénomène, la part de responsabilité des activités humaines ne fait aucun doute : 96 % considèrent qu'elle est importante.

Ils sont aussi une majorité de Français à penser que le réchauffement est scientifiquement prouvé (77 %), même si moins d'un Français sur trois pense que le phénomène est « tout à fait » prouvé (31 %).

Toutefois, la plupart des Français considèrent que les conséquences des activités humaines sur le réchauffement climatique sont minorées (49 %) ou exagérées (33 %). Seulement 18 % des personnes interrogées pensent que les conséquences des activités humaines sur le phénomène de réchauffement sont justement évaluées.

Après l'échec de Copenhague, les politiques n'ont pas la cote: seulement 56 % des personnes interrogées pensent que des mesures seront prises dans les prochaines années pour freiner le réchauffement climatique.

L'Express (lexpress.fr), 19/1/2010

Overview

Read a general overview of the subject.

Irreversible consequences or not?

At the height of its technological progress, humankind is slowly waking up to the fact that the desire for material affluence may be dooming the world we live in to an untimely end.

When did climate change begin? No one knows for sure. For some it is unstoppable; for others, putting it right will cost trillions of dollars. One thing is sure: we are doing incredible damage to nature. From global warming to rising sea levels, from pollution to the decline of biodiversity and the depletion of primary resources, humankind has got a lot on its plate for the next few generations.

Scientists first became concerned about the ozone layer in 1974. Research in 1985 then proved the existence of a hole over Antarctica. Such a hole allows harmful UV rays (responsible for skin disease, reduced crop yields and diminishing marine life) to enter the atmosphere.

Global warming and greenhouse gases also mean harmful consequences for the Earth. The shrinking of the ice packs means more water flowing into the seas and rising shorelines. The seas play an important role in absorbing carbon dioxide pollution. A weakening of this role, as apparently shown by research in the Sea of Japan, means more gas being left in the atmosphere. It is this gas which warms the ocean. That in turn means the migration of marine life which has hitherto thrived in colder reaches. Ocean currents are also diverted and ventilation which causes the mixture of water and gas is hindered.

A diminished biodiversity (biological diversity) would herald a dark future for man, animals and plants. As all living things are interconnected, one broken link in the chain may have irreversible consequences. From sharks to sheep, from bees to bears, the consequences are said to be enormous, recent estimates running from 7 million to 20 million threatened species.

Pollution from industries all over the world is pumping more and more noxious gases into an already overloaded atmosphere, increasing, for example, amounts of carbon dioxide. This is made worse by increased human activity, by people searching for somewhere to live and to grow crops. Making their contribution to society means, for them, carving out swathes of land, hitherto untouched by man. A toll is thus being taken on vast areas of tropical forest, home to so many species – the lungs of the planet and Earth's carbon treatment plants.

Should we fail to see the writing on the wall, the worst doomsday scenario could come true much sooner than we think.

Pronunciation

Listen and repeat.

Reading figures

- 13/30, 14/40, 15/50. • 114, 373.
- 11,380; 15,000,000; 78,923,851.

Chapter 55

Global governance

Language focus

Traduire « devoir »

- Obligation cautionnée par l'énonciateur :
  Tu **dois** le laisser rester. — *You must let him stay.*
- Nécessité du point de vue de l'énonciateur :
  Tu **dois** partir maintenant. — *You need to go now. /You must go now.*
- Nécessité objective :
  Je **dois** y aller. — *I must go I have to go. /I have got to go.*
- Conseil :
  Il **devrait** lui en parler. — *He should tell her about it.*
- Reproche :
  Tu **aurais dû** lui dire la vérité. — *You should have told her the truth.*
- Probabilité :
  Cela **doit** être vrai. — *It must be true*
  Cela **ne doit pas** être vrai. — *It can't be true.*
- Ce qui est prévu à l'avance :
  Il **doit** la rencontrer demain. — *He is to meet her/ He's meeting her tomorrow.*
- Ce qui est inevitable :
  Cela **devait** arriver — *It was bound to happen.*

Wordbank

to achieve equitable development	*assurer un développement équitable*
a backlash	*une réaction hostile*
to boost trade	*stimuler le commerce*
capital flow	*le flux des capitaux*
to close the gap	*supprimer l'écart*
collective action	*l'action commune*
competition	*la concurrence*
a competitor	*un concurrent*
a crushing debt	*une dette écrasante*
debt relief	*un allégement de dette*
to embrace	*inclure*
an engine of growth	*un moteur de croissance*
to establish a system	*mettre sur pied un système*
to establishing lasting peace	*garantir une paix durable*
the flow of population	*les flux migratoires*

global civic awareness	*la conscience d'être citoyens du monde*
global governance	*la gouvernance mondiale*
the IMF (International Monetary Fund)	*le fonds monétaire international*
to institute the conditions for	*créer les conditions nécessaires à/au*
manufactured goods	*les produits manufacturés*
to lag behind	*être loin derrière*
to lobby	*faire pression sur*
on a large scale	*sur une large échelle*
to outsource	*délocaliser*
a pattern of growth	*un type de croissance*
a plant	*une usine, une unité de production*
to prioritize, to put a premium on	*donner la priorité à*
to prove hard to do	*se révéler difficile à faire*
the redistribution of wealth	*la redistribution des richesses*
(a) recovery	*une reprise*
to reduce inequalities	*réduire/diminuer les inégalités*
to reform international institutions	*réformer les institutions internationales*
to regulate the powers of states	*réglementer les pouvoirs des États*
representativeness	*la représentativité*
to respect cultural diversity	*respecter la diversité culturelle*
a shared destiny	*un destin commun*
solidarity	*la solidarité*
to spread	*s'étendre*
to stall	*marquer le pas, s'arrêter*
sustainable development	*le développement durable*
to take on the heavy responsibility	*prendre/assumer la lourde responsabilité*
the Third World	*le tiers-monde*
winners and losers	*les gagnants et les perdants*
the World Bank	*la banque mondiale*
the world trading system	*le système de commerce mondial*
the WTO (World Trade Organisation)	*l'OMC*
the world's political homogenization	*l'homogénéisation politique du monde*

Translation

Translate the sentences into English.

1. Pour parvenir à l'homogénéisation politique du monde, les pays riches doivent réduire le fossé économique entre Nord et Sud.

2. L'organisation du commerce mondial devrait aider davantage les pays émergents pour parvenir à une redistribution des richesses plus équitable.

3. Le FMI va définitivement effacer la dette écrasante des pays du tiers-monde.

4. L'ONU aurait dû mettre en œuvre des mesures pour le développement durable dès les années 60.

5. Les dirigeants des pays riches doivent se rencontrer à Balmoral pour trouver un accord permettant de réduire les inégalités entre pays riches et pays pauvres.

ici londres
Nouvelle formule
www.ici-londres.com
GRATUIT
Tendance
Les flashmobs, vous connaissez ?
Plein air
Suivez Regent's Canal jusqu'à Camden
Gastronomie
Découvrez les wine and cheese tastings
Sorties
Ce mois-ci, ne manquez pas Wax Tailor, Cesaria Evora, Hindi Zahra…
Natalie Dessay
Rencontre avec une diva d'aujourd'hui
n° 134 - mai 2010
INTERNATIONAL REMOVALS RELOCATIONS & STORAGE
DELAHAYE MOVING
DEMENAGEMENTS INTERNATIONAUX & GARDE-MEUBLES
info@delahayemoving.com
London • 020 8687 0400
www.delahayemoving.com
LONDON
PARIS
NICE
NEW YORK

Avec corrigés

EN LIBRAIRIE

ANGLAIS

FICHES et TESTS de grammaire

par Claude Rivière

Cet ouvrage s'adresse aux étudiants de tout cursus entrant à l'université qui ont besoin d'évaluer leur niveau d'anglais et de revoir, préciser et réorganiser leurs connaissances.

Il présente de façon simple **les bases essentielles de la grammaire et de la prononciation de l'anglais.**

Il permet de tester son niveau d'anglais grâce à :

- un test d'entrée et un test de sortie,
- 6 tests de niveau.

Pour consolider ses connaissances :

- 46 fiches de grammaire avec exercices,
- des explications simples mais qui ne négligent aucun détail de la langue,
- un index des mots-clés.

978-2-7080-1223-3
format 14 x 22 cm,
208 pages, 13 €

Claude Rivière est l'auteur d'ouvrages de référence en grammaire anglaise tels que la *Syntaxe simple à l'usage des anglicistes* (éditions Ophrys). Il est membre des équipes de Grammaire et linguistique anglaise de l'Université Paris VII

www.ophrys.fr

Read and answer

Read the article and then do activities A and B that follow.

World Leaders Agree on Timetable for Cutting Deficits

TORONTO. Leaders of the world's biggest economies agreed Sunday on a timetable for cutting deficits and halting the growth of their debt, but also acknowledged the need to move carefully so that reductions in spending did not set back the fragile global recovery.

The action at the Group of 20 summit meeting here signaled the determination of many of the wealthiest countries, after enacting spending programs to counter the worldwide financial crisis, to now emphasize debt reduction. And it underscored the conviction of European nations in particular that deficits represented the biggest threat to their economic stability.

President Obama and Treasury Secretary Timothy F. Geithner had consistently advocated a measured approach to debt reduction that would not stymie growth and lead to a double-dip recession. The United States, however, joined other countries at the summit meeting, which was met by protests and several hundred arrests, by endorsing a goal of cutting government deficits in half by 2013 and stabilizing the ratio of public debt to gross domestic product by 2016. Canada's prime minister, Stephen Harper, had proposed the targets, backed by Germany and Britain.

To assuage objections from the United States, Japan, India and some other countries, the timetable was couched as an expectation, rather than a firm deadline. The G-20 joint statement explicitly stated that Japan, which is heavily dependent on domestic borrowing, was not expected to meet the targets.

The divisions were in contrast to the unity that characterized the previous three G-20 leaders' summits, when the urgency of a potential global collapse produced solidarity and a unified economic approach. Although Mr. Obama insisted emphatically that there was "violent agreement" on the need to reduce debt over time, the final communiqué included a delicately worded call for deficit reduction "tailored to national circumstances." In essence, the leaders were blessing their decision to go their own ways.

The joint statement acknowledged both sides of the debate. "There is a risk that synchronized fiscal adjustment across several major economies could adversely impact the recovery," the statement said. "There is also a risk that the failure to implement consolidation where necessary would undermine confidence and hamper growth."

In a news conference at the conclusion of the summit meeting, Mr. Obama referred only indirectly to the disagreement with Europe, saying, "We must recognize that our fiscal health tomorrow will rest in no small measure on our ability to create jobs today."

His concern about stimulus was echoed by some economists who viewed the pledge on deficits as imperiling the prospects for growth.

"China's growth, specifically, is not seen as sustainable at current rates," Ronald A. Kurtz, professor of global economics and management at the Massachusetts Institute of Technology, said in an e-mail message. "The G-20 declaration therefore amounts to saying 'assume a miracle' for global growth." He said Europe's fiscal austerity plans would also slow growth. [...]

It is the first time the G-20 has set dates for deficit reduction, but the timetable, which is not binding, will probably not require new policy actions. Most of the govern- ...

ments, including the United States, have already put forward budget proposals in line with the targets.

The leaders also discussed banking regulations, but could not agree on a proposal for a global bank tax, supported by the United States, Britain and the European Union, but opposed by Canada and Australia.

And while the G-20 reaffirmed a deadline – their next meeting, in November in Seoul, South Korea – for agreeing on new capital standards for banks, they signaled that several countries might not implement the standards by 2012, as initially planned.

Sewell Chan & Jackies Calmes, *The New York Times* (nytimes.com), 27/6/2010

A. Language

Find synonyms in the first four paragraphs of the article for the following: *stopping the increase, recognised, cautiously, putting schemes into effect, stress, underlined, balance, recommended, to hinder economic progress, supporting an objective, to alleviate, phrased/ described as.*

B. Questions

Answer each of the following questions in 50 words. Use your own words.

1. What agreement has been reached by the G20 members?

2. Describe the different standpoints of America and Europe.

3. Define *The New York Times*' opinion on the agreement.

Translation

Translate the article into English.

Richesse des nations et gouvernance mondiale

On sentait bien que les cartes étaient en cours de redistribution dans l'économie mondiale. Les produits « made in China » sont trop nombreux dans notre quotidien et les délocalisations d'entreprises trop médiatisées pour que nous, Occidentaux, persistions à nous croire le centre du monde.

Mais les plus riches et les mieux lotis, si. Au large de Gibraltar, les noyades d'Africains attirés par les lumières de l'Europe et les flux d'immigrés qui sautent le « mur » américain à la frontière du Mexique nous renforcent dans cette conviction. À la rigueur, nous acceptons la Chine comme exception à notre prééminence, tant ses records en tout genre crèvent les yeux.

Voici qu'il faut déchanter : derrière la Chine et l'Inde, c'est une vaste cohorte de pays naguère dits « sous-développés » qui rattrape l'Occident : en vrac, Malaisie, Vietnam, Kazakhstan, Tunisie, Équateur..., mais aussi une surprenante Éthiopie. La dernière étude du Centre de développement de l'OCDE illustre de façon éclatante que ces pays convergent vers le niveau économique des pays riches. La crise a même accéléré ce rattrapage, alors que certains oracles avaient prédit que les pays en développement en seraient les premières victimes.

Le Monde (lemonde.fr), 19/6/2010

Overview

Read a general overview of the subject.

From globalisation to global governance

Globalisation – a term on everybody's lips. Anti-globalisation groups including trade unions, the unemployed, ecologists and environmentalists gather to protest at G-8 meetings. Today's globalisation is tied up with free trade and the freedom for capital to flow around the world. Advances in technology and transport facilitate communication between buyers and suppliers abroad.

With countries not engaging in protectionism, multinationals have been able to implant abroad and benefit from low-cost labour and resources.

For its opponents, economic and commercial globalisation is nothing less than a nightmare, bringing in its wake relocation, increased immigration, poverty, inequality, outsourcing, the destruction of state sovereignty, unemployment…

Those in favour of further extending the phenomenon argue that there are benefits in the process. Globalisation is a conveyor belt for growth and even if the world experiences a global economic downturn, it is the very notion of globalisation which will mean that the future economic upturn will be felt very quickly throughout the world. Globalisation is put forward as a way of spreading wealth and it is suggested that in a non-globalised world it would have been much harder or even impossible for emerging nations to progress at such speed. In a "globalised" world, peace is also rendered more possible and, indeed, world populations have more to gain by trading peacefully with each other than engaging in costly wars or arms races. World institutions, including charities, find their work easier in a global economic democracy.

This raises a moot point since globalisation itself is inextricably related to the idea of ungovernability given the multiple layers of governance at play – suprastate agencies, nation-states, regional integration projects such as the EU or NAFTA, NGO's, corporate global players, international organisations… Such a multilayered, multidimensional and multi-player system – combined with the states' declining capacity to regulate within their own territories – requires a new political model. Up to now, two directions have been considered: democratic inter-governmentalism which would require a common/ transnational public sphere to elect representatives and enable democratic deliberation; democratic or cosmopolitanism through cosmopolitan institutions like international tribunals or a global assembly.

Unsurprisingly, the failure of the Copenhagen climate summit in December 2009 and the mixed feelings after the G-20 summit in June 2010 have provided ample evidence that setting a common path for the whole of mankind is likely to prove a tall order indeed.

Pronunciation

Listen and repeat.

Reading fractions, percentages and decimals

- ½, ¾, 7/8. • 15%, 0.2%.
- 3.45, 6.015.

Méthodologie : l'essai

La nature de l'essai

• L'essai sert à évaluer votre compétence linguistique de production écrite dans un cadre relativement contraint. Sa longueur peut varier de 200 à 350 mots, soit un volume assez réduit, et il obéit à une triple visée :
– répondre de façon personnelle à une question plus ou moins large ;
– structurer le contenu de façon synthétique et cohérente ;
– proposer un niveau de langue élevé ; vous rédigez une production écrite et vous exprimez à propos d'un sujet de société, tout en demeurant spontané et pertinent.

Les intentions

• Affirmez-vous en exprimant sans détour votre position sur un sujet de société ou une question plus personnelle. Soyez direct, clair et précis, annoncez votre position et gardez le cap sans vous perdre en digressions. Sachant quand même qu'on attend une position intellectuellement tenable sur le sujet, autrement dit, nuancé, convaincant, en évitant jugements à l'emporte-pièce. Par exemple, vous devez évaluer les arguments pour ou contre la fertilisation des océans et cette solution vous semble intéressante : *There are three main basic reasons why French universities should strive to attract foreign students, and more particularly in post-graduate research programmes.*
• Enrichissez de façon convaincante : le volume limité de l'exercice doit vous inciter à rechercher la précision (éviter les mots trop vagues comme *money, problem, like, important, big*…), la densité et la variété idiomatique. Collocations, verbes à particules, noms et adjectifs composés, expressions verbales complexes d'une part, vocabulaire spécifique du sujet (en quantité limité) d'autre part, vous permettent de proposer une production originale de qualité.

Lire et exploiter le libellé

• On distingue six grands types de libellés pour un essai de 250 à 350 mots.
1. La définition d'un terme (ex : *Religion: the opium of the masses).* Il faut commenter, élargir, contextualiser la définition et donner son opinion.
2. Les avantages et les inconvénients (ex : *What are the the good and bad sides of the cyberworld?).*
3. Commenter un paradoxe (ex : *Do VIPs such as movie stars or politicians have a right to privacy?).* C'est le sujet permettant d'utiliser l'approche dialectique « thèse-antithèse-synthèse ».
4. Comparaison et contraste entre deux termes (ex : *Is it possible to vie with the world's best universities while taking on more and more students?).* Convergence puis divergence des deux termes, opinion personnelle à partir de l'actualité ou d'exemples bien connus.
5. Sujet chronologique (ex : *To what extent has the Internet been a revolution?).* Description de la situation (présent simple) ; causes/origines/repères historiques

(prétérit) ; conséquences/bilan/évolution en cours *(present perfect)* ; perspectives (expressions du futur/potentiel et irréel présent).
6. Sujet d'évaluation synthétique (ex : *Draw a SWOT analysis of the traditional press's approach to young readers).* Contextualisation du sujet (*young readers and the press*); *strengths: the press's strong points/assets/benefits; weaknesses: the press's weak points/shortcomings/flaws; opportunities: positive prospects/solutions; threats: obstacles/competition/dangers.*

Mobiliser les ressources

Le champ lexical

• L'important est avant tout de savoir placer les termes les plus souvent utilisés pour évoquer le sujet, non de réciter un lexique complet. Une façon logique de reconstruire une banque lexicale légère mais pertinente est de retrouver les termes les plus courants en répondant aux questions de base :

What?	Qu'est que c'est (le sujet) ? Que font-ils (actions) ?
Who?	Qui agit/subit/est concerné ?
Why?	La cause ? Le contexte ?
What for?	Le but/l'objectif ? La fonction ?
Where?	Les lieux ?
How?	La manière ? Les moyens ?

Les verbes

• Les temps
Pour décrire, contextualiser et commenter une situation présente :
– le présent simple (temps de base) ;
– les aspects *be* + V-*ing* (= *present continuous*) (évaluation critique ou action en cours) ;
– *have* + V-*en* (= *present perfect simple*) (traces du passé dans le présent, notion de bilan) ;
– *have* + V-*en* + *be* + V-*ing (= present perfect continuous)* (évolution en cours).
Pour ancrer votre propos dans une réalité historique :
– le prétérit (simple et en be + V-ing) (= *past simple, past continuous*)
– le plus-que-parfait (*past perfect/pluperfect*)
Les expressions du futur (*will, going to*, etc.)
Le conditionnel (présent et passé : *would* + V, *would have* + V-*en*)
• Utiliser les modaux et les tournures équivalentes, soit pour décrire des caractéristiques de la situation soit pour émettre des pronostics évaluant le degré de réalisation de tel ou tel aspect de la situation.
• Les verbes à particules : une alternative aux termes généraux les plus souvent employés ; utilisation de synonymes plus précis.

Les mots de liaison

– *whereas/while* (comparaison terme à terme)
– *provided/on condition that* (condition impérative dans un énoncé affirmatif)
– *unless* (condition impérative dans un contexte négatif)
– *although/though/even though* + sujet + verbe (contraste par l'opposition de deux termes antithétiques)
– *despite/in spite of* (+ nom/V-*ing*) (équivalent nominal de *although/even though*)
(Voir aussi la liste p. 294.)

Les mots composés

• Les noms et adjectifs composés sont très fréquents en anglais technologique et économique.

Le rythme

• La longueur différente des phrases à l'intérieur du paragraphe est déterminée par la fonction de chaque énoncé (voir ci-desssus). Varier la longueur et la structure des énoncés permet d'établir un rythme contrasté et dynamique.
• Pour écrire des phrases fluides et équilibrées, il faudra éviter :
– les répétitions de mots grammaticaux (pronoms, auxiliaires) mais aussi de termes clés ou d'expressions idiomatiques (pas deux fois dans le même essai) ;
– les juxtapositions de propositions séparées par des virgules. Séparer les deux phrases par un point ou un point virgule ou les relier par une conjonction ;
– les longueurs excessives, que ce soit d'une phrase ou d'un groupe nominal.
Construire un groupe nominal complexe sur le modèle « adjectif composé + nom composé » est une chose appréciée une fois par paragraphe. Accumuler les composés qui rejettent le nom à la fin d'un groupe nominal de plus de quatre termes semblera à la fois lourd et artificiel ;
– éviter les chutes brutales en fin d'essai. Une phrase brève en fin de paragraphe peut signaler de façon convaincante votre accord ou désaccord. Mais la fin de l'essai doit vous permettre de boucler l'argumentation tout en ouvrant la question vers un contexte voisin ou plus général.

La mise en relief d'éléments clés

• Pour mettre un élément en relief, il est important de le placer au début de la phrase mais à l'intérieur d'une tournure emphatique. Exemples :

Hardly/No sooner [+ inversion sujet/verbe] *when/than…*	À peine […] que…
Not only [+ inversion sujet/verbe] *but also…*	Non seulement […] mais aussi…
Never [+ inversion sujet/verbe]	Jamais
Not until now [+ inversion sujet/verbe]	Jamais jusqu'à maintenant
Few are those who…	Rares sont ceux qui...
however [+ adjectif/adverbe]	aussi […] que
Should they succeed/Were they to succeed…	Si (jamais) ils réussissaient…
Had they succeeded/Should they have succeeded/Were they to have succeeded…	S'ils avaient réussi…

L'impact idiomatique des mots courts

• Les mots les plus courts d'origine saxonne (97 des 100 mots les plus utilisés) donnent à votre style une dimension plus idiomatique. S'écarter des termes d'origines latine ou française de deux syllabes et plus pour privilégier les termes courts d'origine germanique vous permettra donc de gagner en dynamisme, en impact et en authenticité. Exemples :

to abandon	*to scrap (a plan/a program)*	*an accusation*	*a charge*
an advantage	*an asset*	*an agreement*	*a deal*
to allude to	*to hint at*	*to be logical*	*to make sense*
to be prejudiced	*to be biased*	*bureaucracy*	*red tape*
a characteristic	*a feature*	*confidence*	*trust to confront*
to face (up to)	*a conspiracy*	*a plot*	*a controversy a row*

to counterbalance	*to offset*	*a depression*	*a slump*
to destroy	*to wreck*	*to divide*	*to split*
to evaluate	*to assess*	*fundamental*	*basic*
interference	*meddling*	*a measure*	*a step*
an objective	*an aim, a goal*	*production*	*output*
to support	*to back*		

Jouer sur les sons

• Comme en français, les jeux rhétoriques sur l'association « sons-sens » viennent à la fois enrichir votre style et valoriser votre propos.

1. Allitérations (jeu sur les consonnes). Exemples :

back from the brink	revenir de loin
back to basics	retour aux bases/valeurs traditionnelles (slogan du parti conservateur dans les années 1990)
a culture clash	un choc des cultures
dark days	des jours sombres
a tall tale	une histoire à dormir debout

2. Assonances (jeu sur les voyelles/diphtongues). Exemples :

to be down and out	être dans la dèche
to cook the books	truquer les livres de comptes

3. Paronomases (jeu sur l'opposition entre sons semblables/sens différents). Exemples :

boom or bust	expansion ou récession
a boon or a bane (= a blessing or a curse)	un bienfait ou une calamité
brain or brawn	de la matière grise ou du muscle
from cradle to grave	du berceau au tombeau (définition du Welfare State britannique)
welfare to workfare	de la protection sociale à la protection sous condition d'avoir un emploi (réforme des aides sociales par Bill Clinton puis Tony Blair dans les années 90)

4. Les rimes internes. Exemples :

a fair share	une part équitable
gloom and doom	de sombres perspectives
lean and mean	compétitif et agressif (reformulation de *streamlining*, le dégraissage d'effectifs)

La compétence socio-culturelle en expression écrite

Au-delà de l'authenticité idiomatique, il nous semble important d'attirer l'attention sur la dimension socio-culturelle propre à l'expression écrite, et plus particulièrement aux différents styles journalistiques.

Répondre de façon précise à une question portant sur un article de la presse de qualité et/ou rédiger un essai sur un sujet d'actualité nécessite de devenir familier avec les composantes du style journalistique (voir pp. 310).

Rédiger l'essai

L'introduction

• 30 à 50 mots.
• L'accroche : contextualiser le sujet soit en citant un événement récent ou bien connu, soit en proposant une généralisation.
• L'amorce : reformuler l'essentiel de l'énoncé et l'axe de votre réponse.

Le développement

• 150 à 200 mots.
• Selon l'énoncé et le plan choisi, votre développement comptera 2 à 4 paragraphes. Chaque paragraphe constitue un ensemble homogène que l'on peut essayer de construire sur le modèle suivant :
– l'argument clé. L'idée force du paragraphe est présentée de façon claire en 10 à 15 mots. On recherche l'impact (vocabulaire précis avec l'utilisation d'un ou deux mots-clés, groupe verbal complexe) ; il faut marquer les esprits. Cette première phrase est un repère dans la progression de l'essai ;
– l'explication. C'est l'étoffement de la première phrase ; vous reformulez en ajoutant idées complémentaires et informations importantes. La phrase est nettement plus longue et vous donne l'occasion d'utiliser les mots de liaison pour relier deux énoncés, de jouer sur les contrastes (synonymes/antonymes/cooccurrents) ;
– les arguments concrets. Il s'agit de renforcer les deux premières phrases, a priori plus abstraites, par des arguments ou des exemples de situations concrètes (exemples historiques au preterit ; bilan d'une évolution connue au *present perfect*) ;
– l'ouverture par l'hypothèse. Désir de changer le présent par le conditionnel présent ; espoirs/attentes raisonnables par le potentiel ; pronostics portant sur le présent avec les modaux, pronostics portant sur le futur avec les différentes expressions du futur.

Les articulations

(Voir la liste d'adverbs et les mots de liaison p. 293-294.)
• Votre essai obéit à une logique interne cohérente ; il convient d'en repérer les différentes étapes. Le lecteur doit pouvoir en repérer les étapes, suivre sans effort votre progression argumentative, sans jamais se demander pourquoi tel argument apparaît à cet endroit-là, pourquoi il a une impression de répétition. Il doit avoir l'impression d'avoir parcouru un chemin entre A et B. Il est sans doute souhaitable de préférer des termes courts et simples pour marquer ces temps de passage d'une idée à une autre *(First, Second, Then, Finally)* et surtout éviter d'alourdir le style et de ralentir le rythme de lecture par des tournures longues et ampoulées.
• Vous pouvez, bien sûr, jouer sur les effets d'enchaînement. Établir un rapport de cause à effet entre deux paragraphes sucessifs en commençant le deuxième par *That's why…* ; ou établir un contraste : *On the contrary…/Conversely…*

La conclusion

• 20 à 40 mots.
• La conclusion est une récapitulation-projection : elle reprend l'argument déterminant/ votre opinion fondamentale sur le sujet en ouvrant vers un prolongement possible de la discussion.

• On reformule l'argument clé (synthèse) en ralentissant le rythme pour marquer l'emphase (tournure longue telle que *The above examples are evidence of the fact that…*). Ensuite, on choisit entre deux stratégies :

– on prolonge en ouvrant vers une piste complémentaire ou parallèle. D'un essai sur *Smoking is bad for you*, on peut ouvrir vers un propos plus général sur les phénomènes de dépendances ;

– on retourne l'argument clé en prenant son contre-pied pour montrer que l'on demeure objectif *(These arguments only offer a partial explanation of… what remains to be discussed is…)*.

Ressources linguistiques

Exprimer une opinion sans recourir à la première personne

• Utiliser ces tournures longues (une fois par paragraphe, deux fois par essai).

It is possible to say…/It could be said that…	On peut dire que
It is necessary to point out that…	Il faut rappeler que
It is plain/obvious/surprising/not surprising/ significant / understandable that…	Il est évident/ n'est pas surprenant/ significatif que/ On comprend que…
There is no doubt/little doubt/ not the slightest doubt that…	Il ne fait aucun doute que
There is no denying that…/ No one can deny that…	On ne peut nier que…
There is no doubting the matter.	On ne peut mettre en doute…
There would be reason to fear…	On pourrait craindre…

• Tempérer une affirmation en utilisant *seem* ou *appear*, qui permettent de se mettre en retrait. Structure à employer une ou deux fois par essai.

Has sport been radically changed by big business? It would appear not/it would appear so.

Le sport a-t-il été changé en profondeur par l'argent ? Il semblerait que non/oui.

• Enclencher une argumentation avec des tournures longues (à utiliser une fois par essai).

The point is that…	En réalité,…
The obvious point to make about… is that…	C'est une évidence de dire que…
The evidence suggests that…	Tout porte à croire que…

• Employer *one*. Fréquent dans le style journalistique, il permet d'avancer une opinion en douceur.

One is inclined to believe (that)…	On peut penser que…
One may sum up by saying that…	On pourrait conclure en disant que…
One must admit that…	On doit reconnaître que…
One may well wonder whether…	On peut vraiment se demander si…

• Utiliser le passif. C'est l'effacement du sujet ; on présente une opinion couramment répandue.

French people, it has been said, like food so much that…	Les Français, dit-on, aiment tant la nourriture que…
It has been estimated that…	On a estimé que…
The situation is said to be worse.	La situation semble bien pire.

Particular notice must be taken of...	On fera plus particulièrement attention à...
It is universally acknowledged that...	On reconnaît généralement que...

• Utiliser des adverbes, soit en tête de phrase soit entre sujet et verbe, pour nuancer une prise de position. C'est un procédé courant en anglais journalistique qui permet d'embrayer entre deux parties, d'avancer ses pions de façon subtile, de modifier le rythme des phrases et gagner en impact.

Arguably	Ce qui fait débat
Ironically, but predictably...	L'ironie veut que... , comme cela était à prévoir
Possibly, ...	Il est possible que...
To be sure, ...	Il faut dire que...

Utiliser ces verbes pour caractériser le propos de l'auteur

to account for	expliquer, analyser
to acknowledge	reconnaître
to add	ajouter
to admit	admettre, concéder
to advance the opinion	avancer l'idée
to advocate	préconiser, recommander
to argue	argumenter, avancer l'idée
to assert	affirmer
an assertion	affirmation forte
to assume	affirmer (sans preuve), présumer, supposer
to claim	déclarer (sans preuve, de façon fantaisiste)
to comment on/upon	commenter sur
to conclude	conclure
to contend	assurer, soutenir, faire remarquer
to demonstrate	démontrer
to dismiss	refuser de tenir compte de
to emphasise	souligner
to expose	révéler (quelque chose de négatif)
to focus on	se concentrer sur
to go on to say	poursuivre en disant
to highlight	mettre l'accent sur
to hint at	faire allusion à
to hold	maintenir l'idée
to insist	maintenir
to maintain	assurer, maintenir
to make plain	déclarer sans ambage
to mention	nommer, évoquer
to note, to observe	observer, faire observer
to point out	faire remarquer
to propose	avancer
to put it	dire (As John puts it [+ citation] – Comme dit John, ...)
to put forward (the idea)	avancer (l'idée)
to report	rapporter
to shed light on	faire de la lumière sur

to state	déclarer
to suggest	montrer que
to urge	dire de façon pressante
to voice (an opinion/concern)	exprimer (une opinion/de l'inquiétude)
to warn (that/against)	prévenir (que/contre)
to raise a point	soulever une question
to stress a point	insister sur une question

Étoffer le style : traduire les tendances avec précision

to crash, to collapse, to dive	s'effondrer
to creep up, to edge up	monter peu à peu
to diminish	baisser progressivement
to edge down	baisser imperceptiblement
to fall off	fléchir
to fluctuate	varier
to hit an all-time high	atteindre son niveau le plus haut
to hit an all-time low	atteindre son niveau le plus bas
to level off/out, to reach a plateau	se stabiliser, atteindre un palier
to nosedive	s'effondrer
to peak	atteindre un sommet
to pick up	se redresser (après une baisse)
to plummet, to plunge	s'effondrer
to reach a peak/trough	atteindre un sommet/creux
to rise steadily	augmenter de façon régulière
to skyrocket, to soar	monter en flèche, s'envoler
to spurt	monter soudainement

Étoffer le style : utiliser des tournures idiomatiques

a. *Success and failure*	**Le succès et l'échec**
a rising star	une étoile montante
hungry for success	avide de succès
like magic	comme par enchantement
not to be up to the mark	ne pas être au niveau
not to have the ghost of a chance	ne pas avoir l'ombre d'une chance
That makes all the difference.	C'est ce qui change complètement les choses.
the sky's the limit	il n'y a pas de limites
the world's your oyster	le monde t'appartient
to fail to deliver the goods	ne pas tenir ses promesses
to go from strength to strength	progresser à pas de géant/marcher de mieux en mieux
to go places	réussir dans la vie
to hit the big time	atteindre le succès national/ planétaire
to thwart somebody's plans	contrecarrer les projets
to win hands down/to pass with flying colours	réussir/gagner haut la main
to work/go/run like a dream	réussir à merveille

b. ***Problems & problem-solving***	**Les problèmes et comment les résoudre**
give it one's best shot	faire de son mieux
in a tight corner	dans une mauvaise passe
it's only the tip of the iceberg	ce n'est que la partie émergée de l'iceberg/visible du problème
to be (left) clutching at straws	se raccrocher à de faux espoirs/ n'importe quoi
to be at a loss	ne savoir que faire
to be caught on the hop	être pris au dépourvu
to be left holding the baby	se retrouver à gérer tout seul
to be out of one's depth	avoir perdu pied, ne pas être sur son terrain
to be up the creek (without a paddle)	être dans le pétrin
to come up against a brick wall/ a stumbling block	se heurter à un obstacle infranchissable
to draw a blank	faire chou blanc
to get someone over a barrel	ne pas laisser le choix à quelqu'un
to get to the bottom of it	aller au fond du problème
to give it a whirl	tenter le coup
to go off the rails	dérailler
to nip the problem in the bud	étouffer dans l'œuf
to pick up the pieces	ramasser les morceaux
to spread onself too thin	s'épuiser à trop vouloir en faire
to throw a spanner in the works	causer des problèmes
to tie up a few loose ends	régler les derniers détails
to wave a magic wand	sortir sa baguette magique
too many loose ends to tie	trop de détails à régler

c. ***Power & authority***	**Le pouvoir et l'autorité**
the movers and shakers	ceux qui font la pluie et le beau temps
to be at someone's beck and call	obéir au doigt et à l'œil
to be on/at the receiving end of	être la cible de
to bend the rules	contourner la loi
to call the shots	décider (de tout)
to carry the can	payer les pots cassés
to get/let someone off the hook	tirer qqn d'affaire
to have friends in high places	avoir des amis haut placés
to lay down the law	to enforce the law
to leave someone to his own devices	laisser qqn se débrouiller seul
to pass the buck	refiler le bébé, rejeter la responsabilité sur
to pull the strings	tirer les ficelles
to throw one's weight around	faire l'important
to be behind someone	apporter son soutien à qqn
to twist someone's arm	persuader qqn

d. ***Danger, safety and risks***	**Le danger, la sécurité, les risques**
a knife-edge situation	une situation qui ne tient qu'à un fil
a leap in the dark	un saut dans l'inconnu
a necessary evil	un mal nécessaire
by the skin of one's teeth	de justesse

to be caught (+ V-ing)	se faire prendre à
to be caught red-handed	se faire prendre la main dans le sac
to be hanging on a thread	tenir qu'à un fil
to be out on a limb	être dans une situation délicate, être en plan
to be safe and sound	être sain et sauf
to cut it/something fine	marcher sur un fil
to fly by the seat of your pants	agir à l'instinct
to have a narrow/close escape	s'en tirer de peu
to lead astray	induire en erreur
to leave something alone	laisser tranquille, laisser tomber
to live dangerously	vivre dangereusement
to play safe	jouer la sécurité, ne pas prendre de risques
to put all your eggs in the same basket	mettre tous ses œufs dans le même panier
to put one's head on the block	mettre sa tête sur le billot, prendre de gros risques
to sail close to the wind	prendre des risques
to set alarm bells ringing	tirer la sonnette d'alarme
to sit on the fence	ménager la chèvre et le chou
to skate/tread on very thin ice	marcher sur des œufs
to stick one's neck out	prendre des risques
to take one's life into one's hands	prendre de gros risques
to tread carefully	avancer prudemment
too close for comfort	trop proche à mon goût

e. *Effort*	**L'effort**
to give your all	donner tout ce qu'on a
to go out of your way	se mettre en quatre
to pull your weight	faire sa part
to have a bash at	essayer
to go through the motions	faire les choses machinalement/par habitude
child's play	un jeu d'enfant
a piece of cake	du gateau
heavy going (n.), a tall order	un défi difficile

f. *Social status*	**Le statut social, le standing**
a (bit of a) rough diamond	un diamant brut (dont les manières frustes cachent beaucoup de qualités)
a high-flier/flyer	un ambitieux, un arriviste
a pillar of society	un pilier/membre important de la société
Anybody who's anybody will be there.	Tous les gens importants seront là.
to be on one's way up	monter dans la hiérarchie
to keep a low profile	faire profil bas
to keep up appearances	sauver/préserver les apparences
to make a name for oneself	se faire connaître
up-and-coming	plein d'avenir, prometteur

g. *Knowledge and ability*	**Les connaissances et les compétences**
to know sthg like the back of one's hand	connaître comme sa poche
to pick someone's brains	faire appel aux lumières de qqn

to rack one's brains	se triturer les méninges
to feel a bit rusty	se sentir un peu rouillé
to be an old hand at the game	être un vieux routier/vétéran
not have a clue	ne pas en avoir la moindre idée
have one's head screwed on the wrong way	avoir la tête sur les épaules
to know/learn the ropes	connaître/apprendre les ficelles
to get the hang of	attraper le coup de

Étoffer le style : utiliser des adverbes

accordingly	par conséquent, convenablement
actually	en fait
additionally	de plus
admittedly	il faut en convenir, certes
approximately, roughly	approximativement, à peu près
(most) assuredly	sans aucun doute
barely, hardly, scarcely	à peine
certainly, surely	sans doute
conversely	inversement
definitely	certainement, sans aucun doute
deliberately	sciemment
especially	spécialement
eventually, finally	finalement
evidently	apparemment, manifestement
formerly	autrefois
fortunately	heureusement
generally speaking	dans l'ensemble
gradually	petit à petit
incidentally	au fait, à propos
increasingly	de plus en plus
namely	c'est à dire
obviously	évidemment
oddly, strangely	de manière étrange, curieusement
particularly	particulièrement
possibly	peut-être, éventuellement
presumably	apparemment
rarely, seldom	rarement
recently	dernièrement
repeatedly	à maintes reprises
shortly	sous peu
similarly	de la même façon
simultaneously	simultanément
slightly	légèrement
unexpectedly	à l'improviste

Étoffer le style : utiliser des mots de liaison

although, though	bien que, malgré le fait que
as well as, also	aussi
because, for	parce que, car
but	mais
conversely	inversement
for example, for instance	par exemple
furthermore, in addition, moreover	de plus
hence, so, therefore, consequently	par conséquent
however, nevertheless, yet	cependant, pourtant, néanmoins
if	si
in fact	en fait
in spite of, despite (+ N/+V-*ing*), *notwithstanding* (+ N)	en dépit de, malgré
likewise, …, similarly, …	de la même façon, …
no matter how/however (+ adj./adv.), *no matter what* (+ N)	peu importe…, quel(le) que soit…
on the contrary, …	au contraire, …
provided (that), providing	à condition que, pourvu que
since	puisque
unless	à moins que
unlike (+ N)	à la différence de
whereas, while	tandis que

Éviter les faux-amis

Voici quelques exemples des faux-amis les plus courants.

Mot français	Traduction	Faux-ami anglais	Traduction
abusif	*excessive*	*abusive*	grossier, insultant
achever	*to finish*	*to achieve*	atteindre
un achèvement	*a completion*	*an achievement*	une réussite, un accomplissement
actuellement	*currently, presently, at the moment*	*actually*	en fait
affluent	*tributary*	*affluent*	d'abondance
un agenda	*a diary*	*an agenda*	un ordre du jour
altérer	*to spoil*	*to alter*	modifier
être apte à	*to be fit for, to be suited to*	*to be apt to*	avoir tendance à
assister	*to attend*	*to assist*	aider
une audience	*a trial*	*an audience*	un public
un bachelier	*holder of a;baccalauréat*	*a bachelor*	un célibataire
une balance	*scales*	*balance*	l'équilibre
candide	*naive*	*candid*	franc
une caution	*a deposit*	*caution*	la prudence

une cave	*a cellar*	*a cave*	une grotte, une caverne
charger qn de…	*to give s.o. the job of…*	*to charge s.o. with…*	accuser qqn de…
la circulation	*the traffic*	*the circulation*	le tirage, la circulation sanguine
un collège	*a junior high school, a secondary school*	*a college*	une université
une commodité	*a convenience*	*a commodity*	une denrée
compréhensif	*understanding*	*comprehensive*	complet
une confidence	*a secret*	*confidence*	la confiance
consistant	*substantial*	*consistent*	constant, logique
courant	*common, usual*	*current*	actuel
une déception	*a disappointment*	*a deception*	une tromperie, une duperie
décevoir	*to disappoint*	*to deceive*	tromper
un délai	*a time limit*	*a delay*	un retard
demander	*to ask, to request*	*to demand*	exiger
un député	*an MP, an elected representative*	*a deputy*	un suppléant, un adjoint
disposer de	*to have at one's disposal*	*to dispose of*	se débarrasser de
une dispute	*an argument*	*a dispute*	un conflit
dramatique	*appalling*	*dramatic*	spectaculaire
éduquer	*to bring up*	*to educate*	instruire
embrasser	*to kiss*	*to embrace*	serrer qqn dans ses bras, adopter une idée
s'évader	*to escape*	*to evade*	éluder, éviter
éventuel	*possible*	*eventual*	final, ultime
une évidence	*an obvious fact*	*evidence*	des preuves
une expertise	*an appraisal, an evaluation*	*expertise*	la compétence
exténuant	*exhausting*	*extenuating*	atténuant
extravagant	*eccentric, unreasonable*	*extravagant*	luxueux, dépensier
fastidieux	*boring*	*fastidious*	pointilleux
une faute	*a mistake*	*a fault*	un défaut
génial	*brilliant*	*genial*	cordial
grand	*big, large*	*grand*	majestueux, grandiose
un grief	*a grievance*	*grief*	le chagrin
le hasard	*chance*	*a hazard*	un danger
ignorer	*not to know*	*to ignore*	ne pas tenir compte de
injurier	*to insult*	*to injure*	blesser
une location	*a rental*	*a location*	un emplacement
la malice	*mischievousness*	*malice*	la méchanceté
maniaque	*obsessive*	*a maniac*	un fou

une manifestation	*a demonstration*	*a manifestation*	un signe
misérable	*very poor*	*miserable*	malheureux
mondain	*society*	*mundane*	banal
une partition	*a separation*	*a partition*	une cloison
un patron	*a boss, a superior*	*a patron*	un mécène, un client
un préjudice	*harm*	*prejudice*	un préjugé
prétendre	*to claim*	*to pretend*	faire semblant
prévenir	*to warn*	*to prevent*	empêcher
propre	*clean, own*	*proper*	adéquat, correct
regarder	*to look at, to watch*	*to regard as*	considérer comme
reporter	*to postpone*	*to report*	relater, raconter
rester	*to stay*	*to rest*	se reposer
résumer	*to summarise*	*to resume*	reprendre
retirer	*to take away*	*to retire*	partir en retraite
une réunion	*a meeting*	*a reunion*	des retrouvailles
une route	*a road*	*a route*	un itinéraire
sensible	*sensitive*	*sensible*	sensé, raisonnable
un stage	*a course*	*a stage*	une étape
un surnom	*a nickname*	*a surname*	un nom de famille
surveiller	*to keep watch over*	*to survey*	examiner
susceptible	*sensitive*	*susceptible to*	sujet à, sensible à
sympathiser	*to make friends*	*to sympathise*	plaindre, compatir
trivial	*crude*	*trivial*	sans importance
truculent	*larger than life*	*truculent*	agressif
versatile	*fickle*	*versatile*	polyvalent

Respecter les différences lexicales entre l'anglais britannique et américain

	UK	*US*
les actions *(bourse)*	*shares*	*stock*
agent immobilier	*estate agent*	*realtor*
appartement	*flat*	*apartment**
appel en pcv	*reverse charge call*	*collect call*
ascenseur	*lift*	*elevator**
automne	*autumn*	*fall*
autoroute, voie express	*motorway*	*expressway, freeway*
avocat	*lawyer, solicitor*	*attorney*
bien immobilier	*property, land*	*real estate**
bilan *(comptabilité)*	*profit and loss account*	*income statement*
billet aller simple/billet aller-retour	*single/return ticket*	*one-way ticket*/round-trip ticket*
billet (de banque)	*banknote*	*bill*

boîte (de conserves)	*tin*	*can**
des bonbons	*sweets*	*candy*
camion	*lorry*	*truck**
car	*coach*	*bus*
caravane	*caravan*	*trailer*
carrefour	*crossroads, junction*	*intersection*
chiffre d'affaires	*turnover*	*revenues*
cinéma	*cinema*	*movie theater*
cité	*housing estate*	*housing development*
code postal	*postcode*	*zip code*
compte courant	*current account*	*a checking account*
courrier	*post*	*mail**
crevaison	*puncture*	*flat tire*
école publique	*state school*	*public school*
employé de banque	*bank clerk*	*(bank) teller*
en vacances	*on holiday*	*on vacation**
essence	*petrol*	*gas(oline)*
gateau sec	*biscuit*	*cookie*
jour férié	*bank holiday*	*public holiday*
lampe torche	*torch*	*flashlight*
magasin	*shop*	*store**
le métro	*the tube, the underground*	*the subway*
pantalon	*trousers*	*pants*
pare-brise	*windscreen*	*windshield*
pare-choc	*bumper*	*fender*
parking	*car park*	*parking lot*
passage piétons	*pedestrian crossing*	*crosswalk*
pharmacie	*chemist('s)*	*drugstore, pharmacy*
placard	*cupboard*	*closet*
plaque minéralogique	*number plate*	*license plate**
poubelle	*dustbin, rubbish bin*	*garbage* can, trash* can*
rez de chaussée	*ground floor*	*first floor*
robinet	*tap*	*faucet*
se présenter aux élections	*stand for office*	*run for office**
société de crédit immobilier	*building society*	*savings and loan association*
téléphone portable	*mobile phone*	*cell phone*
toilettes	*lavatory, toilet*	*restroom, washroom*
trottoir	*pavement*	*sidewalk*
TVA	*VAT (value-added tax)*	*sales tax*

* = les mots américains de plus en plus utilisés en anglais britannique.

Méthodologie : les réponses aux questions

La rédaction de la réponse courte

Les compétences et les attendus

• La question courte (50 mots) permet d'évaluer deux compétences : la compréhension d'un texte de presse et la reformulation.

Les étapes

• Il faut d'abord une lecture rapide du texte pour en prendre connaissance de façon globale et comprendre son organisation. C'est une activité de compréhension globale (*skimming*).
• La deuxième étape consiste à lire attentivement les questions avant de relire le texte une deuxième fois. Chaque question vous amène à restituer un point précis du texte, il faut donc cibler exactement le contenu attendu. C'est une activité de compréhension détaillée (*scanning*). Les questions les plus faciles appellent une réponse simple et directe : recherche d'information, définition d'un problème, description d'un projet. Les questions les plus complexes nécessitent une compréhension plus fine : éléments dispersés dans le texte, sous-entendus ou expression idiomatique à expliquer.
• La troisième étape est la reformulation des éléments vous permettant de répondre de façon précise. Pour reformuler, il faut vous tourner vers les synonymes, antonymes, termes dérivés et les collocations associées à partir des éléments recensés dans le texte de manière à combiner la pertinence et l'authenticité idiomatique.
• La quatrième étape est la rédaction de la réponse de façon concise et synthétique. Il faut répondre en allant droit au but (évitez les phrases amorces longues pour annoncer le point de vue de l'auteur) et en regroupant les éléments reformulés pour les présenter dans l'ordre logique de la réponse.

La reformulation longue

Les compétences et les attendus

• La question longue (de 150 à 250 mots selon les textes et les épreuves) vérifie la compréhension d'un texte de presse complexe et le niveau d'expression écrite. Les attendus sont :
– l'analyse fine de la question qui doit vous permettre de cibler avec précision les éléments du texte vous permettant de répondre avec de façon précise et exhaustive. Il ne faut surtout pas restituer la totalité du contenu du texte, l'énoncé de la question vous amène à définir vos critères de discrimination ;
– la compréhension globale, car il faut comprendre l'organisation des idées de manière à concentrer les repérages sur les parties du texte concernées par la question ;
– la compréhension détaillée, puisqu'il s'agit de relever de façon systématique tous les éléments textuels correspondant à la question (noms, adjectifs, groupes verbaux, mots de liaison, adverbes, temps des verbes, modaux…) ;

– une richesse linguistique importante de manière à reformuler ces éléments de réponse de façon idiomatique et précise ;
– l'argumentation, car il s'agira de restituer de façon synthétique et logique les éléments reformulés.
• Les trois erreurs à ne pas commettre sont :
– citer ou recopier le texte (l'un des attendus est la **reformulation**) ;
– commenter, porter un jugement ou donner votre opinion (vous êtes censé restituer un contenu sans prendre position) ;
– restituer tout le contenu du texte sans sélectionner les éléments précis.

Les étapes

• Première lecture. Lire attentivement l'ensemble du texte une fois en repérant les parties correspondant aux idées ciblées par les différents termes de l'énoncé de la question. Bien repérer la progression discursive du texte (exposition du sujet, explicitation, illustration, hypothèse, élargissement, retour au sujet) ainsi que les enchaînements (rapport de cause à effet, objectifs-moyens, comparaison-contraste-contradiction).
• Lecture-repérages. Le but de cette seconde lecture est de recenser systématiquement les arguments, exemples, reprises, conclusions partielles, illustrations, digressions, commentaires qui vous permettront de répondre de façon aussi précise qu'exhaustive. Souligner/surligner le texte d'un côté tout en prenant des notes en anglais sur une autre feuille. Ces premières notes en anglais sont vitales : attendus lexicaux (les domaines lexicaux renvoyant aux sujets-objets des idées principales, les mots de liaison utiles), outils grammaticaux (variation des temps, modaux, passif, concordance des temps, groupes verbaux complexes correspondant aux actions/directions des idées générales).
• Rédaction. Vous êtes maintenant prêt à rédiger votre texte cible sur un brouillon sur lequel vous aurez tracé des colonnes pour bien contrôler le nombre de mots, en gardant à l'esprit qu'il vous faut mobiliser toutes vos ressources. Voici quelques points qui pourront considérablement améliorer la qualité de votre production :
– morpho-syntaxe du groupe verbal
Le groupe verbal est le moteur de la phrase, son élément dynamique. Il importe donc de privilégier des groupes verbaux complexes (expressions verbales idiomatiques, aspects *be* + V-*ing*/*have* + V-en, passif, concordance des temps, modaux).
– syntaxe des phrases complexes
Utiliser les conjonctions (*whereas/while, if/provided/unless, although* + SV, *despite* + GN, *since/as*...) les mots de liaison *(however, still, yet, so, therefore, unlike, conversely...)* pour restituer l'argumentation du texte.
– richesse et précision du lexique
« *The right word in the right place* » garantit une partie de la concision, notamment lorsqu'il s'agit de termes décrivant l'économie, les sciences et technologies. N'hésitez pas à utiliser des synonymes/antonymes/hyperonymes pour éviter les répétitions et termes trop vagues.
– du bon usage des collocations
Ne pas oublier de procéder par collocations, c'est-à-dire par associations d'un nom et d'un verbe (*danger is looming ahead, to comply with the rules, to abide by the law...*), d'un adjectif et d'un nom (*widespread belief, heavy rain...*).

La compétence culturelle

• S'il vous est interdit de commenter le texte ou de donner votre opinion sur le sujet du texte, vous pouvez en revanche préciser le contexte socio-politique *(the editorial line)* de la publication et le type d'article (un éditorial représente le point de vue de la publication alors qu'une tribune permet à un individu représentant un groupe de s'exprimer sur un sujet donné), notamment lorsqu'il y a une prise de position sur un sujet politique *(immigration laws…)*, économique (*pensions…*) ou social *(abortion, death penalty…)*. La position du *Boston Globe* sur les droits des homosexuels sera bien différente de celle du *Washington Times*; la position du *Guardian* sur le *Welfare State* sera différente de celles du *Times* ou de *The Economist*.
Avoir une idée de la couleur politique et des choix éditoriaux de chaque grande publication (voir p. 305-309) vous permet de démontrer que vous avez une bonne connaissance de la presse des pays anglo-saxons et que vous êtes capable de prendre du recul par rapport au contenu restitué.

L'explication de citation

Les compétences et les attendus

• L'explication de citation est une reformulation explicative concise et complète en anglais idiomatique. L'exercice permet de vérifier deux compétences :
– la compréhension détaillée du texte
Il s'agit d'aller recenser dans le texte les éléments permettant d'expliquer la citation (contextualisation, rapport de cause à effet, mise en perspective). Ceci nécessite une lecture très attentive – au mot près – de manière à effectuer un repérage systématique et précis des quelques éléments concernés. Le candidat devra s'appuyer sur le contexte, mais en aucune manière il n'est censé citer les phrases connexes, ni les intégrer comme s'il s'agissait d'une explication.
– la richesse de la reformulation
L'idéal est bien sûr de ne pas utiliser de termes de l'énoncé. Il faut donc mobiliser vos acquis lexicaux et syntaxiques pour restituer le sens de la citation dans votre anglais. Synonymes, antonymes, termes dérivés, réseau lexical thématique doivent vous permettre de proposer une reformulation idiomatique et pertinente.
• Les attendus sont :
– la précision (expliquer la citation, pas le texte ou son contexte) ;
– la concision (la reformulation en 100 mots est nécessairement compacte. Il faut argumenter avec des mots de liaison courts ou des adverbes, utiliser des adjectifs et des noms composés) ;
– l'organisation synthétique (organiser les éléments de reformulation autour des 2/3 axes présents dans la citation).
Certains termes ou expressions à fort caractère culturel (ex : *Celtic Tiger* dans un texte sur l'Irlande) doivent être expliqués, et ce même si le texte n'apporte aucun éclaircissement explicite. Pour *Celtic Tiger* on pourrait dire : *This refers to how Ireland became a competitive economy after joining the EU by basing itself on the model of the Asian tigers, namely by attracting foreign investors to the manufacturing and services sectors.*
• Les trois erreurs à ne pas commettre sont :
– citer ou recopier le texte (l'un des attendus est la **reformulation**) ;

– commenter la citation (on ne vous demande pas de porter un jugement ou d'exprimer votre opinion personnelle, mais d'expliquer une phrase par rapport au texte dont elle est issue et parfois par rapport au contexte du sujet abordé par le texte);
– restituer le contenu du texte sans sélectionner les éléments précis.

Les étapes

• La méthode la plus efficace:
– segmenter la citation en éléments clés autonomes;
– aller chercher dans le texte les quelques éléments qui expliquent chaque élément clé;
– mobiliser le lexique de reformulation pour chaque terme de la citation et chacun des éléments repérés;
– regrouper les éléments de reformulation autour des éléments clés;
– rédiger en suivant l'ordre d'apparition des termes dans la citation.

Méthodologie : les graphiques

Le commentaire de graphique

Types de support visuel

pie chart/camembert, *graph*/courbe, *schema*/schéma, *diagram*/diagramme, *drawing*/dessin, *breakdown*/ventilation, *chart*/graphique, *matrix*/matrice, *bar chart*/histogramme

A flow chart shows the steps of a process or the succession of operations in a complex activity.
A pie chart displays the size of each part as a percentage of a whole.
A (vertical or horizontal) bar chart is used to compare items of different sorts.
A line chart depicts changes over a period of time, showing data and trends.
A table is a convenient way to show a large amount of data in a small space.
A diagram shows arrangements and situations, such as networks, distribution and fluctuation.

Mouvement général ou absence de mouvement

appreciable	considérable
dramatic	spectaculaire
to fluctuate	varier
to level off/out, to reach a plateau	se stabiliser, atteindre un palier
noticeable	notable
to reach a trough	atteindre un creux
to keep/remain constant/steady/stable	rester stable
to level off/out, to stabilise	se stabiliser
marked	fort
stability	la stabilité
to stagnate	stagner
to flatten out	(s')aplatir
a levelling-off	une stabilisation
significant, substantial	sensible
to stop falling/rising	arrêter de faire le yoyo

À la hausse

boom (n., v.)	une explosion (des prix, des ventes) ; monter/grimper en flèche
to climb	grimper, monter
to creep up, to edge up	monter peu à peu
an escalation	une escalade
to extend, to expand	(se) développer
to go up, to be up	monter
to grow	croître

growth	la croissance
to hit/reach an all-time high	atteindre son niveau le plus haut
increase, rise (n., v.)	augmenter ; augmentation
jump (n., v.)	(faire un) bond
to pick up	se redresser (après une baisse)
to progress	progresser
a progression	une progression
to (reach a) peak	atteindre un sommet
to soar, to skyrocket	monter/grimper en flèche
an upswing	un mouvement à la hausse

À la baisse

to bottom out, to reach a low point	atteindre son point le plus bas
crash, collapse (n., v.)	effondrement, s'effondrer
cut (n., v.)	réduire ; une réduction
decline (n., v.)	une baisse, un déclin ; décliner
decrease (n., v.)	une diminution ; diminuer
to diminish	baisser progressivement
to dive	s'effondrer
a downswing	un mouvement à la baisse
drop, fall (n., v.)	une baisse, une chute
to drop off, to fall off	baisser, fléchir
to go down	descendre, tomber
to hit an all-time low	atteindre son niveau le plus bas
to nosedive	chuter, piquer du nez, s'effondrer
to plummet	s'effondrer
plunge (n., v.)	une chute vertigineuse ; s'effondrer
to reduce	réduire
a reduction	une réduction
slump (n., v.)	chute ; chuter

La causalité

… can be explained by	on peut expliquer … par
… can be accounted for by	on peut justifier … par
… can be attributed to	on peut attribuer … à
… can be put down to	on peut imputer … à/mettre … au compte de
was due to	est dû à
was caused by	a été causé par
was provoked by	a été provoqué par
occurred in the wake of	a fait suite à
was a direct consequence of	a été la conséquence directe de
led to	a abouti à
goes a long way to explaining	explique en grande partie

Commentaires sur in graphique de la demande

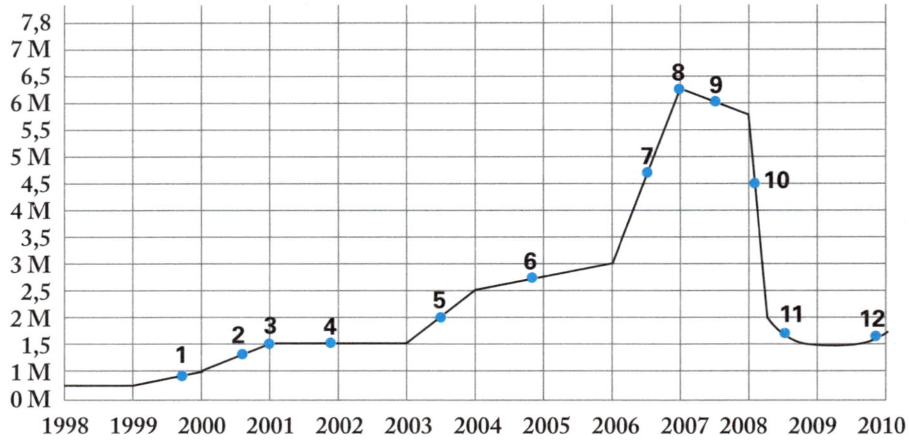

1. Demand began to pick up/to increase slightly in 1999.	La demande a commencé à se redresser/ a amorcé une reprise en 1999.
2. Demand rose substantially between 2000 and 2001.	La demande a grimpé considérablement entre 2000 et 2001.
3. Demand levelled off at the beginning of 2001.	La demande s'est stabilisée/a marqué un palier au début de l'année 2001.
4. Demand held steady between 2002 and 2003.	La demande est restée stable entre 2002 et 2003.
5. There was a marked increase in demand between 2003 and 2004.	Il y a eu une nette poussée de la demande entre 2003 et 2004.
6. Demand rose steadily over the 2004-2006 period.	La demande a progressé régulièrement de 2004 à 2006.
7. Demand soared/rose dramatically in 2006.	La demande est montée en flèche en 2006.
8. Demand topped 6.5 in 2006: an all-time high.	La demande a dépassé les 6,5 en 2006 : un record absolu.
9. Demand began to fall off early in 2007.	La demande a commencé à décroître/ marqué une baisse/amorcé une baisse dès le debut de 2007.
10. Demand plummeted/fell dramatically between 2008 and 2009.	La demande s'est effondrée entre 2008 et 2009.
11. Demand levelled out in the first quarter of 2009.	La demande s'est équilibrée/stabilisée au cours du 1er trimestre de l'année 2009.
12. Demand picked up in the second half of 2010.	La demande s'est redréssée au cours du 2e trimestre de l'année 2010.

La presse anglophone

Tabloids and Quality papers

At the risk of oversimplification, the quality papers (also sometimes called broadsheets) target the middle and upper classes whereas the tabloids – the popular press – tend to have a mainly working-class readership. Originally, "broadsheet" and "tabloid" referred to the page size but now they refer more to the content and style, the term "tabloid" implying extensive coverage of sport and television, as well as stories about celebrities. Articles are short and easy to read and use a lot of photographs. The style is deliberately sensational, using exaggeration and hyperbole to create drama and excitement. Broadsheets devote much more space to serious stories: domestic and international politics, social issues, culture… Their style reflects the assumption that quality papers have a well-educated readership.

Content and structure of articles

Tabloids	Quality papers
Articles show a very obvious bias, giving prominence to views the paper agrees with and dismissing or ridiculing opposing views.	Articles show a less obvious bias, presenting both sides of an argument but nevertheless reflecting the political stance of the paper.
The articles are often written as if telling a story.	Articles are usually constructed around a logical sequence of ideas.
Preference is given to sensational news stories.	Preference is given to fact-based news stories.
The opening paragraph briefly summarises the key facts.	The opening paragraph provides a substantial summary.
The closing paragraph may contain the latest piece of news.	The closing paragraph may give background information.

Style and vocabulary

Tabloids	Quality papers
Headlines are dramatic, sensational and emotive: *May Day Massacre* *X gets off with 5 years*	Headlines are neutral, factual and informative: *PM Defeat at Polls* *X gets five-year sentence*
Preference is shown for short Anglo-Saxon words and short simple sentences.	Long Latinate words may be used as well as a variety of sentence structures.
Simple connectives *(And, But…)* are sometimes used to begin sentences.	Sentences are frequently introduced by link words *(Moreover, However…)*.
Paragraphs sometimes have only one sentence.	Paragraphs are made up of several sentences.

Tabloids	Quality papers
Substandard grammar is used as well as an informal style, thus resembling speech.	Correct grammar and a rather formal style is used.
There is extensive use of puns, alliteration, and words with emotional impact or shock value.	There is use of irony, restrained language and a moderate tone.
Public figures are frequently referred to by their first name or nickname.	Public figures are referred to by their surname or full name.
The reader is addressed in a familiar tone.	The reader is addressed formally and impersonally.

The British Press

The daily broadsheets (quality papers)

The Financial Times

• This daily, printed on pink paper, was founded in 1888 and has a circulation of 400,000 copies a day. The *Financial Times* Group also owns the *Economist.* It focuses on business news, international news and the Stock Exchange. Because it analyses the development of the major companies worldwide, it is considered to be the foremost business daily in the world.

The Times

• Founded in 1785, it has been owned by Rupert Murdoch's ultraconservative News Corp since 1981. It is perhaps the most famous of all British daily newspapers and has a circulation of 600,000. The take-over in 1981 resulted in major changes to the British press notably the creation of *The Independent* in 1986 by some journalists who resigned from *The Times.* Because the paper has become closer to the tabloids in terms of content, many *Times* readers have shifted their loyalty to the *Daily Telegraph.*

The Daily Telegraph

• Founded in 1855, this daily has an average circulation of 900,000. Nicknamed the *Daily Torygraph,* it tends to be the mouthpiece of the Conservative Party both in tone and content. It supports the establishment and the monarchy; issues of law and order are usually placed to the fore.

The Guardian

• Founded in 1821 as *The Manchester Guardian*, it it now has offices in both London and Manchester and has been *The Guardian* since 1959. It has an average circulation of 350,000 and tends to be read by the left-leaning middle-class. It was strongly opposed to the Conservative governments between 1979 and 1997 (under Mrs Thatcher and John Major) and was critical of the New Labour government under Tony Blair. Although regarded as a serious newspaper, it is noted for its numerous misprints…

The Independent

• Founded in 1986 by former *Times* journalists and now owned by the Irish press magnate Tony O'Reilly, it has an average circulation of 200,000. It is a competitor of *The Times* and *The Daily Telegraph*, but changed to tabloid format in 2004. It is noted for its quality reporting and fierce independence.

The daily tabloids

The Sun

• This daily sells on average 3,5 million copies every day. It was founded in 1964 and bought by Rupert Murdoch in 1969. Its politics may be said to be populist and Conservative but it tends to be scorned by the conservative establishment and is regarded by many as belonging to the gutter press, i.e. with a prurient interest in sensationalism and scandal that has nothing to do with serious journalism.

The Daily Mail

• Founded in 1896, it has a daily circulation of 2,4 million. It is a mouthpiece for conservatism but is neither as loud nor as vulgar as *The Sun*. It prefers pictures and sensationalism to in-depth analyses and feeds the general appetite for the "dog-bites-man" sort of news.

The Daily Mirror

• Founded in 1903, it sells on average 2 million copies a day. It used to be the traditional mouthpiece of the working man – the Labour Party and the Trades Unions – but has become more liberal, and appeals now to people who want simple explanations of complex political issues as well as some degree of sensationalism.

The Sunday papers

The Sunday Times,

• The Sunday edition of *The Times* is the most widely read of all Sunday broadsheets. With 10 sections ranging from national/international news to sports and business, and including a glossy magazine, it is a very substantial paper and offers a relatively sophisticated content at a very low price. Its main competitors are *The Sunday Telegraph*, *The Observer and* the Sunday editions of *The Guardian and The Independent,* all of which comprise several sections.

Weekly magazines

The Economist

• This weekly political, economic and financial magazine was founded in 1843, and is very influential in industrial and business circles. Traditionally rather conservative by nature, it has now turned into a more liberally-inclined news magazine focusing on national and international news in politics and economics as well as in cultural, artistic and scientific fields. Its weekly circulation averages 800,000. It often labels itself as the "champion of liberalism", notably in its promotion of "small government" (i. e. very little or no state intervention, low taxes, a minimum of centralised power...) and its belief in the "Protestant work ethic" (i.e. it is up to each citizen to succeed and manage on his/her own by means of a strong work ethic).

The Spectator

• This was founded in 1711 and, as such, is the oldest continuously-published English-language magazine in the world. It began life as a coffee-house periodical for middle-class Tories and is still regarded as very conservative, although satirical and impertinent at the same time. Its articles focus on political and general cultural issues, and the tone is generally thought of as rather "highbrow". It has a circulation averaging 35,000 per week.

The New Statesman

• Established in 1913, and with a circulation of approximately 29,000, it is Britain's oldest and best-known left-wing magazine, with a reputation for independence and for criticising the government. Its articles on politics, science, society and the arts are usually written from a left-wing point of view, and, as such, the magazine may be considered to be the left-wing counterpart of *The Spectator*.

The American Press

Daily papers

The New York Times

Founded in 1851, this the the most famous American daily and is mainly read by well-educated people. Its well-known motto, "All the news that's fit to print" exemplifies the American approach to reporting news: a focus on reporting facts and remaining objective. It has more than a million readers worldwide and has won the most Pulitzer Prizes of all American newspapers (89 times). It traditionally supports the Democrats but is known for being critical of the government, whatever its political persuasion.

The International Herald Tribune

Founded in the 19th century. The IHT was published in Paris by its parent companies *The New York Times* and *The Washington Post* in the 20th century and is known for its serious and thorough news items. It claims today to be "the world's newspaper" because, while still based in Paris, it is printed simultaneously in many places around the world and read by decision-makers everywhere. It was acquired by *The New York Times* in 2002 in an effort to strengthen its international image.

The Washington Post

First published in 1877, it is well-known for its liberal opinions. It was the first to investigate the Watergate story in the early 70s, thus epitomising the watchdog duties of the American press. It is today the top newspaper in the nation's capital and in the rest of the country alongside its arch-rival and former partner *The New York Times*. It focuses on the government's domestic and foreign activities.

The Boston Globe

Founded in 1872, it has been owned by the *New York Times* Company since 1993. Its editorial line is liberal on social issues – pro-choice, against the death penalty, in favour of gay rights – but it holds more conservative views on business and economic issues.

The Los Angeles Times

This daily has been published since 1881. In 2008 it was the second-largest metropolitan newspaper in circulation in the USA and the fourth most widely distributed newspaper in the country. Its political leaning is usually thought to be mostly liberal and centre-left. Other major papers such as *The Chicago Sun Times*, *The San Francisco Chronicle* and *The Minneapolis Star Tribune* are also considered as "liberal left" newspapers. On the other hand, *The Wall Street Journal, The New York Post, The Washington Times, The Boston Herald* and *The Chicago Herald Tribune* hold conservative views

Magazines

Time

This is the leading American magazine with 23 million readers in the US alone, representing 45% of the news magazines sold each week in America. Founded in 1923, it contains information on the economy, politics, science, society, technology and the arts. It is also produced in four international versions.

It has developed a particular style of writing which has come to be called "Timesese", i.e. a unique blend of hard facts, buzzwords and American metaphors. It tends to be regarded as America's mouthpiece across the world and the champion of the American system of values. Its approach to European politics tends to be coloured by the desire to promote the American version of democracy.

Its company Time Inc. joined the film company Warner Bros in 1989 to form the US media and entertainment giant Time Warner, which later bought Ted Turner's Broadcasting System, owner of CNN.

Newsweek

This weekly general information magazine was founded in 1933 by an English journalist, and was later acquired by the *Washington Post*. With 18 offices in the US and across the world, it offers comprehensive coverage of world events with 60% text and 40% pictures. It focuses on US national affairs, international affairs, business, science, technology, society, the arts and entertainment. It is published in 190 countries in four editions and has a circulation of nearly 4 million.

US News & World Report

Founded in 1933, this is a competitor of *Time* and *Newsweek*. It is known for its conservative opinions, and thus tends to support the Republicans. It focuses on socio-cultural issues and analyses of business and economic issues.

Improve your style

Expressions often used in the press

A

the acid test *épreuve de vérité*
across the board *à tous les niveaux*
adamant *inflexible*
to address a problem *s'attaquer à un problème*
ailing *sick*
to aim to *avoir pour but*
the alarm bell *la sonnette d'alarme*
to alienate *se mettre à dos*
to allay fears *apaiser les craintes*
anything goes *tout est permis*
an asset *un avantage*
at the end of the day *en fin de compte*
to axe jobs *supprimer des emplois*

B

to backfire *avoir l'effet inverse*
a backlash *une réaction brutale*
to backpedal, to backtrack *faire machine arrière*
to bail a company out *sauver une entreprise*
a bail-out *un sauvetage*
to be on the agenda *être à l'ordre du jour*
to beggar description *défier toute description*
a benchmark *un point de référence*
to the bitter end *jusqu'au bout*
to blaze a trail *ouvrir la voie*
a blessing in disguise *un mal pour un bien*
to blight hopes *ruiner les espoirs*
a blockbuster *un énorme succès*
to blow out of proportion *monter en épingle*
a blow-by-blow account *ne faire grâce d'aucun détail*
a blueprint *un projet, une ébauche*
to boil down to *se résumer à*
to break new ground *to innovate innover*
to break the deadlock/stalemate *sortir de l'impasse*
a breakthrough *une percée, une avancée significative*
to bring home the bacon *gagner sa croûte*
to broker a ceasefire *négocier un cessez le feu*

C

to call a spade a spade *appeler un chat un chat*
the calm before the storm *le calme avant la tempête*
to cap (health) spending *limiter les dépenses (de santé)*
to cash in on *tirer profit de*
a catch-22 situation *une situation inextricable, un problème insoluble*
to cave in to pressure *céder à la pression*
to champion the poor *défendre les pauvres*
the chattering classes *les intellos*
to clampdown/crackdown on *sévir contre*
to clean up one's act *changer de comportement*
a cog in the machine *une simple rouage du système*
to come to grips with *s'attaquer à*
as cool as a cucumber *d'un calme olympien*
to cook the books *truquer les comptes*
the corridors of power *les coulisses du pouvoir*
cracker-barrel philosophy *philosophie de comptoir, propos de café du commerce*
the credit crunch *la crise du crédit*
a crying need *un besoin pressant/urgent*
cutbacks *des réductions*
to clear hurdles *franchir les obstacles*
contentious *controversial*

D

a dark horse *une quantité inconnue, un candidat inattendu*
a dastardly deed *un acte ignoble*

daunting *redoutable*
dead in the water *fichu*
to debunk a myth *démythifier, démolir le mythe*
a deep-rooted belief *une croyance bien ancrée*
to defuse the crisis *désamorcer la crise*
to deliver the goods *se montrer à la hauteur*
a die-hard *un acharné, un extrémiste*
a domino effect *une réaction en chaîne*
a doomsday prophet- *un oiseau de mauvais augure*
to double-cross *trahir*
to downplay the significance of *minimiser l'importance*
to downsize the workforce *réduire les effectifs*
to drag one's heels *traîner les pieds*
dyed-in-the-wool *invétéré*

E

earmarked for *destiné à*
economic woes *difficultés économiques*
to embark upon an adventure *se lancer dans une aventure*
to explode a theory *démonter une théorie*

F

to face the music *être obligé de faire face/d'assumer*
by fair means or foul *par n'importe quel moyen/par tous les moyens*
the fallout *les retombées*
faltering economies *les économies chancelantes*
the fall guy *le bouc émissaire*
to fan the flames/embers *attiser le feu/souffler sur les braises*
the fat cats *les gros bonnets*
feisty *fougueux, bagarreur*
to have a field day *faire ses choux gras de/s'en donner à coeur joie*
a financial meltdown *un effondrement financier*
a flagship product *un produit phare*
to flare up *éclater*
a flash in the pan *un feu de paille*
a floating voter *un électeur indécis*
to foil an attemp *déjouer une tentative*
to follow suit *faire de même*
friends in high places *des amis en haut lieu/bien placés*
to fuel rumours of *alimenter les rumeurs à propos*

G

to gain momentum *prendre de la vitesse*
to get down to brass tacks/to the nitty-gritty *en venir aux faits*
to be given the green light/the go-ahead *obtenir le feu vert*
to go off the rails *mal tourner*
gobbledygook *charabia*
a golden handshake *grosse prime de départ*
to go green *devenir écolo*
the grassroots *la base (d'un parti, d'un syndicat…)*
the Grim Reaper *la Faucheuse*
ground-breaking *innovant*

H

to hail *saluer*
to be the hardest-hit *être le plus durement touché*
a hardliner *un « dur » (d'un parti)*
to herald *annoncer*
in high dudgeon *furieux/offensé dans sa dignité*
high-flyers *les ambitieux, les arrivistes*
a technical hitch *un problème technique*
it doesn't hold water *ça ne tient pas la route*
hot air *du bla-bla*
to be in the hot seat *être sur la sellette*
a hotbed *un foyer (d'intolérance, etc.)*
to hype something up *faire un battage énorme autour de*

I, J, K

to be in its infancy *n'en être qu'aux balbutiements*
to jump on the bandwagon *prendre le train en marche*
a kangaroo court *un tribunal irrégulier*

to keep the flag flying *maintenir les traditions*
to keep the lid on *maîtriser*
to keep under wraps *ne pas dévoiler*
a keystone *la pierre angulaire*
to kickstart the economy *relancer l'économie*
a knock-on effect *une répercussion*

L

to lag behind *être à la traîne*
a landmark *une étape importante*
a landslide victory *une victoire écrasante*
law and order *la sécurité*
a leading question *une question piège*
a leak *une fuite*
the lesser of two evils *le moindre des deux maux*
to let the cat out of the bag *vendre la mèche*
the litmus test *le test décisif*
to be at loggerheads *être en profond désaccord*
to loom ahead *se profiler à l'horizon*
a loophole *une faille*
the lynchpin of success *l'artisan principal de la réussite*

M

a magic bullet *une solution miracle*
the main thrust *l'objectif principal*
the mainstay of the party *le pilier du parti*
a major setback *un revers majeur*
to make great strides *avancer à grands pas*
to make inroads *faire une percée*
to mar *gâcher*
to massage figures *manipuler les chiffres*
media hype *le battage médiatique*
to mend fences *se réconcilier*
a milch cow *une vache à lait*
a milestone *un événement marquant*
minor quibbles *des pinailleries sans intérêt, du pinaillage*
money-laundering *le blanchiment d'argent*
a mordant wit *une ironie féroce*
to move the goalposts *changer les règles du jeu*

N, O

no pain no gain *on n'a rien sans rien*
off the record *officieusement*
old wine in new bottles *faire du neuf avec de l'ancien*
to open a can of worms *soulever un lièvre*
to oust from power *évincer du pouvoir*

P

it's part of life's rich tapestry *cela forme la trame complexe de l'existence*
to pass the buck *rejeter la responsabilité, refiler le bébé*
to pay lip service to *adhérer du bout des lèvres*
to peak at *culminer à*
to peg pay rises *limiter les hausses de salaires*
peppered with quotations *truffé de citations*
to pick up the tab *payer l'addition*
pie-in-the-sky promises *des promesses en l'air*
to pin one's hopes on *fonder ses espoirs sur*
to pinpoint *établir avec précision*
to be in the pipeline *être en préparation/dans les tuyaux*
to play ball *coopérer*
to play havoc *causer des ravages*
to pledge to *promettre de*
a plight *situation très difficile*
a ploy *un stratagème*
to plug *faire la publicité de*
to be poised to *être prêt à*
a political upheaval *un bouleversement politique*
pork *les pots de vin*
to pre-empt *prendre les devants pour empêcher*
a public outcry/uproar *une tempête de protestations*
to pull the wool over someone's eyes *duper quelqu'un*
to put the spin on *présenter de façon avantageuse*
a pundit *an expert*
to put on the back burner/on ice/on hold *mettre en veilleuse, faire passer au second plan*

Q , R

a quagmire *un bourbier*
to rampage through the streets *saccager dans les rues*
rampant inflation *inflation galopante*

a red herring *une fausse piste*
a red-letter day *un jour à marquer d'une pierre blanche*
to ride out the storm *surmonter la crise*
a rift *un désaccord*
root-and-branch critics *les critiques inconditionnels*
to rule out the possibility *exclure la possibilité*
to be rife *aller bon train*
to run riot *s'emballer*

S

to sail close to the wind *jouer un jeu dangereux*
scaremongering *l'alarmisme*
a scourge *fléau*
to scrap a plan *abandonner un plan*
to scupper *faire capoter*
to see the writing on the wall *comprendre l'avertissement/que la fin est proche*
to sex up a report *rendre un rapport plus intéressant*
to shore up the economy *consolider l'économie*
a showcase *une vitrine*
to slacken (off) *montrer des signes de ralentissement*
to slam *critiquer sévèrement*
to slash prices *casser les prix*
to be slated *être sévèrement critiqué*
sleaze *la corruption*
a soundbite *une petite phrase (en politique)*
to spark off *déclencher*
to spearhead a campaign *être le fer de lance d'une campagne*
to spell disaster *être synonyme de désastre*
a spin doctor *un conseiller en communication politique*
to be split over *être profondément divisé sur*
to spur investment *encourager les investissements*
to stall *être au point mort*
to be at a standstill *être au point mort*
to stem the tide *endiguer le flot*
to step up the fight *intensifier la lutte*
a sticking point *un point de friction*
a stranglehold *la mainmise*
a stronghold *un bastion*
a stumbling block *une pierre d'achoppement*
to be swayed *être influencé*
to sweep under the carpet *passer sous silence*
sweeping changes *des changements radicaux*

T

a tall order *une véritable gageure, un défi difficile à relever*
to take a lot of flak *se faire violemment critiquer*
to take a toll on *nuire considérablement*
to take someone to task *critiquer quelqu'un violemment*
to take the lion's share *prendre la part du lion*
a team player *quelqu'un qui a l'esprit d'équipe*
teething troubles *des problèmes de mise en route*
tense relations *des relations tendues*
the thin edge of the wedge *le fil du rasoir*
a think tank *un groupe de réflexion*
a time bomb *une bombe à retardement*
to toe the line *se plier à la règle, se conformer, suivre la ligne du parti*
to toll the bell for *sonner le glas pour*
to topple a dictator *renverser un dictateur*
the touchstone *le critère, la pierre de touche*
a tough stance *une position très ferme*
to tread/walk on thin ice *marcher sur des œufs, avancer en terrain miné*
a turnaround *un redressement*
to turn a company around *remettre une entreprise sur pied*
a trump card *un atout (maître)*

U, V

to unleash a wave of violence *déclencher une vague de violence*
up to the mark *à la hauteur*
to urge *conseiller vivement*
a U-turn *(faire) volte-face*
with a vengeance *avec passion/avec excès*
to have a vested interest in *avoir tout intérêt à ce que*

to vote with one's feet *montrer son désaccord en partant*

W, Y

to ward off an epidemic *écarter une épidémie*
a watchdog (committee) *un comité de surveillance*
a watershed *un tournant décisif*
to weather a crisis *surmonter une crise*
a wheeler-dealer *un affairiste*
a white elephant *une réalisation coûteuse et inutile*
a win-win/no-win situation *une situation favorable/défavorable aux deux partis*
a windfall *une manne financière*
wishful thinking *un vœu pieux*
to work hand in glove with *travailler main dans la main avec*
to work out a solution *trouver une solution*
a yardstick *un moyen de comparaison*

Frequent expressions involving pairs of words

by and large	*généralement*
by hook or by crook	*de gré ou de force*
come hell or high water	*contre vents et marées*
a cut and dried solution	*une solution toute faite*
to fight tooth and nail	*lutter avec acharnement*
from far and near/wide	*de tous côtés*
give and take	*donnant-donnant*
to go to rack and ruin	*courir à la ruine*
high and low	*partout*
hocus-pocus	*charabia*
the ins and outs	*tous les détails*
to invest in bricks and mortar	*investir dans la pierre*
left and right	*partout*
the long and the short of it	*le fin mot de l'histoire*
more or less	*plus ou moins*
mumbo-jumbo	*charabia, baratin*
the nitty-gritty	*le fond du problème*
rain or shine	*qu'il pleuve ou qu'il vente*
the rules and regulations	*les statuts, la réglementation*
safe and sound	*sain et sauf*
to shilly-shally	*tergiverser*
it's sink or swim	*risquer le tout pour le tout*
topsy-turvy	*à l'envers, sens dessus-dessous*
wear and tear	*l'usure*
willy-nilly	*bon gré, mal gré*
wishy-washy	*insatisfaisant/insipide*

Commonly-used Classical references

an Achilles'(s) heel	*un talon d'Achille*
an Adonis	*un apollon, un beau jeune homme*
the Augean Stables	*la corruption (d'un milieu)*

a Caesar's wife	*quelqu'un dont la probité ne peut être mise en doute*
a Cassandra	*un prophète de malheur, un oiseau de mauvais augure*
chimerical	*illusoire*
a cornucopia	*une corne d'abondance*
a sword of Damocles	*une épée de Damoclès*
delphic	*difficile à interpréter/comprendre*
draconian	*draconnien, très sévère*
the Elysian fields	*les champs élysées, un paradis*
To use Fabian tactics	*jouer la montre*
the Gordian knot	*le nœud gordien*
Beware of Greeks bearing gifts	*méfiez-vous des cadeaux empoisonnés*
a Greek god	*un très bel homme*
halcyon days	*les jours heureux*
a harpy	*une harpie*
hermetic	*hermétique, très difficile à comprendre*
homeric	*homérique, (effort) quasi surhumain*
hubris	*l'orgueil, l'arrogance*
the fall of Icarus	*la chute d'Icare*
Janus-like	*à deux visages*
Junoesque	*(une belle femme) plantureuse*
laconic	*laconique*
a lotus-eater	*un lotophage, un doux rêveur*
nectar	*le breuvage des dieux*
a nymph	*une jeune fille séduisante*
an odyssey	*un long périple plein de péripéties*
olympian	*olympien, très imposant*
Pandora's box	*la boîte de Pandore*
a Parthian shot, a parting shot	*une dernière pointe, la flèche du Parthe*
Protean	*multiforme*
a Pyrrhic victory	*une victoire à la Pyrrhus (que l'on paye trop cher en pertes)*
to cross the Rubicon	*prendre une décision irrévocable*
sophistry	*du sophisme*
Spartan	*dur, austère*
stentorian	*puissant (d'une voix ou d'une personne)*
Stygian	*lugubre, sombre*
a thespian	*un comédien*
a Trojan Horse	*un cheval de troie, un élément infiltré*

Frequently-used proverbs

Actions speak louder than words	*C'est au pied du mur qu'on voit le maçon.*
It takes all sorts to make a world.	*il faut de tout pour faire un monde.*
Beggars can't be choosers.	*Nécessité fait loi.*
The best is the enemy of the good.	*Le mieux est l'ennemi du bien.*
The best laid plans of mice and men (gang aft a-gley, oft[en] go astray.)	*Les plans les mieux conçus peuvent toujours tomber à l'eau.*

Better safe than sorry.	*Mieux vaut prévenir que guérir.*
Birds of a feather flock together.	*Qui se ressemble s'assemble.*
Charity begins at home.	*Charité bien ordonnée commence par soi-même.*
Easy come, easy go.	*Vite arrivé, vite parti.*
Every cloud has a silver lining.	*Toute épreuve cache un bienfait. / Après la pluie le beau temps*
Every dog has his/its day.	*À chacun son heure de gloire.*
Forewarned is forearmed.	*L'homme averti en vaut deux.*
The grass is always greener on the other side of the fence.	*l'herbe est toujours plus verte ailleurs.*
Great minds think alike.	*Les grands esprits se rencontrent.*
Half a loaf is better than none/ no bread.	*Faute de grives, on mange des merles.*
He who hesitates is lost.	*Aux audacieux les mains pleines.*
Honesty is the best policy.	*l'honnêteté paie.*
If at first you don't succeed, try, try, try again	*Cent fois sur le métier, remettez votre ouvrage.*
In for a penny, in for a pound	*Quand le vin est tiré il faut le boire.*
It is a long lane that has no turning	*Tout vient à point à qui sait attendre.*
It's no use crying over spilt milk.	*Ce qui est fait est fait.*
Least said, soonest mended.	*Moins on en dit, mieux on se porte.*
A leopard can't change its spots.	*Chassez le naturel il revient au galop.*
Many hands make light work.	*l'union fait la force.*
Money doesn't grow on trees.	*L'argent ne tombe pas du ciel.*
(The love of) money is the root of all evil.	*L'argent est source de tous les maux.*
More haste, less speed.	*Hâtez vous lentement.*
Needs must (when the devil drives).	*Nécessité fait loi.*
Never say die.	*Il ne faut jamais désespérer.*
Nothing ventured, nothing gained.	*Qui ne risque rien n'a rien.*
Old habits die hard.	*Les mauvaises habitudes ont la vie dure.*
Once bitten twice shy.	*Chat échaudé craint l'eau froide.*
One man's meat is another man's poison.	*Le malheur des uns fait le bonheur des autres.*
One good turn deserves another.	*Un service en vaut un autre.*
Practice makes perfect.	*C'est en forgeant qu'on devient forgeron.*
Prevention is better than cure.	*Mieux vaut prévenir que guérir.*
Don't put the cart before the horse.	*Il ne faut pas mettre la charrue avant les bœufs.*
The proof of the pudding is in the eating.	*C'est à l'usage que l'on juge.*
The road to hell is paved with good intentions.	*L'enfer est pavé de bonnes intentions.*
Lock the stable door after the horse has bolted.	*Prendre des précautions quand il est trop tard.*
A rolling stone gathers no moss.	*Pierre qui roule n'amasse pas mousse.*
Rome was not built in a day.	*Rome ne s'est pas faite en un jour.*
Strike while the iron is hot.	*Il faut battre le fer pendant qu'il est chaud.*

Too many cooks spoil the broth.	*Autant de têtes, autant d'avis.*
Truth is stranger than fiction.	*La réalité dépasse la fiction.*
United we stand, divided we fall.	*L'union fait la force.*
Where there's a will, there's a way	*Quand on veut on peut.*
You can't have your cake and eat it.	*On en peut pas avoir le beurre et l'argent du beurre.*
You can't make an omelette without breaking eggs.	*On ne fait pas d'omelette sans casser des œufs.*

"Inflated" English

Some people want to make themselves sound more authoritative by using what they imagine to be «better» (usually longer) words in the place of simple ones. The following words and expressions can be used to «inflate» written or spoken style.

"Inflated" English	Plain English	"Inflated" English	Plain English
adjacent to *(prep.)*	*near, next to*	expedite *(v.)*	*hurry*
to ascertain *(v.)*	*make sure*	facilitate *(v.)*	*help*
assist *(v.)*	*help*	indicate *(v.)*	*show*
assistance *(n.)*	*help*	initiate *(v.)*	*start*
attempt *(n., v.)*	*try*	inquire *(v.)*	*ask*
beverage *(n.)*	*drink*	in the course of	*during*
commence *(v.)*	*begin*	in the event of	*if*
concept *(n.)*	*idea*	in the vicinity of	*near*
construct *(v.)*	*build*	in the view of the fact that	*since, as*
converse *(v.)*	*talk*		
customary *(adj.)*	*usual*	locate *(v.)*	*find*
deceased *(adj.)*	*dead*	location *(n.)*	*place*
demise *(n.)*	*death*	missive *(n.)*	*letter*
demonstrate *(v.)*	*show*	necessitate *(v.)*	*need*
discontinue *(v.)*	*stop*	remunerate *(v.)*	*pay*
dispatch *(v.)*	*send*	residence *(n.)*	*home*
donate *(v.)*	*give*	subsequently *(adv.)*	*later*
edifice *(n.)*	*building*	sufficient *(det.)*	*enough*
endeavour *(v.)*	*try*	terminate *(v.)*	*end*
evince *(v.)*	*show*	utilise *(v.)*	*use*

Les exercices de prononciation supplémentaires

Syllable stress

Stress the syllable before -tion/-ssion

56 organisation, nationalisation, production, revolution, supposition, recession, possession.

Stress the syllable before -ic(s)/-ical

57 critic/critical, music/musical, mathematics/mathematical, economics/economical. *But:* politics, political.

Stress the syllable before -ient/-ience

58 convenient/inconvenient, sufficient/insufficient, efficient/inefficient, experienced/inexperienced.

Stress the syllable before -ian/-ial/-ialism

59 Russian, politician, especially, imperialism, materialism, superficial, essential, official.

Stress the syllable before -ity/-ety

60 reality, ability, anxiety, variety, society, capacity, possibility, quality.

Stress the syllable before -ious

61 conscious/unconscious, obvious, serious, judicious.

Stress the syllable before -ual

62 Gradual, eventual, usual, intellectual, individual.

Stress the syllable before -ible

63 incredible, sensible, incompatible, possible, impossible, horrible, terrible, responsible, irresponsible.

Do not stress -able

64 touchable/untouchable, valuable, adaptable, desirable, likeable.

Stress the first syllable

65 generalise, specialise, socialism, organise, realise, jeopardise, analyse, capitalism.

Difficult words

66 idea, industry, development, interesting, democracy, necessary, America, Great Britain, probable, percent, England, result.

67 psychiatry, comment/commentary, profit/profitable, succeed/success, final/finally, Europe/European, advantage/disadvantage.

68 government, scourge, plague, nought, event, criterion/criteria, analysis, crisis/crises, area/era/aura, catastrophe, Canada, Australia.

Tongue-twisters

69 What noise annoys an oyster most? A noisy noise annoys an oyster most!

70 A box of biscuits and a batch of mixed biscuits.

71 She sells sea shells by the sea shore. The shells she sells are surely seashells.

72 Brad's big black bath-brush broke.

73 Betty and Bob brought back blue balloons from the big bazaar.

74 Twelve twins twirled twelve pigs.

75 Flee from fog to fight flu fast.

76 Which witch wished which wicked wish?

Reading at normal spead

77 The soaring unemployment rate among young people is a scourge that is affecting every industrialised country.
Fighting crime and violence ranks high on the new government's agenda, while education has been put on the back burner.
Companies must innovate at breakneck speed to improve their competitiveness and keep ahead of the pack.
If the firm hits a rough patch, the CEO is likely to streamline the workforce in order to safeguard the shareholders' profits.
Both the State and the corporate world should provide more funds to enable scientists to break new ground in the battle against fatal diseases.

78 The police will crack down on pub owners and teenage drinkers to oblige them to abide by the law, and to prevent disorderly behaviour.
Management is not about crunching numbers, it is about setting targets, deploying means, benchmarking and assessing performance, and striving to achieve one's goals.

The highly contentious issue of gender equality will lead the Prime Minister to mend fences with his fiercest opponents in Parliament.
The prices of low-cost, easy-to-use, fully-equipped twelve-inch laptop computers are bound to plummet because of the ongoing crisis.
We think it much better to uphold the idea of individual liberties rather than implement a CCTV-based snooper society for the sake of security.

79 Green-minded folk of many shades came to Spain this month, to talk about the need to save from human recklessness as much as possible of nature's bounty of genes, habitats and species. They brought bad tidings. Common birds are in decline across the world. Almost one in four species of mammals is in danger of extinction. If current trends continue until 2050, fisheries will be exhausted. As it is, deforestation costs the world more each year than the current financial crisis has cost in total, one economist argued.

80 And yet here is a place of mystery and imagination, as well as mathematics, physics and imaginative engineering, that promises to take us on a journey into the realm of the spiritual as well as the purely scientific and rational. In this sense, Cern is a modern equivalent of the great temples and cathedrals of the past. It aims to find the point at which creation began.
Ultimately, Cern's scientists may come up against a truly mysterious nothingness – the very opposite of solid architecture – and discover that perhaps we cannot ever truly understand or come to terms with the elusive core and generator of the universe.

IMPRIM'VERT

Imprimé en France par SEPEC à Péronnas
N° d'édition : 005699-01 - N° d'imprimeur : 101008230
Dépôt légal : octobre 2010